AF712376

4-15-93

To Jesus,

For your perseverence and commitment to our profession and its patients, and the important administrative role you played in the Outpatient Clinics and in the Residency.

It has been a pleasure supervising you, and you will do well in both general psychiatry and the practice of psychotherapy.

Looking forward to continued contact,

Ned W

BECOMING A PSYCHOANALYST

A Study of Psychoanalytic Supervision

BECOMING A PSYCHOANALYST

A Study of Psychoanalytic Supervision

Monograph
of the Study Group on Supervision
of the Committee
on Psychoanalytic Education

Edited by

ROBERT S. WALLERSTEIN, M.D.

INTERNATIONAL UNIVERSITIES PRESS, INC.
New York

Library of Congress Cataloging in Publication Data

Main entry under title:

Becoming a psychoanalyst.

(Monograph of the Study Group on Supervision of the Committee on Psychoanalytic Education)
Bibliography: p.
Includes index.
1. Psychoanalysis—Study and teaching—Supervision.
I. Wallerstein, Robert S. II. Series.
RC502.B43 616.89'17 81-8337
ISBN 0-8236-0492-6 AACR2

Manufactured in the United States of America

To Joan Fleming
friend, colleague, mentor
who shared this labor and
whose spirit inspired us all.

THE STUDY GROUP ON SUPERVISION OF THE COMMITTEE ON PSYCHOANALYTIC EDUCATION

Members

Emanuel Windholz, M.D., *Chairman*
Robert S. Wallerstein, M.D., *Secretary*
Daryl DeBell, M.D.
Joan Fleming, M.D. (deceased)
Maurice Friend, M.D.
Paul G. Myerson, M.D.
Sidney Tarachow, M.D. (deceased)
Sarah Tower, M.D.

Consultants

Rudolf Ekstein, Ph.D.
Peyton Jacob, Jr., M.D.
Herbert J. Schlesinger, Ph.D.

Ex Officio

Brian Bird, M.D.
Kenneth T. Calder, M.D.

Invited Participant

Howard Shevrin, Ph.D.

Contents

Editor's Preface

This book is the product of a study of psychoanalytic supervision. It grew out of the activities over a significant span of years, starting in 1965, of an official Study Group on Supervision created within the American Psychoanalytic Association. A central activity and purpose of the Association is the setting and the monitoring of standards of psychoanalytic education to which all the member psychoanalytic institutes adhere in their training practices. This central educational function is carried through a Board on Professional Standards on which all of the member institutes are represented by designated fellows, as well as through various committees of this Board. These committees are almost all action committees in the sense of the ongoing responsibilities that they have for establishing, developing, and accrediting the educational programs of the member institutes and for then certifying the graduates of those programs.

Only one committee of the Board, the Committee on Psychoanalytic Education (COPE), is avowedly a study and not an action group. Without the time and decision-making pressures of the other committees, COPE, designed to consist of a nationally drawn group of senior psychoanalytic educators, all training and supervising analysts, has from the beginning had the charge—and the freedom—to *study* various salient or problematic issues within psychoanalytic education, to do so in whatever way, and with whatever intensity, and over whatever length of time it deemed appropriate or necessary, and, it was hoped, to report the outcome of such studies both to the American Psychoanalytic Association officially and to the wider psychoanalytic world scientifically. That is, the deliberations of COPE, and whatever increments of new knowledge and new educational insight they represent, are basically self-educational activities and consequences for psychoanalysts, to begin with narrowly for those engaged in the study, and if deemed worthwhile enough, to be made broadly available, organizationally and scientifically, to the wider psychoanalytic world both through official committee report and through publication in our professional literature.

This overall function and purpose of COPE has been most systematically pursued by way of study groups set up as subcommittees under the auspices of COPE. It should occasion no great surprise that over the years of its life, COPE established a variety of study groups in areas such as selection, curriculum, etc., before it felt emboldened to turn to the far less circumscribed, and therefore more difficult to encompass, but certainly most central educational arena of psychoanalysis, namely psychoanalytic supervision. A COPE Study Group on Supervision was first brought into being under the Chairmanship of Emanuel Windholz, with Robert S. Wallerstein as its Secretary, during the year 1964–1965 and met for the first time at the Spring Meeting of the American Psychoanalytic Association in April 1965. Its eight original members are those listed on the frontispiece page of this book. It met, as will be described in greater detail in Chapter I of the book, three times each year, usually for two days each time, and over a span of seven or eight years, exploring, with considerable leisure over time and in as much depth as we were collectively capable of, a variety of ways of studying supervision as described in the various chapters of this book. Sidney Tarachow, a vigorous participant in our early deliberations, became ill and died after our very first few meetings, but the imprint of his contributions is nonetheless discernibly (to us) present in the total fabric of the book. Joan Fleming, mentor in study of the supervision process to so many in psychoanalysis across our country, not just to those of us who worked with her in the Study Group, died recently, in 1980, just as the project and the book of which she was one of the principal architects, and far more than just the author of one of its chapters, was being cast into page-proof form. Dedicating the volume to her memory and her spirit pays tribute to her in a way most meaningful to the personal and professional bonds so many of us in analysis have felt to her.

Soon after the Study Group was established by COPE the members made up for critical oversights in its composition by drawing to us, officially as consultants, but really as fully participating members, the three additional senior analytic educators and known devoted students of psychoanalytic education also listed on the frontispiece. One of these, Herbert J. Schlesinger, played an especially signal role in our study as the supervisor who ultimately (after Study Group vicissitudes to be described in the body of the book) provided the very detailed and comprehensive process notes of the first fourteen supervisory hours of a psychoanalytic supervision, covering the first 66 hours of the patient's analysis, which became the data base around which the various perspectives on the supervisory process and the study of the supervisory process developed in the book have been elaborated. The two analysts listed on the frontispiece of the book as *ex officio* members of the Study Group are the two colleagues who served as Chairmen of our parent body, COPE, during the years of our active study and who both gave us the fullest of organizational support throughout our endeavors as well as contributed to our deliberations as more than participant-observers. Howard Shevrin, listed as Invited Participant, is the analytic colleague, then an analytic candidate, who was the student-analyst whose work in supervision is presented in the supervision process notes written by his then-supervisor, Herbert J. Schlesinger. How Howard Shevrin came to participate in this study and contribute to this book is detailed in his own two chapters as well as touched on in the chapters of his supervisor.

Having said this much about what a COPE Study Group is, and how this one was created and its various participants and contributors drawn together, the rest of the account of its activities over time and how they were brought finally into book form with the various members contributing chapters that reflected their own particular area of interest, or perspective on supervision, or special vantage point from which they experienced the process and the events described, all this is the body of the book itself. Though it is a book on psychoanalytic supervision built specifically around the supervision of a beginning psychoanalysis, clearly supervision is equally central, and in many of the same ways, to training in all of the mental health professions, and with modifications, to varieties of other helping professions, in the health and educational arenas alike. In this sense what is generic in the perspectives offered on supervision as a *helping and enabling process* will, we hope, prove to be perhaps comparably useful to supervisors—and supervisees—in other professional helping disciplines as well. In this sense the book is not just for psychoanalysts. It is for supervisors and it is for their students.

At this point, however, I think that the preface still owes the reader two further clarifications. The first is a statement of something that, regretfully, the book is not. The second is some explanation of the gap that the careful reader will have already noted between the seven or eight years of active study of psychoanalytic supervision that the Study Group initiated early in 1965 and the writing of this preface as the book is going to press in late 1980.

First for what the book is not. I have to this point consistently used the word *study*, in the sense of self-education, and of education, to characterize our endeavors. It has *not* been the systematic *research* that we would wish it might have been or perhaps that some successor projects that it may stimulate will in the future be. Considered as a research, this study indeed would have all the methodological flaws and conceptual oversights that Howard Shevrin so clearly points out in his critique and exposition, especially in the first of his two chapters. The research aspects of the study, if any, were only to see if we could collectively describe ways of trying to capture the critical elements of supervision or of the supervisory interaction through some kinds of systematic categorization or systematic focus. Perhaps each of the ways to be described in this book has succeeded in making some progress toward those goals. Perhaps also the way will be clearer for others to go further in the direction both of more systematic study and of actual formal research after their study of our vicissitudes, our dilemmas, and our difficulties.

Second is the issue of the time gap between the completion of the study and the publication of the book. All those who have written books, or have participated in committees that have written books through the assignment of chapters to individual members and yet with the goal of producing a sequentially unfolding narrative, can readily account for much of this gap. There were, however, special additional problems that arose both from the *nature* of our subject matter—the highly private and confidential substance of supervisor and candidate, and of student-analyst and patient, interacting over time with all the properly heightened sensibilities in current times for issues of the guarding of privacy and confidentiality and the securing of properly informed consent—and also from the *particular circumstances* through which stepwise this study was carried out and this manuscript brought into being, circumstances that are indicated throughout the book and that are especially focused on in the contributions by the student-analyst and his supervisor. In briefest capsule, these circumstances stemmed from the fact that the whole study of supervision, including the study of the particular supervision process that is the core data base of this book, evolved stepwise with no intention at the start pointing to any particular direction or kind of publication. When the Study Group as a whole came to the decision that we indeed had something worthwhile to offer the field, that we had achieved a significant self-education and that we wanted to offer and to share what later evolved into this manuscript with the world of our professional and scientific colleagues, we of course had to backtrack, and we undertook to involve the supervisor of the case in a different way, as well as to importantly involve the analyst (now no longer student, but graduate and analytic colleague) as participant and critic, as well as ultimately his patient for her consent to the (suitably disguised) publication of the beginning phase of her analysis.

Mostly, this issue is mentioned here in the preface instead of being properly left for its full unfolding and clarification in the body of the book in order to accord special thanks to a friend and colleague, Jay Katz, who though not listed as one of the contributing authors, is the single person most responsible for the fact that the book has been enabled to appear in print, a tribute to his extraordinarily effective role as negotiator and mediator of all the issues that have surrounded the translation of private study into public book. Jay Katz is both a psychoanalytic colleague and a professor in a law school. Several chapters in the book elaborate the psychological, the legal, and also the ethical problems that he made it possible for us to collectively successively—and successfully—navigate.

A final personal note of credits and responsibilities. The thinking reflected in this book is truly collective in almost every chapter, and yet the various chapters bear the individual authorship and are the individual responsibility of those who selected themselves for particular attention to the task posed by that chapter of the unfolding sequence. As Secretary of the COPE Study Group from the start, I kept very detailed minutes of each of our thrice-yearly meetings, often up to fifteen single-spaced pages for a meeting, and I put together the Outline of Supervision Topics presented as an appendix in this book, culled from the accumulated minutes of the meetings, and designed to serve as organizing foci for developing our various perspectives and perhaps as guides to the evolving structure of our book. I also undertook to edit all of the chapters in the service of eliminating duplication and facilitating the narrative flow, and perhaps even of unifying somewhat the language conventions, without, however, altering in any material way the thinking and the presentations of the various contributing authors. In performing my tasks, I have had the very substantial and invaluable help of Kira Tiedgens, my secretary, who typed, or better retyped, so much of the manuscript, and of Irene Guttman, Editor at International Universities Press, who has so much enhanced the clarity and readability of the manuscript.

Robert S. Wallerstein, M.D.
November 1980

CHAPTER I

The Plan of the Study

ROBERT S. WALLERSTEIN, M.D.

This book is a distillate of the experiences of the Study Group on Supervision of the Committee on Psychoanalytic Education (COPE) of the American Psychoanalytic Association. The Study Group has represented the effort of the organized educational structure of American psychoanalysis to bring together experienced psychoanalytic educators and supervisors with a shared and demonstrated interest and involvement in the advancement of the theory and practice of psychoanalytic supervision into active discussion of the issues of supervision, its (educational) assumptions, its problems of execution and implementation, and its implications and meanings. It was taken for granted—and amply proved to be the case—that the committee members would properly reflect the wide diversity in philosophy of supervision and in operational emphases that characterizes our psychoanalytic educational enterprise today. Much of what has become clarified and better understood through the committee interactions is the result of differing viewpoints, philosophical underpinnings, and pragmatic experiences.

The Study Group[1] has been notably stable and task-devoted since its inception in the Spring of 1965. It has met regularly three times yearly, usually

[1]Emanuel Windholz (Chairman); Robert S. Wallerstein (Secretary); Daryl DeBell, Joan Fleming (deceased), Maurice Friend, Paul G. Myerson, Sidney Tarachow (deceased), and Sarah Tower (members); Rudolf Ekstein, Peyton Jacob, Jr., and Herbert J. Schlesinger (consultants); Brian Bird and Kenneth T. Calder (*ex officio* members, Chairmen of COPE).

for two days at a time, and with much "homework" in between in the form of letters, memoranda, position papers, and illustrative manuscripts, often suitable for separate publication, prepared for group exchange and mutual study. It has studied write-ups of cases and of supervisions, verbatim transcripts of supervision hours, and extensive segments from longitudinally maintained supervisor's process notes of ongoing analytic supervisions. A subgroup within the Study Group,[2] meeting twice monthly over several years, evolved a schema for the organization and classification of the material of supervision processes. In accord with its categories, it has studied in detail several years of process notes of two psychoanalytic supervisions, process notes produced and furnished for the purposes of this inquiry by another member of the Study Group (from another geographic locale). Extremely detailed minutes have been kept of each of the thrice-yearly meetings of the national Study Group. The minutes of the first two years of meetings, which consisted of a systematic survey of the theories, issues, and methods of psychoanalytic supervision and pedagogy, were abstracted and organized into an Outline of Topics in Psychoanalytic Supervision, a detailed guide to the problems and questions that the Study Group had raised and discussed. That outline, which may be of some guiding value to others interested in study of the issues of supervision, is published in full as an appendix to this monograph.

But let us turn first not to outcomes, but to beginnings. The initial charge to the committee was permissively broad and undefined—to "study" psychoanalytic supervision as a crucial element in the psychoanalytic educational process. As a first perspective on the practical problems of analytic education via supervision, the Study Group was given access to a representative spectrum of letters written by supervising analysts to the Membership Committee of the Board on Professional Standards of the American Psychoanalytic Association (with all individually identifying data, of course, removed), letters that attempted a critical appraisal from the supervisory perspective of how effectively the applicant had mastered the clinical practice of psychoanalysis. These letters are one form of data on supervision, data of the kind readily available in every institute in supervisors' regular reports to progression committees, and data, incidentally, most useful for the study of one of the supervisor's functions in particular, that of evaluation.

Expectedly, these letters portrayed a wide range of "learning problems" and of "problems about learning"[3] in the student-analysts, quite apart from the issues of how much or how well they had learned. In fact, only one of the many letters studied stated serious reservations about the adequacy of

[2]Daryl DeBell, Peyton Jacob, Jr., Robert S. Wallerstein, and Emanuel Windholz (San Francisco subgroup).

[3]For the distinction between these, see Ekstein and Wallerstein (1972, pp. 136-176).

the candidate, emphasizing his limited psychological-mindedness and empathic capacity, that he was at best a plodding and mechanical analyst, and (even more rarely ever stated) that he was unlikely to improve much with either further supervision or psychoanalysis.

All the rest of the letters discussed a great variety of problems within the context of generally favorable work toward their resolution. This was to be expected since the letters concerned successful candidates, those who had been graduated from psychoanalytic institutes and were now being proposed for membership in the American Psychoanalytic Association. And if one were to solicit similar letters about candidates who had been dropped during the course of their training, there no doubt would be many more that would stress the graver and less remediable form variants of problems —perhaps the same sorts of problems, just in more extreme form? Reading the letters side by side, one could array the problems that were reported, often into seeming polar opposites. For example, there was (1) the exaggeration of the discerned pathology, the student-analyst who would always see the defensive but never the adaptive aspects of the patient's behaviors, leading to a consistent interpretative bias; and exactly opposite, was (2) the underestimation of the severity of illness deriving, in the particular instance reported, from a countertransference difficulty, namely the student's narcissistic need to prove that he could successfully analyze this too-difficult case. Linked to this pair of problems was (3) the student who was all along too ready to give up in the face of difficulties, persistently overestimating their severity. Another pair was evident in (4) the student who had difficulty in appropriately modifying the classical analytic procedure in response, for example, to severe acute life crisis—that is, the student who too rigidly held on to classical analytic technique even in the face of suitable contraindications—as against (5) the student who tended to fall back on psychotherapeutic rather than psychoanalytic procedures when under stress or in doubt. Another set of opposites that appeared consisted of (6) the student who was overdependent on supervision to the point that he was persistently "analyzing a week late," responding this week with the interpretations that he gleaned from the supervisor as a result of the discussion of last week's material, and (7) the student who resisted the role of student, was stubbornly oppositional about supervision, and had to be taught against his will. Then there was another pair, (8) the student who had such a need to impress the supervisor favorably that he tried to do so at the expense of adequately reporting the process between himself and the patient—lest he reveal too many "mistakes"—linked to (9) the student who tried to make quasi-therapeutic use of the supervision, designated by one supervising analyst in a letter as the use of the supervisor as an "auxiliary analyst." The danger here is of the supervisor being seduced into a personally therapeutic role at the expense of teaching the student how to analyze. That is, here, too, the supervisory process is focused away from teaching the student how to analyze the patient.

And then there were letters that focused more on countertransference problems in the student-analyst: (10) for example, the analytic treatment that lit up specific incompletely resolved neurotic conflicts in the student-analyst (around competitiveness, or dependency, the control of aggression, etc.); or (11) in which the analyst found it difficult to maintain proper analytic objectivity, tending readily to lapse into the assigned transference role; or (12)—another variant—the student who needed to see himself as the objective observer outside of the transference neurosis, defending himself against seeing that he was an integral part of it. And there were single statements about readily recognized common themes in supervision: for instance, (13) the student who was disposed to all-or-none dichotomizations in relation to patient behaviors—a special risk with acting-out behaviors where the student would feel compelled either to interdict the behaviors or to refrain from intervening, counting on just waiting them out. What he would have yet to learn was that there was a third and appropriate way in between, of intervening, not punitively in prohibition, but interpretively. Last (14), there were statements about special problems of terminating cases, about how common good beginnings are, and how rare good endings are. Also revealed in these letters were many hints of how differently the various supervisors had dealt with learning and countertransference difficulties of their students, how they varyingly interpreted their pedagogical, their "therapeutic," and their evaluative tasks. In this they revealed something of their own varying supervisory philosophies.

Clearly, these sample letters reflected a representative range of the kinds of problems and issues that come up in—and for—psychoanalytic supervision. They usually make evaluative statements about *what* the student learned about these problems and issues, in the sense of the supervisor's judgment concerning to what extent they have been overcome or successfully dealt with and the student-analyst freed to progress in his (independent) analyzing ability. However, they are inherently very limited in being able to shed much light on *how* these problems and issues are (successfully or not) worked with. It is with such a survey of problems and issues then that a study of psychoanalytic supervision, as an *educational process,* must begin, not rest.

Within the COPE Study Group on Supervision, different scientific and personal predilections, and consequently different kinds of emphases and selectivities of observational data and methods—and of observer biases—became evident very early in the shared search to learn more about this *how* of the supervision process. Actually, three main trends emerged, three differing methodological orientations, and to an undetermined degree, with perhaps somewhat differing underlying philosophical assumptions about the nature of supervision as a process, or rather how its unique subject matter—analyzing ability—can be learned and taught. These different ways to approach the study of supervision can be characterized as follows:

The task as formulated by the San Francisco subgroup was to devise a longitudinal and parallel schema for the systematic categorization of the major phenomena of an ongoing psychoanalysis and its concomitant supervision, as extractable from the usual kind of available data source—the analyst's process notes of the analysis as regularly prepared for the purposes of the clinical supervision,[4] and similar process notes by the supervisor on the supervision hours, specially prepared for these research and study purposes. If the schema thus devised to represent the phenomena contained in the process notes proves adequate—simple and general enough to be both clinically congenial and not unduly burdensome, while still elaborated and specific enough to differentiate the major categories of study interest—then it will permit coding the essential data of the two processes (the ongoing analysis *and* its supervision) in ways that make possible the study of many (though clearly not all) of the major substantive issues of psychoanalytic supervision. The classification actually arrived at was a six-fold division, extended to cover, and at the same time discriminate, the many events and interactions recorded in the process notes of the two processes, the analysis and the supervision.

Because of the greater feasibility of such a study if it would require only the collaboration of the supervisor and access just to *his* notes on the supervision process and with the hope that the supervisor's process notes of the supervision hour could capture as well the main events and interactions of the ongoing psychoanalysis being supervised, i.e., the subject of discussion and interaction within the supervision, the decision was made to work with only (sufficiently elaborate) supervisory process notes as the way of study and access to knowledge of both processes, the psychoanalysis *and* its supervision. If it could be demonstrated that "good enough" data[5] are thus avail-

[4]By process notes, here and throughout, we do not mean merely an effort at a faithful rendering of the verbal events and interchanges—"he said, I said"—but rather an overall conceptualization of an interactional process, what the patient was driving at, what he was trying to reveal, and what (by inference) he was trying to conceal, what configural sense the analyst made of the patient's material, and the bases on which he decided to intervene when and in the ways he did, deciding what to say and what not to say. Process notes written in this way thus essay to capture the unspoken mental activity of the analyst as well as that of the patient. *Pari passu,* process notes made by a supervisor of a supervision hour try to represent two parallel interactional processes, the therapy as discerned by the supervisor via the presentation by the analyst, and the supervision as conceptualized by the supervisor. Thus they attempt to present three streams of mental activity, that of the patient vis-à-vis the therapist (which is usually the most explicit), that of the therapist (facing two ways, toward the patient and toward the supervisor), and that of the supervisor (reacting to the two processes and to the interactions between them).

[5]I have together with Sampson (1971) discussed at great length the various issues involved in the use of process notes as research data, including the questions of sampling and selectiv-

able to insure adequate study—adequate, that is, in terms of the questions and goals of the particular study—the great advantage in manageability would accrue of a several-fold reduction in the data base (elimination of the four- or five-time more numerous, hence more voluminous, therapist's process notes of the analysis) and also freedom from the need to involve the explicit cooperation of the student-analyst of the case, even indirectly (and hence the lesser likelihood of disturbing his analytic education).

Planned in this way, for study of the two concomitant processes as discernible through the detailed process notes kept by the supervising analyst, and with (for our study purposes) the focus more on the happenings of the supervision than of the analysis being supervised, the six-fold schema was devised as follows: (1) the *analysis,* an account of its themes and contents, its resistances and its transferences, as discerned via the supervisor's process notes based on the material, oral or written, made available by the student-analyst in the supervision hour; (2) the *analyst's understanding of the analytic material,* the assessment of the overall meanings that the analyst grasped in the patient's material, how it hung together in his mind; (3) the *analyst's activity,* or what the analyst did (how he intervened), his tactical and strategic choices; (4a) the *supervisor's understanding of the technical analytic issues,* how *he* understood the unfolding of the case and the technical therapeutic issues posed by it, as well as that congruence of his understanding with that of the analyst (or the lapses in that congruence); (4b) the *supervisor's pedagogic interventions,* or all of the specific "didactic" supervisory teaching, the conveying of technical information, attitude, or insight; (5a) the *supervisor's understanding of the analyst's personal involvement,* his understanding of the other than simple technical or information deficits of the analyst, including the progression (or deviations) of the teaching-learning interaction with all the complexities of the analyst's learning problems (vis-à-vis his patient), problems about learning (vis-à-vis his supervisor), learning style, countertransferences (toward the patient), and transferences (toward the supervisor); (5b) the *supervisor's therapeutic interventions,* the totality of the other than "didactic" supervisory teaching as addressed to the range of educational problems covered under this heading; and last (6) the *analyst's response to the supervision hour,* the evidence of the impact of the supervisory teaching, of both the "didactic" and the "other-than-didactic" as discerned in the subsequent evolution of the material.

The material of the case, its analysis and its supervision, as embodied in the supervisor's process notes, is thus abstracted and reorganized under these six headings on a sequential hour-by-hour basis. The material thus

ity, incompleteness, distortion and bias; counterpart gains in manageability, clarity, and extractability of the themes of central interest; and especially the issues of the conditions under which process notes can be "good enough," "equally good," or even better for the particular research purpose at hand.

organized can then be studied both vertically across headings, or longitudinally over time. Comparative study is possible of particular thematic or topical lines across cases, or of the same case over time along different thematic or topical lines, study, that is, of process and of change. Because the basic data are the condensed and abstracted representation in the original supervision process notes, large sweeps of material, disclosing major configurations and sequence of change can readily be encompassed within this schema. More, it allows, indeed enhances, the detection of recurrent configurations, since they are not buried in such a mass of often deadly detail. At the same time it can be sufficiently detailed to allow rough quantifications (and comparisons) of frequencies of entries (per supervision hour) under each of the headings, so that one could determine (in an actual example) that a serious technical error in the intervention pattern of the analyst (recorded under [3] *analyst's activity*) led to a major intensification of the supervisor's active teaching effort (recorded under [4b] *supervisor's pedagogic interventions*)—a change that might have been noticed, to be sure, by an acute observer who had carefully read the supervisor's process notes, but one which in fact was not noted until this six-fold schema was imposed on the supervisory material, and the entries under the separate headings then compared.

A second major way, conceptually and methodologically, to study the supervision process is that offered by Fleming and Benedek (1966), in their book *Psychoanalytic Supervision,*[6] and represented by one of its authors in the deliberations of the COPE Study Group. Fleming and Benedek undertook the same task—devising a method for the systematic study of an ongoing supervisory process—but by way of a different schema, one focused on supervisor-student interactions rather than on organization into conceptual categories. Since their intent was to study sequences or units of interaction at a micro-analytic level, their preferred data base was obviously the electronic recording of supervision sessions, though the method can indeed be applied (as it has been within the COPE Study Group) to process-note data, provided these data are sufficiently detailed. The method divides the material (whether verbatim transcript or adequately detailed process notes) into sequential interactional units.

To quote from *Psychoanalytic Supervision:* "Our problem in examining the [transcript] data was to find a way of isolating *episodes* that had a beginning and an end, and tracing the theme that related one episode to another to produce the dynamic line of shifting tensions within one hour, between hours, and on a time curve throughout the analytic process. This focus for study referred most specifically to the therapeutic material as reported by the student analyst. For the supervisory process we needed to define episodes

[6]See especially Chapter 3, pp. 35-49.

in the teaching-learning interaction which represented a particular aspect of learning or teaching and which also could be followed through the cycles of changing tensions in relation to the student's progress in learning" (p. 41; italics added). The search is thus for "units of interaction" or "units of exchange" (p. 42) that can be studied in relative isolation: "we have attempted to tease out events in supervision so that they could be observed in *isolation* and thus help us to identify components of the total experience that facilitate the process of learning" (p. 233; italics added). In conceptualizing such process observations, recourse was had both to psychoanalytic theory, particularly helpful in "describing the psychoanalytic treatment experience as a process of interactions with particular motivations" and to social-interaction theory and Bales's problem-solving concepts, a useful framework for "conceptualizing the teaching-learning experience in terms of process" (p. 41).

This method of Fleming and Benedek has distinctive advantages in the study of supervision processes. Because of the micro-analytic and sequential interactional approach, the alert and sensitive supervisor can very quickly make critical diagnostic appraisals of educational difficulties (be they technical or informational deficiencies or emotionally determined impedances) and thus sooner plan his educational corrective strategies. Typical, unusual, or pathognomonic events are more likely to be highlighted early for educational scrutiny. Since the process data are examined sequentially and interactionally rather than being classified into discrete categories (and hence fragmented?) as in the San Francisco schema, they have cause and effect or stimulus and response sequences automatically built in, or rather preserved intact, instead of artificially separated and having to be subsequently reconstructed in a further separate step as in the San Francisco schema. On the other hand, by virtue of that separation and disjunction of elements (of thematic lines and of internal process lines), the San Francisco schema can facilitate a fresh scanning for novel combinations, for cause-effect or correlational connections that would be less evident in the original (unschematized) material.

Each method may have distinct advantages and disadvantages (perhaps complementary to one another), and the two approaches represent differing perspectives about and alternate paths toward a shared goal—an advance in the systematization of clinical supervision (and treatment) data so as to encompass them more comprehensively and render them more amenable to direct study and research.

The third major stance for study of the supervision process was, by contrast with the foregoing two, more directly issue- than method-oriented. Cast in the more traditional clinical mold, it involved immersion in the clinical material, with then identifying (impressionistically to be sure, but with the practiced eye of the experienced clinician and teacher) the substantive problems that warrant more intensive individual and/or collaborative study. It is the method not just of usual clinical teaching (whether built around the oral or the written—process-note—presentation of the analytic material by the student-analyst), but also the method of the usual case report, clinical study, and embryonic clinical research. It is, of course, the historical method, bequeathed to us by Freud, of study of the case material (or supervision material), as reconstructed by the analyst (or, with study of supervision, by the supervisor), perhaps after completion of the case, in more or less detail, and with indeterminate accuracy, omissions, and selective distortions (biases).

The many limitations for the purposes of empirical scientific advance (as opposed to just clinical study) of such an essentially totally private and memory-based method of data generation and study have been by now well documented. These have been stated in a similar context as follows, "The fallibility of human memory is itself the focus of a vast body of research in general psychology. . . . Beyond this issue of fallibility, the reliance on the treating analyst's memory alone as the central (and unsupplemented) data gathering instrument in analytic research is beset by many other equally powerful limitations. . . (1) The unchecked, or at least not systematically checked, subjectivity (countertransferences) of the observer. (2) The unknown systematic biases introduced by any process of selecting data for presentation according to unspecified canons of procedure for determining relevance (an issue linked to but by no means co-extensive with possible countertransference distortion). (3) The lack of public character so that concurrent or independent evaluation is precluded. (4) The lack of repeatability or reproducibility of a forever vanished circumstance. Clearly systematization must begin, rather than rest, at this point" (Wallerstein and Sampson, 1971, pp. 18–19).

Nonetheless, this same case study method, innovated by Freud, has flourished in the hands of its founder and of those who have come after, and has to this day provided a truly extraordinary range of insights into the structure of the mind, the forces at work in the treatment situation, the requirements of technique, and the processes of change. It is a method far from exhausted in the rewards it can yield, and it has been appropriately and richly represented within the deliberations of the Study Group on Supervision and in its distillation into this book.

What then are the kinds of substantive issues, clinical and educational, that such organizing efforts, each of these three approaches, can (each to varying degrees) potentially illuminate? In bare listing (and in the most general way) they include such questions as: What changes take place over the course of the processes under scrutiny in the patient, in the analyst, in the analysis, and (even) in the supervisor and/or the supervision? How do these changes interrelate across the parallel processes and over time? What are the differing effects on the analysis and the analyst of the supervisor's various activities under the categories of didactic teaching and attention to the analyzing instrument in the San Francisco schema? What are the kinds of interventions, amount, timing, phrasing, etc.—discernible in the interactional sequences within episodes isolated for study in the Fleming-Benedek schema—that lead to new learning and integration (as opposed to interfering with learning)? How much light can be thrown on such methodological issues in studying the educational impact of the supervisor's interventions as the question of time lag and of the proper selection of time unit? For instance, is the response to an intervention to be discerned in the association of the next minute, in the reflections of that evening, or the altered activities in the analyzing of the following week (not to speak of even longer-term effects)? Or, put into more technical research language, what are the criteria for linking interventions (independent variables) to responses (dependent variables)?

Such a listing can indeed be greatly extended. However, it might serve as a more informative introduction to the gains in understanding that can be arrived at via the approach to educational and clinical issues through the several kinds of systematizations of method achieved by our Study Group, to illustrate with an actual problem, with both educational and clinical aspects, that the group did explore at some length from its several methodological vantage points. In the fifth hour of the supervision of an advanced control case (the main case discussed throughout this monograph), the supervisor was struck by the fact that the student-analyst responded to the patient's transference position of seeming to have no expectation of the analyst or the analysis, of keeping a definite distance with no quality of either demand or complaint, by in turn taking the counterpart position of objectivity and of similarly defined distance. The supervisor felt this response by the analyst within the transference to be sufficiently marked to be labeled "coolness."

The supervisory materials (supervision process notes) were scrutinized intensely by the Study Group in an effort to elucidate the possible meanings of this hypertrophied analytic objectivity, or "coolness." A considerable range of possibilities was considered: (1) The "coolness" of the analyst could be a reaction formation against a (later confessed) countertransference attraction to the patient. Seen this way, the "coolness" would be the indicator of a *countertransference* problem in the analyst. (2) But the *admission* of "coolness" as a defense, imputed to be a reaction formation in the countertransference, could also be the expression of a *transference* of the analyst to the supervisor, in this instance, an attempt to "disarm" him (*pari passu,* it could simultaneously "arm" the supervisor, enacting with him the transference position in the analysis that was experienced and "perceived," but not cognitively grasped [see Arlow, 1963]). (3) Or "coolness" could be an overall *character disposition* of the analyst that he would defensively like to see as *just* a specific (and circumscribed) countertransference problem (see 1, above). Here one would be confessing to a small difficulty in order to conceal a perhaps larger one. (4) In a wholly different realm of meanings, the "coolness" in the analysis could be the reconstruction of the psychological climate of infancy with the cool and distant father. This would be a compliant transference repetition supporting the transference expectation. If properly sensed by the analyst, the perception of this induced coolness could be turned potentially into the *signal* use of a countertransference affect. (5) And of course the "coolness" could be more *adaptive,* rather than predominantly defensive—a generalized adaptive posture for dealing therapeutically with a still unclear gestalt within the transference. (6) The "coolness" could be, too, a planned *psychotherapeutic* maneuver to reassure the patient against her anxiety. That is, instead of analyzing the burgeoning erotic transference, the analyst would help the patient to repress it. This would be then a therapeutic rather than an analytic maneuver, supporting, or identifying with, the patient's defense. "Coolness" deliberately adopted on such a basis might even not be technically contraindicated; it might enable the patient to feel safe enough to allow her erotic feelings to develop at a more appropriate pace within the transference. (7) Quite the opposite of this, "coolness" could serve as a *seduction,* a come-on, "playing it cool" and inviting pursuit, counteracting in the countertransference. Or, (8) there could be "coolness" out of *technical ignorance,* a misunderstanding or misapplication of the technical precept of analytic neutrality. Last (9), it must be remembered that all the foregoing considerations are based on the premise that the "coolness" discerned by the supervisor was itself a valid-enough perception. It could also be a distortion or a projection by the supervisor, and as such represent an equally full counterpart array of possible meanings from the supervisor's side.

The practiced analyst and supervisor will no doubt have recognized these various possibilities and assessed, from his own experience as applied to the specific data of this case, something of their individual or combined likelihoods. He will perhaps have added some other possibilities not included here. On what basis, then, can one decide which factors are the most operative (and in what combination) in the particular analytic situation being discussed in this supervision? And how can one utilize the various approaches to the study of supervision propounded within the Study Group to throw light on this clinical decision-making process? The balance of this book is an effort to answer just these questions using this example of the analyst's perceived "coolness" as a central paradigmatic instance, the fulcrum around which a many-sided scrutiny of the conceptual and methodological approaches to supervision will be intensively developed.

Chapter II is a detailed exposition of the various general *issues of method* that arise in the study of supervision, of intervention options that present themselves, and of the psychological meanings and consequences that inhere in pursuing each of these possible action choices. The focus is on not just the range of possible methods of approach to the study of supervision, but on the underlying psychological and philosophical assumptions *a priori* built into each method, and on the close-coupled relation of the kinds of substantive data obtained (and obtainable) to the nature of the methods by which these data are derived. In this context the conceptual and methodological assumptions of both the San Francisco and the Fleming-Benedek approaches to the study of supervision are closely examined and compared.

Chapter III in turn represents a focus on *issues of substance.* It is a summary, presented toward the *beginning* of the monograph, of the general *principles* of supervisory practice, which emerged by the *end* of our work together as a consensus, reached by the supervision Study Group, as the achieved outcome of its original wide diversity in stated supervision philosophy and practice when subjected to the empiricism of collaborative scientific scrutiny. These broad areas of agreement on *general principles* (presented in the italicized phrases and sentences in Chapter III) express the commonalities we discovered that knit us together as recognizable supervisors of psychoanalysis, while allowing for differences in application and in implication of the various viewpoints on method and substance that are presented in this monograph.

The fourth chapter presents *specific examples* of how these general principles are viewed and implemented from the various perspectives on supervision philosophy and practice, on supervisory method and substance, that characterize the individual participants in the COPE Study Group project and that, more broadly, reflect the range of professional viewpoints within the field. For sharpened heuristic purposes, these various styles and positions are set up where possible in oppositional terms, or in polarities, as the stance of "say as much as you can" vs. "say only as much as you have to" or the perennial dilemma of supervision conceived as "pedagogy" vs. supervision conceived as "therapy." It should hardly need stating here that for purposes of clear exposition and provocative argument these positions are often presented in "ideal types."

Following this discussion, with its many illustrative clinical vignettes, of the varying viewpoints drawn from the varying backgrounds and conceptual commitments of the Study Group members, Chapter V presents the actual raw material or "primary data" from an ongoing supervision process which served as the arena against which these different viewpoints were tested and interacted in the search for contact and common purpose as well as for exposure of operational difference. This chapter consists of the actual process notes of the first fourteen supervision hours (based on 66 analytic hours) in the case in which the judgment concerning the analyst's undue "coolness" was made in the fifth supervision hour. The fourteen-hour sequence was chosen to cover all the supervision material leading up to and providing the background for understanding the judgment made concerning the fifth hour, as well as providing the continuity and follow-up to this judgment and the intervention decisions based on it with their consequences—all carried to the closure of this logical "meaning unit" of supervision material with the interactions of the fourteenth hour. Since this was the basic material used by all the Study Group members for intensive study from a variety of methodological vantage points, it was felt desirable to render it equally available to the readers of this monograph (with only the alteration of possibly identifying material necessary to insure proper disguise and safeguard of confidentiality)—so that each reader would have the full evidential base for each of the assertions or inferences built up from the primary material, and have data in hand adequate to agree or disagree, to formulate similarly or differently.

Chapter VI, then, is the first of the various systematic "perspectives" on this supervisory raw material—detailed process notes of a supervision process. It was put first because its way of study and its development of the principles involved—those elaborated by Fleming and Benedek (1966)—reflect what is to this point the most systematically formulated treatise on specifically psychoanalytic supervision in the literature. The microinteractional basis of this approach, via the study of discrete units, or episodes, of specific interactions, has been sketched out in preliminary fashion in this chapter. The fuller development of the conceptualization as well as the application to the study of our sample supervision hours is the substance of this chapter.

Chapter VII is from the next perspective, that of the San Francisco subgroup, intensively explored within the framework of the COPE Study Group organization. The chapter consists of the reorganization of the material of the same fourteen supervision hours (Chapter V) according to the six-fold schema presented in this chapter. The fourteen supervision hours are presented sequentially, the nature of each categorized along the six dimensions. Abstracted in this way, the material of the two tandem processes, the analysis and its supervision, can be read in several ways: in temporal succession hour by hour, or any single strand of the six can be read as a sequential narrative in its own right (apart from the other five), or as a comparative study of the separate developments in each of the domains within any hour, or more complexly by studying, for instance, the analyst's interventions in one hour (or a succession of hours), following a shift in the supervisor's interventions in a previous hour.

One kind of application that can emerge from the close study of clinical material organized according to the San Francisco schema is the substance of Chapter VIII. It is an overall summary of what was learned (from the supervisor's perspective) from the San Francisco Project's way of organizing the material of these fourteen supervision hours, comparable to the summary of the same material in Chapter VI, according to the (interactional) perspective of the Fleming-Benedek schema. The two summaries side by side lend themselves to comparative study, for their congruences, and also their disjunctions, thus throwing clearer light, because based on actual clinical example, on the strengths and shortcomings of each approach, on the kinds of data, of information and of inference, that each is best equipped to generate.

The companion Chapter IX is a closely related kind of application that can emerge from the study of the material organized in accordance with the San Francisco schema. In this chapter the focus is not on the supervisor and the processes of *his* work (supervisory), but rather on the student-analyst and the processes of *his* work (analyzing)—as reflected in the view that this way of studying supervision provides of the analyst's normal "working style." That is, the concern is not primary with pathology and deviation—the analyst's personal difficulties and his learning difficulties as evidenced in his "defensive style"—but more with the "normal" functioning of his "work-ego" as crystallized into a "working style," a congeries of capacities reflecting the developmental interactions over time of talents and training (in effect, of nature and nurture). By highlighting the relevant differentiated dimensions of the San Francisco schema study of the same fourteen supervision hours, the general propositions of this chapter are given concrete illustration.

The next chapter, X, then represents a honed-down effort, to take the one focal supervision hour, the fifth, and in the light of this now broader detailed knowledge of the sweep of the analysis and the supervision, before and after, to look at just the one hour from various points of view, seeing what light each can throw on the array of possible explanatory hypotheses proposed for the "coolness" example given in this chapter. Bringing all this effort to bear on the events—and the possible interpretations—of the fifth supervision hour becomes, too, a recapitulation of part of the history of the COPE Study Group effort. This hour was the focus of the most intensive—and multi-sided—study of any hour within the group and at the same time (and actually because of that) was also used as the main focus of the two larger meetings, discussion groups, held by the Study Group with representatives of the various psychoanalytic institutes at the times of national meetings of the American Psychoanalytic Association in 1967 and 1968. It may well be the most broadly known as well as the most intensively studied single psychoanalytic supervision hour.

Chapter XI provides a total other perspective on what has been examined in the previous chapters only from a variety, albeit indeed a variety, of *supervisory* perspectives. It represents the view from the other side, the *student-analyst's* perspective on the treatment of his (supervised) case and the supervision of that treatment as he experienced and undertook to report *both* these parallel processes. He has drawn heavily on his process notes of the analysis and thus provides a different data base from that previously available. In addition, he offers a critical assessment of both the supervisory data and the research approach employed in this study. Unlike the other chapters which, though based on shared experiences, were all written independently of each other, this one was written by the treating analyst after he had a chance to read the chapters written by the others about his work. In that sense, it is a response, a counterconceptualization of the same events as inevitably differently seen. From the point of view of the monograph as a whole, it is then a vital corrective and modification of the total tableau offered by the supervisor and the other presenters, a proper rounding out of the overall effect, the differing versions of the same events as seen from the counterposed vantage points and through widely different personal filters and conceptual standpoints. The chapter by the student in the enterprise alongside the several by the teacher and his colleagues is illuminating and sobering in what it says to us all about how what we do can be viewed in both the giving and the receiving. It is also an assessment of the study as research that raises a number of questions.

Chapter XII is the first of the three more subjective accounts of the supervision studies of the Study Group. It is written from the perspective of one of the group members reflecting on what he felt he had learned about himself as a "supervising instrument" from his participation over the life of the group. The explicit focus of this very personal document is on "how my vistas have altered," though it at the same time fulfills the more *general* aspiration that it presents a typical enough kind of experience to resonate meaningfully with broadly shared fantasies, expectations, and apprehensions of the vicariously involved reader.

A comparable subjective account, this one from the standpoint of the supervisor, is presented in Chapter XIII. It concerns the problems and issues involved in obtaining and reporting detailed clinical material on supervision for this or like study purposes. The chapter is written generally enough to portray the generic problems of collecting this *kind* of material, and in such a way that the considerations it raises could be taken to apply to other such material and situations, as well as to whatever similar material readers of this monograph may be stimulated to gather for process studies (analytic or supervisory) of their own.

The final chapter, by the student-analyst, is an equally candid and perhaps even more difficult self-examination than the two that precede it. Here again, in the completion of the *Rashomon* effect, is the same mix of the concretely personal and the generically applicable. And in this final circling back in such intimate examination to the original purpose of the entire enterprise—the impact of his learning upon the student, learning which after all is the goal of all the supervisory teaching—we trust we shall have brought sufficient closure and provided adequate justification of COPE's heuristic value to the study and the advancement of psychoanalytic education.

REFERENCES

Arlow, J. A. (1963), The supervisory situation. *J. Amer. Psychoanal. Assn.*, 11:576–594.

Ekstein, R. & Wallerstein, R. S. (1972), *The Teaching and Learning of Psychotherapy*. New York: International Universities Press.

Fleming, J. & Benedek, T. (1966), *Psychoanalytic Supervision*. New York: Grune & Stratton.

Wallerstein, R. S. & Sampson, H. (1971), Issues in research in the psychoanalytic process. *Internat. J. Psycho-Anal.*, 52:11–50.

CHAPTER II

The Study of Supervision: Approaches to Method

DARYL DeBELL, M.D.

The COPE Study Group on Supervision concerned itself periodically with the question of how best to study supervision. We recognized early that we were faced not with a single question, but rather with many, and that the method of approach to each must be individually selected. The questions range from those which are mostly practical and administrative, through those that are concerned with the specific didactic problems of supervision, to those that are fundamental and theoretical in nature.

Examples of practical and administrative problems are those involving, for instance, issues of the skill and the training progress of the candidate. We are constantly faced with making just these evaluations, and for the most part we probably do a creditable job of it. However, disagreements within progression committees attest to the fact that our judgmental criteria are at least in need of some standardization, and that a study of the nature of the evidence on which these judgments are based and of the relative reliability and importance of the evidence is indicated.

With respect to all of the many didactic problems of supervision—whether they involve the candidate and his inexperience, his countertransferences, or his particular problems about learning, or whether they involve the supervisor and his corresponding difficulties—all of them require collecting the relevant empirical data, identifying the relevant determining factors, and assessing their complex interrelatednesses.

The more fundamental questions are probably the most elusive. How does learning take place during the process of supervision? What is there about supervision that is unique in its service to the learning process or even especially useful to it? Can we define what usually transpires in a supervisory hour, and if so can we say what is beneficial about it and what is not or is even hurtful? These and the many other similar problems are often difficult to study, and it is clear that each type of problem will be best approached by collecting the kind of data most directly relevant to it.

There are several contrasting strategies that can be employed in such study of supervision. One such set consists of a survey approach to the diverse viewpoints and methods employed by different supervisors and the varieties of administrative practices developed by different institutes. This type of study contrasts sharply with that which attempts to discover basic and generic principles within the learning-teaching situation of individual supervision. Another set counterposes the research study against the scholastic or academic study. The research approach would require the detailed study of the clinical data, i.e., the actual material deriving from supervisory hours, and the attempt to generate general working hypotheses from these data about the dimensions of the teaching-learning process. In contrast, the scholastic approach would study comparatively the conceptions offered by the various serious students of the subject. This dichotomy should probably be considered a false one, however, since any proper research would be preceded and guided by the previous research and theorizing of others. The "single-issue" and the "total-flow" approaches afford yet another contrast in studies directed at the ongoing supervisory process. The single-issue approach selects one dimension of interest in a supervisory process and studies that issue almost exclusively. Case reports about problems in supervision are almost invariably single-issue studies. Such problems as countertransference, or crisis situations, or analyst blind spots are commonplace examples. Total-flow studies would try to follow all of the many identified aspects of supervision simultaneously and concomitantly relate them to each other. Taken literally, of course, such a study would be impossible, but the emphasis is on the idea of considering multiple issues simultaneously.

Among ourselves, we have noticed an interesting tendency to shift from a consideration of the abstract question, "How can supervision be studied?" to the concrete consideration of whatever materials we may be using at the moment to exemplify an aspect of that overall question. This tendency—it rather seems to approach a compulsion—is not limited to the COPE Study

Group, but appears in other groups with similar purpose as well. Even though considerable effort was made to avoid it by forewarning, on both the occasions of the organized meetings of our Study Group with the representatives of the various psychoanalytic institutes, and in each of the sections of those meetings, this same kind of shift was regularly observed.

This general tendency to "regress" from the abstract to the concrete extends to our overall consideration of the supervision process as well. Each time we attempt to study supervision itself, the group becomes concerned with the specific activities of the particular supervisor and each group member attempts to arrive at his own judgments paralleling those of the analyst and supervisor. We in the group have done this so regularly that we have called it, pejoratively, "second-guessing." It is one of the most difficult habits to break, so difficult in fact that we have almost come to accept it as a first stage in the study of any problem, an indulgence we permit ourselves before settling down to our assigned task. When, for example, we read a transcript of a supervisory hour, almost no matter what general question we have raised for discussion, our attention is regularly drawn first to the case. We begin by gleaning from the material presented whatever we can in an effort to make a formulation about the patient. On the basis of this formulation, and what we can reconstruct of the flow of the material, we make plans about the tactical handling of the case, and compare this with the analyst's technical approach, judged by his reported interventions. We then try to estimate how well the analyst understands the case and how tactful and technically competent he is in exploiting that understanding. With these evaluations behind us, we scrutinize the supervisor's efforts in their light, and approve or disapprove, or at least question, those efforts according to the degree of correspondence between our plans and his actions. This progression of attention from the patient, to the analyst, to the supervisor, is striking in its uniformity, and appears to be an essential orienting device for analysts. It is as though the analyst-investigator must obey the dubious biological aphorism that "ontogeny recapitulates phylogeny" and must first repeat his early function as analyst and follow it with his more lately acquired function as supervisor, before he can attend to his announced intention to investigate whatever question he may have raised about the study of supervisory process. When the question is one of candidate evaluation, this sequence is useful; when it is a question of investigating the candidate's problem about learning, its value is more marginal; when we are interested in the effect of the supervisor's teaching activity, such efforts may be largely diversionary.

From time to time various suggestions have been made for the group to focus its study in certain areas. One of the earliest suggestions was that we make a survey of institutes in regard to their supervisors' reports and their methods of evaluating supervision. Another suggestion was to make a survey of recent graduates and their supervisory experiences. We have later, however, come to consider our function somewhat differently and have expressed this as: "The purpose of the Study Group is to formulate a comparative study of ways of conceptualizing the supervisory process." Later we considered doing a comparative study of the work of several supervisors, but again defined our task as being a survey of the approaches to this research. In spite of this position, we have spent a good deal of time studying samples of supervisory material and, at a nonabstract level, in comparing the approaches of different supervisors both inside and outside the group directly and indirectly. We have also discussed at some length the guiding assumptions of the "Fleming-Benedek approach" and have compared and contrasted them with those of the "San Francisco Project approach" and with the more usual case study approach as presented in vignettes offered for study by Study Group members.

A small assortment of other methods of studying supervision has been suggested. The attendance at a supervisory hour by an observer has been mentioned both as a research method and as a means of study by someone trying to learn how better to do supervision. Both activities are extant. The members of the Committee on Institutes of the Board on Professional Standards sit in on supervisory hours, and while their purpose is primarily to evaluate, it could be readily adapted to a research function. In some institutes it has been a practice for both an experienced and an inexperienced supervisor to be present at supervision. If the experienced supervisor does the work, it is the inexperienced one who does the "studying," but when the less experienced one does the work, both can be expected to have a studying and learning experience.

We should now return to the subject for study and the corresponding methods of approach appropriate to such studies. There is no very subtle or complicated methodology required to survey institutes or supervisors' practices, but a study whose aim it is to discover generic principles of supervision is another matter. Mainly we have been considering research approaches to the study of supervision. We have been trying to discover useful methods for studying the actual events of the supervisory process.

Before considering these efforts, however, a brief reference to other kinds of studies is appropriate. First we might group a number of practical items, mostly administrative, which we could call "the practices of the institutes" or "the ecology of supervision." Another collection of items could come from a similar practical level, but would apply to individuals. This would include descriptions of supervision by supervisors or students, and could be titled, "the practices of supervisors." If we turn then to the elements of the supervision itself, we can divide our discussions arbitrarily into at least five general headings: (1) *the phenomenology of supervision,* (2) *the work of supervision,* (3) *supervisory style,* (4) *the supervisor,* and (5) *learning and teaching in supervision.*

The selection of methods for the optimal study of these various issues is indeed very difficult, and the difficulty is compounded when we attempt to study the basis of choice of methodology itself. At one level, to "study" means little more than to "observe." Thus, we may speak of a study of the practices of institutes with regard to supervision. Such a study could indeed be little more than an array of tables listing various practices, such as an indication of the rules of progression of candidates, etc. The method of study would be equally simple and direct. A questionnaire would be sent, and the data received would be tabulated. Such a study would very probably suggest that other studies were indicated, and the methodology would become more complex. It would no doubt appear that different institutes pursued different practices—for example, in the time of assignment of a second case—and one would be impelled to investigate the reasons for this. Again, one could use the questionnaire method, and list the reasons adduced alongside the practices. Often, however, the investigator becomes more ambitious at this point, and hopes to establish some conceptual basis for evaluation. In essence such efforts are doomed to partial success at best, because they rely heavily at some point on observations that are not accessible to the investigator, and on other evaluations that cannot be objectified. Hence, no method exists which is reliable and reproducible and the investigator usually just attempts to evaluate the consistency between the reasons given to justify the practice and the practice itself, and then to assess the strength of the logic of the position taken. It is fairly clear that in such a study the major gain comes from the active consideration of the merits of all the arguments, and very little can be expected from the rigor of the methodology. Unfortunately, to a variable but large degree, this is the fact with all studies of supervision. However, even in the absence of a rigorous method, such active consideration of the counterposed arguments is often of considerable value.

No matter what the methodology, its first task is the accumulation of empirical data. Next, this is organized and evaluated; hypotheses are generated and the data re-examined for evidence of their confirmation or refutation. Fresh data are then obtained and the hypotheses thereby more rigorously tested. When the subject of study is supervision, there is much concern about the nature of the basic data. To pursue this question, we may consider first the topic of *the phenomenology of supervision.* The word "phenomenology" carries the proper connotation for the first step in the pursuit of a proper research approach, i.e., we should be able to say unequivocally "what happens." At once, however, we are plunged into confusion, because it is not easy to say what happens in the supervisory situation. In every instance worth considering our description of what happens includes important assumptions—for example, about the motives of the participants. A trick of method (for which I have no name, but methodologists probably do) we employ is to consider larger rather than smaller portions of material, with the result that the cumulative impact of the data warrants certain conclusions when the smaller portion would not; e.g., we may be warranted in concluding that the supervisor is bored when we assess the tenor of his responses throughout the hour, although no single response would justify such a conclusion. We are so accustomed to this practice in our conduct of analysis that we may overlook its existence, but it is one that is constantly used and yet virtually impossible to document, or even to justify or defend against determined, skeptical attack.

There are, however, some methods that minimize the number and magnitude of organizing assumptions and subliminal evaluations. The use of transcripts of supervisory hours is a good example. All of the verbal material is available for repeated review, and even though the nonverbal communication is lost, a tremendous amount of information is available. It is just this volume of material that drowns most efforts to use transcripts. Some method of selection of the data must be employed; but if the direct observation of the phenomena of supervision is the intent, then this selection must introduce at least a minimum of bias: bias should be contrasted in this usage with artifact.

We should certainly want to avoid introducing artifact by the use of a particular method, but bias should be compared to perspective or viewpoint, and is therefore inevitable to some degree whenever the data have been ordered according to any method chosen to be appropriate to the study of any given hypothesis. Thus the Fleming-Benedek method considers the material from the vantage point provided by the conceptualization of the dyadic system of supervisor-analyst interaction. The perspective thus afforded enables them to see certain kinds of problems very clearly, but if Emerson's law of compensation holds, there will be elements of the process that will be concomitantly rendered more difficult to see from within that framework. The use of the transcript is somewhat deceptive because it creates the illusion that the basic data are all at hand. Most of the important basic data are, to be sure, but particularly when fragments are presented (as, for example, in the Fleming-Benedek [1966] book) the diagnostic conclusions of the supervisor clearly rest not only on the evidence presented, but on a considerable amount of additional data available to the supervisor but not presented. Still, when data from transcripts are used, it is usually appropriate, less ambiguous, and more convincing as far as it goes.

Another possible method of using transcripts would be the arrangement of supervisor-student exchanges according to their content and apparent purpose. Such labeling followed by tabulation would provide a relatively clear view of the kinds of transactions taking place during supervision as well as something about their frequency and pattern of occurrence. Such a method might provide a means of largely avoiding the evaluative tendency and the second-guessing which is sometimes such a distraction in our effort to study supervision processes generically.

A method of reducing data from supervisory hours to manageable proportions was devised (the San Francisco Project) to avoid preconceptions as much as possible and still provide a broad view of the events of supervision. It was applied to process notes written by the supervisor amounting to several pages for each supervision hour, but with some modifications it could be applied as well to transcribed verbatim interview data. In brief the method is as follows. There are six rubrics under which the supervision data are categorized:

I. The analysis—its problems
II. How the analyst understood the analytic process
III. What the analyst did
IV. The analytic process
 a. supervisor's understanding of this process
 b. supervisor's actions in response
V. The educational process
 a. supervisor's understanding of this process
 b. supervisor's actions in response
VI. The evidence of the impact of the teaching.

According to this schema, category IV includes all didactic teaching, and category V includes all other kinds of teaching.

For each category a summary of the material of a single hour is prepared with the intent of preserving the essentials in as condensed a form as possible. The six categories provide the framework for a record of the important supervision phenomena in both discrete and accessible form. The phenomena of each hour can then be studied as a cross-section of the supervisory process, or any one of the categories can be studied longitudinally, either individually or in relation to any of the other categories. It is believed by its devisors to introduce a minimum of influence from preconceptions and to provide coded data on the phenomena of the supervision in a form making for ready exploration of a wide variety of hypotheses.

Once the phenomena of supervision have been delineated, the study of the other areas of interest will have been greatly facilitated. For example, let us consider *the work of supervision.* What does the supervisor actually do? If we have the data available, we can devise ways of labeling each action of the supervisor and can ultimately determine, almost virtually by inspection, what the supervisor's work actually has been. It is self-evident that some kind of interpretive weighting of his interventions would be necessary, and for that purpose statements from the supervisor about his intentions would be useful. Still, it is probable that there would be systematic differences between his understandings of what he had been attempting and actually doing and the conclusions on these matters reached by others by means of such study of the supervision.

Supervisory style might be approached in a similar manner. Again the kind and frequency of the supervisor's interventions would be the evidential base on which to build conclusions about his style. Obviously a good deal beyond mere tabulation would be required, and special attention would need to be given to the manner in which interventions were made, i.e., phrasing, tone, etc. The subject of *the supervisor,* himself, hardly requires the formal application of a method, although whatever might be learned about work, style, and particularly the problems of teaching could be well applied in this area of knowledge about the supervisor.

Learning and teaching in supervision are both the most basic and the most difficult to study. The teaching effort can be observed objectively, and it can be approached by questioning the supervisor about his general concerns and his specific intention in each given instance. There is also much information available from whatever studies have been made of work and style. The study of teaching will probably be most fruitful when it is intimately correlated with the study of learning. However, it is often difficult even to determine that learning has occurred, or at least that it is functional learning. We are all familiar with the candidate who has good theoretical and technical knowledge and can discuss cases with great facility, but who overlooks obvious opportunities for interpretation or who makes clumsy or incorrect ones. It is also common experience to explain something about a case and have the candidate appear to understand it perfectly, only to have almost the same material misunderstood subsequently. For this reason we are justifiably cautious about the evidences for learning. Even when we as supervisors are satisfied that learning has indeed taken place, we may sometimes suspect that our judgment is more in accord with Festinger's concept of the reduction of cognitive dissonances than based on solid evidence. For these reasons, methods of studying learning need to establish specific criteria by which it can be decided that something specific has been learned. For this purpose we must go beyond the usual practice of assessing some gestalt on the part of the supervisor of the analyst's overall level of analytic sophistication and compare it with later such gestalts. The most common of such approaches has been that of diagnosing and "treating" a learning problem, and using subsequent observation of comparable material to determine that something taught was learned. It is a more subtle problem of observation to detect general learning in the absence of focused problems, although again the usual evidence comes from the supervisor's first having noticed some defect or awkwardness which is subsequently no longer discernible. These are single-issue approaches. We have no examples of comparable evidences from a total-flow approach because such studies have just not been made or at least not reported. However, our San Francisco Project should be able to provide just such evidence from the sequential study of its categories II, III, and VI and possibly even IV and V.

We have often discussed the interrelation of the kind of data secured with the method of its collection, the manner of its presentation, and most basically, even the questions which led to its initial collection. It is prerequisite that there be some preliminary hypotheses for it to be possible for any selection of data to be made at all. Even if a verbatim transcript is used, there is an implied assumption that all of the *relevant* or necessary data are contained in the verbal exchanges, and that the nonverbal communication can essentially be neglected. Any other method of reporting (i.e., data collection and presentation) increases the influence of either intentional or unintentional selectivity and emphasis and represents then the effect of implied hypotheses. In fact, in most problem-centered reporting the data are intentionally preselected and ordered in such a way as to form a brief for the conclusions. This is characteristic of all analytic case presentations, and the fact that analytic audiences are adept at discovering alternative or contradicting hypotheses usually influences authors to focus their presentations even more. Thus, case presentations are invariably illustrations of evidence collected and organized to prove a point, to support a hypothesis; and they are virtually antithetical to the requirements of usual scientific method. The Study Group, fully realizing this, is emphasizing beyond that, that even the most rigorously unbiased method of collecting and organizing data will nevertheless be built on certain guiding assumptions and inescapable hypotheses. The usual difference between the clinical psychoanalytic approach and the hard-science approach is that in the latter the assumptions are more easily spelled out or are fewer in number and more generally consensually accepted. For our work we should make the attempt to seek explicit understanding of and agreement on the particular guiding assumptions.

The nature of the data and the purposes for which they were collected thus automatically influence the nature of the study and any conclusions that can be drawn from it. For example, recollected and recounted supervision will have been subjected to secondary elaboration (as will the analyst's account of the ongoing analysis). These data will show the effect of defensive maneuvers and probably of idealizations as well. It is also reasonable to assume a counterinfluence, i.e., the idealizations that occur under the influence of the wish to tell it "better than it is" will probably likewise influence subsequent thought and behavior such that the report will more closely approach the established ideal. Such a feedback effect could be very important to the learning experience for both analyst and supervisor and would depend entirely on the creative reporting of the analyst (or the supervisor if it is his learning that is being considered). Such "creative reporting" might even be mistakenly censured as dishonest if its operation and proper function were not understood.

For there to be a careful study of the teaching-learning process during supervision, there must be available adequate data, and no one source can be deemed sufficient for all purposes. For certain purposes a transcript will be necessary, plus process notes, plus full commentary by both the supervisor and the analyst. The transcript would be particularly necessary to check the so-called secondary elaboration previously postulated. The selection process and the secondary elaboration by the supervisor when he prepares process notes on supervision constitute limiting factors on such data, and would tend to affect the judgments of independent observers in a similarly constraining way.

We do believe that neither verbatim transcripts of recorded supervisory hours, nor process notes, nor any other notes recalled by the participants can ever by themselves give even an approximately theoretically complete account of the supervisory process. The recorded data would indeed supply information which might be overlooked in verbal reporting by both of the participants, but they can hardly supply the thoughts of either of the participants in the process. Such information can only come, if at all, from their notes, yet it is often essential for a proper assessment of what is transpiring.

We turn now to the ways that selection of data and of the units of observation will influence the conclusions reached. According to Fleming and Benedek (1966), the data are perforce both selected and simplified for purposes of explication. This results in such reduction of information comprehensiveness that the reader is precluded from formulating, or at least hampered in his efforts to construct, alternative explanatory hypotheses. This should be acceptable if one is merely studying the hypotheses developed by the writers, but it will often be objected to by those who wish to systematically consider alternatives for themselves. Even if this objection were not made, it is usually impossible to present enough supporting evidence to make every conclusion self-evident or inescapable.

It is important to distinguish between the method of study applied to supervision and the conclusions arrived at on the basis of that method. In the Fleming-Benedek study, for example, the selection of supervisor-analyst interactions as the primary unit for study does allow for a very wide range of conclusions about both the learning and teaching processes. However, the use of this method should not necessarily influence how rapidly these conclusions are drawn, let alone what actions are taken on the basis of those conclusions. The major possibility of influence by the method on the conclusions should be the fact that a specific verbal interaction has been chosen as the basic unit of observation. This fact is very likely to lead to conclusions built on interactions, or responses of one of the two members to the other. A bias in this direction might be expected when the results are compared to methods whose unit of study was not specifically interactional.

A vexing problem of methodology is that of trying to decide when the "evidence for" something becomes "convincing" evidence. It is clear that in matters involving so many factors, each of which may be defined differently by different judges, no complete agreement will ever be reached by any representative group of analysts. It is clear at the same time that the greater the agreement on basic definition, the greater the chance of then reaching agreement on the degree of conviction appropriate to any given body of evidence.

It is instructive to compare two methods of approach to the study of supervision, the Fleming-Benedek approach and that of the San Francisco Project. The San Francisco Project is not in itself a study of supervision, but rather an effort to devise a method for its study. It has, however, been applied to the study of supervision to a degree that allows some kind of comparison between the kinds of finding to which it gives rise and those that derive from the Fleming-Benedek approach. The latter approach is designed to force attention on specifically educational problems and objectives. It virtually requires attention to teaching problems and to actions regarding them. In contrast, the San Francisco Project method affords no such specific focus. Since it is primarily an indexing and codifying process, it is itself designedly neutral with respect to such questions. It would be expected, however, that it could reflect the varied interests of its users and permit such material a prominent place if that is the specific focus of study.

The fact that the Fleming-Benedek approach is so problem-oriented can be considered to be either an advantage or a disadvantage. It becomes an advantage to the degree that it focuses attention quickly on problems that interfere with proper learning and with the proper conduct of the analysis. In doing so it can give the supervisor early warning, and allow him to begin indicated remedial action quickly. It can be a disadvantage if "problems" are inevitably found when the method is applied, and are even to some extent artifacts produced by the application of the method. Even if artifacts are not produced, the emphasis on problems may produce a skewing of the observations or of the attention of the observer such that the nonproblem learning processes are given relatively less attention. There is a middle ground that holds that even though the method is problem-oriented, this orientation need not necessarily produce such skewing effects. If the observer is careful enough in his application of the method, even the skewing produced by the method's problem orientation can be minimized or avoided.

The San Francisco method has been exposed to complementary criticism. Because it fragments the interactional sequences, it makes "educational diagnoses" more difficult. The method does indeed fragment those sequences, but again it can be argued that an observer who wished to emphasize educational diagnosis could preserve in the codified material whatever data he needed for such diagnosis. If this is true it would suggest once more that this method, like most others, depends for its operation and results on the attitudes and interests of the investigators who employ it.

REFERENCE

Fleming, J. & Benedek, T. (1966), *Psychoanalytic Supervision.* New York: Grune & Stratton.

CHAPTER III

General Principles of Psychoanalytic Supervision

HERBERT J. SCHLESINGER, Ph.D.

From the beginning of its investigations, the Study Group has tried to focus on the actual work of the supervisor in the supervisory situation. It has proceeded inductively for the most part, staying close to the data, whether a vignette of a supervisory encounter, a tape recording of a supervision hour, or a supervisor's process notes of a large segment of a psychoanalytic supervision experience. Each of these kinds of data highlighted the advantages and disadvantages of various strategies for the study of supervision and each led the Study Group to focus on different aspects of the supervisory situation. While the main thrust of the Study Group's work was to explore the usefulness of different paradigms for studying the supervision process, a preoccupation clearly reflected in this monograph, there were also many important by-products for the members of the group individually as well as for the group as a whole.

One of these additional and unexpected benefits was that the members of the Study Group, who at the outset differed considerably in their attitudes toward and practices in supervision, moved closer together in their views about the nature of psychoanalytic supervision. In effect, the members of the Study Group, while far from identical in outlook at the close of this project, nonetheless could by then subscribe to a common and consensually agreed on set of principles of supervision.[1] The listing is presented at this point in order to aid in evaluating the actual supervisory material to be presented in detail in Chapter V, and to help the reader assess the cogency and utility of these principles themselves after studying the expositions of the Study Group as conveyed in succeeding chapters.

To what extent general agreement on this set of principles represents actual change, i.e., convergence either in the doing of supervision or the thinking about it, or represents only agreement to use a common vocabulary in talking about it, remains a still open question. In discussions of this issue, however, several members of the Study Group stated they could detect changes in the way they actually conduct supervision, not merely in the way they talk about it within the group.

Nevertheless, the fact that the Study Group could arrive at such a common "language," one that allowed analysts of differing orientations to discuss both the intimate details of psychoanalytic supervision in some depth and to relate these to an overall conceptual framework about supervision, was in itself an achievement of considerable worth. It permitted the Study Group to get past the point at which so many discussions founder, the point at which it is not yet possible to distinguish issues of substance from preferences in usage.

After studying many examples of supervisory encounters, examples that represented a range of conceptions of what the ideal supervisory stance might be, the members of the Study Group found themselves converging on a single model for which they chose the felicitous phrase—*supervision as an enabling process.* Inherent in this point of view is the recognition that the supervised analysis is at the crux of psychoanalytic education. It is in this experience of conducting an analysis under the tutelage of an experienced colleague that the candidate has the opportunity to integrate what he has learned emotionally and cognitively about himself and about the analytic process from his personal experience in analysis with what he has learned about psychoanalysis from his experience in the classroom and in his reading. *It is the function of the supervisor to facilitate this process of combined personal and professional growth in the candidate.* Thus, the main idea captured by the term "enabling process" is that the activity of the supervisor must be governed by his understanding of what the candidate needs to know at any given time and what sorts of clinical experiences will permit him to learn what he needs to know in optimal fashion.

We concede that candidates can learn from a broad range of experiences, not only from manifestly gratifying ones, and that learning and teaching processes are not necessarily isomorphic. All of us have had the experience of learning from teachers who were less than adequate, and many of us

[1]The "principles" are denoted by italics.

have worked with students who were able to learn only through opposition. Nevertheless, the good supervisor, according to this model, will be concerned with such questions as, "Will interrupting the candidate to ask him to clear up this uncertainty about what he or the patient meant be helpful at this time?" or, "Should I call to the candidate's attention the poor timing of his interpretation or wait and let the events of the analysis show it to him—to see if he can pick it up himself?" etc.

A clear implication of this sample of the interior monologue of a supervisor is that an important (if not the most important) source of his capacity to assist the candidate is his position outside of the process between analyst and patient. From this uninvolved position, above the fray and after the fact, the supervisor can more easily remain objective and see things in their proper perspective. The advantages of his position vastly enhance the probability of his being the more correct in his assessment of the analytic process. If he voices his assessments frequently and indiscriminately, he may so reinforce his own sense of mastery (with the awe of the candidate also contributing to this effect) that the difficult task of supervising may seem deceptively easy. For the supervisor to be "right" and for him to be an effective teacher are not always equivalent.

Another implication of the term "enabling process" is that *consistent with the candidate's level of analytic development and skill, he should be encouraged to be as active as he can be in the pursuit of his learning objectives.* A hierarchy of general learning objectives can be delineated: As the candidate can sense where and how he got into trouble and can begin to develop his own resources to understand the problem and extricate himself from it, as he can come to recognize his own learning needs and can formulate his own goals to be accomplished in supervision, so will he be on the way to developing mature professional independence as an analyst.

Among the specific learning objectives the candidate will have in undertaking a supervised case are the following:

(a) To experience in the position of analyst the common phenomena of a psychoanalysis. These are phenomena that one hopes he has already experienced first-hand in the position of patient, but to encounter them second-hand, as it were, is an experience of a different order.

(b) To allow the analytic situation to develop so that the patient can experience these phenomena himself. He must also learn how and when to facilitate the achieving of these experiences and when to assist the patient's mastery of them through interpretation.

(c) To learn to conceptualize what he experiences, to arrive at tentative dynamic and genetic formulations and to learn how to test these out, while holding them in abeyance, by making use of the emerging data of the analytic situation.

(d) To use the occasion of supervised analysis to continue to develop his capacity for self-analysis, to gain the special insights into a patient's experiences that come from permitting himself to resonate with the patient and to associate freely even as the patient does. He should also be able to allow himself to associate freely in the supervisory situation when necessary in order to explore with the supervisor the meaning of the patient's productions and his own reactions to them. The ability to exercise this skill is essential not only to deepen his understanding of the analytic meaning of his own activity (or lack of it) and to widen the range of options open to him, but also as a tool to investigate the enforced narrowing of these options by the blind spots that may occur from time to time.

These general learning objectives apply to any supervised analysis. They are not meant to exclude the special opportunities that may occur to learn more about clinical theory, when the case material illustrates a theoretical point, or to learn more about metapsychology, when the phenomena of the developing analysis and the candidate's learning readiness permit these kinds of useful, if more peripheral, excursions.

The candidate's learning objectives are spelled out here as a way of pointing as well to the supervisor's teaching tasks. For *the supervisor may be called upon to teach in any of these areas, to help the candidate experience the analytic situation more deeply in an affective sense as well as to help him take sufficient distance from it to conceptualize better what is going on, and from that conceptualization to develop a rational approach to the patient based both on his own intuition and on a sound psychoanalytic understanding.*

Here a conflict between principles may arise, for while the supervisor may consider it indicated to teach actively in a particular area, the concept of supervision as an enabling process implies that the supervisor should limit his teaching interventions to the minimum that will enable the candidate to learn from his own experience. The synthesis of this potential conflict lies in the principle that *the supervisor must adopt a diagnostic point of view toward the candidate's learning process.* While as an experienced analyst he will hear a great deal more than the candidate is aware of reporting, and will appreciate the clinical process in greater complexity and on many levels, as a supervisor he will be able to make use of far less than what he hears. Thus he will always have to choose from the array of analytic material the particular points he would like to (or needs to) raise for discussion with the candidate. But he will also need to choose those issues he will himself pay closer attention to, in accordance with what he believes to be the line of the ongoing supervisory process as well as the concomitant line of the ongoing analytic process. The supervisor needs to diagnose not only the events in the analytic process, but also the events in the supervisory process. Just as the candidate learns to begin with the patient where he is, so *the supervisor must begin with the candidate where he is.* He must diagnose what the candidate needs to learn and consider how he can best learn it. The use of "best" here implies that the supervisor should understand the pace at which the candidate can assimilate new ideas and new skills in a way that will make them his own, i.e., in a way that will permit him ultimately to become his own teacher rather than to remain dependent on supervisors to discover what the material really means.

The supervisor must recognize that while the process in which he is engaged with the candidate is designed to facilitate the candidate's growth, it will sometimes happen that elements in the supervision may seem to impede that growth. The paradox here is the same one we are accustomed to in the analytic situation. The phenomena we conceptualize under such headings as resistance, defense, identification, and transference can occur in supervision as well as in psychoanalytic treatment. It is one of the unique features of psychoanalytic education that conducting an analysis of a patient, the capping experience of the educational process, occurs only after long preparation through the candidate's own psychoanalytic patienthood. *One of the major criteria for deciding that the candidate is ready to undertake the phase of analyzing a patient is that he is deemed ready to make use of the supervisor as a teacher with maximal openness to learning and with minimal tendencies toward neurotic distortion of the supervisory relationship.* But this state, like all ideals, is achieved only relatively. Thus *it falls to the supervisor, as part of his diagnostic task, to assess to what extent the candidate brings unresolved neurotic problems to the supervisory situation (as well as to the clinical situation) and also to assess to what extent he, the supervisor, may unwittingly be contributing to the candidate's (clinical and supervision) difficulties.* Among the phenomena of the analysis the supervisor will register are some that hint at the analyst's transferences and countertransferences with his patient. Whether the supervisor points these out or even alludes to them will depend, of course, on whether they interfere with the analysis of the patient or if a teaching point useful to the analyst can be made by referring to them at that time.

As is true for the clinical situation, the fact that the supervisor is aware that resistances, defenses, etc., are intruding into the learning situation does not necessarily mean that he will make explicit use of this information in his work with the candidate. Whether and how he does so depends on his assessment of the supervisory situation in terms of what the candidate needs to know at this time, and how he can best learn it. Again, "best" implies that the goal is not only to facilitate the acquiring of a piece of information but also to enhance the capacity to become an independent learner.

It is in just this area that the perennial (and largely sterile) argument about whether supervision is teaching or treatment tends to arise. The argument, of course, has much less to do with how the supervisor understands what he hears and sees than with how he understands his options for making educational use of this information. There are a number of ways of making use of such observations (assuming for the moment that some use must be made of them). A way of ordering the modes of intervening that derives from the supervisory function itself is to consider that the candidate's problem is an educational one (in the narrow sense) until proven otherwise. To state this idea in the form of a principle, *the supervisor who feels it necessary to intervene in an area that seems to involve the candidate's countertransference, or other neurotic difficulty, will in general first adopt the working hypothesis that the candidate's difficulty stems from lack of knowledge. Only when the candidate shows himself unable to make effective use of information to correct whatever is disturbing his functioning as an analyst will the supervisor point to the possible contribution to the difficulty of dynamic factors within the personality functioning of the candidate.* The supervisor who adopts this working hypothesis will often enough find that the candidate will himself call attention to intrusive countertransferences and bring his self-analytic skills to bear upon them. It is worth noting here, however, that some candidates find it more comfortable to plead guilty to countertransference than to admit ignorance. Others seem to feel more sensitive about their emotional involvements and prefer to plead cognitive ignorance. Either plea may be true, and both may express resistance to learning as well as the beginnings of insight. We have here another instance where the highest educational diagnostic skills of the supervisor are called upon.

We mentioned above that the supervisor might unwittingly be contributing to the candidate's neurotic distortion of the supervisory situation. We know that in the establishment of the psychoanalytic situation the clear expression of transferences and their crystallization in the transference neurosis depend on the proper analytic behavior of the analyst. This need not imply, as has sometimes been said, that the transference is *induced* by the analyst. We stress rather that clear manifestations of transference and the development of an unobscured view of the transference neurosis do depend on a clean analytic technique. The relevance of this statement here is that the appearance of such interfering transferences in the supervisory situation must also depend, at least to some extent, on the behavior of the supervisor. If the supervisor behaves with the supervisee too much like the analyst he also is, he may promote the defensive use of himself as a transference object and in effect replace the patient as the object of chief concern to the analyst. If his behavior is too expectant, too noncommittal, if he is too much concerned with preserving his own anonymity, he may foster unwanted regressions in the candidate with the effect that the relationship with the supervisor will perforce become the main object of mutual scrutiny by supervisor and candidate.

Perhaps we should make clear that the reactions that concern us are not, for instance, the resentment of a candidate who feels his supervisor is too opinionated, too eager to tell him how to treat the patient, or turns his attention to things other than the ones he wanted to discuss. These reactions, while they may have affective components and may also interfere with learning, are more superficial, more realistic, and also probably more easily dealt with or disposed of. They can more readily be put aside by the candidate than the reactions that properly would be called transferences.

One of the vital conceptions implicit in the foregoing discussion is that of the "learning alliance." *The criterion* (mentioned above) *for entering the phase of supervised clinical work would be restated as whether the candidate is sufficiently capable of forming a learning alliance with his supervisor,* one that will permit him to trust the supervisor, to openly look at his own reactions to analyzing, to permit himself to associate freely not only when he is with his patient, but also in the presence of his supervisor, when this is necessary to explore the meaning of events in the analysis. We recognize that in describing the learning situation between candidate and supervisor in these terms we are also describing an ideal that practical supervisory situations only approximate. In describing an ideal, however, we do not mean to imply that there is only one kind (or level) of learning alliance that can be effective. Clearly, candidates can learn usefully under a variety of circumstances, some far from ideal. Nevertheless, we believe that *part of the supervisor's task is to become aware of the nature, strength, and vicissitudes of the learning alliance between himself and a given candidate and to attune his teaching methods to the readiness of the candidate to learn in this context.*

Referring to identification among resistances to analysis and to learning should not obscure the fact that this process is also one of the normal phenomena of development and often a useful, if temporary, phase in both the therapeutic and learning situations. The analytic supervisor will frequently notice that the candidate makes use not only of what he tells him, but also of the way in which he tells it. He can hear in the candidate's report reflections of previous supervisory interactions—not only of concept, but also of style. Sometimes these reflect frank "borrowings" or imitations recognized by the candidate as such, while at other times they occur without awareness. As trial identifications, these imitations can be useful ways for the candidate to try out something new to him. That they may also represent incipient resistances to learning will, of course, also be considered by the supervisor. In particular, adaptation to the supervisory situation, in the sense of telling the supervisor what (the candidate thinks) the supervisor wants to hear, can be a formidable impediment to learning. In any case, *the supervisor must recognize that he serves the candidate as a model in terms of how he would handle the clinical episode under discussion and also in terms of how he reacts and associates to, and reflects on, the material the candidate reports.*

To state that the *supervisor is a teacher* may seem to be belaboring the obvious. But perhaps this statement will not seem so banal if certain of its thus far unmentioned implications are considered. As a teacher, the supervisor is not engaged in the private practice of teaching; he teaches by virtue of his position on the faculty of a psychoanalytic institute. His responsibilities are two-fold—to the institute whose educational program he represents and is implementing, and to the candidate whose education is entrusted to him. A third direction of responsibility must also be mentioned—that to the candidate's patient. To be truly responsible to three masters would be difficult indeed; the task is of course somewhat lightened by the fortunate practice in institutes to select cases for their candidates very carefully, at least the beginning cases. The educational purpose of this care in selection is to provide the candidate with optimal clinical material on which he will be able to experience, in the position of analyst, the phenomena that occur in a "standard" analytic situation. In addition, he should of course have the experience of conducting an analysis that is terminable. These needs provide reason enough for such careful selection. But a useful by-product, one that is not usually mentioned, is that a well-selected case reduces the pressure on the supervisor, as a conscientious physician, to concomitantly have to actively look out for the welfare of the patient of his supervisee. Needless to say, the proper initial selection of the candidate and the general care taken in his training up to this point also work to this same end.

To put these issues in more general terms, one can say that the possibility of establishing and maintaining an adequate supervisory situation is dependent on the earlier processes of selection of both candidate and patient and the successful completion of the earlier stages of the candidate's education, not least of them a successful (i.e., sufficient to that point) personal analysis. The selection of an appropriate supervisor by or for a candidate at a given point in his development, in some instances, could also turn out to be crucial.

If the patient is not well chosen, or if the analyst is not sufficiently skillful or is too involved in his own neurotic distortions of the treatment situation, the supervisor will not be free to teach in an optimal way. He will be forced in turn to introduce distortions of the supervisory situation either to rescue the patient or the analyst, or in other ways to make the best of a bad situation. These aberrations, it is sad to say, are through error or misfortune not uncommon in psychoanalytic education.

But assuming the adequate case, which fortunately is also the more usual case, i.e., the patient is well-enough chosen for supervised analysis and the candidate is well-enough educated and ready for that undertaking, then the supervisor as teacher is still responsible both to his supervisee and to his institute. His responsibilities as a teacher to the candidate have to some extent already been spelled out. In attempting to relate himself primarily to the learning needs of the candidate, many a supervisor has discovered that it is a far more difficult and complicated task to teach someone to conduct a psychoanalysis than it is to do it oneself.

The supervisor's corresponding responsibilities to his institute as a teacher involve, first of all, educating the candidate about the case that is presented to him. We have noted that, as part of that responsibility, the supervisor engages in continuous educational diagnosis. One facet of this diagnostic process is evaluative: It considers the supervisee as an individual for whom a unique learning situation is to be created, one which will enable him to develop his maximal potential analytic skills; but we must also remember that the candidate is one of a class of candidates, each of whom is expected not only to grow to his maximum potential as an individual, but also to meet the educational and performance standards of the institute. Thus, in addition to the need to evaluate the supervisee as part of his ongoing educational diagnosing in the service of supervisory teaching, *the supervisor must transmit his evaluation of the candidate to the institute as well as to the candidate himself.* In accordance with these principles, the candidate should share the responsibility for evaluating his own work to the end of making as accurate as possible self-evaluation an integral part of his analytic skills.

The idea of evaluation implies not just "grading" (although the evaluative stance implied by the necessity to give a grade does seem distasteful to many analysts, and not least to those who become analytic supervisors), for grading can indeed become perfunctory if not supported by a thoughtful critique of the strengths and weaknesses of the candidate. Just as important, if not more so than an evaluative statement that summarizes how well (in quantitative terms) the candidate has met the institute's educational expectations, is a description of the specific areas of strength and weakness that the candidate shows—a statement of the supervisor's "educational diagnosis" of the candidate that can be used to help tailor the candidate's further educational experiences. What is required, in short, is an evaluation geared not just to the question of "pass" or "fail," but one that can promote the continuation of the candidate's education both by the present supervisor and by others. The communicating of the supervisor's evaluation to the candidate, at the very least, or far better, the sharing of the evaluative process itself with him, is an essential aspect of proper supervisory teaching.

It is clear that in order to provide such an educational evaluation *the supervisor must have an overall conception of analytic education into which his particular experiences with the candidate can be placed.* It would be desirable, of course, that the conception of psychoanalytic education be one that is shared by the entire faculty of the institute, to say nothing of the educational community of psychoanalysts at large.

This collection of principles, maxims, and homilies represents a distillation of the experiences of the members of the Study Group in their own teaching and practices, as well as with each other around the study of the supervisory process. As a statement of consensus, it lacks any distinctive pattern of emphasis that would distinguish the working philosophy of any single member of the group. Yet around this list of principles, as for supervising itself, the members of the Study Group gained a renewed feeling of respect for the complexity of the function and the difficulty of conceptualizing it.

None of us was trained to be a supervisor. In comparison with the care given to our education as analysts, our elevation to supervisors was largely a function of seniority and the impressions gained by others of our competence as analysts, and perhaps as seminar leaders. For the most part, then, each member of the group was self-taught as a supervisor, and showed it at the beginning of the study in the individuality, even idiosyncracy, of his working style, in his particular patterns of insights and oversights, and in the conviction that he knew the way in which supervision should be done, or at least was comfortable with his own way of doing it. The experience of working together as a group had an important educational benefit, one which in advance of our joint effort most of us were not even aware of lacking.

It is just this unexpected by-product of studying the process of supervision in a group, its capacity for enhancing the supervisory skill and breadth of outlook of the members of the group, that may be among the most useful, or at least the most easily transferable, aspects of the Study Group's work. While our explicit aim was to learn something about the supervisory process through exploring different methods for studying it, we also discovered an effective way of teaching and learning about supervision. We hope that those interested in the problem of selecting and educating supervisors may find something to emulate in our experience.

CHAPTER IV

Supervisory Styles and Positions

DARYL DeBELL, M.D.

Personal style, in supervising as in all behavior, is multiply determined, and we have by no means treated the matter exhaustively. Style at this level of consideration is largely representative of the supervisor's personality as expressed in his work. In this respect, we can assume a shared set of principles and aims for a variety of supervisors and still observe a variety of means of applying those principles in order to accomplish those aims. For example, the goal assumed might be to ascertain what the analyst thought about reported transference material. Even the question, "What do you think about that?" can be read with a great variety of inflections from the most neutral to the most challenging. Some supervisors in pursuit of the same goal will lead the witness and ask, "Do you think this is father transference material?" Such variations require no difference in goal, but they may well have a tendentious effect on the reply. During the course of the supervision it is apparent that the fabric of interaction between supervisor and analyst will develop in quite different ways, and that those differences will depend to a significant extent on the style of the supervisor.

If we consider the determinants of style, we may imagine a spectrum represented at one end by the personality of the supervisor, and on the other end by his theories, or perhaps more accurately, his convictions. It will become more clear when specific issues are discussed, but it can be mentioned now that differences in method will inevitably be generated by differences in theoretical positions. Whether we should call those differences in method stylistic is open to question. Whatever one's preference, however, it will be recognized that every intervention by the supervisor must be influenced on the one hand by his personality, and on the other hand by his theoretical position, his philosophy, his convictions, and his chosen frame of reference. Whenever a clear-cut theoretical position (rather than a rationalization) is recognizable as the major determinant of a supervisor's action, we should characterize it in some way other than "style." We should do this not because "style" is wrongly applied, but because in spite of correct denotation, the connotation may be inadequate. In lieu of another term, we propose to qualify our statements to make it clear in such instances that theoretical considerations are especially prominent.

Style, of course, does not apply only to the interventions themselves or to their means of presentation. It will be evidenced as well by the preferences of the supervisor for dealing with certain kinds of material. Every supervisor has his own style as an analyst. He tends to approach cases in a characteristic way, to prefer certain kinds of formulation and to make his interventions accordingly. This style as an analyst is almost certain to be expressed in his supervisory work. Where one supervisor will pay particular attention to transference material, another will emphasize resistance aspects. Such preferences about viewing the material of the case with an individual perspective automatically influence the supervisory interventions, and these variations contribute also to the supervisor's style.

There are a number of specific stylistic issues, some of which can be described in polar or antithetical form.[1] Some of them overlap and are to a degree, therefore, redundant, but the advantage of listing them in this way seems to outweigh the disadvantage of the repetition. A quick listing should begin with the classical dilemma of supervisors: the issue, stated in variant versions of "teaching versus treatment." The next issue to be considered will be that of "expectant teaching versus active teaching" (on the expectant side we may add the related designation of the supervisory attitude of leniency and even the somewhat pejorative description, passivity). Another pair of contrasts to be considered is that of the supervisor who forces his concepts versus the one who virtually refuses to give the analyst any formulation of the case at all. Closely related, but not always correlated in practice, is the polarity of the supervisor who forces his own interpretations versus the

[1]In this chapter the device of a series of polarities has been employed, together with the use of dialogue between the proponents of the two extreme positions. This device tends to produce an artifact, the appearance of polarized views within the committee which do not in fact exist. Likewise, critical editorial comments are directed at certain extreme examples which are in all probability fictional, but are presented for their heuristic value and without desirable qualification.

supervisor who will not give even any model interpretations. Somewhat related to the "lenient" supervisor is the one who tries always to be encouraging, or perhaps unfailingly solicitously helpful. These behaviors contrast respectively with the tendency always to find something to criticize, or, as antithesis to the helping attitude, to be regularly challenging. A close relative to the supervisor who forces his concepts and/or his interpretations is the supervisor who tends to "take over the case." However, the particular antithesis is different and consists of the supervisor's insistence by word and deed that it is the analyst who is in charge of the case, that he and he alone has the full responsibility for its conduct.

A number of other stylistic qualities are not amenable to such categorization and require a different type of discussion. The first of these is the matter of identification of the analyst with the supervisor and the means by which it is promoted or discouraged. The second of these considerations is whether the focus of the supervisor is predominantly or inflexibly patient-centered, analyst-centered, or process-centered (we hope not supervisor-centered). A variant of this is the consideration of whether the supervisor attends primarily to the analyst-supervisor interaction, the analyst-patient interaction, or whether he is less concerned with the interactions and more attentive to the dynamics of the case or to the technical questions raised by the interventions of the analyst. We also wish to consider the relation of style to the analytic and teaching philosophy of the supervisor—the influence on his style of his frame of reference regarding supervision.

The topics listed above provide a series of dimensions by which we can measure, however roughly, the style of any supervisor.

Perhaps one of the earliest and most persistent questions about appropriate supervisory activity is how much one should treat the analyst versus how much one should simply teach him. This is a peculiar question, and becomes more strange the more it is discussed. For one thing, it is difficult to find proponents of the explicit "treatment" of candidates during supervision; certainly no one in the group advocates analyzing the supervisee. Still, every member of the group agrees that it is sometimes necessary to point out to the analyst certain obstructive behavior patterns, and even on occasion to comment about and even to inquire into their possible meaning and motivation. Such interventions by the supervisor are not necessarily thought to be unacceptably intrusive, i.e., "therapeutic." There is rather a tacit acceptance that such actions are often both useful and salutary. There is also common agreement that as supervisors we expect that ideally candidates will become aware of their own emotional or transference-determined responses, and that they will be concerned about the effects of those responses on their analytic work and bring them into the supervision. Stylistic differences determine how these are brought to the student's attention, and include the supervisors' varying convictions about the feasibility and utility of self-analysis. Those who feel the most opposed to "therapeutic" activity nonetheless appear to accept a certain amount of it when the primary intent is clearly a pedagogic confrontation. The supervisor is demonstrating the existence of faulty technique, and is then permitted to pursue the matter by illustrating the possible origins of the error. To state the matter in extreme terms, everybody appears to oppose "treatment" of the supervisee, and yet everybody does it. Some do it with misgivings, and some without. It appears from the discussion of actual supervisory material that the range of behavior is far narrower than the range of espoused philosophical position. There is disagreement about the *why* and sometimes about the *how*, but not so much disagreement about *what* should be done.

For example, a situation was reported and discussed in which a student was giving up prized research time in order to treat another analytic patient who, however, treated the analysis most cavalierly, frequently skipping hours. This behavior was expectedly repetitive of a chronic life pattern. The patient came to the analysis having jilted a lover, and was now "jilting" the analyst. It was clear to the supervisor that the analyst was irritated with this patient who was treating so flippantly the analysis for which he, the analyst, had given up so much. The analyst seemed not to be aware of his irritation, and the supervisor pointed it out. He indicated to the group that he felt the proper supervisory stance was to point out the irritation, but that he did not feel it proper to inquire into its sources. He was asked why this would not be a proper question, since it seemed to the questioner to be quite proper. The variety of possibilities in this situation was then discussed. Is the student aware that he is irritated? He may be aware, and may not be expressing it to the supervisor, or he may not be aware. The first question would be, "Could you be irritated with the patient?" If it turned out that he was not aware of the irritation, then the evidence for it should be demonstrated to him. On the other hand, if he was aware of it, one could go on discussing its nature and its source from there.

There is still another possibility. He might not have been aware of it, but the question directing his attention to his irritation might have brought him to a sudden realization of it or, on the other hand, might have resulted only in a perplexed disclaimer or a defensive denial. Even more complex, the analyst might not have been aware of the irritation, but might have had a "symptom" that reflected it, for instance, an inordinate fear of losing the patient (a projection of the vengeful desire to be rid of her).

This condensed account of a spirited discussion implies the range of opinion within the group as to the appropriate amount of probing of the analyst's thoughts and feelings. There was unanimous agreement that the supervisor should pay attention to the distressed feelings of the analyst. In this case he should note the evidence, direct or indirect, that the analyst was irritated with the patient who was treating his own sacrifice lightly. All agreed also that it would be appropriate for the supervisor to inquire into the analyst's feelings toward the patient, and even to suggest the possibility of a reaction to the patient's provocative behavior. Individual differences in style would become evident in practice, although all agreed with the philosophy that as long as learning objectives were being served, one might proceed. At the same time, the general rule was expressed that as long as the analysis was flowing properly, the supervisor ought to do the very least by way of intervention and confrontation. As the treatment process ran into difficulties, the supervisor would be called upon to "do" more and more as needed.

Further, the type of supervisory intervention employed is apparently very much influenced by the supervisor's degree of belief in the possibilities for self-analysis. Those who accept as a matter of fact the existence of self-analytic processes make regular and consistent efforts to promote this work as part of their supervisory task. Those who do not believe that it occurs, or who deem it a rare and relatively limited event, make little or no effort to make the kinds of confrontations which would promote it. Thus in the example given, those who do not believe in self-analysis tend to stop sooner in the sequence of probings than those who do. The believers would sometimes be willing to confront the analyst with the fact that his anxiety about losing the patient might be related to his repression of his irritation at her provocativeness. The doubters would be very reluctant to go so far, even if the candidate were in analysis, perhaps particularly if he were. Such observations may be misleading, however, and the influence of style may be less than one might suppose. At least some observers in the group felt that there was considerably greater defense of principle than there was difference in actual practice, and that rather similar confrontations were made by most supervisors if the analyst was still in analysis. Even if he were not, it appeared that most would still confront[2] the analyst with his interfering stereotypical errors.

When actual supervision processes were considered, for example, the thirteenth supervisory hour in the Fleming-Benedek (1966) book in which the "cockroach dream" was discussed, we found that questions were raised about therapeutic possibilities which would not at first be apparent. In this supervisory hour the analyst referred to the patient's vague feelings from childhood. The supervisor first tried to get the analyst to react to those feelings. When he could not, she decided to follow her own associations and reveal them to the student-analyst with the intent of helping him thereby to mobilize his own feeling responses to the situation. This action was questioned by some because of the possibility that it might have a distorting effect on the whole future course of the supervisory process, all the more

[2]"Confront" is used here to describe the neutral presentation of previously unrecognized facts to the analyst by the supervisor, and is very close to the usage employed to describe the similar technical act in psychoanalysis itself.

because it occurred so early.

The pedagogic intent in this example was to forcefully demonstrate to the analyst the existence of his own inhibition of associative thinking by contrasting it with that of the supervisor, as well as to provide him an identificatory model of analytic behavior. The authors and some members of the Study Group clearly felt that it was possible to come to an early decision about the inhibition shown by the analyst in his work and whether to intervene. The critics of intervention felt that there was danger it might lead to a skewed emphasis which focused the supervision too much on the analyst and too little on the patient. A reconciling point of view held that the difference could be resolved by invoking the dimension of time; i.e., those who criticized the intervention did so mainly on the basis of its being presumably too early. Even they could imagine doing the same thing, but only after the evidence for the inhibition was stronger and could be presented convincingly to the student. Another view held that such relatively early efforts should not properly be called confrontations (or therapy at all) because, in this example at least, it was given in the form of an invitation which could be easily declined by the analyst. There is indeed a strong implication that the supervisor is promoting this kind of thinking, but it is only in her concluding remark to the candidate that she became directive: "Next time try to get closer to the patient's feelings." At this point some group members expressed reservations about the effectiveness of such an injunction, believing it to be too directive and evocative of resistances or evasions. In addition to the question of timing, it is also true that for some it is comfortable to teach in this personally revealing way, while for others it is not.

The issue of treatment versus teaching arises in a special way when countertransference problems become evident during supervision. (Although our discussions were conspicuously concerned with countertransference as the paradigmatic problem, the same general considerations could of course be applied to all of the psychologically determined interferences with the analyst's functioning.) Those who adhere most strongly to the pedagogic position contend that the only tenable course, even in the face of visibly interfering countertransferences, is to adhere strictly to the procedure of pointing out the dynamics of the case, the therapeutic requirements, the technical considerations, and the array of appropriately available interpretations or other interventions. They believe a critique of the analyst's formulations can be made, and defects pointed out to him—at the proper time. Similarly, he may not only be told something about the interpretations he might have made, but the interpretations which he has made can be critically examined. All of these activities should of course be carried out in such a way as to illuminate the interference with the proper conduct of the analysis caused by the countertransferences.

Supervisors toward the other end of the spectrum might start with the above-described course, but they would be willing to go considerably further. They would be more pointed in their suggestions about the nature of the analyst's mistakes, and they would call his attention to behavior that was determined by his countertransferences. Under some circumstances they would pursue the matter by asking leading questions about his inappropriate course of action, or by demonstrating that he had consistently failed to recognize specific important material, or if he had seen it, that he still made characteristic errors in formulating or interpreting it. It is sometimes fairly easy to arrive at the point where the analyst recognizes that he makes a consistent error which may be variously attributed to ignorance, inexperience, countertransference, analyst transferences, psychoneurosis, or character problem. When the analyst does raise the question, "What is it that makes me make the same mistake repeatedly?" or he says, "I know that was a foolish [or serious] mistake, but I don't know why I did it," the supervisor most committed to a purely pedagogic role is apt to say, "Perhaps you should take it up in your analysis." Others would encourage the analyst to explore the question further then and there. For example, if they thought it relevant, as in one of the examples cited above, they might wonder aloud if the analyst recognized his feelings of irritation at the patient's provocative behavior. And some would cite evidence from the reported material supporting such a conclusion.

A less direct supervisory approach to this issue is sometimes employed. The supervisor may instruct the analyst that his feelings can be used as an indicator of the patient's unconscious intents. Upon reflection, the candidate notices his own irritation, for example, and seeks evidence of the patient's unconscious purposes in provoking him. Once his attention has been directed to his own responses, it is a shorter step to the recognition of stereotyped responses, or feelings for which no corresponding unconscious purpose in the patient can be detected. Then it is quite a short step to a consideration of the nature and source of the analyst's psychologically determined interference. Those most inclined toward this "therapeutic" position will try to explore this question thoroughly as it expresses itself in the analyst's work with the patient, and even as it may express itself in the supervisory work.

No one in the group advocates efforts at genetic reconstruction or even the pursuit of the analyst's associative connections which would lead in the direction of such reconstructions. These efforts we all consider to properly belong in the student-analyst's own analysis. There is strong support among members of the Study Group, however, for an effort to explore the relation of the student-analyst's mistakes and shortcomings to his psychological impediments, and then in varying degrees to acquaint him with those observations. Sometimes the questions of the supervisor will result in a condition of "the thing speaks for itself "; sometimes the supervisor must spell it out. The argument for pursuing this effort rests mainly on the contention that it is primarily "educative," and that although the supervisor's actions are indeed virtually indistinguishable from the common psychoanalytic technical activities of confrontation and clarification, they are only employed in supervision to prepare the supervisee for subsequent associative processes and genetic reconstructions either in his self-analysis or in his personal or training analysis, but not within the supervision. It is further argued that it may be only during supervision that these kinds of impediments become visible; the supervisee may himself not be aware of them, and is hence unable to report them to his analyst. It is all the more the supervisor's responsibility to detect and deal with these problems, at least to the point of bringing them unambiguously to the supervisee's attention, lest the analyst remain forever handicapped. Some indeed hold the opinion that it is a major task of supervision to discover and help remove these sometimes very subtle but potentially disruptive psychologically determined work interferences.

Even if there are no gross psychologically determined impediments to the candidate's doing good psychoanalytic work, it is contended by some that the optimal development of any analyst's analytic instrument usually requires the kind of reflective self-examination which the supervisor's explorations and confrontations would stimulate. Most of the group agreed that the analyst cannot be successfully confronted with his psychologically determined "blind spots" until a firm working relationship has been established within the supervision. To be sure, some were confident that they could establish such a relationship rather quickly, while others expected it to take months. The latter group tended concomitantly to also have the impression that psychologically challenging confrontations could be highly stressful both to the analyst and to the supervisor-analyst relationship, and were therefore doubly hesitant in making them.

The dilemma of supervisors about confronting may be made less painful if they recognize that it is not necessarily a favor to the analyst to be overly considerate of his feelings. It can indeed be a disservice to him to fail to confront him with his mistakes or his ignorance. It is a particular disservice for supervisors to fail to recognize these defects because such failure makes any realistic and appropriate teaching effort impossible. That tact and even indirection may be required goes without saying, but a too-cautious approach can be as self-defeating as an overly accusing one would be.

These issues concerning the kind and the tenor of confrontation represent a transition from the general questions of "teach or treat" to the ones related to "How active should the supervisor be in any given circumstance?" In the discussion of supervision hour 5, detailed in Chapter X, the analyst is judged to be too "cool" and detached in his analytic work. There was general agreement that this behavior was analytically inappropriate and nearly general agreement about the early steps that might be taken to correct it. First, of course, the consequences to the patient of the analyst's inappropriate behaviors should be discussed with the analyst. If this proves insufficient, the supervisor may put it more directly and strongly, saying in effect, "Look, you are being too distant and dry with this patient. She needs to feel more of a sense of compassionate concern." It was recognized that such a direct course could serve to intimidate some candidates, but in this particular case it was agreed that something along these lines might have been appropriate.

Our discussion of the book on psychoanalytic supervision by Fleming and Benedek developed the same spread of opinion about the degree of appropriate activity and intervention by the supervisor and about how soon it might be undertaken. A major focus of the Fleming-Benedek book is on sequential interactions between the supervisor and analyst, with emphasis placed on increasing the awareness by the analyst of his own emotional responses during the conduct of his work, to the end that these responses can be used to better advantage. Major emphasis was placed on the importance of working through the candidate's inhibiting work difficulties by using appropriate psychological means. The use of psychoanalysis, i.e., interpretations involving reconstruction, was however not considered appropriate to the supervisory situation.

In our discussion of the example of Case 1 (Fleming and Benedek, 1966, p. 59) one opinion was expressed that it might be too early in the supervision to come to such a firm diagnostic assessment of the student-analyst's learning problem. An additional question was raised as to the advisability of acting so quickly on such an assessment, even if accurate. The opinion advanced earlier that the analyst might rather be inhibited by such supervisory activity was repeated, and an additional warning was made that the analyst might experience such close interaction with the supervisor as unduly intimate and therefore seductive, again with the potential consequence of inhibition and perhaps withdrawal. Although these consequences were considered to be possible, the majority felt that within the stylistic dimensions illustrated in the book, these were not probable outcomes. Again, it was observed that subtle differences in style, involving only nuances of timing or exactness of phrasing, might influence the outcome significantly, particularly if the varying susceptibility of different students is taken into account.

The group studied a supervisory hour contributed by another supervisor in which he was also exceedingly active. Nearly every item of the analytic material was responded to strongly by this supervisor. He supplied an interpretation for each item, and was equally ready to evaluate the analyst's interventions. Material that could be recognized by the group as indicative of ambivalence or perhaps as mildly hostile was at once labeled by this supervisor as evidence of "murderous rage," and he was diligent in his attempts to prove this to the analyst. (There was, incidentally, later material that tended to confirm his thesis.) Such torrential supervision certainly represents a "style"—one about which most of the group felt rather critical. There is no doubt, however, that it gave the analyst a continuous exposure to the workings of the supervisor's mind, both regarding the case and his handling of it. If this were combined with an equal capacity to draw out the analyst to comparable free expression, there would be little to criticize. In a single sample no conclusions could be reached, but the fear of the group was that any or all of the bad effects listed above might be elicited.

The opposite style may produce a potentially equally bad result. The studiously noncommittal supervisor (or even worse, one who merely casts doubt on the analyst's ideas and interventions) leaves the analyst in limbo. The competent analyst-candidate might work effectively under any of these varying conditions, but the one most in need of supervision is likely to be thrown into difficult transference reactions, or at least into a state of critical dissatisfaction with the supervision. At neither of the extremes of this particular polarity does the candidate have both the proper stimulus and the real freedom to produce his own ideas and to test them against the material of the case in a spirit of mutual inquiry.

There was general consensus that there were some common attitudes and actions by supervisors that could have bad consequences. An example was discussed in which the candidate was caught between opposed demands from two supervisors. The first supervisor consistently wanted only an overview of the main trends of the case and was impatient with detail. The second supervisor was equally insistent on always hearing minute detail. It was agreed that these extremes were undesirable and would be likely to evoke effort by the analyst to satisfy the demands of the supervisor rather than be free to concentrate on the most fruitful consideration of the case material. He would clearly be prevented from feeling free to present the case in accord with his own style and to review it himself with any sense of benevolent criticism while he felt so constrained to anticipate and satisfy the essentially opposite and generally unreasonable demands of his supervisors. The second supervisor was also quite strict in both his personal and teaching style and, for instance, pressed the analyst for more information about the patient's sexual habits. It was quite early in the analysis. The candidate did not yet know much in this area and was unwilling to question or press his very reticent patient. The supervisor insisted, and the candidate protested that he could confront the patient with her reticence, but that pressing for details was wrong. The supervisor ended this exchange with, "I can see that you don't want to learn anything from me. You had better take this problem up in your own analysis." Such insistence that the candidate follow every opinion of the supervisor, we all agreed, was not helpful and probably wrong; and it would pose an almost insoluble problem for most candidates.

A similar episode was reported of a patient who asked the analyst for a tissue, which he provided. The candidate was then severely reproached by the supervisor, who said this was a gravely significant interaction which must be dealt with interpretively immediately in that hour. Few would dispute the possibility that the supervisor might be correct in his assessment, but we could all agree that it sounded as though the supervisor was being portentous, and excessively rigid in his demand for action by the analyst.

The shading over of acceptable stylistic variation into undesirable but harmless foible and then into unacceptable peculiarity is hard to assess precisely, but the foregoing examples and the one following are almost certainly in the last category. In this tale, three candidates, each with a hysterical woman in analysis, all had the same supervisor, who was quoted as giving each of them the same major injunction, "You don't have to take all that garbage from your patient."

A similar coercive attitude concealed by a more seductive manner can be observed in some supervisors, but it is difficult to exemplify in a short account. This is the supervisor who is pleasant and patient, but who is subtly coercive and demands that his idea be adopted completely by the student, who is never given credit for a capacity for independent judgment. A related subtlety is that of the supervisor who is drawn too easily and without awareness into a rescuing operation. More frequently early in their training, candidates may be quite uncertain and may be seductive in their attempts to get help and reassurance from the supervisor. The supervisor who is susceptible may discover (and perhaps some never do!) that he has been conducting a monologue about the case which he had been led to think all along was a dialogue. The frightened and insecure candidate may prove to be a very good listener whose appeal to the narcissistic exhibitionism of the expansive (often otherwise coercive) supervisor results in the latter's giving extended discussion, formulation, and advice. Sometimes the candidate is less subtle but no less effective when he presents the case in such a way as to alarm the supervisor and thereby move him to overly directive "rescue" operations.

The same result, the monologue effect, can occur whenever the supervisor responds invariably to presented case material with his own immediate thoughts and formulations. It is not uncommon for enthusiastic supervisors to listen intently to the evolving case material and then break in with a statement about how this confirms "our" formulation of last week, or some other idea or conceptualization. This can often be a very constructive pedagogical procedure, but its regular use risks the possibility of critically intimidating the candidate. Or it may merely fail to adequately stimulate him to bring his own ideas forward, in which case the supervision is also not fulfilling its purposes.

This brings us to the question of how much the supervisor should tell the analyst. We have been describing the pitfalls awaiting the supervisor who says too much. We hardly need to express our doubts about the helpfulness of those who rarely say anything. Within the acceptable range of variation along this dimension we have set the polarity: "Say only as much as you have to" versus "Say as much as you can." The "say only as much as you have to" stance is governed by the assumption that the effort to be actively educative or "rescuing" is in opposition to the student's need to (and freedom to) come to grips with the problems of conducting an analysis on his own terms, whether or not those problems are cognitive or technical problems or emotional problems activated by doing analytic work. The "say as much as you can" stance is held by those who are clearly not so impressed by the dangers implied above. They believe that that stance ought to be modified to provide several additional choices, e.g., the supervisor can explain the dynamics; he can indicate how he himself thinks about the situation; or he can attempt to catalyze the student's own associative processes. This latter effort virtually comes full circle and matches the aim of the "say only as much as you have to" position, except that it is more active in its attempt to elicit responses from the student.

The position of saying only as much as you have to in order to give the candidate the most freedom possible to develop his own approach could be paraphrased as follows: "I do not wish to burden the analyst with alternative formulations. The active teaching of the dynamics of the case, or of anything else for that matter, may well make it harder for the analyst himself to learn how to become analytically reflective. The optimal balance is to have adjusted one's activity so that only that information is supplied that is necessary to promote such reflection. I may agree with the analyst's formulation if I think it is correct, or raise a question if I think it is not. I prefer to wait until the evidence from the presented material is very strong before suggesting a formulation, and generally I would not suggest interpretations, preferring to have the candidate come to his own conclusions and present them in his own way. I think that candidates are too often overloaded with possibilities contributed by supervisors, and it is more confusing than helpful. I do try to help him *find an approach* to conceptualizing the various possibilities that might be present in the patient and in the analysis, and to selecting the criteria that will best guide him in making his choices. I expect a candidate to have the capacity for growth; my task is to provide a supervisory atmosphere which will foster that growth. When he has trouble because of countertransferences or a reaction to supervision, I try to minimize the tension, counting on his psychoanalytic orientation (and his own analysis) eventually to catch up with his neurosis."

The reply by one who holds the position of saying as much as you can could be paraphrased as follows: "I recognize the possibility of overloading the candidate, and of confusing him by providing a multiplicity of choices, but those choices do exist and an analyst should be aware of as many of them as possible. He should be able to contend with such a smorgasbord without suffering either bewilderment or indecision (or indigestion). The supervisor should not present all of his ideas as having equal probability. He should maintain perspective, and label both his speculations and his relative certainties. By presenting a wide variety of ideas and at the same time suspending his judgments, the supervisor provides an appropriate model for an analytic approach to the material of the analysis. Occasional theoretical discussions provide a bridge between theory and the concrete clinical material with which both discussants are thoroughly familiar. The same is true of discussions of technique and of its theoretical basis. I think that it is valuable to use the case material to help nail down theoretical concepts to concrete examples, and it is the unusual student who on his own initiates such discussion. I think such offerings of my own speculations can be presented in such a way that they facilitate rather than inhibit the associative activity of the analyst. If it is done competitively or if the analyst's speculations are depreciated, it will of course be unproductive. If I think the analyst has made a mistake, I say so. If it is a clumsy interpretation or if it is something that stops the patient momentarily, I point it out directly and at once. If it is a more serious error, I try to bring it up more gently, but in either case I think our alliance should be strong enough to bear the strain of legitimate criticism."

Supervisors vary with regard to the amount of dynamic formulation about the case which they expect from students, particularly early in the case. This issue of formulation versus nonformulation may well be a specious one, or one which can be resolved in terms of the following considerations. Formulations are in effect hypotheses. As such they create an order for the analyst. Within the framework of this order it is possible to allocate the innumerable facts of the case material and thereby make them more available to recall. Without such an aid to long-term memory, the number of recallable facts will be very severely curtailed. At the same time, this ordering has a tendentious effect on the conceptualizations that will ultimately emerge. Or in other words, the final conclusions reached are inevitably influenced and perhaps even determined by the early and the intermediate and intervening hypotheses. Since in both empirical science and in clinical psychoanalysis the goal for the final theoretical formulation and the final genetic reconstruction, respectively, is to correspond as congruently as possible to reality, it is crucial that hypotheses be held loosely enough to be refuted or at least modified by the development of relevant evidence. In practice all psychoanalysts apply the general formulations of psychoanalysis to the developing case material. However, it is the detailed formulations that are at issue. It may be a false issue if we can agree that the effort to avoid premature formulation is misplaced and it would be better to persuade the analyst to use his hypotheses properly—that is, to hold to them as mnemonic devices and as guides to the probable future development of the material, and to be willing freely to modify them or even abandon them in the face of new evidence. It would appear that formulations of some kind are inevitable, and that the real issue is the degree of their appropriate use versus the misuse to which they can be put by those who use them either to defend against their sense of confusion in the face of the enigma posed by the patient or against their sense of anxiety in the face of the demand posed by the supervisor.

These variances in supervisory demand for explicitness in formulation correlate loosely with the positions supervisors take about how much they should tell the analyst. Those who hold to saying "only as much as you have to" tend not to require much formulation by the candidate; those who say "as much as you can" tend correspondingly to require active efforts at explicit formulation by the candidate. There is general agreement that the analyst should have some degree or level of tentative formulation. However, those who tend to oppose this emphasis or to not encourage it doubt the advisability both of extracting an early formulation of the case from the analyst and of presenting their own formulations to him. This position is taken because they believe that to present or elicit such formulations would set up a very detrimental supervisory tone from the beginning. The concern is that the options of the student would inevitably be curtailed, that his freedom to listen and react to the unfolding material of the analysis would be constrained too early into a set form of his own making (i.e., his formal structuring of the case) or alternatively would fall under the shadow of the supervisor's expressed formulation. This dual influence is felt to be deleterious to both the capacity to work freely with the patient and the ability to communicate freely with the supervisor. The opposed group does not believe these dangers weigh so heavily, and considers that initial formulations, though necessarily tentative, should not thereby be blurred. Furthermore, they should be discussed with the supervisor and compared with his formulations for concordance and divergence. The two sets of formulations will then be subjected to amplification and correction as the analysis progresses. Some supervisors find it useful to take particular care to find out from the analyst precisely what the material meant *to him*. It should be stressed that this does not necessarily mean a detailed formulation, but it especially avoids providing those answers that would tend to discourage the candidate from divulging his impressions, his speculations, and his hunches.

It may be useful to consider this question of how active the supervisor should be by using a bit of actual case material. The positions taken in this discussion are comparable to those taken by the opposed proponents of "say only as much as you must" versus "say as much as you can." In our discussion of supervision hour 5 (see Chapter X) the members of the group attempted to be as stringent as possible in their critique of the supervisor's activity. In so doing, it may be assumed that their own stylistic preferences were being expressed. One position taken was that the supervisor was overactive in his questioning and his explaining. This critic would have been more passive, expectant, and nurturing, with the hope that in such a supervisory climate the analyst could feel freer, would venture more, and that therefore his natural talent would find better room to expand. The critic likewise felt that there was an overly intense intellectual effort to comprehend and to advise, and that this kind of "overactivity" tended to focus the attention of the analyst on the supervision and the interactions within the supervision rather than on the patient and the interactions within the treatment, where his attention more properly belonged.

This viewpoint was buttressed by the observation that even if it were granted that the interventions of the supervisor were put tactfully and tentatively or even hesitantly, still the supervisor may have been proposing too many foci for attention. The "overactivity" consists then also of providing too many concepts for the analyst to fully comprehend and absorb. In contrast, this critic would have limited himself more to manifestly evident material. He would perhaps have drawn attention to such things as the patient's having missed an hour, or her summery dress on a wintry day, or her familiar tone in her telephone conversation with the analyst. The specific stylistic preference expressed was for this kind of initiative or activity by the supervisor rather than the actual supervisor's discussion of the possibility that some of the patient's productions were screen memories covering primal scene material, or his discussion of the analyst's use of oversimplified identification models. The actual supervisor had also tried to consider in a recapitulation of the whole week's work such matters as the patient's withheld affects, the overall transference position, and the state of her object relations. He had questioned the analyst more or less strictly, "Are you overstressing your analytic objectivity to the point where it could be felt by the patient as indifference?" And in addition, the supervisor made a statement to the effect that the patient was not very empathic with her own suffering, that she was describing her problems as though in the third person. He figuratively used the phrase, "There is no patient here." Each of these five major interventions by the supervisor was felt by this critical observer to be an overloading and more than the situation or the analyst was ready for.

Even those whose approach was most in accord with that of the supervisor were able to find points of difference, as would the supervisor himself had he had the same opportunity to review his reported material with the proverbial 20/20 hindsight. The defenders against the criticism of "overactivity" felt this depended on an on-the-spot estimate of the analyst's capacity to absorb the kind and the number of supervisory interventions offered. These supervisors felt that some candidates are well able to pick and choose among the supervisor's offerings, and that the more that is made available, the greater the opportunity for learning. Here there is a matter of elusive judgment by the supervisor as to what in a particular instance constitutes overloading or intimidation of the analyst. They felt that as long as the analyst maintained a true spirit of dialogue there was no real danger of overloading. Conversely, if the analyst responds with a defensive or provocative attitude, or if he becomes silent or otherwise unresponsive—for example by a perfunctory agreement followed by a quick change of subject—then the supervisor should consider that he has exceeded the saturation point and reduce his output. Another possibly ominous or at least dubious sign is a too ready or too effusive agreement followed by a feverish though possibly furtive search for material that will confirm the then-to-be-considered omniscient pronouncements of the supervisor. Such an approach to dosage of supervisor intervention depends on a kind of titration, with the use of the above indicators and a reasonable degree of intuition on the part of the supervisor.

This implies that the supervisor will tailor his approach according to its reception. With some candidates he will need to be sparing and careful all of the time; with others he may be much more generous, or challenging, depending always on his estimate of his impact. Such an ideal of variability of approach to accommodate to the shifting immediate needs of the analyst is of course generally subscribed to by the members of the Study Group, even though they do not all read the reported evidence in the same way.

A yet different approach was made by another discussant who thought that this supervisor had not been active enough. This opinion was based on the fact that, in the supervisory report at least, there was no mention of an effort by the supervisor to ask the analyst more about his understanding of the material. Much of the supervisor's opinion and intervention seemed to be based on inference from the analyst's presented material, and there seemed not to be enough supervisory activity to probe more fully the exact level of the candidate's comprehension of his material. This same discussant, however, reported experiences of his own in which he felt that just such probing had had adverse effects on the learning process.

The term "evocative questioning" has been used to describe an approach to teaching which is neither didactic in the directive or lecturing sense nor laissez-faire. This approach has been linked with the phrase "enabling teaching" and could be considered a middle ground or an alternative to the more extreme forms of expectant or of directive styles. It can pursue questions in a very diligent way and it permits judgments to be made. It can even raise issues of the analyst's neurotic and countertransference problems by asking him increasingly pointed questions.

Such evocative questioning can offer the supervisor as a model for the analyst, particularly when it is used to illustrate the reflective qualities of the supervisor and the ways they are made use of in his consideration of the analytic process. Ideas may be offered with the suggestion that they be "tried for fit." Such use of the word "suggestion" offers us an example of the range of effects of which different supervisory styles are capable, however, i.e., the suggestion can be made in a most natural and tentative way or it can be stressed in such a way that the analyst is given to understand that there are really no tenable alternatives. Between those extremes the supervisor may convey his conviction of the degree of "fit" but still leave the analyst room to make his own decision (the fit being of course the double one of fit for the analyst and fit for the patient).

One of the ideas about the supervisor's role which would modify the style of the supervisor is the conviction that the emergence of a teaching alliance should be just as self-consciously facilitated as the emergence of the therapeutic alliance. Some in the group were dissatisfied with the terms "teaching alliance" and "learning alliance" because they believed the terms presume a still unproved point-by-point congruence with the therapeutic alliance. Nevertheless, all agreed that it was desirable to promote a working relationship based on rapport and mutual respect. The advantages of doing this seem self-evident and will not be detailed. Possible disadvantages are more subtle, and derive from either mutual or unilateral seductive actions, their gratification or frustration, and the complex transference-countertransference developments that ensue. A simple example, observed all too often, is the supervisor who finds a candidate particularly attractive and promising, and in consequence enters into a mutual-admiration-society relationship with him, only later to become disillusioned either by the candidate's inevitable shortcomings or perhaps by some inkling that the student is in some way disenchanted with the supervisor. When this happens the supervisor has been known to behave "like a woman scorned" with unfortunate results for the supervision. Short of such extreme and neurotic interactions, an overly close relationship still presents similar but less dramatic opportunities for difficulty, and clearly should be avoided. Those who take the most authoritarian stance make no effort to foster any kind of alliance or special rapport. A relationship does develop of course, and it may be no less strong and potentially disruptive of learning simply because it is unplanned. The problem of "split transferences" is encountered with heightened frequency at both these extremes, i.e., with both the seductive and the authoritarian supervisor.

The degree to which a formalization of the approach to supervision is desirable was discussed, and again a range of viewpoints emerged. It is not surprising that in general those who have thought and written the most about the problems of supervision tend to consider the problems in a more systematic and formal way. There was not, however, a true polarization within the group, but rather an interpenetration of the formal approaches with the more usual clinical intuitive or impressionistic approach. Such formalization and its modification are exemplified in the following overly schematized descriptions. The supervisor first considers the case and both his and the analyst's understanding of it. Next he tries to conceive the ideal treatment strategy. Then he considers the student-analyst's understandings in both his defensive and his adaptive working, and finally, the supervisor considers the necessarily altered treatment strategy and how to teach it, based on the maximal feasible adaptation of this particular student, given his stage of learning, experience, and freedom from neurotic distortion, to this "ideal treatment strategy." A modification of this approach would start from the focus on the student's level of understanding and development and would avoid trying to approximate any theoretical ideal. The major consideration would be the analyst's level of understanding of the case, then his level of understanding of technique (particularly the analyst's operational capacity as determined by his defensive and adaptive working). The supervisor would then work out a treatment strategy tailored to that student's capacity with that specific case. The supervisor's teaching strategy would be tailored specifically to the assessment of the learning requirements of that student-analyst.

There are certain styles which the members of the group generally agree are undesirable. An authoritarian style is condemned by its very appellation. By this token, the coercive supervisor and the rigidly didactic supervisor are highly suspect. Nevertheless, it was noted that it is still possible to learn from a position of opposition. In such an instance a "learning alliance" might be a misnomer, but some kind of working learning relationship might still exist. A less extreme condition obtains where the supervisor is simply challenging, in the Socratic sense. Under these circumstances it appears that a certain proportion of students mobilizes to meet the challenge, and even enjoys the intellectual adversary role. In principle it might even be held that a degree of opposition as well as independence is necessary or desirable in the learning situation. At least it is a common observation that there is an optimal level of tension present during maximal states of learning. A subsidiary consideration is that when the supervisor is too passive, expectant, or noncommittal there may be an increased risk of fostering undue transference developments. On the contrary, if the supervisor is overly aggressive, controlling and/or opinionated, we may expect and indeed hope for appropriate resentment from the student-analyst.

Supervisors vary in their willingness to formulate the cases and in the degree to which they communicate such formulations to the analyst. This issue has already been discussed in part under the headings of saying "only as much as you must" versus "as much as you can." At this point the dichotomy being considered differs somewhat: those who formulate and communicate extensively, as opposed to those who formulate little and communicate little or nothing of this to the candidate. At their extremes, these positions become parodies, and there are cogent arguments against taking either position dogmatically. Those who caution against the supervisor explicitly formulating the case point out that when the supervisor does this, he correspondingly discourages the analyst from doing it. It may also be seen as intimidating the analyst or, conversely, as promoting unprofitable and unhealthy rivalry by him. This may lead to a subtle but definite distancing between supervisor and analyst. A different result can be that the analysis is guided by the supervisor to such a degree that the analyst neither thinks much about the case nor has to take much responsibility for its conduct.

There are differences in supervisory style that influence the nature and extent of the identification of the analyst with the supervisor. The Study Group agreed that some degree of such identification is both inevitable and desirable. It is inevitable to the degree that students always identify with their teachers, and it is desirable to the degree that the supervisor approximates the model of an ideal analyst. Even if the supervisor provides an unsatisfactory model it is still possible for the analyst to profit from the experience by responding with an identification negating the recognizably unaccepted aspects of the supervisor. This relatively superficial and conscious reaction is unfortunately probably less common than the less desirable identification with the aggressor which can regularly be observed as a kind of "hereditary" trait in the more susceptible descendants of such recognizable supervisors. The mitigating effect on blind identifications is probably one of the best arguments in favor of multiple supervisors. If we ask how favorable identifications with the supervisor are fostered, we have a rather more difficult question. An approximate answer is: by having a capable supervisor who can lend himself as a model, who demonstrates in the supervision his own way of exploring the analytic material and his own efforts to comprehend and bring order to it. The supervisor, both by his way of studying the analytic material and his method of conducting the supervision, serves as a model for: (1) a mode of listening, (2) a method of weighing and thinking while suspending judgment and action, and (3) in periods of emergency or crisis, a way of getting out of a regressive jam and back to a constructive course.

The focus of attention of the supervisor may be directed to the patient, the analyst, or the analytic process. It may on occasion be directed to the supervisory process as well, but this is not common except among those supervisors with a special interest in this direction. We take it to be self-evident that this focus should shift in ways appropriate to the circumstances and that each choice deserves adequate attention. Overemphasis on one at the expense of the other would have predictably unfavorable consequences. Those whose approach is generally most didactic are most likely to focus largely or even exclusively on the patient. Those who lean toward the "treat" end of the "teach versus treat" polarity will naturally focus more on the analyst. Those who attend primarily to the analytic process will perforce take note of both elements of the process and hence have a built-in balance. The supervisor who is completely patient-oriented runs the risk of taking over and managing the analysis, with the analyst becoming his mere agent. This pitfall can be encountered also within a process orientation, but the risk is smaller. The learning of the analyst may suffer because of this, and if he is overly anxious to "complete" a case he may fall in with the supervisor's thrust all the more readily. The effort of both analyst and supervisor becomes limited to the immediate demands of patient dynamics. The case may progress, but the analyst can complete the analysis with a minimum of attention to his own activities, their meaning, and even their consequences except in the most immediate sense. He may even lack perspective about the case itself, if the supervisor's view is excessively limited to immediate dynamic and technical problems.

The opposite problem is encountered by students whose supervisor is preoccupied with his "countertransference problems." The group was again unanimous in its opinion that such preoccupation provides but a travesty of proper supervision. The student, unless he rebels and leaves supervision, is compelled to submit his own management of the case to tendentious analysis, with the result that discussion of the case itself is virtually abandoned, and the treatment process is viewed only from the limited perspective afforded by a consideration of the therapist's own feelings and actions. Although this extreme probably is never reached by supervising analysts, some risks are always evident when the analyst's reactions occupy the center of the stage, however briefly. These have already been covered in the "teach versus treat" section, and will not be repeated here, except to note that the analyst may adopt a *mea culpa* attitude as a defense, or he may simply become very secretive about his interventions and report only those he has learned will pass muster. In either case, satisfactory conditions for learning are sacrificed.

It is a special instance of the supervisor focusing predominant attention on the case when he has the idea that the patient is his responsibility. There are those who feel strongly that this is so, and this attitude does not seem to correlate precisely with levels of supervisory activity as might be expected. Particularly if it is a clinic case, supervisors are often inclined in this direction, and are moved to give quite specific advice, amounting virtually to a rescue activity if the case appears to be in danger of what is deemed a serious acting out or other disruption. The rationale is that the supervisor is the more expert, and when the patient's welfare is at stake, the most expert intervention possible should be made. The virtue of this position is self-evident, particularly as regards patient care. The disadvantages of it are cited by those of the opposite persuasion. First, the independence of the candidate is directly breached. He is normally an able psychiatrist who should be capable of making sound clinical judgments if in possession of the proper information. If the supervisor usurps his judgment, it implies either that the student-analyst cannot understand the issues well enough, or that he cannot be trusted to arrive at the proper judgments about them. In either case infantilization is threatened, or the analyst may simply sabotage the supervisor's intervention and develop either a covert or overt state of rebellion.

Those opposed to taking ultimate responsibility for the case contend that the case is in fact the analyst's. He comes to learn about psychoanalysis and to discuss its application to the case, but it is his judgment and his responsibility that must obtain. His analytic growth cannot be augmented if control is wrenched (or teased) from him at crucial moments. The "rescue" issue is also relevant here. If the analyst really is floundering, and the case endangered, then the difference between the two positions narrows considerably. It may be virtually effaced when the analyst asks for help. Supervisors of both persuasions would then be willing to give advice and even active direction. Those who feel the most sense of responsibility, however, are less likely to discuss alternatives. It is also harder to make a distinction when the case is in danger of being lost because of patent mismanagement and misunderstanding by the analyst. It is very hard in such instances even for the "nonresponsible" supervisor not to make direct suggestions about how the situation might be remedied. The purist among them will mention that it is at just these times that it is most important to maintain the clarifying rather than the directive role. If the analyst can be instructed sufficiently and at the same time persuaded that it is his job and he is trusted to do it, the crisis should result in an experience of enhanced analytic growth and maturation.

By this point perhaps enough illustrations have been offered of the diversity of supervisory stances that can be delineated within the behavioral spectrum ranging from idiosyncracy and perhaps even uniqueness of style, which is genetically and characterologically rooted, through to explicitly thought-out scientific choice and conviction with its anchoring in theoretical study and in clinical training and experience. This spectrum from extreme of intuitive style to extreme of formulated scientific position indeed allows sufficient intervening points to provide ample explanatory base for the whole range of acceptable supervisory practice of "good enough supervision."

REFERENCE

Fleming, J. & Benedek, T. (1966), *Psychoanalytic Supervision*. New York: Grune & Stratton.

CHAPTER V

The Data: Process Notes of Fourteen Supervision Hours

HERBERT J. SCHLESINGER, Ph.D.

"Process notes" is a term borrowed from the supervisory language of social work, describing the notes written by the caseworker following an hour with a client, with the intent of recapturing the interaction between them either verbatim or in paraphrase. This set of process notes resembles the social work prototype to the extent that I, as the supervisor who wrote them, have tried to record something of the interaction between myself and the analyst, but I also undertook to convey enough of the interaction between the analyst and his patient, as discerned through the analyst's report, so that the reader would obtain sufficient grasp of what it was that I was interacting about with the analyst.

For purposes of research in supervision, process notes taken alone have some advantage in that the voluminous verbatim analytic material is preselected and predigested by a presumably experienced analytic teacher. But this advantage creates a correlated drawback in that this process of selection and condensation may make it difficult to see past the supervisor and to arrive (with any sense of conviction) at conclusions other than those the supervisor anticipated. Tape-recording would of course capture everything that had been said, but would omit the highlighting of issues and the reflections of the supervisor that adequate process notes afford.

Probably no one form of supervisory material would provide adequate data to answer all the questions one might find it useful to study. It would be best in each instance to settle on the questions to be investigated and the methods to be used and to delineate the appropriate data in terms of these more primary considerations. Since the Study Group's project was in the nature of a pilot study, process notes of supervision, obtainable to begin with, with less intrusion on the analytic process, seemed both a good place to begin and also to promise data adequate for these initial purposes.

I decided that I could prepare such notes for the Supervision Study Group, providing the anonymity of both the analyst and the patient could be adequately assured. Further, I thought that since my own interest in preparing these notes was being served by the agreement of the Study Group to focus mainly (though not exclusively) on the supervisor's activity, and since I would not be tape-recording but merely making my own post-hour notes, I felt no necessity at the time to inform the candidate-analyst of my participation in the COPE Study Group's project. I should add, however, that my interest in studying supervision was a matter of general knowledge in my institute.

I also gave some thought to how I would prepare the notes for the Study Group so as to maximize the likelihood of a useful result from this collaboration both from the Study Group's perspective and my own. Since the group had as yet no worked-out method for conducting a study of supervision (indeed, to develop such methods was one of the purposes of the project that was being planned), I decided to assign myself some methodological ground rules:

1. I would observe and report as faithfully as possible what I actually did as supervisor and to record, also as much as possible, what I thought during the supervision when this was not directly reflected in what I said to the analyst. Thus, my focus would be on the supervisor's activity while reporting enough of the events of the analysis, as the analyst reported them to me, to provide the background necessary to understand the supervisory process.

2. The effect of this reporting bias (to preserve the supervisory interventions as comprehensively as is useful) is that since the candidate talks much more of the time, his interventions will be much more subject to condensation in the reporting than will mine. This bias is even truer of the ratio of participation by the analyst and the patient in the analytic hours although, as I have remarked in the supervisory notes, this analyst tended to report to me only a fraction of his interventions with the patient. The balance of the reported material in my process notes represents much the larger proportion of what I did, much less of what the analyst did, and still less of what the patient did. I have reported my own comments in full if they were short, but if they dealt with the standard analytic ideas or obvious teaching points, I have only summarized or alluded to the content that I am sure any

supervisor would be able to fill in for himself. I would dictate these notes as soon as possible after the supervision hour so as to minimize the retrospective distortions, and then send them off to the Study Group unedited, except for correcting typographical errors.

3. I would also ignore what the Study Group actually did with these reports lest their thinking interfere with my primary role which, as I saw it, was to be the subject of their study. Neither would I review these notes myself until I was ready to relinquish my role as subject. Although the Study Group thoughtfully sent me write-ups of their discussions as well as discussions by the San Francisco Project group, I did not look at these until the Study Group indicated that they had enough material so that further notes by me were no longer desired.

4. I made my bias about the intended focus of my notes explicit because I wanted to concentrate on the events in the supervision process and not make it easy to explain what went on in supervision by events "outside the field." Thus, I gave the Study Group at the outset a bare minimum of information about the candidate and his patient. Only after they had completed the "first round" of their study of the first fourteen hours of supervision did I make available to them the more complete account of the complexities of the teaching situation as I experienced it (recorded in Chapter XIII). Many of these supervision notes were dictated immediately following the supervisory hour described. Sometimes this was not possible, and a note could not be dictated until some hours had elapsed. The persons most immediately concerned in these notes are:

The Patient. A single woman in her mid-twenties, attending college, who supports herself by working part-time for a small business firm. She applied for help to a community mental health agency. The agency staff, thinking she might be in need of psychoanalytic treatment, referred her to the psychoanalytic institute's clinic. Her presenting complaint was that she was not doing anything constructive with her life. Specifically, she would like to be married and was engaged to quite a suitable fellow, approved of by her family. As the wedding date grew closer, she began to feel more physically repulsed by him, felt compelled to hold wedding plans in abeyance, and to suspend the engagement. Though she stated she was fairly certain that she did not want to be married to this man, neither could she give him up. In effect, she has been living with him in a largely asexual relationship. At the same time, she has had occasional affairs with other men, which she claimed to enjoy so long as they did not threaten to become serious. Her pattern of affairs with men has been that she would get quickly and deeply involved with only those who were not suitable marriage prospects and would then break off with them herself as this became apparent.

The patient is the youngest of four children, with a sister two years older, a brother four years older, and a sister six years older; the others are all married and have children, and none have sought psychiatric help. The father's job often took him abroad, and the family had moved with him, living in different countries for short periods. Military service kept the father away from the family for several years during the patient's childhood. The mother has been described as alcoholic since the patient was eleven, and has dominated her husband. Both parents have had affairs known to each other and to the children.

The Analyst. A man who has had good clinical training and has an active practice of psychotherapy. He also holds a part-time research position at a local institution. This is his second supervised psychoanalytic case, the first being a difficult male patient.

The Supervisor. A male who had been supervising psychoanalysts for over five years and who is interested in the learning and teaching of psychoanalysis. He prepared these notes at the request of the COPE Supervision Study Group.

PROCESS NOTES OF SUPERVISION

SUPERVISION HOUR 1 (ANALYTIC HOURS 1–3)

I agreed to start working with the analyst because the patient was waiting and he had the time, although I did not have a regular hour open. I told him I would have to fit him in where I could, and he accepted on this basis. Our initial discussion about the patient was over lunch. Since he seemed comfortable about starting, I suggested he go ahead, and we would discuss the case further after he had begun. He had the patient on the couch during the first hour, and when he saw me in passing once before the next appointment we had set up, he let me know that he thought things were going pretty well.

When we met, he had process notes typed for the first three hours, but gave me an informal summary of what he thought had taken place before I looked at them. His observations about the patient were that she seemed to be conveying that, "yes, she sort of had these problems that were bothering her and could have a happier life, but on the other hand, maybe they weren't really that bad." He called it a kind of self-justifying tendency. He said she was talking fairly easily, but not really in a very free manner. She only alluded to things that would be difficult to talk about. He said at one point she became reflective, and said though she had always wanted a captive audience, indeed, had wanted to be an English teacher so that she would have a captive audience to whom she could talk about the beauties of literature, now that she has one, she can't seem to use it. He said she was reflective in wondering why she could not talk about things that really were bothering her when she had the opportunity. I asked the analyst what he had been doing about his observations He said, "Nothing, just listening," and he went on to stress his inactivity. This led me to ask if his stress on it meant he had been told by someone that he ought to keep his mouth shut during the initial phase of the analysis. He said, "Well, not exactly, but perhaps." Then he added he knew that his own tendency in psychotherapy was to be rather too active, to jump on things as soon as he saw them, and he was trying to hold this tendency in check.

After some discussion of this kind, I asked if we should look at the notes, and we did. I read them quickly and found things about as he had described them. The analyst's comments in the beginning were rather neutral, asking for clarification from time to time. He explained the analytic situation to the patient well enough, without too much detail, and allowed her to struggle a bit with the request for associations. There were occasional reinforcers, asking what came to her mind or asking for a bit of clarification about what she meant. But for the most part there was no further intervention than this. I did discuss a bit what he might do if her tendency to balance off her problems with self-reassurance turned out to reflect not just the usual initial anxiety, that she may have gotten herself into more treatment than she needs, and he indicated some awareness that he knew how he could handle it.

My own observations were that the patient's associations jump around quite a bit. She doesn't stay too long on one subject and consciously seems to have the feeling that she is not talking about anything important. Nevertheless, the material is about her life, and there is a consistent flow to it. The resistances show, but they do not seem excessive. The analyst does nothing specific about them other than offer occasional appropriate mildly facilitating comments. In view of his statement that he was doing "nothing," I made it clear to myself that his understanding of the analytic situation was the same as mine, that the beginning phase of analysis would be handled differently from psychotherapy in that he was hoping to achieve a deeper level of regression, and that he would avoid interpretive comments or other interventions that would tend to abort the tendency for the patient to regress.

He noted at the beginning of his note for each hour how the patient was dressed. Her rather plain clothes the first hour gave way to an attractive suit in the second and to considerable perfume in the third. He mentioned too that she brings her coat into the office and takes a while removing her coat and putting it on again, although the coat could be left outside. He also mentioned, although he did not put it in the notes, that she uses every opportunity to look at him. When I asked what the quality of her looking was, he said he thought she was trying to see what his reaction was to what she was saying. When he asked me what I had in mind, I said I wondered about differentiating that motive from the possibility that she was trying to hold on to him as long as possible, to "memorize him," or possibly to "take him in with her eyes." There is no direct evidence for these other possibilities yet.

The analyst recorded that before leaving the office the patient asked him where he was going (in response to his earlier announcement that he was going to be gone for three days next week). Thus, there is more evidence of a developing pattern of the patient's investment in the period before and after the hour.

Toward the end of the third hour the patient reported she felt the room was just spinning, and she raised her head from the couch momentarily. This incident followed talking about her older sister for the first time (in whose footsteps she had followed and with whom she probably felt competitive). I shall come back to this after this next point, because I recall that something occurred earlier that should be mentioned here in sequence.

Having read the three hours quickly, I had the feeling that he was handling things pretty well, that events were developing and there wasn't much he needed in the way of technical advice. I did suggest a way he could handle the possibility that she would get stuck for a while around the question of whether she really wanted to invest herself in this much treatment. He seemed to understand the quite superficial interpretive moves that could be helpful in such a situation. We then looked at the flow of material itself, and I started to talk aloud as I tried to reconstruct the flow of her associations, showing that when the qualifications and connections were removed, the material had some quality of free association. Particularly in the third hour, there was a hint at some transference when she said she liked seeing a piece of sculpture of mother and child on the analyst's shelf, and mentioned she would like to have a child but never permitted herself to get herself into a "situation" in which she could have one.

Following a long pause and complaints that there was nothing else to talk about, she talked about her current affair disturbing somebody else (a man) who lives in the same house. The possibility that the analyst would approve of her wish to have a child, countered by the fear that he would not, was followed by references to having a captive audience, which seemed to reflect her own fear of being captive herself. After she said she had a captive audience, the analyst told her he would be away for three days. She immediately countered by saying she planned to be away at Christmas. There followed a discussion of her plan, and the analyst mentioned she would be charged during her absence. This seemed to be an unnecessary intrusion of reality, and I wondered if the analyst had responded unconsciously to being described as captive (I had not known before he started that he had plans to be away so soon).

Following this was a story about her older, married sister (who has "everything," all sorts of electrical gadgets) having a broken extension cord, which is dangerous to her children. The story seemed to involve following in the sister's footsteps, taking what her sister was no longer interested in, trying to compete with her, and so on. But these ideas were countered by others which said she gave as good as she got. After mentioning that her sister was more aggressive, had a louder voice, and had a role in a play that the patient wanted and then turned it down and gave it to the patient, the patient's head started to spin.

The analyst and I discussed some of the possible significances of the relationship to her sister for a bit.

The first supervisory hour seemed comfortable, and the analysis off to a good start.

SUPERVISION HOUR 2 (ANALYTIC HOURS 4–12)

Supervision continues on a catch-as-catch-can basis. I saw the analyst once over lunch last week, when he brought me up to date. It seemed to me he was handling the beginning phase pretty well. My impression was that the patient seemed analyzable and that the flow of the material had the proper ring to it with one important exception—there were no indications of any expectation of the analyst from the patient. Shortly after beginning with the patient he told her he would be away for a few days. The patient instantly responded that she had plans to go away Christmas. Also, she "forgot" to come the next hour by coming at a time different from her appointment. The analyst mentioned she had had a dream she wanted to bring into that hour, but told in the next one, about a great big black cat. (These first two supervision hours will run together because he brought the same material in to me today in addition to hours 4 through 12. I did not have time to read all this material, but he asked me to look at hour 5, which had the black cat dream in it—slightly more than three pages of single-spaced notes that I shall not try to summarize.)

I had the impression, though, from what the analyst said and from skimming the notes, that the state of the patient at present is that she has come to see in her life that she does things she does not understand and gets into "messes." Even though she knows what she is going to do will cause her trouble, she does it anyway. It was this realization that brought her to treatment. Having begun treatment, she tells the analyst that things are really a little better now. The material of this hour includes many associations to cats that are untrustworthy, sneaky, and sly, but there are also associations to a cat of her childhood that she loved very much. This mother cat died, leaving kittens behind that also died despite everything she could do. She has never wanted to go near cats again. In the same hour, she reported two dreams of the past, one of a gingerbread man or sandman who got little and big as if made out of wet sand, and another following being told her mother was an alcoholic and hospitalized, in which she called to her mother and was awakened as she screamed for her.

There are other stories in the hour of enormous risks she took because of being apparently unaware of the danger she was in. There seems to be a fear of becoming dependent on the analyst—a fear of helplessness one might say at the moment—which parallels the awareness that has been dawning on her that she is really helpless in her own life. As she comes to the analysis, however, she starts to take charge of her own life as if she were jumping from the helplessness of the fire in her life into the frying pan of the analysis and were very much afraid of her impending dependency on the analyst. His news of impending departure is countered by her own plans to leave and her forgetting an hour after having a dream in which a big black cat comes at her with his claws outstretched, and the hour has, as I mentioned, hints of the dangers and messes in which one can get into out of dependency. There was also the hint in these hours that the patient's rather disorderly life may partly be motivated by a wish to master her fear of dependency through casual affairs that she permits or breaks off at her own will.

The analyst and I spent most of the hour developing this understanding. The analyst also called my attention to another dream in the eighth hour, which was something of a nightmare. There was not time to look at the entire hour, but in the dream she was in an apartment with old-fashioned windows, broken up into little panes by wooden strips. There were two windows with a wooden partition between them, and a person behind this partition, so that all she could see were the shoulders and hands. The left hand was pointing at the ring finger of the right hand. It was the wedding finger, but on the wrong hand. The patient's associations were to the huge diamond ring that her mother has wanted to give her, and she had the horrible thought that maybe she wanted mother to die. She has to watch out in admiring anything of her mother's because her mother would want to give it to her. We had no time to discuss this further.

I had one or two minor technical suggestions for the analyst, mostly about his asking unnecessary questions. At least in one instance he had communicated a proper understanding, but in the form of a question. Rather than confront the patient with the fact that she had left something out, he asked her a question about the missing material. I also suggested that he make his notes a bit shorter, suggesting a maximum of one page.

The analyst still seems to be handling the case quite well; he suggested himself that the patient was seeing him as a "nice guy" who tended to give her too much and thus make her feel helpless, in the manner of several incidents with boy friends and by implication as she described her mother in some of these hours.

SUPERVISION HOUR 3 (ANALYTIC HOURS 13–15)

There are only three hours this week because the patient has been away. The analyst brought three notes. He handed them to me, but I did not look at them immediately. He asked if I would like him to summarize what took place, and I said I would. He gave a cogent and concise summary of the events of the week, mentioning the patient's recital about her visit to her family in another city. A discussion followed of her ex-fiancé, whom she cannot marry but cannot give up either. During the last hour the patient alluded to her distrust of psychiatrists and psychologists. He summarized the events indicating that movement we had been looking at previously seems to be continuing. Except for the last hour there are no references to the treatment process itself but a good bit of metaphoric communication about the difficulty in getting together with people and an increase in the amount of (covert) reference to her distrust of or reservation about the treatment.

In my discussion of these events with the analyst he spent some time talking about the relationship with the ex-fiancé and the allusions to distrust of psychiatrists, mentioning that the patient said she had had an affair with a psychiatrist, a married man with children. She therefore had good reason to realize they are no better than other men. Also, her brother-in-law is a psychologist and shows some very peculiar behavior. In among these references the patient mentioned that not only did she have her own trouble with her ex-fiancé, but she had also gotten a good look at her sister's marriage and had almost decided that marriage was not for her. The lives of her sister and brother-in-law are totally taken up with the children, they have no time to themselves, and so forth. It seemed to me as I listened to this that the patient was saying that inasmuch as she came into treatment because of her inability to wed her ex-fiancé and her desire to be married, she now wondered if it would not be a better idea to give up her plans to be married and hence her need for treatment. One hint that this is not the entire truth is that the patient in the last hour said that, unaccountably, she was feeling better and felt that she was getting somewhere in therapy though she had no idea how therapy works. She pragmatically welcomed the change in any event. As we discussed these events, I ascertained that the analyst had been continuing his quite conservative approach to the patient, limiting his own interventions to an occasional question for clarification and comments about what the patient is or is not talking about.

In discussing the patient's apparent distrust I tried to point out to the analyst the possibility that indications of displaced mistrust may be secondary to her feeling more comfortable with the analyst—in other words, might be secondary to positive feelings which might be frightening to the patient.

In the discussions of the patient's sexual life I found out through questioning him that she referred to her behavior in nonvulgar terms using the euphemisms "intimate" or "sleep with," but she had not mentioned whether she had any feeling for the people with whom she was "intimate." Rather, she seemed to view herself as a "liberated" woman and, as the analyst noted, her attitudes toward sex seemed rather "masculine" in the sense that she took it where she found it and was a little annoyed at men who tended to make these things more complicated than they need be. She seemed to regard herself as having sexual needs which she wanted to gratify like any others. Missing from her account was any investment in the person of the partner or, indeed, any mention of pleasure. We know from the intake that she thought she had a problem with frigidity, achieving orgasm perhaps one in four times. Neither had she mentioned any intimacy with the ex-fiancé, only mentioning that she was not sexually attracted to him and therefore could not think of marrying him. There were some references in the notes that she was "panicked" at the idea of marriage and also showed some "panic" the other night when she visited the ex-fiancé and could not stay with him, but had to have a friend call him and say that she was not coming back. (There are little hints at increasing anxiety symptoms even as the patient is feeling better in the hours.)

After much of our discussion, I did read through the notes. I thought the analyst had handled things quite well, but I made a few suggestions about how his comments could be phrased to educate her a bit more about what is useful in the analytic process. I also commented that she did not seem to need even as little intervention as he was applying, and I noted there were increasingly long pauses which the analyst was inclined to break by picking up the last topic rather than by wondering about the silence.

He had recorded that in the second hour he had told the patient he would be away again over Friday and Monday. He told her this just before the New Year's vacation. Thus there have been several interruptions in this beginning. The analyst had to go to another city to attend a family wedding. Since the analyst was aware of it, I did not comment further on the undesirability of the interruption, but we did spend a few minutes at the end anticipating what the next moves might be. I tried to alert him to any likely ways in which the patient's increasing transference feelings might show themselves. He had some questions about how psychological-minded the patient was based on some data in the intake. I did not have much to say about this. Clearly the flow of the patient's material was quite coherent and very rich in metaphor, but there was no indication as yet that the patient had any idea of what she was talking about.

SUPERVISION HOUR 4 (ANALYTIC HOURS 16–18)

There were only three hours this week because of the analyst's absence to attend a wedding. After a few comments about his trip, he started talking about the patient, saying a bit humorously that she made her first "transference interpretation" this week, i.e., she wondered if her difficulty in talking was related to feelings about the analyst. He felt encouraged about the way things were going. The patient was showing a bit more psychological-mindedness, was being reflective about what was going on, and commented spontaneously on the difficulty in trying to say everything that came to her mind. He mentioned something he had recorded in the notes, that she had surprised him by saying she thought the agency that had referred her to the psychoanalytic clinic was paying part of her bill and that she felt indebted to them. He said he intervened, probably inopportunely out of his surprise, but he counted this as an error against himself. (I noted to myself that he had been very meticulous about the handling of the case in its beginning phase, and while his handling of the case had been adequate, I thought I would note to myself the possibility of overconcern about making mistakes.)

The analyst also mentioned that, although he had told her he would not be here on Friday, the patient had showed up and was told by his secretary that he was not there. She then remembered he had told her he would be away. She did not mention having come to this hour when they did get together again. The analyst wondered if perhaps this parapraxis shocked the patient, who might have felt she was more "open" than she would like to be. We talked about the trends he had outlined in a general sort of way. It seemed as if the analysis was moving in a proper way, considering the interruptions, though it was clear the patient was not saying everything that came to her mind (he mentioned that this was beginning to concern her too).

I then looked over the material at his invitation and noted there were long silences showing up. I asked him if this was new. First he said no, they had been intermittent, then realized as he looked at the material that the silences were increasing. I talked to him a bit about the probable meaning of these in terms of the growing awareness by the patient of her relationship to the analyst and the increase of resistance.

A quick glance at the material showed the following themes: She is thinking of moving, taking a roommate; she characteristically makes bad decisions about who she rooms with. Documenting this, the girl she is planning to room with has attempted suicide and is in treatment. She gives many examples of people in treatment who have turned out badly, yet she needs treatment; she has read about the efficacy of will power, how things suddenly change for people, she doesn't think it would work for her; then her feeling of indebtedness to the referring agency because they are paying part of her analytic bill; then about people who don't take care of themselves such as her boss who goes around unpressed with holes in his shoes. She has been spoiled and is sloppy because she has always had maids. She has some difficulty with someone at work into whose area she overstepped, then after a quarrel they became good friends. She recalls a month she spent together with her father. He and she were actually going to college together, he to fulfill a lifelong ambition, and they enjoyed each other's company in her mother's absence. This led to her recalling an attraction she had for a bartender in a club who seemed like a knight in shining armor; later she was disillusioned in him when she looked him up in his home neighborhood (the analyst wondered about transference implications here). She then went on to how difficult it was to talk about herself and how much she needed to, and how she realized how difficult analysis really was. At first she had thought it would only take a few week because, after all, that was all one could talk about oneself. Clearly she was refraining from talking about something at that point, and the analyst tried in a properly nonspecific way to help. She went on to talk about how difficult it was for her to stop smoking and eating too much with no implication at this point or later that she was asking for help from the analyst. There are some hints of a fear of dependency on the analyst.

After this hour the analyst was gone for a few days. The patient did not mention his absence when he returned. There were more thoughts about her difficulty in talking, which she related to people in authority, but she could not make the link to the analyst. She seems to feel like low man on the totem pole; she, like her grandmother and her ex-fiancé, has psychosomatic problems, a perpetual stomach ache. Then follow some thoughts about a folk song about telling an analyst about a dream in which she is the only one left after an atomic war. She then seriously said that she did not know how she would get help if she did not talk about what was on her mind.

As our discussions went along, partly as I was reading the material, we were able to sketch a plausible growing transference paradigm having to do with the patient's fear of dependency, but also her making of the analyst an authority with whom she found it difficult to talk. She made this comparison with her father some time before. Although he was warm and rather open, she found it very difficult to talk to him. I could see in the patient's silences and particularly in her remonstrances toward herself for not saying everything that came to her mind a hint that the analyst "authority" should enforce the basic rule, and I pointed it out to the analyst, who could see that what I meant was an invitation to counteract in the transference. On the other hand, the patient's silences were quite revealing, since they came at points when one could see that a train of thought was being finished in her own head. I showed him at several points how one could be thinking how one could intervene without actually suggesting that he do so. He asked specifically if he should be interrupting these silences now. I said probably not, except that since she had told him she was worried about not saying everything that came to her mind, he could remind her at some such time that this was one of the points she was concerned about—in other words, that there are ways of facilitating her communicating without getting into an authoritarian position with her. I also picked up the phrasing of one of his interventions, which had several things latent in it, and showed him how he could put it much more simply. The issue had to do with the point I had made before with other candidates about the effect of asking questions on the patient's free associations, and how what is essentially the observation he wanted to make could be best stated as an observation rather than a question.

We both noted that the talk about the affairs had dropped away, the boy friend had come into the picture and gone out, and now her attention was turning to the analyst and her father.

SUPERVISION HOUR 5 (ANALYTIC HOURS 19–22)

The analyst told me there were only four hours this week because the patient had called in sick. He handed me the notes, but I did not look at them, as he described briefly what had gone on during the week. He mentioned that the patient continues to talk, and I recalled (several hours after our meeting) his stressing that although she was absent for an hour, she made no reference to it the next time. She had called in to say she would not be coming. He said she came in the following hour wearing a bright summery dress although it was one of the coldest days of the year. There was no mention of this either. The following day the patient could not get her car started and called in to say she would be late. Since the analyst's secretary was ill, he took the call himself. She identified herself by the diminutive of her name, the analyst noted, like a little girl. The conversation was straightforward, but again when she finally came only five minutes late she did not mention this unusual event. When she left that hour she said, "Well, I still have to get my car started," leaving the implication that she must have come by some other means.

While summarizing most of the details of the hour, the analyst quoted this remark, but gave no sign of why he thought it significant. In context, the remark struck me as implying that she had fulfilled her duty to the analyst by getting to her hour and now had to go back to deal single-handedly with her *own* problem. I wondered to myself if the analyst had heard this too.

The analyst also mentioned that the relationship with the ex-fiancé was coming much more into the picture. Also her distress about being unable to stay with him or leave him alone was becoming more important. The ex-fiancé was out of town, and she was longing for him, but she felt that when he came back she would be unable to get together with him. The analyst linked this up with other events in the patient's life she had told him about, particularly a memory relating to her teens when her father, who was usually long-suffering with her mother's excessive drinking and extravagant spending, one day, as the patient recalled it, was choking the mother on a couch in the living room when she came across them. She was used to her parents' quarrels and sympathized with her father because the mother really treated him badly (it was only the mother who talked about divorce). She was shocked to see the violence.

We discussed this memory briefly. The analyst had been trying to see in it some explanation for the patient's difficulty with her ex-fiancé. The memory, along with other incidents we had been discussing, led me to suggest in passing that it might have some characteristics of a screen memory relating possibly to primal-scene material.

Later in this hour, after I had looked over the typed material he had given me, I tried to help him clarify his thinking that the patient was revealing a considerable identification with her mother. He based this inference partly on her shock at seeing the violence toward her mother and on parts of several dreams in which she put on clothes (incidentally, summer dresses) that belonged to her mother. He reminded me that the mother was generous to a fault and would give her, as the patient said, "the shirt off her back," if she knew she liked it.

While I saw what led the analyst to his opinion, I was not impressed that it was the most important feature in the material. As we talked about his thinking regarding the material, especially after I read it, I kept noticing the even way in which the patient told her story. In connection with her ex-fiancé, whenever they tried to have intercourse, she would become so stiff that he would get furious about her unresponsiveness. Once he walked out on her, then came back. The ex-fiancé would also cry as a way to win her back. They finally decided to give up trying intercourse. (The analyst also mentioned to me in passing that the first fellow she had intercourse with, she had deliberately tried to get pregnant by in order to win him back from another girl he was interested in. This information is in the history, not mentioned by her in the recent hours.) The last time she and her ex-fiancé had intercourse she was unwilling, and when he persisted she became "hysterical."

My point in recording these details here is that the patient talked about these and other matters about which she must have felt distress in a way that did not invite the analyst to be sympathetic or to help. There appeared to be very little of what I would call "demand quality" in her speech during the hours. One might say she allowed herself to expect very little of the analyst, but put up with the relationship, including the problems of getting there when the car would not start, without complaint. In this connection, she described in the last hour of this week her first meeting with her ex-fiancé. She could get no sympathy from him. He seemed so objective at a time when she needed someone to be on her side against the world. It was after this statement that the patient left the couch with a smile, saying she still had to get her car started.

I called the analyst's attention to my observations, noting that the qualities she was acting out seemed to be closest to those she had described in her father (whom she also described during these hours as being absent much of the time during her early adolescence when she felt she very much needed him). After the analyst saw this pattern, I moved a bit further with him in two directions: I wondered if there was anything in his effort to be analytically correct that led him to overstress objectivity in his attitude, possibly to the point of conveying indifference. On the other side, I noted that I thought it very likely that the patient's projection of a father imago onto the analyst could also include identification with what she would construe as his objectivity toward her problem. I said that the patient may not really feel herself to be a patient because neither she nor, as she perceives it, the analyst conveys much empathy for her actual distress. I linked to this figurative observation the lack of demand quality in the hours and the patient's apparent willingness to put up with the difficulties in coming for analysis without complaint.

The analyst looked thoughtful as he listened to my comments, but made no direct response to them. Nor did I act as if I expected any from him. He did comment on the patient's character and resistance problem reflected in this behavior, and we discussed possible ways in which he could interpret this attitude when it seemed relevant to do so. The analyst continued to feel that the patient was coming more under stress, with which I would agree, and he would have to keep aware of the necessity to intervene at some point. In the meantime, the patient was talking steadily, filling in a good deal of her background, indicating her willingness to work, for instance, on dreams, and showing a bit more psychological-mindedness than we had anticipated at the beginning.

Another theme the patient talked about is worth mentioning. At one point she described her older sister as being more of a mother to her than her actual mother. The sister was quite compulsive and ritualistic. The patient recalled a childhood memory of being so angry with her sister that she ran down the stairs and kicked her in the stomach. There were in her dreams several references to stairs, and suggestive hints of pregnancy fantasies and fears of being damaged in intercourse, none of which was interpreted by the analyst, who continued to handle the hours technically in a very adequate manner.

SUPERVISION HOUR 6 (ANALYTIC HOURS 23–25)

The analyst told me he had only three hours to report because the patient had missed one hour and he did not have the notes for yesterday's yet. His presentation was completely oral, although he had detailed notes on each hour typed and placed them on my desk. We started right in talking about what had been going on, and I did not look at the typed notes at all.

The analyst mentioned that his impression was that the patient was trying to be continent, to go back to her ex-fiancé although she had a feeling that this "wouldn't work." He had been out of town. She was looking forward to his return, wanted to be with him, but, as she described in these hours, could sleep with him but not have intercourse. In one hour she described having a dream of intercourse with him while lying next to him. As the analyst told about his observations and inferences it started to become clear to me that a pattern of resistance was developing in which the patient was attempting to master problems as fast as she saw them as a way to minimize her involvement with the analyst. We talked about this briefly, the analyst bringing in confirming evidence.

In the course of this discussion he had mentioned the patient having missed an hour, saying that his recollection was that she told him she might be late, even very late, because of a school examination she had to take. But when she came in the next hour she mentioned nothing about having been absent. When he brought it up, she said she thought she had told him she would not come in, and in further discussion between them, she was able to link this tendency to things other people had told her, to the effect that perhaps she is not definite enough in the arrangements she makes. The analyst in reflecting with me said he thought he saw in this pattern a difficulty in making mutually satisfactory arrangements with men, and he tried to link her various unsatisfactory heterosexual arrangements to it. Throughout the hour the analyst had this same overall point of view of trying to see in the transference the larger implications for the patient's life and neurosis. In regard to the missed hour and her blandness about it, I suggested there was also a resistance pattern to be seen—the patient's willingness to admit only to a kind of "technical failure" in not having made herself sufficiently clear. The analyst confirmed that she did not entertain any thought that the absence might have been motivated.

There was a theme associated with this last point that I raised as the analyst talked about the various affairs and engagements. Particularly with regard to her present "ex-fiancé," I asked if there had ever been a satisfactory sexual life between them. The analyst started to speculate, saying he thought so, and reminded me of some details we both could recall. I noted in his account, however, that he was unclear and that his tendency was to make some assumptions to fill in the gaps in the patient's account. I warned him about this, saying I wondered if the patient were not being as "general" in her account of this important area as she was in other areas, and suggested that he and she were both acting as if she had told what in fact she had not. I suggested this could be made the content of a resistance interpretation. I warned him about the possibility of simply adapting or accommodating to this style of communication in the patient. The analyst said he suddenly remembered something she had told him in this connection about her experiences with a teacher who gave the patient grades of B for work she considered quite as good as that of a friend who got A's. One day she said she overheard the teacher talking, and knew she was talking about her when she said that there was a pupil in the class who always wrote her papers as if the teacher would understand what she was talking about, for instance, would be as fully familiar with the poem about which the patient was writing. The patient said that after this she got A's from this teacher. The implication was that the teacher "caught on" to her way of writing rather than that the patient became more explicit.

As the analyst went on with this account of what had been taking place, new light was shed on some of the events described above. He had mentioned the patient's discomfort at her job. There was an older man in the office whom she admired exceedingly but with whom she had the greatest difficulty in talking. It was not just that he was an authority, because there were people above this man with whom she had an easy relationship. The analyst told me this story to try to demonstrate the transference trends and, in particular, to tell me what he had done at one point—an intervention with which he was not altogether pleased. He said the patient had surprised him in her discussions of the difficulty in talking with this older man by recognizing that she had difficulties in talking with the analyst. She really startled the analyst when she said she wondered if the difficulty she had in talking to the analyst did not have something to do with what she had to say and also with her problems in general. The analyst laughed as he said that he felt that she was "going too fast." She really ought not to have been at that stage yet. He quoted himself as saying something that struck me as kind of "bookish," the general effect of which was to say to the patient, "There, there, you mustn't pay more attention to this than to that." (I do not recall the exact words, and I am not going to look up in the notes what actually took place, as I dictate this.) I mentioned my impression of what he had said to the patient and wondered why he thought she was going too fast, indicating that he could, through some nonspecific encouragement or more direct intervention, see how far she could go with that idea, since the patient had said she had been thinking about these matters outside the hours. The analyst hesitated a moment and then grinned and told me the fantasy he had had in connection with this event, that he felt kind of like the Wizard of Oz, and that he was concerned that it was too soon for the patient to see the mechanics of how the Wizard's illusions were created. I laughed with him, but also pointed up the implication that he must feel that the analytic process was a fragile affair and that if the patient would "see how it works" she would become immune to the "magic" (it occurred to me that this might be one reason for the analyst's obvious efforts to be delicate in his handling of the case). I commented that analysis was a natural process and a quite sturdy one, etc., and mentioned in the course of this that perhaps the patient was going too fast for him, not for her.

At another point in our discussion he came back to this story about the older man at work and this time made closer reference to his notes. Some additional details came into the story. During the hour in which she described the difficulty in being close with this man (in subsequent hours she described how she was working on making herself talk more freely to him—note the theme of trying to solve the problem herself) she mentioned as a kind of confession that what was getting in the way of her talking to this man were some sexual feelings she had about him, and in a worried way the patient went on to wonder if perhaps that was what was interfering with her ability to talk to the analyst (whom she also sees as a large, older, and "vital" person, and her father with whom she has had the same difficulty, but who does not strike her as large or vital). After making these tentative connections, the patient trailed off. The analyst did not do anything with this material, which came at the end of the hour. It was the next hour that she missed, and during the following hour, according to the analyst, her mood was rather depressed: nothing was going to turn out right for her, etc.

I called the analyst's attention to the amendment to the story, showing him the probable link between the emergence of troublesome sexual thoughts toward the analyst, her staying away the next hour and then returning to make no further references to these feelings except through this sense of hopelessness that I tried to weave into this. I tried to show him the sequence of emergence of a forbidden wish, the denial of the wish—she doesn't *really* want that, as a matter of fact she doesn't really want anything in life—depression. I did not comment to the analyst, in part because I did not see it clearly until I started to dictate this note, that he had crossed the same point in his interaction with the patient three times in his telling it to me, each time adding more data.

One other aspect of the hour stays in my mind. He described the patient at one point suddenly sitting up and stretching herself before lying back on the couch. When he asked her about this, she said she had a crick in her back. The setting was one in which the discomfort could be related to what she was talking about. At another point in talking about the third hour, he said she was wringing her hands and showing obvious tension. The analyst's intervention dealt only with the words she was saying, however, and I noted he seemed to ignore what he was seeing in favor of what he was hearing. I tried to show him that what he had said would have been much more effective if he had been able to link it with the way she was feeling in the hour at that point, and indicated how the trend of the hour was going. I mentioned that, from an analytic point of view, if her associations were flowing "properly" they would move from the events in her life outside to the way things were in the hour. The implication was that if he could connect these two, the patient's associations would turn to her past. He said he had never tried to use the material he saw as opposed to what the patient said, but got the gist of what I was trying to tell him.

There was more to our discussions. In particular, the patient related a number of dreams during this last hour, with which the analyst tried to work. She dreamed that someone, probably a black boy, had put some needles and drugs in her gym locker; she was attracted to a lifeguard at the swimming pool and went off with him on some sort of trolley ride to an oriental place; tonsillectomies were about to be performed on her and others without any anesthetic. The last dream led back to recollections of a tonsillectomy she had had to have at age four. Her sister, two years older, was required to have hers out at the same time, although hers were not diseased. After surgery the patient felt fine while the sister felt rotten. The patient wheedled the sister's applesauce away from her only to have the sister want it after the patient had finished it. The sister has never let her forget this event. There was also a dream about spiders, of which the patient is not afraid as long as she does not see them. This led to a childhood recollection of being unable to go through a door because a ladybug was there. An aunt squashed it with her bare foot and then led the child through the door.

There are also hints in this hour that it is when the patient reaches a stalemate with her ex-fiancé that she feels she has to go to bed with somebody else.

While the analyst's account was completely nonsequential (as is mine!), I had the feeling that I had a grasp of the overall situation.

SUPERVISION HOUR 7 (ANALYTIC HOURS 26–31)

The analyst had a good deal more on his mind than his patient, and wanted to talk about some other concerns. Since he was all wound up about this, I thought it best to allow him to continue. We spent approximately half of our time clarifying a matter having to do with his research ambitions until he seemed satisfied and switched topics by saying, "But we have other things to talk about."

He had his notes with him, but I suggested he simply tell me about what had been going on. He took only an occasional glance at his notes. He started, saying he had six hours. He thought there was a special kind of transference reaction developing—the patient cried for the first time and showed more difficulty in talking. He said she noted herself that she had never discussed in any detail what her sexual life was like with her ex-fiancé and stated that it was satisfactory enough in the beginning, but then when he kept wanting intercourse daily, she did not wish to comply. Even though he agreed finally to a lesser frequency, their pattern of breaking up and getting together, which became the rule, began. The analyst went on to say that the patient told him she had been talking to an old friend about her dreaming about intercourse with her boy friend when she was lying next to him and mentioned wryly that he had asked her if she had enjoyed it in the dream, to which the patient said she answered "no." The analyst said he confronted her with the apparent ease with which she talks about quite intimate subjects with un-named old friends compared with the obvious difficulty she was having talking about these things with him. The patient was quite aware of this, and her associations led into a line of thought to the effect that she knew where she stood with this old friend, whom she then named (M.). She could see him when she talked to him. She was afraid she might get too attached to the analyst if she permitted herself to talk freely. At this point she broke into tears.

The material then led into her early experiences at home, or rather her early experiences which involved the absence of a home, as her father's work took the family to cities around the world. The patient believed she suffered most in the family from this moving around. After a while she refused to make any attachments at all. She remembered being unwilling to make any real friends among boys. The patient then recalled that her father always seemed to be uncomfortable around her and had difficulty in talking to her. She recalled many telephone conversations when she called home when she used to think perhaps his reticence was because a long-distance call was expensive, but recently she called and father hurriedly offered to get her mother for her. She also recalled an incident at about nineteen when she was quite prudish and was dating a man somewhat older than she who wanted intercourse. They had argued about it in her house, and he had stamped out. Her father then suddenly asked her if she was pregnant, a thought which startled her. The analyst noted that she did not give any indication of what her response to her father was. She said, with a chuckle, that she told him, "Only if it was another Jesus Christ." She went on to say that her father bought her a typewriter after this, after having gotten a portable for her older sister. The patient wanted an office typewriter, not a portable, because the keys are spaced more widely apart, and commented that her father got her the one she wanted after some difficulty, but always brought up to her that he did not feel he got a good buy. She did not know why he felt that way. (Both the analyst and I wondered if it was true that an office typewriter has a larger keyboard than a portable one.)

In the next hour the patient came in and was the picture of dejection, turning her face to the wall. She was apparently much moved by the previous hour, talked more about her loneliness, and made many references to her childhood experiences when the family moved from place to place. She could not understand how her sister could so easily give up the things she had acquired and move cheerfully to another place. She told the analyst offhand that she had broken off with the fellow with whom she had been having an affair during her ex-fiancé's absence. As she told the story, it seemed she just provoked him into being angry with her and, in a way, said good riddance to him. She said he was a hypocrite anyway—not believing in premarital intercourse but indulging in it. She was back with her ex-fiancé. The analyst at this point dealt with the matter-of-fact or once-over-lightly attitude with which she said such things, and the patient indicated her awareness that this was a defensive attitude. The analyst digressed and mentioned in response to my question that the ex-fiancé seemed to know that during his absences she had affairs with other men. She did not tell him about them, but they moved among a closely knit set of friends, so that he heard about them. He did not seem to make much of a fuss about it. The analyst mentioned in connection with this last story that he had been commenting on her reluctance to go into any detail in the story when she first told it to him. He mentioned to me that he thought it was an error on his part at that moment not to link this confrontation of defense with the motive she had given him the other day about her fear of attachment, and so at the next opportunity he put these things together. The patient agreed with this observation and interpretation, and at this point went into talking about the way her father seemed reluctant to become involved with her.

The analyst mentioned to me that he thought she was afraid he would become seductive or overinterested in her and not be able to control himself if she "let herself go." The analyst brought in some other details of the hour to support this notion, including that when she left her friend M.'s house, he had given her a very sweet kiss. She did not want to stop him from doing this lest she hurt his feelings, but if he had indicated he wanted to go to bed with her she would not have known how to handle that. The analyst thought that he and M. were supposed to be intellectual buddies to the patient.

After some discussion, I suggested that it sounded to me that she feared the analyst might mistake her interest or sense of attachment to him and would sexualize this (projection). In such a predicament she would be stuck, neither wanting to hurt him nor lose out on the opportunity for help. The analyst thought this was a more precise version of how she probably saw the problem.

The analyst mentioned a number of other details that the patient had filled in about her life, including that she had mild tuberculosis from age four to six and had to stay in a lot and rest. She told about an instance in her childhood, when she was about three, when her mother was forced to tie a rope around her ankle to keep her in the back yard. She would plead with her mother not to do so and that she would not run away. But no sooner would the mother turn her loose than the patient would bolt out of the back yard and try to cross the street with her mother chasing after her. The patient also mentioned that when she was twelve or thirteen she had a problem with weight and thought she was fat and ugly. She would not go near the swimming pool when the rest of the family was in enjoying themselves. The patient was also a thumbsucker until age six and wet the bed till five.

There were a number of dreams during this period. The analyst mentioned some of them, but I do not recall them well enough to record them here. Apparently he did not do much with them.

As you can see, the six hours were covered quite sketchily during the brief time the analyst and I had together. I did not look at the notes he gave me at the end of the hour until, in trying to reconstruct what he did, I felt I had to check a couple of things where my recollections were vague. I noticed the sequence of things he told me was not always the same as happened in the hours, but as he told them they seemed coherent enough. As the analyst talked about what he had done with the patient, his interventions seemed to the point, tactful, and adequately sensitive to what was going on. At a couple of points he was able to integrate what the patient was feeling at the moment with the sequence of her thoughts, and by putting these together he was able to help her over some anxious moments when she was stuck.

SUPERVISION HOUR 8 (ANALYTIC HOURS 32–36)

The analyst had his notes prepared as usual and handed them to me; I put them on the desk. He said he would summarize the developments for me, and I asked him if he would prefer to report in that way rather than having me read what he had written. He said he would, and went on to say he wanted to talk about some things that had happened that he did not think were too good. I asked if he meant in the analysis or, recalling last week's digression into other matters, if it was something outside the analysis. He said no, it was some things he had said to the patient that, on reviewing his notes, he had some question about.

On Wednesday the patient was fifteen minutes late, apologized, but said nothing further about her lateness. She talked about a friend who had told her she looked up to her, that at one point in her life the patient and her mother were her only "contacts with reality," and that she had even contemplated suicide. The patient felt that people should not say those things to their friends. There was always something uncomfortable about being that important to anybody.

After a moment of silence the analyst noted that although she had apologized for coming late, she had chosen not to talk about why she was late. The patient said this was characteristic of her. She did not like to excuse herself or offer explanations for her transgressions—a matter of pride. She went on, however, to say that it was her birthday, and that at work people were very kind, kept coming by to congratulate her and drop off little gifts, and she had quite forgotten about coming until the sales manager had reminded her that she had to be elsewhere. After this, the analyst said that he did not know why he did it, but he asked her how old she was. He then congratulated her, and she thanked him. The patient went on to say that when she was a child, she was taught not to tell tales.

The analyst commented on the sequence of her communications, and said that she found it difficult to talk about things that were troublesome as well as things that were pleasing. The patient again said this was characteristic of her, sighed, and went on to say that in her intake interview, when she was asked to tell her happiest as well as her worst childhood experiences, she could not remember either one. Again, she recalled the episode in grade school when she had "infantigo" and tried to keep it covered up. The analyst commented that it seemed to be a matter of pride for her not to make excuses, and the patient commented about her pig-headedness. At the end of the hour she was talking about how she tried to remind herself to leave in time for her hour but did not remember.

I note as I dictate this summary of the supervision hour that I had intended to take up with the analyst his congratulating the patient on her birthday but let it pass at the time since he did not indicate that this was really the matter he wanted to talk about.

The analyst went on to talk about Thursday's hour. There were many silences he said. In between silences she talked about having received some roses from her parents for her birthday. They called later to say they were planning an anniversary party over the weekend and they wished she could be there. Her ex-fiancé had taken her out for her birthday; she had wanted a card from him. The analyst noted she reported the reactions of several people to her birthday and that she had been reluctant to mention to him that it was her birthday yesterday. He wondered whether she was concerned about his reaction or had some hesitancy about how he would react to the news of her birthday. She went on to talk about how difficult it was to talk to the analyst, as it had been also to the examining psychiatrist, but how easy it was to talk to other people, noting that she was not sexually attracted to them. The analyst brought these things together to say that she found it difficult to talk to men to whom she felt sexually attracted, to which the patient, surprised, exclaimed, "You mean to you?" She was silent and then said if it was true for the analyst it would also be true for her father. She seemed anxious, wringing her fingers, finally saying she could not deny it was true. Then, after despairing about ever straightening things out with her ex-fiancé, she told another story. A boy she had once been interested in scared her, and she had to run away when he told her he was in love with her and wanted to marry her. She could not stand him when he got serious.

The patient began Friday's hour by saying she had thought a good deal about what they had talked about the day before. She went on to say that one of the boys who was interested in sleeping with her had come around, was very friendly, and finally suggested they fall in love with each other. In the past, she would have become upset by this, but she did not this time. She listened to him and was nice and did not say much. He talked himself out of it finally. The analyst asked about this, and mentioned to me that he had clearly in mind that she was describing her identification with the analyst. She said she thought she knew herself a little better now. At eighteen, when a boy had proposed to her and shared a fantasy that he could see her coming up the stairs pregnant and that she looked beautiful, she was terrified.

Then the analyst, with a significant look at me, said at this point he thought he had better bring her back, but he was afraid he did so rather sharply. He quoted himself as saying, "I noted that you [the patient] started the hour with what you considered to be an important observation of your difficulties here in talking with me; however, you have gone on to talk about other circumstances and not about what happens here." As he quoted himself, the tone did seem rather sharp. He reported the patient's reaction was to get more obviously anxious.

I asked him then what he thought needed responding to in the hour at that point. He mentioned that she was drifting into identification with him. I asked him what about that needed attention from him at that moment. He said perhaps he should not have said anything; it was too early. I noted that all the alternatives he seemed to be able to consider included saying something to the patient; the only question was what or when. The analyst saw that, but did not know quite what to make of it. I tried to show him then where things were as I saw them—that the patient was still quite shaken by the interpretation he had given her the day before and the insight of the relation between her inability to talk to him and her feelings of sexual attraction. The patient was now showing the ways in which she was knitting herself back together, partly with the effort at identifying with him. But she was also talking about some events of the past. Thus, at a point where he might be reaping some of the effects of his interpretation, he in effect stopped the patient from going on.

The analyst saw this and entered into the discussion, mocking himself a bit as he held up his hand as if to the patient, saying he had acted like a traffic cop. Either I or he earlier had said that it was as if he were trying to rub her nose in what they had talked about yesterday rather than seeing what she would make of it.

At the end of our brief discussion he summed up his involvement in it by saying he felt he was trying to undermine her defensive efforts but in doing so was trying to sharpen the distinction between himself as the analyst and her as the patient by going right after her defense of identification. But he said the patient went on to talk about childhood events, after mentioning that the education courses she was taking told her that teachers should try to analyze themselves before they try to help students. He then reported that he followed up his earlier intervention with another one which was quite a bit more verbose and intellectualized, calling her attention to her identification with him and how it was hard for her to deal with those wishes. I commented about the sequence of interventions beginning with last hour's interpretation, which tended to deepen the analysis, and his later rebuke and intellectualized summary, which had the opposite effect of aborting the process he himself had started with his interpretation. The analyst seemed to get the idea, but did not go further into what might have led him to do that until close to the end of our hour.

After our discussion the analyst summarized the rest of the hour briefly, commenting that the patient had mentioned she had a conflict with one of her analytic hours that she would like the analyst to change. This was a first for her; usually she had not thought to ask the analyst to accommodate to her. When he called this to her attention, she said she felt perhaps she was a bit more important than she once did, but that if it was a choice between the hour and the activity with which it conflicted, she would choose the hour.

The analyst went on directly to the Monday hour. The patient had come at 11:30 instead of at 3:00. He learned this from his secretary. When the patient showed up at 3:00, she did not mention she had come earlier, nor did he mention it. The patient came in and said she had had a horrible Saturday evening. It turned out that her ex-fiancé was out of town and she missed him terribly, tried to reach him by phone on Friday and Saturday but could not, felt very anxious and alone—her mood changing for the worse when she saw that the roses her parents had sent her had died. The analyst reminded me that it was her parents' wedding anniversary that evening. She also looked out and saw squirrels in the yard and thought of the squirrels that had been killed by some kind of poison put out for rats when she was a child. The analyst said there was something Proustian in the way the patient described her shifting moods and perceptions. Unable to get her ex-fiancé, she called B., a man to whom she had been engaged some years ago, who lives in another state. She told him she was in analysis and he was surprised, regarding her, of all his acquaintances, as least needing analysis. While still in this state and not feeling any better after the phone call, she was visited by J., a black man who was a friend of B.'s and hers (this was Sunday). This fellow had had a sad history. After an automobile accident, he seemed to have deteriorated; his conversation always got around quickly to his sexual exploits, which it did again. He mentioned his plans to rape a girl—which the patient thought odd because it was a girl with whom he had been having an affair and who hardly needed to be raped. She said that she was perhaps the only female acquaintance this fellow had with whom he had not slept. After she and B. broke up (with some implications that he had thrown her over) she planned to have an affair with J. They spent the weekend together, but she felt repulsed, and he respected her feelings. J. was contemptuous of white girls who joined the civil rights movement, said all they were interested in was the "big dicks" of the black men, and he and the others were willing to oblige them while "screwing" them to show up the white folks. Part of the story about J. was that he had grown up in a small town where he had experienced no discrimination at all, he said, until high-school days, when the boys started dating and then did not want him around. He retaliated then by dating only white girls.

The analyst observed that he had made an equation in his mind between J. and himself. He said to the patient that she had reported difficulties in talking with men toward whom she felt sexually attracted, and wondered if the instance with J. was another of these. The patient agreed, but then went on to say that perhaps her feeling of depression and panic had something to do with homesickness. She had a longing to be at home, and recalled childhood incidents of that kind. The analyst then mentioned she had sounded homesick in her account of Saturday, and reminded her about the roses she had received from her parents. The patient said she was not aware of having felt that way on Saturday, but had been expecting a package from the folks that did not come. She would have liked to have been at their party, but she did not think about these things on Saturday.

The analyst and I talked a bit about his equating himself with J., and I asked him then if he had noticed that something was missing in the hour. I mentioned then that the patient had not said anything about wanting to call him, though I was certain it had crossed her mind. The analyst agreed, and we talked some more about the events of last week, linking up the developments with the interpretation of last Thursday and showing him the different themes of sexuality and dependency in various combinations that were developing.

The analyst went on to report the Tuesday hour in which he thought some countertransference had shown up. She talked about getting some packages of shoes from her parents, exchanging them at the store where there is a shoe salesman who reminds her of the psychiatrist with whom she had an affair. She was taking a life-drawing course for fun, and so forth. It turned out the package of shoes was just a bonus, not the one she had been expecting from her parents. The shoes kind of gave her a lift, though they were neither very expensive ones nor the kind she would have bought for herself. She was clearly feeling better and mentioned she had gotten in touch with her ex-fiancé. When the analyst asked, she said she did not know why she was feeling better except she has become interested in things other than herself. To this, the analyst said he thought he gave her a slap on the wrist when he replied—"I said this is apparently your way of getting over these feelings, but it doesn't help us understand how you got into them." The remark, when I looked at it later in his own notes of the hour, did not look quite as bad as he made it out to be, but during our discussion, he was very dissatisfied with it. I asked him what made him think of countertransference in that connection, and he answered that he felt he had taken a position with her like a stern taskmaster and indeed linked it to the "traffic cop" remark I had called attention to in an earlier hour. He wondered if this was his way of handling the sexual attraction that the patient had for him. He said she was a good-looking woman who said in many ways that she was available. He had the feeling that this remark was a way of closing the door on those thoughts and keeping them down to business. He felt that the remark, however, had the effect of closing the doors he had opened with his own interpretation. It also had the effect, he thought, of keeping her little, and thus less sexually threatening. I listened to this account, merely commenting that what he said sounded plausible, but I wondered if he was convinced that it was so. He said he thought it was. I just nodded and let it go at that.

We had no more time, but after he left I glanced at the notes for the rest of the hour, and in response to this comment of his, the patient went back to the Saturday when she felt very upset. She talked about doing some boring work and of being bothered that she had no family or children or husband and was getting to the age where she should. She was "hung up," and yet she was aware that after she spends a few days with her ex-fiancé she wants to get away from him. She spoke of the peculiarly ambivalent relationship she has where she longs for him and has to be able to reach him when he is away, even though she feels glad when he goes because then she is free to make other dates. She recalled the period when he asked her to marry him—how panic-stricken she was. But during a storm when he was away, she kept calling him about what to do. Her parents had approved of their marriage, but she just could not go through with it, and finally told him that she would have to get psychiatric treatment. She mentioned that her ex-fiancé does not quite fit into the family as she sees him. He is conscientious, hard-working, a good provider, has a sense of humor, her parents like him. But he does not go in for the partying, joking around, or drinking; nor is he an athlete, which are all characteristics of her family.

SUPERVISION HOUR 9 (ANALYTIC HOURS 37–41)

The analyst began by saying he felt he had not handled a dream in this first hour very adroitly. The patient dreamed that she had done something praiseworthy and her father had kissed her, but it was more than a fatherly-daughterly kiss. Her mother then said something sarcastic. The patient continued to talk, though not specifically about the dream, mentioning the visit of a girl friend who had a picture of her graduation day with her father and how happy they seemed with each other. The patient has no such picture—only one with mother, father, and herself. She went on to talk about other things, saying it was a lousy day, how irritated she was, and so on, with further associations. The analyst said that he was dissatisfied with his intervention, which brought her back to the dream by asking her what came to her mind about doing something praiseworthy. His self-criticism had to do with the feeling that he was intruding. I asked him what he thought would have happened if he had not brought her back to the dream. He said that was a good question; probably she would have come back by herself sooner or later. Thus he felt he had interfered with the path she was taking, which involved day residues of the dream about which she had many feelings, and which seemed to be about the theme that, unlike her friends, she could not enjoy her father. Instead, he got more sexual feelings expressed in the transference. I said he probably wondered whether this would have happened if he had not intruded himself, and the analyst agreed. I made a little bit more of the point that such an intrusion itself could aggravate an eroticized transference and that even though the patient might be fleeing to the past to avoid transference feelings, there was no need to rein her in. The analyst listened but went right on when I stopped, as if to say that he did not really need all that explanation.

The analyst went on to report, referring to his typed notes, that the patient had written to her two-year-older sister, with whom she had always been close, telling her about being in treatment and implying it was easier to write to her sister than to talk to the analyst. She told of an incident when she came upon her sister crying and telling mother, "All right, he was drunk," referring to her father. No one would ever tell her what had happened. She mentioned that during mother's menopause she insisted the girls go around the house more covered up than they were accustomed to being. The analyst went back to refer to his error of intruding. It struck me that the error was not all that bad to deserve this much attention, and I thought I detected a perfectionistic streak in the analyst. I just mentioned to him, however, that while I thought it would have been better to let the patient proceed the immediate results might not have been any better. I said the aim would have been merely to get a less disturbed view of where her thoughts might go as she tried to defend herself against her transference feelings.

The analyst nodded agreement and went on to the next hour. She had told him she had a wonderful day, her ex-fiancé with whom she has been spending much time showed her his new car. The boy who lives in the same rooming house, who had been trying "to make her," apologized and left her a rose. She was pleased, but wondered if there was any obligation involved in accepting it. The package she was expecting from her parents finally came. She and her ex-fiancé had been debating the merits of Leonardo and Michelangelo, and she talked about her art class and how busy she was. This was interspersed with little misadventures like allowing a pot to burn and her feeling that she and her ex-fiancé are drifting apart.

The analyst offered a resistance interpretation to the effect that she was trying to see things in a good light, but every now and then a contrary feeling entered. The patient became a bit angry, saying she guessed that's the way life was. She went on to say the package from her parents was not all that nice, and then she said she started to lose her sense of accomplishment. After another version of the same "resistance interpretation" the patient said she wondered why she was reluctant to tell her negative thoughts, perhaps because she did not want to seem ungrateful to the analyst. The analyst noted to me that this was the first time she had ever said anything like that. The theme then seemed to switch toward the question of dependency on the analyst or family and the need for her to remain independent or autonomous. He noticed that her posture, which was usually quite feminine on the couch, suddenly seemed to him more masculine. He demonstrated how she changed from what he called a feminine style, with one knee over the other and her hands crossed under her bosom, to a more masculine style, with her legs crossed at the ankles and her hands under her head. He had the definite impression that her posture changed in this way when she talked about wanting to do things for herself and be autonomous. The patient, after this shift in posture, told him she had the feeling of being guided all her life, not being able to do things on her own, and that she should be having a baby, as her friends were doing. But she was not sure she meant it. She would not be able to have a career and children too because she would feel obligated to the children.

As the analyst was talking about the sense of the need for autonomy that he picked up, I wondered if his constantly bringing her back to a topic might be experienced by her as too much guidance. The analyst thought yes, and went on to say that he had been hypothesizing at the end of this hour that she was retreating from the incestuous feelings that had come up in the previous hour toward this need for autonomy—that she can't stand any attachment including marriage because it would also be involved with incestuous feelings.

The analyst went on to the next hour. She came in smiling and with a new hairdo. After a silence, she began. He thought she was concerned about the issue of autonomy and was trying to find a comfortable position for herself. She finally quoted a line of poetry that occurred to her, one that she and a former boy friend would quote to each other—a line from Ferlinghetti that goes, "What can you say to the fabulous fuli bear after lying lush in the luli flowers./ What can you say to your mother, brother. . ."—and the analyst said she was more in a masculine than feminine position as he experienced it. When he asked her about the "bear," she said she always associated that with this boy friend, but now that she was lying here, it could be the analyst. The analyst's associations were that she was unable to convey to him the positive aspects of lying there on the couch. Her interpretation of the poem was the difficulty of conveying a unique experience to anyone.

The way in which he quoted the poem and recounted the first part of the hour made it sound to me as if there were some element of wooing him in it. I mentioned this, and the analyst agreed it could be true. I went back to the masculine versus feminine positions, as he saw them, suggesting there was a difference in conceptualizing feminine feelings versus defenses against them and feminine versus masculine feelings.

The patient went on to talk about her education, her fondness for the classics and that sort of thing, with the feeling she had already told him about these matters (she had not). The analyst felt she was saying sex was not important, that there was a world of ideas to share. The patient said she and the former boy friend used to love to read poetry to each other. She mentioned another poet, a woman who had suicided after the birth of a baby. This story, as the analyst was telling it, sounded to me as if the patient were struggling over the issue of being involved, and was both trying to put some distance between herself and the analyst and to woo him. The analyst agreed and included also the alternations between the wish for help and the wish for autonomy. The analyst went on to say he thought she was retreating from the sexual feeling she had encountered by stressing her own role as a helper, wondering whether treatment was the only way to do any good for people. He interpreted that she needed to stress her reservations about coming, etc. The patient agreed and said she had had that feeling before she came that day. She did not want to find out any more about herself which, with a little more interrogation, she stressed had to do with the sexual feelings that had been coming up that were hard to take. They interfered with her self-concept, and she wondered if she would like herself better if she found out more.

At the end of the hour the analyst indicated he had done a good deal of talking and pushing and had not allowed the patient to express her feelings associated with not wanting to know any more. I had the feeling from the way he described the hour that he had been too eager with defense interpretations. He agreed, and I suggested there might be a link between his pushing the patient along defense lines and his wondering the previous hour about whether he was troubled by his attraction to the patient. I asked if his pushing or prodding her to get down to business might not also be an expression of his wish to control these feelings in himself. The analyst agreed this might be so.

The analyst said on Monday the patient again made the mistake she made last week, coming at 11:30 instead of 3:00, but did not mention it during her hour. She came in sad and preoccupied, could not remember her dreams. She spent a lot of time with her ex-fiancé, sleeping with him over the weekend. They both wanted intercourse, but she could not bring herself to do it. Sunday afternoon, while in bed studying, she had a sudden impulse to have intercourse, told him, and they did, but she insisted on no foreplay. She did not know whether either of them enjoyed it. He wanted to talk about it, but she did not. She said that he feels she has improved since being in analysis, and that things are going better between them. She doesn't know. She then said that she felt she owed it to her ex-fiancé to have intercourse with him. When she told him this, he said it was ridiculous. She did a lot for him, like preparing meals.

After a bit the analyst asked about the foreplay issue, and she said that was always the problem before. She never liked passionate kissing—only brotherly kissing—nor did she like the other things that go along with foreplay. Intercourse itself she did not mind, but the other things, while she could tolerate them with others, she could not stand them with him. There were a number of other associations having to do with feeling guilty for not helping people enough. The analyst pulled these things together and commented on her feelings of letting people down, mentioning the ex-fiancé, himself, and others who had come into her associations. All the people she let down were men. After some silence she said that she felt the same way about her boss, whom she had previously described as a seedy, run-down fellow. Now she said, "Poor guy has so much to do." She wished she could help him more, and felt it may be her fault that "he is the way he is."

The next hour she came in happily, reminiscing about childhood events. She took what the analyst calls her masculine posture and went into incidents that took place between the ages of three and eight. Once she was Queen of the May in a crepe paper dress and was taken off by a little boy to look for tadpoles in a pond. When they found her they said he had thoughtfully pinned up her dress so it would not get wet. There were further associations about this boy's family and a visit they made to them only to find them down and out. Her father felt sorry for them and bought them a huge sweeper they did not need. She seems to have it now, and has a storage problem with it. Another incident was about a fire when her mother and a neighbor managed to carry out their stove, a feat that they could not duplicate later. The patient went on to say that swimming was always important to her; there were a number of memories about various pools. When she was feeling like this, only time could limit her—in other words, she could do anything. But perhaps people cannot stand being happy for too long. There were more associations about riding the waves at a beach. She and a boy were side by side when a wave unsettled them; they never could return to the position they were in. This had stayed as a symbol in her memory of the impossibility of retrieving the past. She quoted a line of poetry from Wordsworth: "Although we cannot bring back the hour of the splendor in the grass. . . ." She had wanted to sew a sampler for her ex-fiancé with this poem on it—how difficult it was to recapture childhood—then associations to pleasant memories on verandas and porches and some childhood songs.

When the analyst paused I asked him what he had been doing during this hour. He replied he just sat it out, but he said at one point that she was reminiscing, and toward the end of the hour told her that when she was feeling happy she thought she could do anything. She responded philosophically, that was a problem with life itself, so much to do and so little time, etc. He said obviously he need not have said either of the things he did. He noted that she was talking freely and nearly all the material was new.

We discussed the events of the week, noting how the patient had gotten off the hook of the transference. In the course of this discussion we got back to the odd intercourse experience and I mentioned that I thought he could have asked her to be a bit more specific about the problem with foreplay.

The analyst had a number of hypotheses about what was going on, noting the identifications with the helper and the feelings of guilt she had been talking about. I asked if her other affairs had terminated. The analyst said he thought so; she had not mentioned them. He said also she had mentioned during the week that her ex-fiancé reminded her very much of her brother. This may relate to some feelings about her father. She has been close to her brother and added that he had been promised a brother for himself and that he too had been promised to their older sister as a sister for her to play with. She said her brother was a good sport about having gotten a sister instead. I reminded him about the feeling he picked up that she was always letting people down, etc.

Our discussion went back to technical matters and the point got across that the patient did not need quite so much of what the analyst called defense interpretation. I noted that this seemed to take the form of his telling the patient what she *was not* doing and one can be just as effective and less stern-sounding if one looks for the adaptive purposes of what the patient *is* doing. I said in any case she was moving along pretty well and he probably did not need to intervene as much as he did. We discussed what a defense interpretation is since I noticed that some of the things he called defense interpretations were simply tending toward constructions leading to transference interpretations. In the course of this I had occasion to mention to the analyst that the patient herself was concerned enough about the unrealistic nature of some of her feelings and that some of his comments to her sometimes put her a bit on edge about this rather than facilitating the expression of things that were difficult for her to say. At the end of the hour we both agreed that things were going pretty well and the analyst, who is not inclined to be optimistic, thought he had a good patient. I recalled he turned down the previous case which had been offered him.

It occurs to me now that the analyst is also one to whom poetry means a great deal but he has not mentioned this in connection with the patient's demonstrations of her interest.

SUPERVISION HOUR 10 (ANALYTIC HOURS 42–46)

The analyst said he had several things to talk about and that he had gone over the notes before our meeting and had made a brief summary. First of all, about the patient's "real world": she was becoming more intensely involved with her ex-fiancé, practically living with him—had intercourse both Friday and Saturday nights but was not sure whether either of them had enjoyed it. I recalled she had spoken similarly of an experience the previous week, and I asked the analyst if he understood what she meant. He said it was not clear and he did not inquire. He went on to say that she was reporting new feelings about her ex-fiancé in addition to admiration and feelings that he was the right man for her, though for some reason she could not think of marrying him. She was also noting that she felt irritation and jealousy. This seemed to be related to what she considered his "philistine" tastes—a generally materialistic orientation which at bottom seemed to refer to his having considerably more money at his disposal than she had. He was able to buy a new car while she rode around in an old wreck, and so forth. The mixture of envy and disdain for some of his values led to a bit of conversation between the analyst and myself about her bantering complaint that she was an "unsuccessful philistine." Then the analyst went on to say that when the patient was close to her ex-fiancé she felt she wanted to get away and "raise hell." This expression meant to have affairs with other men. She said she would not do it and either stated or implied she was going to try to stick it out with her ex-fiancé and work in her analysis.

I commented to the analyst that it sounded as if living with her ex-fiancé represented "homework" from the analysis. The analyst chuckled and agreed, and wanted to go on describing what was taking place. I asked him his opinion of that pattern. He thought a moment and said she was giving up pleasure and so forth in the hope of getting more than she has ever had before from the analysis. At the same time she was saying she was not sure either that it would work with her ex-fiancé or that she would get what she wanted from analysis. In the last hour of the week she voiced some tentative criticism of the analysis—about having reached a plateau, comparing it to trying to lose weight, and having to find a "new path downward." She was willing to put up with the feeling that she was not getting anywhere at the moment, but wanted to remind the analyst that she was covering old ground about her feeling that she could not really be close to her ex-fiancé. He said in this connection that she drifted into a story in the most recent hour about a man among her acquaintances who was very rich, but who would not look at women. At a party, she and some girls took the most eligible among them and tried to make a real play for him, but he would not give the girl a tumble. The analyst linked this metaphoric communication to her feelings of reproach for him for not responding to her sexual feelings. He said she seemed sad and angry, and he mentioned that she had told some of her dreams. I noted to myself that the analyst had not addressed the question I had asked him about the analytic significance of the pattern he had been describing, but was going on descriptively and semi-associatively on the level of clinical detail. I decided to let him go the way he wanted to for the time being.

Before describing her dreams, the analyst reminded me that during the last week he had told me that the patient had reported feeling responsible for disappointing many men, ranging from her ex-fiancé to men who came to the door asking for information. In these dreams, her ex-fiancé was doing things wrong. In one dream she and her ex-fiancé were married, and he was runnng around with other women. In another dream her ex-fiancé had done something terrible and was either going to prison or to the electric chair for it. She saw the projections in these dreams and, in her associations, mentioned having reproached him jokingly for once having made a play for another girl. The analyst said there were other dreams that were of interest—one in which she saw a tornado through a window in a hospital. The tornado was strange in that it was horizontal rather than vertical. Her associations led to an image of a black ribbon. The analyst reminded me she had had other dreams involving looking through a window, mentioning particularly the one in which she saw someone wearing a ring, whose middle was hidden by a partition in a window. The analyst went on to mention that she had lost things in a great storm, and that she was obliged to move and felt unsettled after that. She had had the thought of going home to her parents in another state. When she called them, her father answered and sounded drunk. She knew instantly that she could not go home. She remarked that he gets uninhibited when drunk, and the analyst reminded me of the disturbing incident of her coming across her sister crying after some mysterious event and excusing her father because he was drunk. He was surprised when the patient said that perhaps she did not want to share mother's affection with her father—that she would go home if he were not there, that, as the youngest child, she felt spoiled by mother.

In the next hour she gave a clear oedipal dream. She was in a classroom, taking an English course with a lady professor, whom she named. Sitting next to her was another English instructor who, like the professor, was elderly but did not quite have his Ph.D., toward which he has been working for a long time. This instructor had his arm around the patient. It turned out that the students were supposed to pair off for a kind of game with sexual overtones, and they were to dress in clown robes. She turned away from him toward a younger boy on her left, but found he was already taken. When she turned back to the instructor, she found it was too late, and she was alone. The professor then talked about a present for her niece, which was to be a lamp made to look like an antique. It had secret compartments in which jewelry was kept; the lamp was fascinating. There were some associations about the instructor and the campus gossip that the professor and he had been going together for years though they did not marry. Some students went to the professor's house to peek in and watch them have dinner one Sunday. The analyst said the patient did not see the oedipal significance of the dream. He was reading his notes and commenting about them. He said the patient associated to the instructor another man with the same name, a young and handsome speech teacher whom she had last seen through the glass door of a classroom. The analyst said he tried to work on the replacement of one name for another, but that she sighed and demurred that she had no interest in the younger man.

He next tried to work on the feeling tone belonging to being left alone, and this led her to recall some additional details about the dream, the most important of which was that she thought the professor was mad at her because the instructor had his arm around her. The analyst mentioned at this time that he forgot to tell me that instead of chairs in the classroom there were lounges arranged informally in a kind of semi-circle. This was one of the connections he saw to the hour, the lounge equaling couch. He asked what came to her mind about the lounges, and she talked about their qualities as furniture. When he commented again on the feeling of aloneness, she said, after a pause, that she felt it would be like death to get married, going on to say that when she thought of marriage she also thought of suicide.

The analyst associated to this an incident the patient told him happened before. She and her date drove out to the country. After intercourse in the car, she walked nude through a stream in what may have been a kind of dissociated state and would have walked over a waterfall had the man not caught her. She wondered then what her parents would have thought if they found her nude at the bottom of the waterfall. I asked with what kind of tone she said these things, and the analyst said, "As if it were meaningful, with some pain, and a sense of confusion that she knew it shouldn't be so but it was." The patient went on, he said, to tell a Feiffer joke about a little girl who urges a boy to come out and play. He demurs, but finally he gives in, and it turns out that the play is for the little boy to be hanged. The analyst said he did not understand the joke when it was first told him, but now as he tells it to me, he does. Marriage is just a small thing to most people, she said, but she just cannot see it.

After a silence the analyst thought he would take a stab at bringing some transference into the hour. He commented on the lounge; perhaps it was like the couch. The patient sighed in response and said that everybody had someone in the dream except her; perhaps it meant that she was lying down talking to the analyst, but she would really prefer to be alone. Her associations then led to a story she said she told the analyst before about how, on a previous job, her immediate superior, a woman, was having an affair with the director of the department. A psychologist who worked in the department advised the patient to try to take the director away from her. She said it was ridiculous because she did not want the director. And anyway, how could she? The girl was not as attractive as the patient, but she was very intelligent and she just would not mess around with people like that. This reminded her of the girl who took away the fellow she was engaged to (this was her first engagement). She was plain-looking but very intelligent. The patient would rather tangle with a good-looking, sexy, but dumb girl. The analyst and I talked about the sequence of events during this hour, noting the switch in theme toward competition.

The analyst went on to say that following this there were some hours of resistance. It was then that she reported having had intercourse with her ex-fiancé over the weekend and that "it didn't bother her or make any difference." When I asked the analyst if he had inquired about this, he said he had not, and began to justify his reasons for not doing so at some length. I let him go on. He mentioned that she was saying more and more about her sexual experiences and he just thought he ought to let her proceed. When I asked him how he meant that, he said she gave considerably more detail about it now than when she had first started. He said at first she would simply say she went to bed with someone. He went on to detail how she was talking more about her experiences. I said it sounded to me as if he had a stereotyped idea of what I had in mind when I asked him if he had inquired. He seemed to think that what I had in mind was that he should inquire into the details of her sexual experiences, when what I had in mind was the anomalous feeling tone she announced about these experiences. I mentioned the importance that this peculiar announcement of hers might have and the ways he might work with it. In contrast, he seemed to be afraid of intruding on her private experiences.

The analyst looked at me oddly and said it occurred to him that maybe what he was trying to avoid were some voyeuristic tendencies of his own associated to the window theme. He then flipped through the notes and read me a section he had not mentioned before, following the patient's stating that if her father weren't around she would have her mother to herself; the analyst had compared this with the dream in which she sent her ex-fiancé off (to prison); then who would she have? The patient said she would not know, and the analyst commented that she said this very sadly. From this she went on to say that last night she had come across a stack of old letters she had written to her ex-fiancé two or three years ago and was struck by how free and affectionate they were and how much they referred to the physical aspect of the relationship. As she read them, they seemed almost vulgar to her. The analyst then said he wondered in what way they were vulgar. He read from his notes: "I asked this question rather unreflectively and it might have been an intrusion of some voyeuristic impulse." We talked about this attitude and I commented on observations I had made during previous hours. I told him it was hard to ascribe any specific meaning to them because the analysis at this stage seemed to be going very well with minimal intervention on his part, but there seemed to be an overriding attitude not just to adhere to a sound technique but to strive for a kind of elegance—a kind of perfectionistic tendency. I put this together with the possible attitude toward his own voyeuristic tendencies which amounted also to a reaction formation resulting in intensified restraint on his part. The analyst reflected about this and compared what was going on now to his first case, in which he felt he was much too active and had been seduced by the patient into wrangles with him—feeling constantly challenged. He said in this analysis he is trying to slow down and not intrude unless he is certain—and besides the analysis seemed to be going well this way.

After some further discussion on this point, I said I would like to return to the beginning of his report when I asked him what he thought about the significance of the "homework" her return to her ex-fiancé seemed to imply. I mentioned that I asked him about this at the time and that he went on to give a good deal of material but had not really dealt with my question. He seemed puzzled and could not see what I was after. I tried to sketch for him the pattern of transference and resistance that was implied here. The patient was assigning herself the task to be a good girl, to live an organized life, to return to her ex-fiancé although this was painful to her. In return for being "good" in these ways she expected something from the analyst. The analyst seemed pleased to see this pointed out to him. Clearly he had not seen it in quite the way I was pointing it out to him, and he started to respond associatively to the idea, mimicking the patient's reproaches: "How long do I have to be good?" Or "Look, I'm on my diet the way I ought to be." The analyst then reflected suddenly that actually, though she talked about the necessity of dieting, she also seemed to him to be getting fatter. He wondered about the implications of this for the sketch that I had drawn him. He then asked me if I thought the analysis was moving into the pattern I was talking about or whether it was already there. I said I thought it was quite deeply into it, and we could be seeing the beginning of a crystallization of transference into something we were both calling the transference neurosis, at least in its early phases.

The analyst had questions about whether he should do something about this. I paraphrased his request, linking it to the countertransference issue we had discussed earlier, saying that it sounded to me as if he were asking if I thought he should interpret and destroy this development, implying that he would rather keep hands off. The analyst nodded, saying he feared I would recommend that he plunge into it. We discussed under what circumstances interpretation would be necessary, noting that in any such development there was a balance between forward movement and resistance and that whether he would interpret would depend on his understanding of which factor was predominant and why. But then I noted that there were many things that could be picked up and conveyed to the patient which would have a facilitating effect, e.g., minor, superficial patterns of resistance. This could also have the effect of helping him to see how ready the patient was to go more deeply into the material. But I emphasized that I did not mean these things had to be taken up unless there was some indication to do so.

We seemed to run out of things to talk about, and it was close to the end of our time. I said I had one more reason for picking up this "homework" theme again: he had mentioned his restraint as possibly referring to a reaction against voyeurism, and I noted that the patient was living out a kind of contract she had made with him to take her sexual feelings to her ex-fiancé and do her work in the hour with him. What the analyst just told me was that he suspected one of his unconscious motives might be that he would wish her to do just that to keep him from being tempted. I linked this to the theme about fearing her father's "uninhibitedness" and the feeling she could not go home again. I emphasized that I was just bringing these possibilities together for him to look at, but he seemed quite grave as he reflected silently about the matter for a moment.

He then jumped to another topic altogether by saying he was intrigued by the marriage-suicide equation the patient had made, and started to speculate about it. I said quietly, but with a smile, that he could ask *her* to associate to the idea. He saw my point and stopped. I reminded him also that the patient had given us some other earlier indications that marriage and death went together, recalling that when she announced her first engagement to her parents, while her father took it phlegmatically, her mother acted as if it would kill her. The analyst first misunderstood me and tried to correct me, saying that they really wanted her to marry this fellow. Then, before I could correct him, he said, "Oh, I see, you meant the first engagement." The analyst left looking rather thoughtful.[1]

SUPERVISION HOUR 11 (ANALYTIC HOURS 47–51)

It looked for a while as if we were not going to be able to get together because of some conflicts in the analyst's schedule, but then he took the initiative to arrange things so that we could meet at a different time.

The analyst began by saying he had an uneasy feeling that he could not justify fully. He did not feel the sense of steady movement he felt formerly. He did not know if his feeling was accurate or, if he was correct, why it was so.

He summarized how things had gone. He began by saying he had touched fairly directly on what he and I had talked about during the last hour—the theme that she was doing her part, but what was the analyst doing? He said when he did so, she tried to get the analyst "off the hook." He said there was an example of this in the Wednesday hour, and he summarized the hour briefly (and I shall do so even more briefly). She had been having many dreams she did not remember. This seemed linked to the dream of father kissing her in an unfatherly way, which she did not like; maybe she did not want to remember her dreams, and so forth. She was finding it hard to be cooperative. He interpreted her "cooperation" outside, which he and I had discussed the week before, and her feeling of disappointment at being on a plateau. She tried to excuse the analyst, who, she knew, was following the proper procedure for psychoanalysis: it is not his fault if she cannot free-associate, etc. She was not really complaining, just informing him about her inner state of mind.

When the analyst concluded, I said she was getting not only him off the hook but herself as well. He looked surprised and said, "How?" I paraphrased what he had told me to show that not only did she tell him he was

[1] *Note to Study Group.* Both this and the last few reports of the supervision hours have been reconstructed from notes I took during the hour. I knew I would not have a chance to work on them until quite late the night of the supervision hour or sometimes not till another day. Although I do not like to take notes during a supervision hour, I felt I needed them in order to prepare these summaries. My recent notes follow the sequence of the supervision hour closely, and I have not been reading the analyst's extensive process notes, amounting to over nine single-spaced pages for the week. I have referred to them, however, to pick up the sequence when I noticed the analyst was reading from his typed notes rather than reconstructing what took place associatively or working from a handwritten summary of the week he had prepared from his typed notes. When I have looked at the typed notes, I have noticed that the sequence he reports there is often quite different from the sequence he gives me in the supervision hour. Thus, the material he presents to me for supervision is a kind of associative, theme-linked, synthetic account rather than a sequential one. What he tells me makes a kind of sense, and I can see what I think are significant trends and pick up opportunities for teaching, but I am also aware that there probably are many other things that are not reported. I am content to go along for the time being, but I wonder how satisfied I would be with the analyst's reports if I were not taking notes and concerned about making a summary for the Study Group.

doing the right thing, but she specifically did not want him to change and and do more to help her. There were no expectations that he should meddle in her inner state, and there were the references to her father's unfatherly behavior and a high-school teacher's "unteacherly" behavior to show him she did not want any Ferenczi-like behavior from him. The analyst got the point, and we discussed the implications of the hour from that point of view for a while.

He wanted to go on, but I said I wanted to add more to another point; while he had made use of the resistance pattern I had pointed out last week, I thought he had missed one important link in it, that is, that she was cooperating by making a tacit bargain with him to live a regular life outside the analysis instead of living up to the "formal contract" she had with him to associate freely. The analyst at first thought she would have understood that, but when he looked back in the material he saw that it was not explicit and there were added indications, as he thought about it, that an isolation had taken place between the hours and her outside life. He meant the forgetting of her dreams and that she had said she even forgets the hours now when she leaves. She tries to bring notes in order to remember her dreams and feels she should cooperate more, but does not. As he brought the other details in, I showed him that another way of looking at what she was doing was that she was making "work" out of the psychoanalysis. I pointed out that while it is a common expression that the patient is "working well," the attitude of working is in a way antithetical to analyzing.

The analyst mused a bit, apparently dissatisfied with himself, and frowned, wondering why he did not see that and pick it up. Having in mind the perfectionist pattern I had noted previously, I wondered aloud, "Why the self-reproaches?" He said he saw it clearly now, he did not see why he could not see it before, during the hours. I said I could not tell from the way he put that whether he was merely marking himself down for having erred, or whether he wanted to look into why he might have missed these themes. He said it was the latter, and perhaps he had been too much interested in her dreams for their own sake and had let the thread of the analysis itself slip. He mentioned that she had had a number of dreams with implications that her relationships with men are not proper. In one he said a black man was to come and pick her up to go bowling in a pick-up truck, but she did not go. She had associations to the first fellow she was engaged to, whom her parents, mainly her mother, would not allow in the house, and there were other associations to incidents in high school when her behavior would indicate to a boy that she was interested in intercourse but she would refuse to go along. This was at a time when she was still virginal.

I interrupted the analyst to ask with what kind of affect did she tell these stories, and he replied, "with a kind of chuckle." I asked him further what he thought about that. He said he smelled a transference pattern there in that she seemed to be teasing him and not "putting out" either. He did not say this to her, but (I later checked his typed notes) mentioned that in these examples she gave she was not "cooperating"; she agreed laughingly.

I noted in regard to his readiness to hear the transference implications in her remarks that there were two elements he ought to consider—the formal similarity between the events she was describing and the transference situation, and the affect, reminding him that the underlying primary-process connections were drive- or affect-organized links. What stood out was the chuckle with which she gave these reminiscences. I reminded him that the train of associations led from her discomfort about cooperating with the analyst, her inability to remember dreams linked to the dream of father kissing her in an unfatherly way, and other quite uncomfortable associations. The discordant affect could be made the center of his intervention by noting where she had started and where she came to, pointing out the change in her feeling tone.

We discussed this possible intervention a bit, the analyst wondering aloud what she might do if he would have said that. We sketched out some of the threads in the hour and showed how this might have tied things together again, raising the issue of when and where interventions would be necessary and to accomplish what.

After this the analyst launched into an account of what was evidently the material that was disturbing him during the week—on Thursday the patient had had confirmed for her that her ex-fiancé, with whom she has been practically living, would be going out of town to visit his parents on Saturday. The analyst did not hear about this till Monday, when she told him of the feeling of relief she had had when she heard this and that she immediately started to plan to have an affair while he was away. She could not stop herself, she did not want to and could not fool herself—felt tense until she did do so, then felt relieved—"so good it almost hurt"—knew she had not done a good thing and was wondering why the relapse into the old pattern. Some details were at variance with her feeling "so good" because after intercourse she could not sleep and even the sheep she tried to count started to mate. She also mentioned in passing that she had spent the night with this fellow but could not sleep as long as she was in contact with him.

The story was that she had invited herself to a party to which a girl friend was going, "quite aggressively" made a play for a man there she decided she wanted to sleep with, and went home with him. He was a good-looking stranger. It is apparently important to the patient that the men she goes to bed with are good-looking masculine specimens. She did not plan to see him again and she did not feel guilt about what she had done until her ex-fiancé came home again and brought her a quite thoughtful gift. I asked the analyst how he had reacted to all this, and he said he just listened. The patient went on to talk about how she had developed precociously as a girl and had been ashamed of her body, but that after she had started to have intercourse she felt better about herself and very much liked to have men tell her that her body was nice, etc. Her associations went to a time when she shared a room with her sister and she awoke to hear her parents in intercourse making animal-like noises; her associations were to pigs grunting and squealing—it was revolting. Another association was to a fellow she knew when she was very young, with whom she would occasionally neck, and who now looked her up and clearly wanted to have intercourse. But she could not possibly do so because he would be somebody who would be talking again to her parents. The analyst picked up out of all this the difficulty she had in getting involved with anybody with whom she had intercourse and vice versa.

I asked what led up to his remark (which, as I check back in the typed notes, occurred in the last of the hours he had brought—that is, what I just mentioned picks up highlights from the Monday and Tuesday hours). He filled in some additional material we discussed as we were talking about it. There were a number of dreams, for instance, one which she told on Monday about an old-fashioned key which was three-fourths the height of the analyst's door, like a skeleton key, but which somehow opened up by splitting down the middle. In it were lots of crawling things like spiders, and way in the back some gold. He said the patient made of this an allegory for the analysis. (When I checked over the hour, she had told this before telling him about the affair.) Later in the hour she told him of a dream about a gathering of spiders. Each spider had a wedding ring, and they were all throwing the wedding rings into the middle of their gathering. I asked the analyst what he made of these dreams, and he said he saw in them the caricature of masculine sexuality he had mentioned to me some hours before. He linked the patient's behavior in having the affair as being very masculine, going out deliberately to the party looking for someone to go to bed with. He saw the key also as a phallic symbol, as something with which she could open doors. I asked him what he made of the three-fourths the size of his door, and he had no thoughts at first. I noted it would be just about his own height. The analyst agreed, and went on to say that he did not really comment on his thinking about her own possible sense of loss about her ex-fiancé going away for the weekend, which he regretted, and also mentioned that his association to "ring" was the dream in which her mother was wearing the ring on the wrong hand. He said the patient wondered why she was not married to her ex-fiancé; they were married all but in name. I asked him about the rings being thrown, and finally I asked him if he had heard of the game in which married couples throw their keys into the middle of the floor and find a partner for the night by picking up any key other than their own. He was surprised to see that this was just what she did with her affair.

Later we talked some more about the dream, and I showed him the formal characteristics of the dream and the multiple condensations that were obvious. I sketched in the patient's transference dilemma: trying to keep the analysis and her outside life apart, which only worked temporarily as they kept drifting closer together again. I showed him how this theme showed up in the dreams, too.

Before we ended he said there was one more thing he wanted to tell me. After he took up the matter of sexuality versus involvement, she suddenly sat up and said she just had to go urinate and was the hour about over? It was, just about, and she fled to the bathroom. He wondered what this meant, and I asked him if he had noticed with other female patients that a sense of sexual excitement and the wish to control it could be experienced as an intense need to void, pointing up the other implications of what had happened.

SUPERVISION HOUR 12 (ANALYTIC HOURS 52–56)

The analyst mentioned that the patient goes through a weekly cycle. Then he thought for a minute and said perhaps he goes through a weekly cycle of reviewing the patient's progress.

The patient had received news from mother that she was going to have a D & C, with implications of a hysterectomy if cancer was found. She mentioned it just that once, at the beginning of the week. She also had seen the fellow she went to bed with when her ex-fiancé was away, and found she could not stay uninvolved with him. She met him once again accidentally, went to a party with him, etc. He offered to fly her—he is a pilot—to where her sister lives, and she was irritated to turn it down, though she thought that was the right thing to do.

Within the analysis, he said he worked with her on her pattern of "being good" as an alternative to analyzing. After a pause the patient went on to see where that pattern might apply elsewhere in her life. I interrupted the analyst to note a similar pattern to the one I had described the previous week. Rather than considering *if* what the analyst says is true, she makes a tacit assumption along the lines, "if it's true, then it should apply elsewhere," without ever looking to see if indeed it is true. The analyst agreed, but went on to say that her associations led to experiences in another country, where a respected older man in charge of their cheerleading squad was discovered by them to be involved with a number of girls, and another incident when seeing people praying at a huge religious statue, she walked behind and found it hollow and covered inside with the usual graffiti. The analyst said his associations ran to expectations on her part that if she would let herself become more open, the analyst would prove untrustworthy. I asked where he saw the grounds for that, noting that her associations at this point seemed only to speak in general of good appearances hiding inner corruption. He said he had gotten the idea from me during our last hour, but there was other confirming evidence. He went on to talk about natives of other countries who in her opinion were polite on the surface, but the bitterness showed after you got to know them. She learned a few phrases, just enough to get into trouble because people thought she knew the language. The analyst and I tossed this metaphor around a bit in its transference implications, and then the analyst reported that he went on referring to the idea that being "good" for her was easier than analyzing. The patient protested that it was because tension kept building up and had to be discharged. The analyst was about to go on, but I asked him if the affair with a man she had picked up was still going on, and the analyst said, "Not yet, but it will." He mentioned that she had talked about having received an invitation to go to a party with him.

She came to the Thursday hour wearing a great deal of perfume and dressed in pastel colors that suggested baby clothes to him. She was carrying a pink sweater; instead of dropping it on a chair, she laid it down next to her on the pillow, suggesting to the analyst a baby. He looked at me, as if bringing confirming material, saying that her first association was, "trying to think how things were when I was a small child again." He called to my attention her peculiar syntax in which the misplaced "again" implied reliving, rather than a renewed effort to recall. The patient's associations then went to her childhood when the marriage between her parents was very bad. The mother would come to her at night sometimes to say, "No matter what happens, remember your father is a good guy." It turns out that the patient was the mother's confidante because, she thinks, unlike the other children, she gave no advice. The patient said she noticed that people generally do what they want to do anyway, and so she has made it a personal rule to offer no advice. She then talked about the party she had gone to with this fellow and how sad it was to see all these young men drinking too much and trying to act like Casanovas, and all the young women, some of whom had been married before, trying to look their sexiest. They all knew each other, but they weren't friends, and she found herself being drawn more and more to her new boy friend, getting involved with him against her wishes. She talked about the feeling of involvement and, in the course of this, as in describing the party, she showed great sensitivity to nuances in relationships. She described how she had become involved with the psychiatrist with whom she had an affair. Their eyes just met when she was working in a store and she knew, and later confirmed with him that he knew, if they ever got together, something would happen. She tended to "assimilate" to the other person with whom she was involved.

I asked the analyst if there were any explicit references to the possibility of he and the patient getting together. He said he guessed they were there, but he had not seen them yet. And after some further discussion, I asked if he made any use of the defensive pattern of getting involved in other relationships. It seemed that the analyst had stayed on the "being good" interpretive line but had not yet brought in the patient's efforts to control her involvement with the analyst by "discharging elsewhere."

The analyst went on to say that the patient had tried to tell her ex-fiancé about what was going on with this new fellow she had met, but had a very difficult time. When she tried to tell him, he merely reassured her and urged her to go to sleep. The circumstances around this point were not altogether clear, and I asked if the ex-fiancé and she were still living together. He said he thought so, but not quite as much as they used to, because she had been out several times with this other fellow. I asked also if the phrase he had reported her using (that she had been trying to tell her ex-fiancé just as she had tried to tell the analyst) was accurate, and if so what it meant. The analyst checked his notes and found this happened the way he had reported it, and I pointed out that the implication was that she had not succeeded in telling her story either to the analyst or to the ex-fiancé. I came back to this point later on.

The analyst went on to say that she was becoming more involved with the new boy friend and had reflected that though she could get involved easily, she could not get married. Apparently what makes it easy with the boy friend is that he is soon to leave the city. When she told him that she liked him, he said she should not because he would be leaving soon. She said that was just what made it possible. (I am not sure if these details were reported at this point or not.) In response to her talking about the troubles of involvement, the analyst compared this to her coming to psychoanalysis to "get straightened out" while finding to her dismay that she tended to become involved. The patient confirmed this, mentioning how irritated she was that everything she seemed to get into always came back to her involvement with the analyst. Finding herself involved led her to efforts to get away. She, and possibly the analyst, referred to the efforts to be "good" in this context, and I reminded the analyst that her being "good" amounted to being quite bountiful indeed with her sexual favors, again alluding to the factor of displacement in the service of resistance, not merely the pattern of compliance that we call "good."

In the Friday hour, the analyst saw a sharp change in mood. The patient showed no more bounciness. Her ex-fiancé was ill, and she had been caring for him. She received an invitation to fly to her sister's home and turned it down. The analyst said he felt that during this hour he pushed things too far and fast. In regard to turning down the flight, when he mentioned her feelings about the sacrifice, she shrugged it off, indicating that no heroics were involved. She went on to talk about a childhood incident when she wanted badly to go to a movie and mother forbade it because she was too young, and mother had then given her a doll instead. The patient felt guilty. She thought she had been spoiled. She should not have received a gift for simply having to conform to a realistic demand. I asked the analyst about this pattern when the patient reported herself feeling guilty; it seemed like a sophisticated interpretation rather than a reported experience. Also, I wondered if it contained a reference to guilt that she might feel for indulging herself now. The analyst was unsure about this, but he said his associations ran to the dream about the key, in which she was rewarded with gold for her search. I said I did not recall the dream quite that way, and he said that in that dream the spiders and other monsters had suddenly been transformed into gold.

As he read this section of the hour he had used the word "reward" and taken it back in talking to the patient. In the hour itself, he was very "talky," and as he finished reading the section to me he said he himself thought that he was too didactic. I tried to get from the analyst what the point was of his interventions there. He claimed he was aware that she was becoming increasingly involved with the analysis and the analyst. She was invited by her mother to come visit her during Easter, but she regretfully turned down the invitation because she did not think she should be away from her hours that long. She had also asked for a change in an hour so that she could go to a business luncheon. She mentioned it once, and the analyst forgot to do anything about it. She raised it again with irritation, saying he could have done something about it if he had wanted to. The analyst said he did not have much success in suggesting that she could have raised it once again. The next hour, however, he was able to change the appointment to a more suitable time. (I asked the analyst what might have happened if he had not. He replied she would have just canceled the hour as she had once before, when she had a final exam.) When the patient came for the next hour, however, the one he had changed for her, she said she was gratified, but then was considerably blocked, with ten- and twelve-minute silences.

During that hour she said that the life-drawing instructor had made a number of coarse remarks about the male models, which she thought embarrassed some of the younger female students in the class. After a long silence, she mentioned that the new boy friend had called and wanted to visit her. She thought he should not because she had some work to do, but she agreed to visit him for a while, and they had intercourse. It might have been at this time that her conversation with this boy friend about her liking him and being permitted to like him because he was leaving occurred. There was a little more talk about the affair, and the patient went on to talk about a girl at work who had just gotten married and was obviously pregnant but did not wear maternity clothes and thought nobody noticed her pregnancy.

When the analyst finished talking about the hour, I went back to the pattern of silence and then telling him about the affair; I then gave him some of my associative connections between that and his pattern of forgetting about a request to change the hour, and the patient's response to that. The analyst's understanding of what I was trying to say was that he should have taken up with her the fact that she had feelings she was not talking about. I indicated this was a possible approach, but I was suggesting that there was another way to think about the resistance pattern. I pointed out that there were several indications in the patient's associations of a kind of tacit understanding with others—her mother, the psychiatrist with whom she had the affair, and the analyst with regard to the change of hour. After her long silence and her telling him the bare details about sleeping with the boy friend, there seemed to me a tacit expectation on her part that if he wanted to help her go into this he would say something. I reminded him that after the first such incident she had been quite open about the conflict she felt and the awareness that she was not forced into it but wanted to for some reason, and the guilt she felt, etc. I compared her relationship with the analyst to that with the ex-fiancé, who "didn't want to hear" her confession, etc. I tried to show him various ways in which he could have picked up what I would think was her unconscious expectation (perhaps a correct understanding of the analyst's countertransference, his unwillingness to intrude), to show her the use she made of his silence as reflecting his agreement that she should not talk about such matters.

The analyst seemed to understand this idea, and so I went at it from another point of view, noting that the "being good" seemed to be coming into the hours as well and that after the long silence she told what she had done, in that way obeying the letter but not the spirit of the basic rule. This aside was stimulated by the analyst's mentioning to me that she had *told* him this and *told* him that. I tried to show him that there was a difference between analyzing and telling, and that the tacit expectation of the basic rule is that the patient will not only tell, but she will listen to herself telling and reflect on what she says. The latter implications of saying what comes to her mind were clearly missing in these most recent interchanges with the patient. We also brought into this discussion the pattern about the mother spoiling her by rewarding her for undergoing frustrations which were simply age-appropriate rather than excessive burdens.

SUPERVISION HOUR 13 (ANALYTIC HOURS 57–61)

The analyst took a few minutes to discuss a matter that had nothing to do with the case, and I was a bit surprised both to have him bring up the question and even more to find that he agreed with me in general. My experience with the analyst has been that when he raises such issues it is because he expects to differ with me.

He had his notes prepared, but as in recent weeks did not offer them to me. Indeed, at the end of the hour, I had to ask him to leave them. This seemed merely a matter of oversight.

He began by saying that he was really getting a sense of the pathology that the patient has in the area of affect expression. She seemed most unwilling to face the sad side of life. She had told him, as if in passing, that her mother had called and confirmed that the examination had shown she did have cancer of the uterus and would require a hysterectomy. I asked the analyst how he responded to that. He laughed and said he felt his countertransferences welling up. He felt like saying, "What's the matter with you?" He did confront her more about the absence of feelings, and it was clear that she did not seem to feel the lack of them, and gave him more details about what had occurred instead. When he got closer to the point, he said she responded with a Latin quotation meaning, "the fear of death disturbs me." He sketched in the line of associations the patient gave regarding her mother, who had always said she was not long for this world because of her drinking. The patient then offered some new material regarding her childish feelings, i.e., as long as her older sister was around, a little bit of her mother would always be with her, and that she would not feel the loss of her mother. But cancer equals dying. The analyst said his association at this point was to the story the patient had told about having been given a doll by her mother because she had not been allowed to go to the movie. He was struck by the childish ability to accept a substitute gratification in order not to feel a loss. I voiced one of my own associations here, asking if the patient also drank. The analyst said no, nothing in what she said or in her history suggested drinking as a problem, though he saw the drift of my thinking.

The analyst went on to say that he noticed that associations about the ex-fiancé nearly always lead to associations about the mother. He said in regard to the ex-fiancé, during the week she had a talk with him and indicated she wanted to break off with him, there is no future, it is either break off and cease all communications or get married, and she could not see the latter. She was still unable to tell him about the affair she was having off and on, and the analyst felt that since she had tried several times to tell him, the ex-fiancé must have some inkling of what she wants to say and probably does not want to hear it. At one point he told her something she had never heard before, that when they are apart he goes out with other girls, but that he does not want to break up with her because she is the only one who can satisfy him sexually. The patient threw up her hands at this, said the analyst, at the irony that she was the only one for him and he was the only one who could not satisfy her. At the same time she was concerned about the man she was having the affair with, and commented on the shallow people he goes with, mentioning again the empty kind of drinking parties they go to.

I asked if she had made any association between the shallowness she sees in this man's friends and her own avoidance of affect. The analyst said she had not, and repeated what he called his countertransference feeling of, "My God, what's wrong with you, girl?" We made it clear that his feelings were not about what she did, but about what she did not feel. She said in this regard her ex-fiancé congratulated her about being more open in her feelings, because after their serious discussion about breaking up when he wanted to go to bed with her, she said she was too concerned about all this and did not want to sleep with him. He said he would much rather hear that than, as in the past, that she was tired or some other irrelevant excuse, or crying. I asked about the crying, and the analyst was not clear about how much there was of this. I recalled the patient once reported "going into hysterics," but I could not recall any episodes of real sadness. The analyst remarked again that the older sister was becoming much more important in the patient's associations.

The patient had had a dream that impressed him, the first one in which he appeared as himself. He summarized it as: He wanted to look at some object she had, like a tassel, or which had a blond tassel at the end of it. At the end of this blond tassel there was the name Mary, which the analyst said she pronounced so that it was hard to distinguish it from the word "marry." When in the dream she tried to look, it was painful and her face "screwed up." The patient's associations went to her sister, who once, when they were young, wore a tasseled cloth over her shoulders. She remembered a photograph showing her sister and her at the piano. She said she had asked her mother about that picture and learned that it was one her father took when she was about eleven, when the children were dressed up for Halloween. The analyst thought there was more "primary process" in the dream. When I looked inquiringly, he said the dream was much more loosely hung together and the patient's associations went freely in many directions. He mentioned some of them regarding the tassel—she thought of squashed houses, a girl friend who was tall and thin, long skinny houses, a bedroom in one of their homes that was long and thin, parents' bedrooms, her sister, who is a tall, slim girl. She said her mother had been told she should have a hysterectomy twenty years ago, and she went on to talk about what it means to a woman sexually to have this operation. She said that mother would have had it, but father thought that she "wouldn't be a woman anymore." Subsequently mother had a lot of trouble, including ectopic pregnancies, hemorrhaging, miscarriages (the analyst noting in an aside here that there were certainly other ways to prevent some of these disasters than having the operation). The patient said that while she would be inclined to advise mother to have the operation, if she were in the same boat, she would feel the same way as mother did. She did not want to lose part of her body. She wished to have children. I asked the analyst if she ever mentioned the possibility that she might be sterile following an unsanitary abortion. He said she had never mentioned this.

The analyst sensed a lot of depression not far from the surface. He repeated to me one of the patient's associations that sometimes life seemed more frightening than death, and he recalled to me the equation between marriage and suicide. He said he also heard more from her about symptoms. When the family lived abroad, there was a tower at the edge of town with an outside staircase and no rail. Her older sister could scamper all the way to the top, but she would get scared and stop when she was only half-way up. She has always been more fearful than her sister, who could stand on the very edge of the Grand Canyon. She also mentioned claustrophobiclike feelings, when they were playing games, of being wrapped up in blankets; as a child she could not stand to have her arms confined close to her sides.

The analyst looked up at this point, and obviously had finished his summary. I said I agreed with him that the defenses against affects were indeed important and I wondered how he intended to approach them. He said he would like to read a portion of an hour so I could see. He read a portion of the fifty-seventh hour, mentioning the party she had gone to with the most recent boy friend, associating to the *dolce vita* quality of these parties with her own pattern of trying to prepare for an examination by distracting herself. Instead of studying she would find a reason to scrub the floor or wash dishes, etc. The analyst commented on the avoidance pattern there and tried to link it to her pattern of jumping from one idea to another in her analysis, having the idea that she was trying to "keep moving," a phrase she had used in regard to others. Her associations were to the psychiatrist she had had the affair with, who also wanted to keep moving, then to the picture *Georgie Girl,* which she had seen recently. Her ex-fiancé thought that she was like the heroine, about whom the title song says that she should change but actually she does not.

There was an aside here in which the analyst asked me if I had seen the picture, and I said I had. He said he did not see what people thought was so wonderful about it. Again I was surprised, because the analyst is one very much involved in poetic and artistic things, with a tendency to be accepting if things are sufficiently off-beat. There was a bit more discussion in which we both agreed that the heroine's performance was excellent, but the other characters (the two psychopaths) left him unmoved.

There were more associations from the patient about moving around, and then came the episode of her trying to talk to her ex-fiancé seriously about breaking up. She mentioned, in a sudden change of mood, a humorous recollection of a fellow who lives in the same house as she who has fixed up a bedroom in Persian style with drapes, wallpaper, cushions on the floor, etc., and invites girls up to this "den of iniquity." I asked if the analyst had responded in any way to the shift from a worrisome, serious mood to the breezy one of the last memory. He said not directly, but he tried to link the dilemma she was having with her ex-fiancé with the dilemma she felt in the analysis—the feeling that she wants to buckle down versus the feeling of being unwilling to look, as was shown in the "tassel dream," and so forth. He mentioned her feelings in this, but the idea was submerged in the complexity of what he was saying. I said that I thought he was trying to be too ambitious and crowd too many things into his interpretations. The analyst nodded instantly as I started to say this, saying he had the same feeling. I stated that if the affect was the problem, he ought to take it up more directly, and I demonstrated several ways in which he could have called the shift in affect to her attention.

The analyst agreed with these possibilities and after a bit said he wanted to show me how he had done something like that with regard to the mother's call about having cancer. It seemed to me the second example he gave, while more direct on the affect side, really was chiding her about the way her thoughts jump around. I said, inasmuch as the charge to her is to associate freely, he can hardly pick her up for jumping from one thing to another. The point anyway was not *what* she talked about, but *how* she talked about it, and again I tried to demonstrate how to separate these and how the line of interpretation could lead to her awareness that an unwitting motive is the wish to avoid feeling deeply. In this connection I suggested he should anticipate that it is not just sad feelings she is trying to avoid but good feelings as well, that he would probably find an equilibrating tendency. The analyst looked doubtful for a minute, and I told him how the patient wanted to avoid the feeling of involvement even though she would speak of this new affair as being fun. The analyst said he had noticed that she speaks of fun, but he has no idea of what is fun in the relationship. He even asked her and got no decent answer. I said it might be worth further inquiry.

I added a suggestion as we closed; he might anticipate if he followed this line that the patient would interpret it as the analyst "wants her to feel bad." I also noted that the patient had already implied, with regard to what the analyst had called her infantile ("childish") pattern, that she does not have to feel bad if her mother dies because she has the illusion of mother's presence in her sister. As we closed it was clear that we were in agreement about what had to be done next.

SUPERVISION HOUR 14 (ANALYTIC HOURS 62–66)

The analyst had some extraneous matters to take up first and, after these were settled as well as they could be, stated it had been a very interesting week with the patient. He summarized the week's events in the way that had by now become familiar. He had a tendency to represent the week as a single event, as if it were frozen in time rather than an unfolding process. This is only a tendency because the other aspect does come in, but the effect of listening to him is quite different from listening to someone who presents in strict historical sequence.

The patient mentioned her mother's operation, but again with few reactions. Then she described her menses, noticing a clot of blood which contained, she thought, an "ovum." She had first noticed something like this at age seventeen, which was a very disturbed time for her. (The analyst in an aside reminded me of the mother's menstrual history.) Her attitude in describing her clot was intellectualized, objective, disinterested, one which she parodied as, "Oh my, isn't it interesting what comes out of me?" At seventeen she had wanted to show this clot to her mother, who was not around, and offered to show it to father, who declined. Now also she wanted to show it to someone, but there was no one. He came back to this later on and added some more details. She went on to talk also about the abortion, what a horrible experience it was, and she laughed as she told about it. She also laughed as she told about the end of the sordid affair she had had with B. that ended after the abortion. The analyst pointed out to her the laughter and how it contrasted with the horror in the story. She left the hour looking sad, but also a bit angry.

The next hour there was a dream which he said he would come back and tell me, but in fact never did. She talked about how disorganized her life was; she was having insomnia, and got up at night with the feeling that she "had to do something." She has compulsively been knitting a sweater for her mother and works on it at night when she wakes up. In order to prevent herself from doing this she has had to leave the sweater at work. Her associations turned back to mother; even the associations to the dream, which he had not told me, kept turning to her mother. The patient continued to be distressed about how unhappy her life was. The analyst added that in the next three hours she seemed to be trying to combat her feeling with various acts of denial. She wore a new springlike dress to each hour. It turned out the dresses were part of a package her mother had sent her, the second time she had gotten such a "care" package. I asked about the reason for these packages, and he said she had very little money to live on and her mother seemed to know this.

He went on to say that the patient was aware she was trying to get over her mood of depression and instability. She mentioned that her recent boy friend had left town and that she was more affected than she thought she would be. She was able to compare herself to his friends, whom she described as shallow and avoiding any kind of feeling. She also considered her relationship to her ex-fiancé, saying that it would be better to separate permanently, and yet she could not. She was afraid of the guilt she would feel because of his reaction. The first time she tried to break off from him, which was only a short time after she knew him, he cried for three days, lost ten pounds, and she finally had to give in. In an aside, the analyst told me that her mother used to tell her as a girl that she should stop crying or she would make herself sick. He mused about her identification with her ex-fiancé as an abandoned child, seeing the relationship as having a mother-child coloration. Another reason for her inability to break with her ex-fiancé was the great security she felt in the relationship. He was always there whenever she wanted to see him, he was interesting to talk to, he indulged her in every way, when she criticized him for not reading he built a library, etc. Also, she did not have to sacrifice anything for him. The analyst said he took a lead from one of my suggestions and asked her what the problem was, then, since she seemed to have everything figured out. The patient said she felt puzzled and alluded to vague feelings that her ex-fiancé seemed "too delicate." She could not think of him as the father of her child. The analyst said specifically she could not think of him as the father of her son. She did not enjoy sleeping with him, and she thought if she loved someone, she would want to sacrifice for him. I noted as an aside that she did not seem to count the considerable sacrifice she was making by remaining neurotically bound up with him, and the analyst agreed.

The analyst reported that in the last hour she talked about her depression at seventeen, saying she felt "strange," and alluded to thoughts and feelings that were not quite clear to him. The depression seemed related to the death of an uncle, from cancer. It was known as soon as they diagnosed it that he was going to die—it was just a matter of time. Mother's cancer came in, but no reference to the possibility of dying and, although she mentioned the objective condition of mother, who had just come through her operation, there was no feeling about it. I asked the analyst what he did here, and he replied he picked up her "objectivity." She shifted back to age seventeen and her uncle's cancer, and how strange and withdrawn she was. She stayed in her room and read a lot, avoided people, and again mentioned thoughts and feelings she did not specify. When she felt better she went back to school, but avoided taking any psychology or sociology courses lest they remind her of that painful time. She only took such courses when they were absolutely required.

The analyst asked about the relationship of her entering psychoanalysis now to the revival of these fears, and she said enough time had passed so that they no longer seemed quite so horrible. The analyst again pointed out the "objectivity," and said that by the end of the week she had become more aware of the depth of her denial and avoidance, especially around the issue of mother. He said he wondered what his part in her life was and thought that he was more like a mother to her, feeling that her implicit hope was that he would understand without her having to say explicitly what goes on and "send her packages." She spoke of how difficult it was to get away from her ex-fiancé. Other fellows she went with, it was no trouble. They'd just get the hint that she was no longer interested in them. But her ex-fiancé avoids seeing these things and gets very upset when he cannot escape them. I asked the analyst if he got any feeling that she wanted him to go away. He said no, and recapitulated the feelings he thought she had about wishing he would understand and take care of her. I pointed out that her relationship to her ex-fiancé is that he makes her comfortable and secure, and he agreed this was so, but there did not seem to be anything yet in the material to support the possibility that she also hoped that the analyst would disappear.

The analyst paused, but I was not sure whether he had finished the report of the hours. I commented that his major activity seemed to be focusing on the disturbance in her affects while avoiding content. He said that was true, and he went on to say that he thought a lot of the phallic talk she indulged in seemed to defend against oral conflicts. He went back to the menstrual clot; she had told the boy across the hall about it. This is the fellow who is a patient in a community outpatient clinic who wanted to have an affair with her. She did not feel attracted to him; thus they shared only an "intellectual intimacy." The fellow laughed and told her that an ovum is a single cell and could not be seen. She bristled at his reaction, and said it needed something to feed on; she told him that after all sperm come out in a kind of glob too. The analyst wanted to point out to me her naive notions about biology and also the oral idea intrinsic in this phallic-competitive interchange. As an association to this, the analyst thought she must have been quite depressed at about seventeen. I commented that I was struck by the ease with which she talked about these matters to this friend, and the analyst also noted the willingness to show and tell her father, which struck him as odd and which would seem to underline at least the intellectualized defenses against her feelings.

The analyst went on to say that there were some more details about abortion, mentioning the abortionist's rusty tools that he washed in the sink in front of her and the infection that resulted. Also B. had married her girl friend S. right after this. She was only interested in marrying B. after she found him interested in S. She lost her interest in him after the abortion. Then he went over the hour itself during which these things came out and read the material. I asked him about the tone in which he commented on the inappropriate affect. It seemed to me to have a note of "primness" about it. I mentioned this to him. He looked sad, wrinkled his forehead, and said, "It might be so." I commented also on the disapproving tone he had used. He said he was aware of his difficulties in dealing with material of this kind, and then read another portion of the hour in which the patient had said, in response to one of his comments, that if she did not laugh she would cry. When he pointed out that she must be feeling something, for she was kneading her fingers together, she instantly withdrew them and put them behind her. She had never done that before.

I asked the analyst what he had done about this and he said, "Nothing." I showed him she had acted as if she were reproved or scolded and how he could have picked up this reaction and put it into the series of her denials, his comments about them, her feeling reproached, and so forth. The analyst seemed chagrined to have overlooked the opportunity, and recognized his difficulty. He said the laughter was uncontrollable, kind of compulsive, and did not reflect the ego's comfortable position with regard to what she was talking about. He mentioned the phrase, "If I don't laugh, I'll cry," and I commented that this seemed also an intellectualized statement under the circumstances. The analyst agreed and went on to describe the pressured, strained quality of her laughter. He went back to talking about the time of the abortion, and I asked whether her parents had known about it, because he had mentioned that they had urged her to go visit her sister. He said he thought so, no, he did not think so, he did not know. Maybe they were aware something was going on and they did want her to break up with B. She had told him that after the abortion, when she was going to see her sister, B. wanted her to leave him the key to her house so that he could stay there with S., the girl he later married. The patient demurred at this. She just could not stand the idea of the two of them running around in her house and sleeping in her bed, but she laughed when she told this. B. was so mad at her for her uncooperativeness that he slammed the door and broke a light fixture. Again I had the feeling that we had come to an end in his account, and I said she had not just told him this. He said no, this happened the first hour when she talked about these things and mentioned she was sick of the whole business and did not want to think about it.

The analyst noted we had some time left, and mentioned that she told about her recent boy friend's experience of going home to visit his parents and finding a party in progress. While he was getting a beer from the refrigerator, his father wandered in and told him he and his mother had been divorced and that each of them was remarrying, and he introduced him to his secretary, shortly to be his wife. Her boy friend was indignant, called another girl friend of his, and left as soon as he could. The implication was that this whole crowd was involved in retaliating against each other in kind. She complained that her boy friend told her about important things only over the telephone or at a crowded party. It seemed to be against the rules for him and his crowd to show any emotions. She wondered if she was like them. I asked the analyst if there was any direct reference to the analyst during the week; there was none except for his question to her regarding her avoidance of psychology and sociology courses. The patient said her sister also was a denier and, in her last letter, did not mention the mother. Even when mother called her to tell her about the operation, they were chit-chatting. Her mother and father were thinking of going abroad after the surgery and asked whether she would be able to take care of their dog. The patient mused about what strange things people worry about under such conditions.

We noted the similarity between this pattern and what goes on in the analysis. The analyst reported a further incident about a girl at one of the parties her boy friend took her to who seemed to be playing around with many men. According to the patient, however, you would have to understand more about her, that she just lost her husband in an accident and she was left with three children, and she needed to have some kind of fun. I tried to contrast this attitude with the patient's attitude toward her own "playing around," noting the moral stand of condemnation followed by understanding and forgiveness compared with her own casualness and her "liberated" attitude. The analyst did not quite get this at first, and I tried to tie it into the way she dealt with her feelings; there was a good deal of projection going on. The patient's moral attitude was being shown in connection to her awareness of other people's behavior.

The analyst spontaneously went back to talking about the prissiness I picked up in his tone of voice. He mentioned musingly that last week he had felt "outraged" at her attitude toward her mother. This week his feelings were more sad and touched, as he felt the limitations she had. He reminded me that his first feelings toward the patient were of concern about sexual attraction. He said these feelings had disappeared entirely as it became clear they were just his fantasies and that the patient seemed like a much more sad and limited person. I did not mention here that his own attitude had become "motherly." I thought I would just let this ride.

We talked more about the style in which he confronted her with her denials of feeling, and I said that a likely misunderstanding on the patient's part would be the feeling that the analyst thought she "ought to feel bad." Indeed there was some of this, possibly conveyed by the analyst himself. I tried to indicate that I did not think that any particular way of phrasing his comments would avoid that necessarily; indeed, to strive for too much perfection in the way he phrased things would in itself be precious. Rather, he ought to be ready to interpret the patient's reactions to his interpretations. Along that line, we discussed the technique he was using. Both of us agreed that he should not badger her, but I also recommended he watch the results of his interpretations and suggested different styles of reaction that might occur. One of them, apparently, she had already shown. In response to one of his comments, she was silent, and one might have thought she was reflecting on what he had said, but then after a "decent interval" she went on along a different tack. I said this involved a kind of isolation and withholding of associations which he could comment on or ask for. On the other hand, he should not assume that because she did not respond immediately his comment had no effect. He might look to see what line of associations eventuated. I suggested as a possibility that rather than responding directly she might give him additional examples of the same kind of thing, or *conversely* she might follow with a series of examples that implied a refutation of what he tried to tell her. We were involved in this discussion and I did not notice that time had run out until I was in danger of being late for my next appointment.

EPILOGUE

Since these notes of the supervisory process and the supervisor's reflections about them (see Chapter XIII) cover only the first few months of a psychoanalysis that lasted about 750 hours over close to four years, the reader who values a sense of closure may wish to know something of the later developments.

In the period reported upon the analysis was stormy, with a great deal of acting out of the patient's need to defend herself against a dependent relationship to the analyst. The patient's coolness and aloofness toward the analyst and her caution about having any expectations of the treatment contrasted sharply with her hypersensitivity to the analyst's activities, particularly to his several absences early in the treatment. As the analyst became more convinced about this impact that he had on the patient and could see the need for some shift in his approach, the difficulties gradually subsided. The patient became better able to voice her fantasies that the analyst would "straighten her out" without her participation or involvement. As the analyst and the relationship became more real to her, her investment in analyzing, as opposed to attending and reporting, increased sharply. The development of a workable and increasingly reliable therapeutic alliance was succeeded quite rapidly toward the end of the first year by the emergence of a transference neurosis.

As the analysis proceeded, the patient's life outside the analysis concomitantly settled down. She began to experience some success at analyzing when an annoying phobia, one that had not been mentioned among her presenting complaints, suddenly yielded to accurate interpretation. The awareness of the hostility that had been expressed in that symptom entered the transference and she was able to express through fantasy and direct accusation her rage at the analyst, focused at this stage mostly on interruptions of the analysis, such as through ordinary holidays, which formerly had led to spells of self-destructive acting out. The turbulent feelings and behavior that had formerly disturbed her life now came completely inside the analysis. The patient was able to hold a job, complete her education, and finally embark on a new career.

The first major theme of the transference neurosis involved rage at the analyst, many feminist concerns, and mistrust of men, and led to the recovery of moments of early disappointment by her father. Gradually, the transference neurosis shifted to expose more fully the patient's lifelong clandestine, dependent, and nurturant relationship with her mother. The analysis of the layers of fantasy that permitted her to avoid her oedipal anxieties by maintaining a regressive relationship with her mother then came into focus. The analysis of the oedipal fantasies and the family romance led to the understanding of her self-defeating behavior and permitted her to give it up. The homoerotic aspects of the transference neurosis gave some temporary difficulty, but with careful and sensitive work by the analyst were resolved successfully.

The analysis moved into a classical termination phase in which, over the course of about a year, the patient worked through these themes in several contexts, was able to separate herself from a man with whom she had been intimately involved for many years, but whose function had been to support her neurosis, and was able to make new and more satisfying arrangements, ultimately to marry. The termination phase demonstrated that structural changes had occurred. Her sense of herself improved considerably, degraded relationships were no longer possible for her, and the patient demonstrated a capacity for pleasure, sexual and otherwise, that had formerly been unavailable to her. Relationships with both men and women deepened and became more mutual. Termination was agreed upon by patient and analyst and sufficient time was allowed to work through these issues once again.

The candidate learned a good deal from this case. He was able to experience how the patient's character and pathology, as well as his own initial defensiveness about recognizing how his own behavior impacted upon her, all fed into the patient's mistrust and supported her acting out. As he became able to appreciate this interaction, he was able to relate differently and change his technical approach. As these initial difficulties were resolved, the analyst's own gift for analyzing was freed to develop and contributed to the later development of the case along generally classical lines. The initial difficulties experienced by the analyst were perhaps intensified by his feeling that the supervisor expected much more of him than he was able to deliver at that time. The "learning alliance," which, during the phase reported upon, was less than the best, also improved as the case continued. The analyst was able to make use of the supervisor in a different way and to take far more responsibility for his own learning. The candidate went on to successfully complete the requirements of the institute and was graduated within a year after the completion of this case.

CHAPTER VI

Perspective: The Fleming-Benedek Approach

JOAN FLEMING, M.D.

In introducing a description of the method and procedure I used in studying the material available to the COPE Study Group on Supervision, let me state first that I believe that there are many ways to approach the problem and many different procedures for collecting the data for such a project. In general, the choice of procedures and of the methods for analyzing the data will be determined by the questions the investigator wishes to answer. But, before going further with this point, it seems important to me to highlight some of the problems inherent in the necessary overlap when one supervisor "investigates" how another supervisor "does it." The study of supervision is a very different task from the doing of it.

Supervision is one of the main ways of teaching clinical psychoanalysis. Until about 1952, what went on in a supervisory situation was considered almost as private as what went on in a training analysis. Since then, supervision sessions have been audited by visitors from the Committee on New Training Facilities and the Committee on Institutes of the Board on Professional Standards of the American Psychoanalytic Association, and by the survey directors of the Survey of Psychoanalytic Education as well (the latter fully described by Lewin and Ross, 1960). Supervision hours have also been recorded on video tape and have been transcribed from audio tape records (see Fleming and Benedek, 1966). Sharing the material of supervision and the experiences encountered in studying it offers many advantages to psychoanalytic educators interested in learning more about teaching clinical skills. It also presents many pitfalls. Probably the more serious of these are the narcissistic exhibitionistic anxieties and defenses which are stirred up by situations of exposure and examination for both the supervisor-observer and the supervisor-observed.

This is such a prevailing and potentially obstructive problem that I feel it is important to call attention to the danger and to emphasize some ways of dealing with it. First, it is essential to keep constantly in mind that the investigator of supervision is neither the analyst of the patient nor the teacher of the student whose material is being studied. He is an observer of their interactions with each other and must maintain a position of objectivity toward what he observes. It is often very hard to remain in the position of the objective investigator outside of the private and affect-laden supervision situation. The observer finds himself drawn all too readily into the role of critic of both analyst and supervisor. This is especially easy because any supervisor must necessarily function as a critical evaluator of his student's analytic technique, since evaluation and correction of errors are part of any teaching-learning relationship.

Consequently, the critical role of the supervisor becomes part of what an investigator observes and necessarily must also evaluate. The investigator, however, must make an effort to avoid "one-upmanship" as he, too, notes the student's errors and realizes he might have made a different choice of teaching tactics had he been in the supervisor's shoes. This kind of investigator reaction is properly more a part of the doing of supervision than the studying of it. Yet, notation of these comparisons with all of their similarities and differences is part of the secondary data of this kind of an empirical, clinical study. These secondary data add to the information about supervision and are, therefore, valuable for study in themselves. Actually, the investigator cannot and should not avoid making evaluative observations as his research progresses, but he should steer between the Scylla of personal criticizing and the Charybdis of aseptic fact-finding devoid of assessment of contextual meaning. He can do this by maintaining an attitude of self-criticism which subjects his own investigative evaluations to the same critical scrutiny he applies to the data he observes.

Today, the range of supervision material available for study is a wide one. The possibilities run from video tapes and transcribed electrical recordings to "process notes" made by the supervisor, material in anecdotal form, and administrative supervisory reports. Given this range of data possibilities, the first step in establishing a method of approach is to decide what question among the many that could be asked about supervision is the one to be investigated first. The question decided upon will influence the form of the basic data which will, in turn, influence the procedure for obtaining them. For example, the question, "What happens within a supervisory session?" requires a more verbatim account of the interaction between student-analyst and supervisor than the question, "What learning problems are most frequently encountered in the supervision of a first case?" The answers to the former question would require the data obtained from tape recordings or "process notes." The latter question could be answered by collecting a series of vignettes reported by several supervisors of first cases. The vignettes would describe the learning problems that were found in first cases and the protocols for study would be in anecdotal form, each representing but a small segment of any one supervisory session. Or, another supervisor might ask the question, "How do I recognize problems of countertransference and what do I do about them?" For this purpose, his summarized comments about several students would constitute his beginning data base.

The difference across this range of questions is a difference in focus which varies from the wide-angle view of the whole supervisory situation and teaching-learning process to a deliberately narrowed-down view limited to a particular class of events or level of experience. The wider the area covered by the question to be studied, the more closely the basic material needs to approximate the full events of the actual supervisory experience. When a limited focus is chosen to begin with, such as the most frequent learning problems in first cases, the next step involves collecting the data and then finding a classification scheme that will order the problems into appropriate categories. For example, they might be classified according to causal factors, such as inexperience, lack of aptitude, inadequate theoretical knowledge, or personality problems. Once this is done for a sufficient number of first cases, the learning problems in a given category can be counted, the one occurring most frequently can be noted, and an answer to the question as it applies to the cases studied will have been found. The same procedure could be used in studying second, third, and fourth cases, if desired.

Such additional studies would naturally pose another level of question, e.g., "How do the frequencies of the various learning problems vary with the level of experience?" The procedure then would require a different ordering of the data and the application of more complex statistical methods for their proper interpretation. From each proceeding, new derivative data emerge, new questions and new problems for study appear, leading eventually to broader generalizations and new theoretical constructions about supervision as an educational method. For example, after the question on learning problems in first cases has been answered, the investigator may want to know how a given learning problem was handled by a given supervisor with different students or by different supervisors with the same student. For this project more verbatim data would be required, which, in turn, would stimulate new questions and provide more answers for understanding more of the supervisory process as a whole.

We can conclude from these comments on the relation of issue to method and to data that one can begin a study of supervision at different points, study it from different angles, and move from one point to another, either limiting or expanding the field for investigation.

When I began the study of the supervisory material provided through the COPE Study Group on Supervision, the primary question seemed to be: *What is happening within this supervision?* This is a very general question, more oriented toward the larger view of the events and the phenomena plus the process in accord with which they unfold than toward a more circumscribed problem, such as countertransference phenomena or supervisory teaching interventions. Of importance in trying to respond to this general question is the form in which the events of a supervisory experience are being presented. Sometimes the data are inadequate to the questions, and either the data or the questions have to be modified. Often identification of areas of inadequacy leads to new questions and changes in the form of data presentation, which add to the understanding of what happens in supervision, explicitly and implicitly, and to the better definition of the elements of the process.

In this instance, the Study Group data were available in the form of summarized accounts of the events that occurred between the student-analyst and the supervisor, as they were recalled and written up by the supervisor after each supervisory session (Chapter V). I had already worked with a procedure and a point of view derived from studying similar data (Fleming and Benedek, 1966). Turning to the Study Group material, it was of interest to me to see if our own procedure for studying supervision could be applied to the protocols offered by this supervisor. Another investigative interest was to observe the kind of events discerned in this "process-notes" recorded supervision compared with what we had seen in the study of our verbatim transcripts.

My orientation to studying any data from the therapeutic or the supervisory process is anchored in the idea that the essence of both processes is the sequential flow of communication that optimally follows certain basic patterns. In the analytic process the basic pattern involves a regressive reproduction of the infantile conflicts, the transference neurosis, coupled with the gradual working through to new integrations. This pattern is facilitated by the analyst's skill in identifying the resistances to the development of the transference neurosis and in assisting the patient to overcome them. In the supervisory process the basic pattern involves watching this regressive movement and especially the analyst's activity in facilitating it. His aptitude, his skill, his mistakes and counterreactions, his learning to conceptualize the process of psychoanalysis—all of this is the material for supervisory consideration. The obstacles to learning are comparable to therapeutic resistances and can be seen in a lack of sensitivity and empathy, general ignorance of dynamics and technique, inexperience, and counter-reactions rooted in the analyst's intrapsychic conflicts, which are for whatever reasons not well enough worked through.

With this orientation in mind, I was interested in observing and understanding the flow of communication between *A* (the analyst) and *P* (the patient) as it was reported by *A* to *S* (the supervisor) and the exchanges about this between *A* and *S*. I wanted to see if the stimulus-response sequences of the therapeutic process could be differentiated from those in the teaching-learning relationship. Could particular learning problems be identified in the exchanges between *A* and *P*? Could particular teaching objectives and techniques be identified in the exchanges between *A* and *S*? Could the vicissitudes and progressions both in the analysis and in the supervision be followed and evaluated?

I read the data presented and made marginal notes, attempting to isolate episodes of teaching exchanges, i.e., units of something taught (see, for example, Fleming and Benedek, 1966, pp. 38–48). This was more easily done in some of the supervision hours at hand than in others. The records of *A*'s report to *S* about the events in the analysis varied, depending on whether *S* read *A*'s summarized notes or *A* presented his material orally. The account of the interaction between *S* and *A* also varied in the amount of evidence given on which *S* based his inferences and evaluations of *A*'s work. The specific form of *S*'s activity with *A* also varied in the detail with which it was reported. Sometimes it was summarized so that the sequences of stimulus and response were not available and, therefore, the effect of supervisory teaching could not be so easily identified in relation to a given episode. I came to the conclusion that these "process notes" did not provide as adequate data for responding to the question, "What happens within a supervision session?" as a transcript of one electrically recorded.

The most obvious difference between the two is in the sheer amount of verbatim detail and the vividness of the interaction between *A* and *S*. The specific words used by each party are significant data at this level of question and will be fully reproduced only in the recordings. A second difference is one which is reflected in the structure of the supervisory learning situation. In our material of transcribed audio tapes (Fleming and Benedek, 1966), the student reported orally on his perception of the analytic process and used his notes only for review in preparation for supervision or to refer to in case of need. This procedure was emphasized by us as a part of learning how to analyze, and the pattern of reporting was used as a vehicle for evidence of learning needs and learning difficulties. This procedure was part of the way we *did supervision*. It naturally became a target for investigative evaluation.

A different procedure was used in the Study Group protocols. Consequently, notations on specific learning problems had to be made more often from the supervisor's summary of what *A*'s notes contained or in the discussion about them. This difference could itself be a topic for discussion about varying learning objectives. But, in spite of my opinion about the inadequacy of the Study Group data in this respect, they did provide information about the supervisor's reactions to both *P* and *A* and his evaluative thinking during a supervisory session which transcript data cannot do, unless there is dictation of such material after each supervisory session. Of course, our delayed retrospective recall of these data is subject to all of the possible errors in remembering anything.

When a second level of notation and classification was attempted on the Study Group data, it was possible to observe over a series of hours that the most frequent teaching tactics consisted in explaining to *A* how *S* understood the meaning of *P*'s associations and behavior and of suggesting changes in *A*'s manner of intervening. It was clear from *S*'s comments on his own reactions in the supervisory relationship that he was aware of countertransferences and resistances to learning which became problems in the supervision. Vicissitudes in the learning alliance were observable, as well as what *S* eventually did about them. His approach to countertransference issues was indirect in these early hours and he cautiously avoided confrontation, except where defensiveness toward himself as the supervisor was noted.

The next section in this chapter presents my summarized observations and inferences derived from detailed study of the first twenty-five analytic hours of this case (supervision sessions 1-6, Chapter V). These derived data were written down in a form that emphasized the following points:

1. Based on the principle of "process" or flow of interactive communication, the time sequences in the flow of interaction in the analytic relationship and in the supervisory relationship were noted.

2. The responses of *P* and *A* to each other and their reciprocating effects were observed as I would do if I were the supervisor. The way these responses increased or decreased resistances, the form the defenses took, and the signs of developing transference phenomena were noted but not detailed in this summary, since it is the interferences with optimal, expectable flow that need the most supervisory attention. These interferences indicate the learning needs and learning progression of *A*. In my summary I focused on the main learning needs as I discerned them.

3. The supervisor's teaching focus and teaching tactics were noted and the results of his teaching efforts were observed over a series of hours in order to discover the effect on *A*'s understanding of *P* and his developing skill.

4. Comparison between supervisory sessions which gave clues to *A*'s

progress in learning as it was reflected in changes in his work with *P* and in his communication with *S* and with himself were included.

The summaries of each hour contain observations on both the learning needs and the teaching tactics. I have placed within brackets my evaluative commentaries on these supervisory events.

SUPERVISION HOUR 1 (ANALYTIC HOURS 1–3)

Exchange 1 (through paragraph 3). Good beginning by *A* who observed and reported well as far as this exchange goes. *S* interrupted with what I felt was an intrusive-sounding question *regarding his activity* which might put *A* on the defensive. *A* did seem to be in a hurry to get *P* on the couch.

One bit of evidence of a learning need is *A*'s reply that he has been *doing nothing* except listening. [These words might have little significance or they might indicate that he has not yet learned that listening is a very active part of an analyst's work and that it is far from *doing nothing.* This is a matter of choice of learning objectives. It could provide an opportunity for teaching which *S* did not pick up, preferring to focus on "activity," meaning responses and interventions of various sorts communicated to *P.* It seems that *S*'s intervention was premature since, as he read the notes, he discovered that *A* had not been "too active."]

Exchange 2 (paragraph 4–end). *A* continues to associate to *P*'s material in the *S-A/A-S* interaction, giving nonverbal cues, etc. *A* was able to report some of his diagnostic thinking when *S* asked for it.

Another possible learning issue appears around *A*'s announcement of an imminent three-day separation. It seems poorly timed relative to *P*'s wish for a "captive audience" and *A* appears insufficiently sensitive to the possible effect on her. *P* reacts with, "I'm going away, too." *A* counters by saying that she will be charged if she leaves him (a possible retaliatory impulse?). *S* recognizes this as an error but does not discuss it on the level of *A*'s "instrument" (his sensitivity) but rather as an unwitting counterreaction to being called "captive." [This could be a countertransference. If not, the educational diagnosis is more a matter of inexperience and "dumb spot," i.e., an insufficient sensitivity to unconscious meaning even though he is adept at observing manifest behaviors. He seems to be preconsciously aware of significant meanings but does not integrate them yet by an empathic identification, e.g., the question, "What does her need for a 'captive audience' mean and how is it related to events involving separation in childhood?"]

[This exchange between *A* and *P* seems to color much that follows. The basic transference expectation seems to be anaclitic with intense separation anxiety and regressive pull for *P.* Her defensive transference then revolves around the issue of how to keep from getting too involved with *A.*]

SUPERVISION HOUR 2 (ANALYTIC HOURS 4–12)

Supervision continues irregularly. *S* reports he is satisfied, with one exception, namely, *P* does not seem to expect anything from *A*. [I wonder about this since she has already talked about experiencing *A* as a "captive audience."] The next reported material also refers to transference expectation, e.g., *P* says *A* is not a "captive audience." He is not dependable or trustworthy, but is like the cats she has known. She loved them and cared for them in childhood, but the mother cat left and the little ones died. [This material certainly refers to a deep-seated separation anxiety. *P*'s history would offer some clues in the family's frequent moving from place to place and the alcoholism and infidelity of her parents. The significance of these events for *P*'s dynamics is not yet clear, but I think one can expect *A* to be especially alert to signs in this direction.]

Following the material about cats comes the dream after she learns mother is hospitalized; in the dream she awakens screaming for mother. *P* speaks of fear of dependency on *A* and fear of her own helplessness. This intense concern she associates with possible death wishes toward mother. Mother is also giving "things" like diamond rings [which only intensifies the ambivalence and anxiety about her rage over her frustrated needs].

A is aware of the references to him as someone tending to give her too many "things" [but he does not seem to see the mother transference here in terms of a sequence involving separation—helplessness—rage—conflict—anxiety—resistance, stimulated by *P*'s problems but reinforced by the actual separation from *A* and a reaction to *A*'s handling of this separation in the first three hours. *A*'s acceptance of *P*'s image of him as a "nice guy" but somewhat frustrating is correct as far as it goes. It is not yet an understanding of the deeper levels of this material and its transference meanings. This points toward a possible learning need in the area of transference phenomena, a learning need that, if present, may indicate insufficient preparation in terms of theoretical knowledge. Such a need may or may not be something *S* can do something about in the supervisory situation. Of course, he may choose to let it alone until the problem becomes further clarified.]

SUPERVISION HOUR 3 (ANALYTIC HOURS 13–15)

A reports well and recognizes the continuing and intensifying transference resistance and defense against the transference, expressed in *P*'s "distrust and reservations about the treatment process she has gotten herself into."

S associates to the analytic material and recognizes the resistances. *S* also sees *P*'s conflict over a developing positive transference which *P* longs for but is threatened by because she feels she cannot depend on anyone. [I feel the anaclitic needs are predominant in this patient, and her sexual yearnings at this point are only a means to that end. Other aims and associated conflicts are there, too, but not in focus at present. The "panic at the idea of marriage and intimacy" signals other levels of conflict that also seem to stir up her fear of progress. Is this fear rooted in security gratification which she is afraid to lose if she cathects objects on another level of development?]

[*A* seems to be doing all right, as measured by the fact that *P*'s material flows on in a consistent manner. The chain of her associations and the stimulus-response pattern can be followed in terms of the rise and fall of anxieties and resistances, the ebb and flow between present and past, and the transference and genetic inferences that can be made. *A* is certainly not overactive and does not interfere with the analytic process in the patient. My question at this point is whether he understands clearly enough *P*'s problem of anaclitic need and separation anxiety and the concomitant developing mother transference. There is another analytic interruption by *A*, and our data do not reveal his analysis of it. Anxiety and resistance have not become intense enough yet to require interpretation in order to keep the analysis going, but *P*'s confusion over appointments and her not talking about this would point to a resistance that could become serious. This situation presents a *teaching problem.* Should *S* explore the level of *A*'s insight more actively or simply let things develop?]

SUPERVISION HOUR 4 (ANALYTIC HOURS 16–18)

Again we see *P*'s reaction to interruptions. Tentatively, they seem related to a basic conflict over separations. How her reaction is expressed in her behavior and in her associations is revealed in the material. *A* recognizes the connections quite clearly in these hours, sees the phenomena of parapraxis and depreciation of analysis, but he does not seem to independently recognize *P*'s silences as evidence of increasing resistance or how the interruptions in treatment make her "feel like low man on the totem pole." He seems not to recognize adequately the increasing affect of despair and the underlying rage.

P is clearly trying very hard to handle her anxieties and to perform her task in analysis. The therapeutic alliance is still effective, but is put under strain.

This transference situation is discussed between *S* and *A*. The data we have seem to emphasize *P*'s image of *A* as authoritarian and her attempts to comply with this "transference" image which run into difficulty in the silences. *S* also gives some technical suggestions in the area of interpretation, i.e., facilitating interventions. [Still not in the therapeutic focus are *P*'s reactions to the separations from *A* and an attempt to bring out the affect involved in the underlying mother transference.]

SUPERVISION HOUR 5 (ANALYTIC HOURS 19–22)

The analytic material continues in the same vein, with *P* acting out her conflict over dependency by getting sick and having car trouble. She does not recognize the resistance function of her own "objectivity" (not complaining and not verbalizing any affect about these events) and it is not clear how much *A* does. At least he does not interpret these manifestations of defensive need to her.

P turns to the past and recalls anxieties over separations from father and over the quarrels between father and mother. *A* correlates evidence in dreams of identifications with mother and signs of conflict about this which *S* relates to possible primal-scene significance.

S focuses with *A* on *P*'s pseudo-objectivity as a defense and wonders if *A*'s own objectivity is interpreted by *P* as meaning he is cold and unsympathetic. *S* discusses the resistance problem as being intensified by *A*'s apparent lack of responsiveness. There is some discussion of the mothering experiences of *P* and the split mother image created by the older sister's mothering role. [Most of the teaching technique consists of *S* pointing out his own explanatory inferences to *A* and what they might mean in terms of *P*'s "character and resistance problems." The learning alliance seems in good equilibrium. *A* can give his own evaluation of the situation, e.g., "*P* is getting more under stress, but she continues to work analytically."]

SUPERVISION HOUR 6 (ANALYTIC HOURS 23–25)

P talks of her fiancé and her conflict over being involved and close without a threatening genital intimacy. *S* sees this pattern as an expression of defense against transference involvement. This is discussed with *A*, who offers confirmatory evidence. *A* also reports his interpretive activity. He confronts *P* with her failure to mention the missed hour. He tries to link this with her generally confused and unsatisfactory relationships with men. His report also reveals his effort to see "larger transference implications."

S confronts *A* with his tendency to accept *P*'s habit of being overly general and assuming she has said something when often actually she has not. *A* responds with recall of *P*'s story of the teacher who graded her down because *P* seemed to assume a shared knowledge which was not necessarily so. [This is an excellent bit of supervisory process in which *S* interprets a counterresistance by *A* which tends to perpetuate a character defense by *P*.

The intervention by *S* mobilizes *A*'s associations to *P*'s material, and he recalls evidence that *P* is reacting with him as she did with a teacher in the past and that, when the teacher confronted her with the inappropriateness of her behavior, she was able to change. *P* is preconsciously aware of *A*'s fitting in with her old pattern. *A* has not perceived this on his own, but he is able to do so when *S* confronts him with his own empathic interpretation of the *A-P* interaction. *S* does not need to go further into the motivations and roots of *A*'s blind spot, but to confront him with it was necessary for the analysis and helpful for *A*'s development. I would call this a pedagogical "treatment" of a possible learning block in *A*.]

The next exchange in the analysis involves *A*'s response to *P*'s developing some observing ego and making connections between her behavior at work with one authority figure (an older man) and her problems in general. *A* was somewhat surprised and felt she was "going too fast," telling *S* he had a fantasy that it was too soon to learn the magic of Oz. His countertransference clearly influenced his message to *P*, although we do not know just what he said.

S handled this defensive reaction in *A* very gently and in the end made an interpretation that *P* seemed to be "going too fast for him, but not for her."

P gives more information about her relationship with this older man. She has sexual feelings when she talks to him. She then describes him as resembling *A* and her father, and wonders if there could be similar difficulties in talking to *A*. She makes these tentative connections with evidence of some tension and anxiety. *A* makes no direct response, and *P* misses the next hour and is depressed in the one following. [The increase of resistance following this breakthrough and the defenses of flight and depression are clear, but seem not to have been picked up by *A*. *S* notes this partially, but explains the dynamics without confronting *A* with his counterresistance. This counterresistance shows itself also in his less adequate understanding of *P*'s nonverbal behavior and affectivity. He registers these clues, but cannot correlate them well enough with her words or other analytic events.]

Space does not permit listing each observation I made and the classification of each under the headings I used, such as learning alliance, learning needs, learning difficulties, and teaching tactics. It seems clear as I compare my approach with what I know about the approach of other members of the Study Group on Supervision that I pay less attention to the minutiae of *P*'s material, but do emphasize the repetitive themes that indicate the dynamic line of the conflicts and the developing transference. I feel that *A*'s degree of awareness of these two lines in the process of the psychoanalysis indicates his level of learning. Consequently, these observations are given significance in my study of supervisory data only as they are understood or misunderstood by *A* rather than in the analysis by itself. In other words, my focus is on *A*'s understanding of the therapeutic process rather than simply the phenomena that constitute it. Emphasis was given to the evidence of *S*'s recognition of what *A* is responding to, how he understands *P*, and how this understanding or lack of it influences *A*'s responses to *P* and thereby affects the development of the transference in a positive or negative direction. How *S* helps *A* to understand his patient more accurately and to understand where and why he might have been incorrect was also what I concentrated on, attempting to observe not simply *S*'s teaching tactics as he noted them in the protocol, but also to infer the reasoning in back of his choices and to follow the effect of his teaching efforts as they were reflected in the analytic process and in the evidence for *A*'s learning.

At this point it seems important to add three comments on methodology, which also differentiate the *doing of supervision* from the *study of it*. First, as an investigator reads a series of protocols of supervision sessions, he must keep in mind that he has an advantage over the supervisor, since he is observing the whole of a session (or a series of sessions) after the fact and at a distance from the position of immediacy. On the front line, so to speak, in the conduct of a supervision, it is harder for the supervisor to keep the story of the process in perspective than it is for the outside investigator. Many choices of intervention might have been made differently had the supervisor been able to "see" as broad a view of the data as the investigator can. Second, when an investigator looks at the protocols of only one or two sessions, he may observe what appear to be omissions or a lack of understanding on the part of the supervisor which will be explainable later as subsequent protocols indicate that the problem had indeed been recognized, but had not been dealt with explicitly until the future time. Third, it is clearly not possible to bring into focus everything that might be discussed in a given supervision session. Consequently, a supervisor must give priority to some points and let others wait. This fact will color the manifest picture in any protocol, whether it be in the form of transcripts or "process notes," and awareness of this fact must be kept in mind by the investigator.

In formulating this statement of my encounter with the COPE Study Group on Supervision project for this study of protocols of "process notes," I have clarified a number of points in my thinking on proper methodology for the study of supervision, as well as the application of a specific method of approach. What stands out sharply in my mind are three issues that represent a culmination of what I have learned from the years of experience in working with the Study Group. First, the form in which the data of observation are collected is determined by the question for which answers are sought. Second, a study of supervision can begin at a variety of different points but will always lead to new questions and require new data, since the basic data for one project will not be adequate for other projects. Third, the sharing of data on supervision in whatever form it is presented offers an opportunity to the investigators not only to learn about how to study supervision, but also how to conduct it. The differences between how an observer would conduct the supervision and the way the protocol demonstrates it was conducted can stimulate the supervisor-investigator to examine his own practices and to sharpen his own thinking by forcing him to be more explicit about the rationale for his own behaviors as a supervisor. This last point is a very fertile field for future studies of supervision in which differences between investigators and between investigators and the supervisor under observation can be defined, compared, and evaluated in a common effort to objectify and improve our teaching skills.

REFERENCES

Fleming, J. & Benedek, T. (1966), *Psychoanalytic Supervision.* New York: Grune & Stratton.

Lewin, B. D. & Ross, H. (1960), *Psychoanalytic Education in the United States.* New York: Norton.

CHAPTER VII

Perspective: The San Francisco Project

ROBERT S. WALLERSTEIN, M.D.

Chapter V, the detailed supervisory process notes of the first fourteen supervision hours, represents the data base from which the San Francisco subgroup within the Study Group[1] essayed, via the scheme it devised, to systematize the study of the phenomena of the supervision process. Further, as stated in the first introductory chapter in this monograph, because in theory the supervisor's process notes of the supervision would also capture the main events and interactions of the ongoing psychoanalysis that was the subject of discussion within the supervision, these supervisory process notes could be simultaneously a way of study and access to knowledge of the therapeutic process in the psychoanalysis. But clearly in these notes the ongoing psychoanalysis will be only very selectively described in order to highlight the specific supervisory issues and problems discerned by the supervisor, and in the schematic categorization of the process-note data by the San Francisco Project, the phenomena of the analysis per se, recounted in no matter what detail, serve only as the substantive subject base on which learning and teaching how to analyze—the specific focus of this

[1]Daryl DeBell, M.D., Peyton Jacob, Jr., M.D., Robert S. Wallerstein, M.D., and Emanuel Windholz, M.D.

whole study of supervision—takes place.

In keeping with this, the six-fold schema, outlined in Chapter I, that was devised by the San Francisco Project for the categorization of the supervision hour process notes allows only one category, the first, for the description of all the events of the analysis, an account of its thematic flow, its resistances and its transferences, as discerned through the supervisor's process notes based on the written material (process notes) and verbal presentation of the student-analyst in the supervision hour. Since, however, with rare exceptions, so much of the actual time of the supervision hour is necessarily taken up with the conveying of the events of the analysis to the supervisor, and since in order to present and render comprehensible the learning problems evident in this material and the teaching interventions employed to deal with them, the supervisor in his notes must describe the analytic treatment situation, both comprehensively and in adequate detail, it turned out that this category 1, *the analysis,* bulked the largest in the following schematic categorization.

The other five categories seek, in more detail, to discriminate the events and problems of the supervisory process, the issues in learning around which the teaching takes place. Categories 2, *the analyst's understanding of the analytic material*, and 3, *the analyst's activity,* refer to the thoughts and the actions of the analyst qua analyst and apart from the direct role and involvement of the supervisor. In theory, the two are conceptually distinct from one another: the one, what the analyst *thought* of the material, the meanings he grasped in it or imposed upon it, and the other, what the analyst then undertook to *do* (and not to do) in response to those meanings. Practically, the evidence fitting under these two headings is often commingled in the supervisor's process notes and separations have sometimes had to be made quite uncertainly and arbitrarily. Actually, category 2, *the analyst's understanding*, though in theory a more comprehensive category since it should encompass *all* of the material of the analysis as presented (compared to category 3, *the analyst's activity* [or actual interventions], which could be very discrete and limited), often enough turned out to be more difficult to specify and sometimes even sparser because, unless specifically drawn out *and reported* by the supervisor in his notes, the analyst's understandings had often to be inferred through the layerings of the supervision process notes, whereas his specific interventions were more apt to be directly evident—in his verbalizations or actions—and recorded as such.

Categories 4 and 5 refer specifically to the teaching problems and issues as focused by the supervisor. Here, too, a clear distinction conceptually, often however more ambiguous in the material actually reported, was attempted between the more didactic issues of the learning and teaching (areas of ignorance, lack of experience, specifically needed technical advice, etc.) and the more personally involving issues of the learning and teaching (those deficits in understanding, technique, or activity based on other than simple informational lack—the whole complex of the analyst's learning problems and countertransferences vis-à-vis his patient, and problems about learning and transferences vis-à-vis his supervisor, as well as the related issues of style, predilection, and character). This distinction has been stated by Jacob as that between the handling of "dumb spots" and "blind spots." The categorization here attempted is as follows: 4a, *the supervisor's understanding of the technical analytic issues*; 4b, *the supervisor's pedagogic* (in the sense of more "didactic") *interventions* (note here the same effort at distinction between understanding and activity, or intervention based on that understanding, as attempted in the categorization of the student-analyst's analytic conduct); 5a, *the supervisor's understanding of the analyst's personal involvement;* and 5b, *the supervisor's therapeutic interventions* (therapeutic in the sense of other-than-"didactic" though not personal therapy in the many ways this distinction is made through the course of this monograph—see especially Chapter IV). Where the evidential basis was inadequate in the supervision process notes to confidently assign material between categories 4 and 5 (the "pedagogic" and the "therapeutic"), the maxim was followed of considering a problem a reflection of a "dumb spot" before a "blind spot"—that is, a "dumb spot" until proved otherwise. This no doubt led at times to the material in category 4 being artificially inflated at the expense of what might subsequently turn out to be the more proper categorization of some or perhaps even much of it within category 5.

The last category, 6, *the analyst's response to the supervision hour,* is the only specifically interactional category in the schema. It is meant to convey the evidence of the impact of the supervisory teaching, of both the "didactic" and the "personally involving," on the subsequent unfolding of the events in both the supervision and the analysis, either immediate or delayed. Expectedly, evidence in the category would in some hours be either very sparse or very general (as inferences about the climate of the supervision).

The manner of categorizing the material of the supervision process notes under these six headings was quite simple. Each member of the San Francisco Project subgroup separately read through the process notes of each supervision hour and marked each sentence or thought unit with the appropriate category number. These accounts were then compared line by line in the subgroup sessions and reconciled into group consenses. All the units belonging in category 1 were taken sequentially and woven into a coherent narrative account with minimal elaboration, beyond making sensible connections and transitions, and minimal inference building as well. The effort was to adhere very closely to the original data so that the thoughts and sentences in category 1 would as much as possible be recognizably in the language of the original process notes—though at times condensed to eliminate redundancy and repetitiveness. The same procedure was of course followed for each of the other categories. At the end, all of the phenomena revealed and recorded in the process notes of each hour should have found their way into one of the six subject headings of the categorization for that hour.

What follows is this categorization in accord with the headings of the San Francisco Project for each of the fourteen supervision hours reported in full detail in Chapter V. The kind of thing that can then be derived from this schematic categorization in inferences and conclusions concerning the issues and problems of teaching and learning by way of supervision is demonstrated by example in Chapter VIII.

SUPERVISION HOUR 1 (ANALYTIC HOURS 1–3)

1. *The Analysis*

The patient started in analysis, on the couch during the first hour. The patient stated that she certainly had problems but that perhaps they were not too bad. She alluded to the fact that she expected she would have difficulty in talking and expressing herself. She had always wanted a "captive audience" (part of her interest in teaching as a career) but now that she had one, she could not seem to use it. When the analyst said that he would be away for three days the very next week, the patient countered with her plan for a brief Christmas vacation, to which the analyst's response was that she would be charged.

The patient's associations jumped around a bit and seemed unimportant to her, but the material was about her life, and there was a consistent flow to it. Over the several hours she dressed more attractively (and seductively) each time. She used every opportunity to look at the analyst as much as possible. She remarked that she liked seeing a piece of sculpture (mother and child motif) on the analyst's shelf. She would like to have a child of her own, but never permitted herself to get into a situation in which she could have one. She talked of her current affair and of her concern that the analyst would not approve of her wish to have a child.

2. *The Analyst's Understanding of the Analytic Material*

The analyst promptly took an expectant, neutral, "inactive" stance. He evinced no special effort to formulate the initial material into an overall conceptual framework. He thought the patient's intense visual fixation on him expressed her apprehensions concerning his initial reactions to her.

3. *The Analyst's Activity*

The analyst stressed his "inactivity," that he was observing, "just listening." When he did comment it was for the most part in neutral requests for clarification. He explained the nature of the analytic situation to the patient well enough (according to the supervisor), without too much detail, and allowed the patient to struggle a bit with the request for associations. Right after the patient commented on her pleasure in at last having a "captive audience," the analyst responded with his announcement that he would be gone for three hours the very next week (no captive he).

4a. *The Supervisor's Understanding of the Technical Analytic Issues*

The supervisor felt that the analysis was off to a satisfactory start and the supervisory situation was a comfortable one. He felt that for the most part they had a shared understanding of the initial analytic material. He wondered whether the analyst did not feel overly constrained perhaps in responding to the patient. But all in all, he felt that the analyst was handling things pretty well, and that not much was needed in the way of technical advice.

4b. *The Supervisor's Pedagogic Interventions*

With regard to the analyst's stress on his analytic "inactivity," the supervisor wondered whether the analyst had been told to keep quiet during the initial phases of analytic work. The analyst said, "Well, not exactly but perhaps." He knew that his own tendency in psychotherapy was to be rather too active, to jump into things as soon as he saw them, and he was self-consciously trying to hold this tendency in check. The supervisor agreed that the avoidance of premature interventions would facilitate the deeper regression being sought in psychoanalytic as contrasted with psychotherapeutic work. The supervisor did point out other possible meanings in the patient's intent gazing at the analyst (trying to hold on to him as much as possible), and pointed too to the hint of transference manifestations in the patient's pleasure with the mother-child sculpture on the analyst's shelf.

5a. *The Supervisor's Understanding of the Analyst's Personal Involvement*

The one issue that could be potentially discerned here centered on the analyst's announcement of his pending three-day absence in response to the patient's stated pleasure in at last having a "captive audience" and then his further (punitive?) response that she would be charged when the patient countered the analyst's announcement with her own plan for a Christmas holiday.

5b. *The Supervisor's Therapeutic Interventions*

The supervisor wondered whether the analyst had counterreacted unconsciously to being described as captive. There is no mention of the analyst's response to this query.

6. *The Analyst's Response to the Supervisory Hour*

The climate was a cooperative one between colleagues with a shared understanding of the case.

SUPERVISION HOUR 2 (ANALYTIC HOURS 4–12)

1. *The Analysis*

The patient "forgot" to come to the very next hour after being told of the analyst's planned three-day absence the following week, by coming at a time different from that of her appointment. She brought a considerable amount of dream material to these analytic hours. The most emphasized was a dream of a large black cat coming at her with claws outstretched. Her associations were to cats of her childhood, cats she loved but that died, a mother cat leaving kittens behind that also died. The patient has avoided cats ever since. From the total material, one could discern that the patient has come to see in her life that she does things she does not understand and gets into "messes." Even though she knows that what she is going to do will cause her trouble, she does it anyway. It was this realization that had brought her to treatment. Having begun treatment, she felt that things were a little better.

There were other dreams reported as well: a dream from the past of a sandman made of wet sand growing alternately big and little; another dream from the past of screaming in fright for her mother (after learning that mother was in a hospital for alcoholism); a nightmarish dream of an old-fashioned, spooky apartment in which the terrified patient could see someone's shoulders and hands, pointing to a wedding ring which was on the wrong hand. Associations were to a wish for mother's large diamond ring and the horrible thought that she harbored a death wish.

There was talk too of the risks and the sense of helplessness in life, of the fear of becoming dependent on the analyst and the dangers and messes one can get into out of dependency. The patient presented also a picture of a rather disorderly current life, marked by casual affairs.

2. *The Analyst's Understanding of the Analytic Material*

The analyst wanted the supervisor to focus in detail on the hour with the black cat dream and its associations, and presented process notes of that hour that occupied three and a fraction single-spaced pages. The analyst saw the link between the patient's expression of helplessness in her life and her fear of becoming unduly dependent on him. He felt that the patient saw him at this point as a "nice guy" who would tend to "give her too much" and thus make her feel helpless.

3. *The Analyst's Activity*

Nothing of special note in this category. The general analytic stance was unaltered from the previously described material of the initial week.

4a. *The Supervisor's Understanding of the Technical Analytic Issues*

The supervisor felt that the analyst was handling the beginning phase of the analytic work pretty well. The patient seemed analyzable, and the flow of material had a proper analytic ring to it. There seemed one important exception however—there was no indication of the patient having any expectation of the analyst. With regard to the patient's disorderly current life, the supervisor felt this to be at least partly motivated by a wish to master her dependency strivings through casual sexual relationships.

4b. *The Supervisor's Pedagogic Interventions*

The supervisor developed his views of the possible meaning of the patient's disorderly life style in discussion with the analyst. He made a number of minor technical suggestions, mostly about asking unnecessary questions, pointing to at least one instance where he communicated a proper understanding in question-form. He made a suggestion that the process notes of the analytic hours be shorter—perhaps a maximum of a single page (single-spaced) per hour. There was no noted response to this request.

5a. *The Supervisor's Understanding of the Analyst's Personal Involvement*

Nothing recorded relevant to this category.

5b. *The Supervisor's Therapeutic Interventions*

Nothing recorded relevant to this category.

6. *The Analyst's Response to the Supervision Hour*

The climate and nature of the supervisory interaction (interventions and responses) continued as stated for the previous session, a cooperative venture between colleagues with a shared understanding of the case.

SUPERVISION HOUR 3 (ANALYTIC HOURS 13–15)

1. *The Analysis*

The patient had taken her Christmas holiday and had visited with her parents in another city. She was preoccupied with her relationship with her fiancé whom she could neither marry nor relinquish. She alluded to her distrust of psychiatrists and psychologists. While she made no direct reference to the treatment process, there was a good bit of metaphoric communication about her difficulty in getting together with people and increased reference to her reservations with respect to the treatment she had gotten herself into. It turned out that she had had an affair with one of the local psychiatrists and had good reason to believe that they were no better than other men; her brother-in-law was a psychologist who behaved most peculiarly; and a good look at her sister's marriage convinced her that the demands of marriage were not for her.

Despite all this the patient was unaccountably feeling better. She felt she was getting somewhere in treatment, though she had no idea how the treatment was working. Nonetheless, she welcomed the change. In her attitude toward sexuality, she expressed herself as a "liberated" woman who could take sexual activity where she found it. But missing was any evidence of emotional investment in people or any mention of pleasure (it was known she had a problem of frigidity). She was vague about her sexual life with her fiancé and said she was "panicked" at the idea of marriage or any kind of enforced intimacy with him.

2. *The Analyst's Understanding of the Analytic Material*

The analyst in his own conceptualization comprehensively drew together the various expressions of distrust and reservation concerning analysis and professional people, and the complex (attracting but repelling) relationship with her fiancé. It was clear that the patient was a "liberated" woman, who nonetheless had sexual difficulties with her fiancé and anxiety attacks about staying with him.

3. *The Analyst's Activity*

Again there was mention of the analyst's continuing conservative approach, of his limiting interventions, for the most part, to occasional questions for clarification and comments on what the patient was or was not talking about. During the middle of the week, he notified the patient that he would once more be away for two analytic hours in the immediate future.

4a. *The Supervisor's Understanding of the Technical Analytic Issues*

The supervisor was impressed by the evidence of increasing anxiety in the patient (the "panicky feelings" over her sexual behaviors) even as she stated she was feeling better. He felt too that the patient's expressed distrust of treatment and analysts might be fueled by the analyst's absences ("unreliable"). He felt that the patient was saying that, yes, she had come to treatment because of her desire to be married coupled with an inability to be so, but perhaps it might be a better idea to give up her plans for marriage, and thereby her need for treatment.

4b. *The Supervisor's Pedagogic Interventions*

The supervisor asked the analyst to summarize, not to read his overly detailed process notes, though later in the hour, the supervisor himself read them through. In relation to the overall analytic events, the supervisor offered the interpretation that the patient's professed distrust might be a defensive move against positive feelings for the analyst which might be more frightening to her. The supervisor again thought that the analyst was handling things quite well; he made a few suggestions about how the analyst's comments could be phrased to educate the patient a bit more about what is useful in the analytic process. The supervisor felt the patient could use perhaps a little less intervening than the analyst was applying. The supervisor noted too the patient's increasingly long pauses, which the analyst was inclined to break up by picking up the last topic mentioned rather than wondering about the silence itself.

5a. *The Supervisor's Understanding of the Analyst's Personal Involvement*

The supervisor was uneasy about the number of interruptions just at the beginning of this treatment. But since the analyst himself seemed aware of this, the supervisor refrained from further comments on the undesirable consequences of such interruptions.

5b. *The Supervisor's Therapeutic Interventions*

The supervisor tried most gently to deal with the issue posed by the analyst's absences in more didactic terms, in anticipating what the patient's responses might be, the likely ways that transference responses could manifest themselves, etc.

6. *The Analyst's Response to the Supervision Hour*

The analyst responded readily to the supervisory request that he lay aside his detailed process notes and rather present an overview of the analytic situation; later in the hour, however, for clarification, the supervisor read through the notes.

SUPERVISION HOUR 4 (ANALYTIC HOURS 16–18)

1. *The Analysis*

The analytic hours were marked by a pattern of increasing silences and withholding during this period. The material showed the following themes: The patient was thinking of moving and taking a roommate. She characteristically made choices that turned out badly. She mentioned many people she knew in treatment who also turned out badly. She had read things about the efficacy of will power, but did not think it would work for her. She came for her hour on one of the days the analyst was gone and, only on being informed by his secretary, did she remember being told of this absence. She made no mention of this happening when she came to her next scheduled hour.

The patient talked about people who do not take care of themselves properly, a boss who goes around unkempt, with holes in his shoes. She recalled a month she had spent with her father when they both attended college at the same time; they had enjoyed each other's company in mother's absence. She was attracted once to a bartender at an officer's club, but was later disappointed and disillusioned when she met him under other circumstances. Mostly, she was coming to realize how difficult it was to talk about herself and how difficult psychoanalysis really was. She remarked on how difficult it was to stop smoking or to stop eating too much. The patient then surprised the analyst by a statement that an agency would be paying part of her analytic bill and that she felt indebted to them. She returned to the difficulty in talking, and related it to problems with people in authority, but she did not connect this with her relationship with the analyst. She just didn't know how she would obtain help if she couldn't bring herself to talk about what was on her mind. She compared this situation with that with her father. Though he was warm and rather open, she found it difficult to talk with him.

2. *The Analyst's Understanding of the Analytic Material*

The analyst expressed himself as being encouraged that the patient was psychologically minded to a greater extent than he had thought, more reflective (commenting spontaneously on her difficulty in saying everything that came to mind), had made her own first transference interpretation, etc. He wondered how much she was taken aback at her own parapraxis in coming to the cancelled hour, thus finding that things slipped through more openly than she was yet comfortable with. He felt that the patient was concerned (like the analyst *and* the supervisor) that she was not saying everything that came to her mind.

3. *The Analyst's Activity*

The analyst felt that he intervened inopportunely and probably too brusquely out of his surprise at the patient's revelation that she had a third party probably paying part of her analytic expense (though the precise nature of his intervention was not specified), and counted this an "error" against himself.

4a. *The Supervisor's Understanding of the Technical Analytic Issues*

The supervisor saw in the patient's talking about all the difficulties in her life (with speaking freely, with curbing her smoking and her overeating) a barely disguised plea for help. He saw, too, in the silences and in the remonstrances toward herself for not saying everything, a strong hint that the analytic "authority" should enforce the basic rule.

4b. *The Supervisor's Pedagogic Interventions*

The supervisor indicated that the analysis seemed to be moving in the proper way, considering the interruptions, even though it was clear that the patient was not saying everything that came to her mind. The analyst was surprised when the supervisor called his attention to the pattern of lengthening silences in the analytic hours—a growing awareness by the patient of her relationship to the analyst and an increase of her resistances? The supervisor sketched out a plausible evolving transference paradigm—the patient's fear of dependency countered by her relating to the analyst as an authority with whom she found it difficult to talk. He pointed out to the analyst the invitation from the patient for the analyst to counteract in the transference (*enforce* the basic rule). He also pointed out how worried the patient was about not saying everything that came to her mind and indicated ways of facilitating communication without getting into an authoritarian position with the patient. He showed the analyst how he could simplify his interventions, make observations as observations rather than as questions, etc.

5a. *The Supervisor's Understanding of the Analyst's Personal Involvement*

The supervisor noted that the analyst was overly meticulous in his handling of the beginning phases of this treatment, and seemed so overconcerned with the possibility of making mistakes (perhaps, some displacement of guilt feelings for his absences?). He felt, too, that the analyst's appearance perhaps left something to be desired, at times not neatly enough groomed (and wondered if there was perhaps some implicit reference to the analyst as some other person the patient was sorry for—like the boss who was unkempt and had holes in his shoes).

5b. *The Supervisor's Therapeutic Interventions*

The supervisor's expressed concern to show how the patient's transference (to create an authority to resist) could exert a pull on the analyst to counteract was stressed because the supervisor feared the analyst might find this a pitfall.

6. *The Analyst's Response to the Supervision Hour*

The analyst and supervisor jointly took note that the patient's preoccupation with her casual affairs had dropped away, that her boy friend had seemed to come in and then out of the picture, and that her attention was starting to turn in the direction of the analyst and also her father.

SUPERVISION HOUR 5 (ANALYTIC HOURS 19–22)

1. *The Analysis*

The patient called in sick one day and made no reference to this when she came the next day. The very next hour she wore an out-of-place summery dress, though it was one of the coldest days of the year, but made no mention of this either. And again the next hour, the patient called in to say she would be late, she could not get her car started. The analyst took the call himself, and the patient identified herself by the diminutive of her name. When she came, there was no mention of this, except when the patient left that hour, remarking, "Well, I still have to get my car started."

In the week's material the patient's relationship with her fiancé came more to the fore. She was distressed that she felt unable to stay with him *or* to leave him. She spoke about her parent's fierce quarrels where her sympathies all lay with the father; the mother treated him shabbily and talked often of divorce. The patient was shocked when she came upon her father driven to reactive violence (choking the mother on the living-room couch). With her fiancé, whenever the patient tried to have intercourse, she would be stiff and he would be furious at her unresponsiveness. Once he walked out on her and then came back. He would also cry as a way to win her back. They finally decided to give up trying to have intercourse; the last time the patient was totally unwilling and, when her fiancé persisted, she became hysterical. She recalled her first meeting with her fiancé. She could get no sympathy from him; he had seemed so objective at a time when she so badly needed somebody to be on her side against the world. At the end of that hour, the patient left the couch with a smile, making the remark about still needing to get her car started.

The patient talked of her older sister who was more of a mother to her than her mother. The sister was compulsive and ritualistic with her. The patient recalled a childhood memory of once getting so angry at her sister that she ran downstairs and kicked her in the stomach. Linked to this were dream references to stairs, hints of pregnancy fantasies, and ideas of being damaged in intercourse.

2. *The Analyst's Understanding of the Analytic Material*

The analyst was searching in the material of the tension, and the violence between the parents, for the clues to the patient's difficulties with her fiancé. He saw the patient as revealing more clearly her identification with her mother (the shock at the violence visited on mother, the several dreams in which she clothed herself in mother's dresses, etc.). He felt the patient was getting more under stress.

3. *The Analyst's Activity*

The analyst made the link between the patient's relationship with her fiancé and many episodes between her parents during her teens, in one of which, the father, usually long-suffering in the face of mother's excessive drinking and extravagant spending, was driven to the violent attack upon mother.

4a. *The Supervisor's Understanding of the Technical Analytic Issues*

The supervisor was most impressed by the "even way" in which the patient told her story. The patient talked about the most distressing events in a way that did not invite the analyst to be sympathetic or to help, or anything else. The supervisor felt there was very little "demand" quality in the patient's speech. She allowed herself to expect very little of the analysis, "putting up" with the relationship, including the problem of getting there when her car would not start, without any complaint. Despite these concerns, the supervisor felt the analyst was, for the most part, continuing to handle the analysis in a technically adequate manner.

4b. *The Supervisor's Pedagogic Interventions*

The supervisor offered the view that the patient's memory of the violent assault by her father upon her mother contained characteristics of a screen memory relating possibly to primal-scene material. He also brought to the analyst's attention all his concerns about the nature of the patient's attitude toward, and lack of expectations of, the analysis. He compared this to qualities the patient had described in her father, who was often not there when she very much needed him. He wondered whether the patient was projecting a father image upon the analyst and then identifying with this *father* in what she would fantasy as his objectivity toward her problems. It was as if, in this sense, there were no patient here, in that both the analyst and the patient could be construed as not having much empathy for the patient's lack of demandingness, her apparent willingness to just "put up" with the analysis.

5a. *The Supervisor's Understanding of the Analyst's Personal Involvement*

The supervisor wondered to what extent the analyst might be contributing to the patient's transference development (no expectation, objective distance, etc.), or, counteractively, be falling into the counterpart role.

5b. *The Supervisor's Therapeutic Interventions*

The supervisor raised the potential transference-countertransference issue underlying the observed behaviors (no expectation, objective distance) by asking (in addition to the question of the *patient's* projections, and *her* identifications) whether there was anything in the analyst's behavior and attitude, in his efforts to be analytically correct, that overstressed his "objectivity" to the point of seeming to convey indifference. Here, too, the supervisor's concern was relevant. For the patient, it was as if there were no patient present, insofar as neither she nor, in her perceptions, the analyst appeared to have much empathy for her actual distress.

6. *The Analyst's Response to the Supervision Hour*

The analyst saw the character and resistance problems of the patient, as delineated by the supervisor. The analyst and the supervisor disagreed on the assessment of the patient's most salient identifications: the analyst saw primarily the identification with the mother; the supervisor was more impressed by the identification with the father.

SUPERVISION HOUR 6 (ANALYTIC HOURS 23–25)

1. *The Analysis*

Through this period the patient was trying to be sexually continent and to get back with her fiancé, although she had a feeling this "won't work." She can sleep with him, but not have intercourse, can dream of intercourse with him while lying next to him. She hinted at one point that it is when things did not work out sexually with her fiancé that she felt driven to go to bed with someone else. During the week, the patient again missed an hour and, characteristically, did not mention this spontaneously when she came the following hour. When this was discussed with her, she blandly denied any idea that the absence was in some way motivated and related to the analysis.

The week's material began with the patient's expressed discomfort with her job, which then focused around an older man whom she admired tremendously, but with whom she had difficulty talking. She linked this to difficulties with the analyst and wondered if it was part of a problem with men in authority in general. She stated, as a kind of confession, that what was getting in the way of her talking to this man were some sexual feelings she experienced toward him and, in a worried way, wondered if perhaps that was what was also interfering with her ability to talk to the analyst (also an older "vital" man). She alluded to the same difficulties with her father and then trailed off to the end of the hour.

It was the next hour that the patient missed, and in the following hour her mood was depressed; nothing was going to turn out right for her, etc. On one occasion, the patient suddenly sat up, stretched herself before lying back on the couch, and attributed this to a crick in her back. On another occasion she was wringing her hands in obvious tension, though making no verbal reference to it. In the last hour of the week a sequence of dreams was reported, ranging from one of being attracted to a lifeguard at a swimming pool, with whom she went off on a trolley ride, to one in which tonsillectomies were about to be performed on her and others without anesthesia. The patient associated her own tonsillectomy at age four, when her older sister, who did not really need one, was also made to have the operation. The sister suffered more postoperatively, and once the patient wheedled some of the sister's food away and ate it, which the sister then regretted. The sister "never let the patient forget this."

2. *The Analyst's Understanding of the Analytic Material*

The analyst comprehensively linked in his own mind the many "difficulties" the patient presented during the week: the difficulty in arranging to be at all her hours, the difficulty in working out satisfactory relationships with men, troubles with men in authority, in the office, and in the analysis. He felt, in fact, that the patient was reaching for these same connections, but "too fast" (and he tried at one point to dampen this interpretive effort by the patient in a way that seemed somewhat "bookish" to the supervisor).

3. *The Analyst's Activity*

The analyst took up the patient's missing an hour (which she would have tried to pass over). She put it down to a misunderstanding and to her tendency not to be definite enough in discussing arrangements, for instance, that she was not going to be able to come for that hour. The analyst tried to link the patient's various unsatisfactory sexual arrangements to this pattern of not being able to work out satisfactory, mutually understood arrangements with men.

4a. *The Supervisor's Understanding of the Technical Analytic Issues*

The supervisor discerned the development of a resistance pattern (based on the way the patient presented material), in which the patient would attempt to master problems as fast as she saw them as a way of aborting her involvement with the analyst over them. The supervisor also felt the resistance aspect in the patient's writing off the missing of the hour as only a "technical failure" in not having made herself clear. He noted a tendency in the analyst to relate only to what the patient was saying, and not enough to what she was showing behaviorally (the evident distressed affect—the episode of wringing her hands).

4b. *The Supervisor's Pedagogic Interventions*

The supervisor discussed the discerned resistance pattern (that of "solving problems" in order to minimize involvement with the analyst about them) with the analyst. He inquired for clarification as to whether or not there had ever been a satisfactory sexual life between the patient and her fiancé. The analyst's reply was speculative, making assumptions to fill in the gaps in the patient's account. The supervisor warned about this tendency. He pointed to the patient's overall pattern of being "general" in her accounting; perhaps she and the analyst were falling into jointly acting as if the patient had been more specific. The supervisor pointed out that this could be the content of a resistance interpretation, cautioning at the same time against simply accommodating to this style of communication.

The supervisor added to the analyst's efforts to link together various facets of the presenting material. He drew a connection between the threatening emergence of troubling sexual thoughts toward the analyst, the immediately following missed hour, and the subsequent depressed, useless feeling. The supervisor also pointed out how the analyst did not always make use of all the material that was available, tending to pay attention only to what he heard (the patient's verbalizations), and not enough to what he saw (the distressed behaviors—hand-wringing). All in all, however, the supervisor conveyed that the overall trend of the hours seemed to be moving properly from events in the patient's life on the outside to the way things were in the hour, with the implication that, if these two could be connected, the patient's associations would then naturally turn to her past.

5a. *The Supervisor's Understanding of the Analyst's Personal Involvement*

In connection with the discussion with the analyst of the latter's concern that at one point the patient was moving "too fast" in making connections, the analyst revealed his own fantasy of feeling like the Wizard of Oz and his concern that it was "too soon" for the patient to see the mechanics of how the Wizard's illusions were created. The supervisor's concern here was that if something was moving "too fast" in the analysis, it was more likely too fast for the analyst than for the patient.

5b. *The Supervisor's Therapeutic Interventions*

The supervisor discussed the issue of "too fast" and the accompanying Wizard of Oz fantasy from the standpoint of the implication that psychoanalysis is a very fragile thing, that if the patient would "see how it works" she would become immune to the magic (hence, perhaps, the analyst's studied efforts to be so delicate in the handling of the case). The supervisor conveyed his own view that psychoanalysis is a natural process and, for the most part, quite a sturdy one. He then said that evidently the analyst's concern was that the patient might be going too fast for him.

6. *The Analyst's Response to the Supervision Hour*

The pattern has been established that the analyst brings very detailed process notes of his analytic hours, but that he makes an oral presentation of the week's material without reference to his notes; on some occasions during the course of the supervision hour, the supervisor would turn to them for particular study.

The analyst confirmed the supervisor's picture of the resistance pattern of "overgeneralization." He remembered the patient's story from her schooldays of overhearing her teacher talking about a pupil who always wrote her papers as if the teacher knew all the things she was writing about, without her having to explain them specifically. With regard to the supervisor's injunction to pay attention to behavioral as well as verbal material, the analyst indicated he had never really tried to use such material (what he saw as opposed to what he heard), but that he got the idea of what the supervisor was trying to convey.

SUPERVISION HOUR 7 (ANALYTIC HOURS 26–31)

1. *The Analysis*

The patient had never discussed in detail what her sexual life with her (now called ex-) fiancé was like. It seemed that it was satisfactory enough in the beginning, but, as he continued to press, it became increasingly distasteful to her, and grew to be a fight between them. At about this time, their pattern of breaking up and getting together was resumed. With regard to such matters, the patient acknowledged she could often talk more freely with her friends (with whom she felt she knew where she stood) than with the analyst. With him she felt that, if she permitted herself to talk freely, she might become overly attached to him.

The patient talked about her many childhood moves, with her father assigned from one post to another. She felt she was the one who suffered the most in the family from the incessant moving around. After a while, she refused to make any attachments at all. She felt that her father was always uncomfortable around her and had difficulty talking with her. She recalled his anxiety when he once jumped to the conclusion that she might be pregnant, at a time when she was still totally inhibited and prudish in her sexual behavior. Again she came back to the dejection and loneliness with the childhood experiences of being shifted from place to place. She followed this with an off-hand account of how she provoked the breakup of the casual affair she had had during her ex-fiancé's absence and had now gone back to him. He seemed to be aware that she had transient affairs with other men during his absences, but did not make a fuss about this.

More details about the patient's childhood emerged. She suffered "mild tuberculosis" from the ages of four to six and had been confined to home a lot. Once, when the patient was three, her mother had been forced to tie a rope around her ankle to keep her from running off. She was a bedwetter until five, and a thumbsucker till six. At around twelve or thirteen she had a problem with her weight, thought she was fat and ugly, and avoided going to the swimming pool with the rest of the family.

2. *The Analyst's Understanding of the Analytic Material*

The analyst felt that a special transference position was developing. The patient cried for the first time in an hour (when she talked about her fear of getting too attached to the analyst if she permitted herself to confide too freely), and she showed more difficulty in talking. The analyst also felt that the patient was afraid he might become seductive or too interested in her and not be able to fully control himself if she should "let herself go."

3. *The Analyst's Activity*

The analyst called the patient's attention to the apparent ease with which she talked about intimate subjects (her sexual difficulties with her ex-fiancé) with un-named old friends, compared with the obvious difficulty she was having talking about these things with him. He pointed out the very casual, once-over-lightly way in which the patient confessed her very cavalier treatment of her interim lover, and the patient responded with her awareness that this was a "defensive attitude." Most important, the analyst firmly linked the patient's reluctance to talk about her sexual behavior with her fear of attachment to him; the patient concurred and followed by talking about the way her father had always seemed reluctant to become involved with her.

4a. *The Supervisor's Understanding of the Technical Analytic Issues*

The supervisor, in reviewing after the hour the notes the analyst had left with him, noted that the sequence of material, as reported verbally in the supervision hour, was not always the same as recorded in the notes, but the supervisor felt that things had seemed coherent enough as they had been presented. In fact, as he and the analyst had talked together about what had been done with the patient, the analyst's interventions had seemed to the point, tactful, and adequately sensitive. The analyst had indeed been able, as needed, to integrate what the patient was feeling at a given moment with the sequence of her thoughts and, by putting these together, was able to help her over some anxious moments when she was stuck.

4b. *The Supervisor's Pedagogic Interventions*

Regarding the analyst's concern that the patient would see him as unable to control himself should she "let herself go" in the analysis, the supervisor said it sounded as if the patient feared the analyst might mistake her interest or sense of attachment to him and would sexualize this (projection). In such a predicament, the patient would indeed feel stuck, not wanting to hurt him nor to lose out on the opportunity for help. Mostly, the supervisor was more passively expectant, waiting to see what use the analyst was making of the more active teaching of the preceding supervisory hours.

5a. *The Supervisor's Understanding of the Analyst's Personal Involvement*

Nothing recorded relevant to this category.

5b. *The Supervisor's Therapeutic Interventions*

Nothing recorded relevant to this category.

6. *The Analyst's Response to the Supervision Hour*

About half the available time was spent on some of the analyst's administrative concerns ("a combined request and protest") regarding his research activities before switching to talk about the analytic material. Again, the analyst (as per their understanding) presented the material extemporaneously, with only an occasional glance at the notes, which he then left behind for the supervisor after the hour. Regarding the issue of the patient's fears of the analyst's potential sexualized interest in her, the analyst agreed that the supervisor's formulation seemed a more precise version of how the patient probably saw the problem at the moment.

SUPERVISION HOUR 8 (ANALYTIC HOURS 32–36)

1. *The Analysis*

The patient came fifteen minutes late one hour and made no comment about this. In response to the analyst's inquiry, she said she did not like to explain (and excuse) these kinds of things; it was a matter of pride—or pigheadedness. In connection with her birthday, and people's gifts and congratulations, the patient indicated she felt very uncomfortable about being important to others. She contrasted her ease in talking with other people to her difficulties in talking with the analyst, and accepted the transference interpretation concerning her social difficulties with men to whom she felt sexually attracted. She was upset at this (obvious) interpretation of the erotic element in her feelings about the analyst, saying that if it was true for her analyst, it could also be true for her father and then stating, with much show of anxiety with hand-wringing, that she "couldn't deny it was true." She came at a wrong time one day (11:30 a.m. instead of 3:00 p.m.), but made no comment about this in her hour.

The patient spent that weekend without her fiancé, anxious and alone. She called her black ex-lover (to his surprise), and she flirted dangerously with another black friend (a mutual friend), but this was not sexually consummated. She was homesick for her parents, this being the time of their thirty-fifth wedding anniversary. She was touched by a gift they had recently sent her. She felt confused in the relationship with her ex-fiancé, peculiarly ambivalent toward him, unable to be comfortable with him or away from him. She longed for him when he was away and had to be able to reach him, but was also glad when he left and she could be free to have other sexual contacts. She recalled how panic-stricken she was with his formal proposal of marriage. Her parents approved of him, but she could not go through with it, and finally told him she would have to get herself into psychiatric treatment over this.

2. *The Analyst's Understanding of the Analytic Material*

The analyst was impressed that the patient was identifying with him (as, for example, in her recounting of her "therapeutic" dealings with a would-be suitor) and that this was a defense against her burgeoning awareness of the eroticized father transference. He felt a great need to make something of this interpretively. He was aware, too, that his transference interpretation had shaken the patient, and also that there was something not wholly appropriate (his "countertransference") in the way he rather sharply brought the patient back to his concept of where they were supposed to be right now, rather than letting her drift into developing associated images and memories linking to related adolescent fantasies.

3. *The Analyst's Activity*

The analyst felt he had done a number of things that were not too good during the week, although he did not specify what they were. He took up the patient's silence about her lateness very directly. He congratulated her on her birthday. He made an effective transference interpretation proceeding from the patient's difficulties in talking about unpleasant things, but also about pleasing things, to her special difficulties in talking with men to whom she was sexually attracted, which readily linked to both him and her father. Afterward (in the next hour) he felt he was unduly sharp with the patient when he cut off her flow of developing memory images (into adolescent experiences) in order to bring her back to their central theme (as he saw it), because he felt she was defensively identifying with him in his therapeutic role and he had to "go after this defense of identification." He followed this tack with a rather talky and intellectualized interpretation, pointing out the ways in which he felt the patient was identifying herself with him. His further activity in the hours was of a piece with these deflecting tactics, and in discussing it with the supervisor, he used such phrases as acting like a traffic cop, rubbing the patient's nose in it, slapping her wrist, etc.

4a. *The Supervisor's Understanding of the Technical Analytic Issues*

The supervisor felt that the analyst had indeed made an appropriate transference interpretation and linkage between erotic attraction, men, himself, and father. This triggered a flow of nostalgically tinged memories from adolescence. But then the analyst had had to "bring the patient back" too sharply when he thought she was wandering from the point. The analyst's rationale was to go after the patient's "defensive identification" with him. Actually, the supervisor felt it to be an expression of the analyst's desire to control things so as not to let his countertransference slip again (the birthday congratulations earlier in the week). But the effect of his "bringing the patient back" was to block his own efforts and abort the patient's unfolding response to his transference interpretation. His intervention in its effect was a rebuke followed by an intellectualized summary.

4b. *The Supervisor's Pedagogic Interventions*

The supervisor questioned the analyst's rationale for his overly sharp confrontation and wrenching back (the need to tackle the "defensive identification"). He indicated his own understanding, that the patient had been much shaken by the interpretation and insight into the relation between her inability to talk to him and her feelings of sexual attraction; the analyst had subsequently deflected the material and, just when he might be reaping the benefits of his interpretation, had in effect aborted the very process he had started. The supervisor encouraged the analyst not to push the patient, but to give her a chance to react to his interpretations, and to be willing himself to follow her response.

5a. *The Supervisor's Understanding of the Analyst's Personal Involvement*

The supervisor had noted the analyst's congratulations on the patient's birthday (the initial countertransference slip), but had let it pass at the time since the analyst had indicated that he had something else on his mind that he especially wanted to discuss (although what it was was never made explicit). In the discussion of the effect of the analyst's blocking the patient's flow of associative responses to the interpretation, it seemed clear that the analyst had persisted in his stance with the patient and, during the supervision hour, himself suggested that his own difficulty with controlling his feeling of attraction to the patient might be at the root of his "traffic-coplike attitude." To the supervisor this seemed like something carefully thought out and, while plausible, seemed to reflect a willingness to call himself down and be self-critical which, in addition to its characterological roots, could also be a way of controlling the supervisor by anticipating (and thereby warding off) criticism.

5b. *The Supervisor's Therapeutic Interventions*

There was considerable discussion of the analyst's countertransference defensive needs (to ward off his own feeling of attraction) which might have played a role in the analyst's overly sharp confrontation and ostensible "bringing the patient back" to the subject, which actually blocked rather than furthered the associative response to the anxiety-arousing (both for patient and analyst) transference interpretation. But the supervisor saw this discussion also in its defensive meanings and did not enter into the possibility that the analyst's very self-criticalness might also be a way of disarming the supervisor's effectiveness. Instead, the supervisor rather gently tried to refocus the issue pedagogically in terms of the impact of the analyst's behavior on the patient, like the failure to think of the analyst as someone she could call when she was anxious, linking it to his previous thoughts about the absence of conscious expectation of the analyst. The supervisor was unsure as to whether he had done right in letting the birthday congratulation remark pass by (again, not from the standpoint of countertransference meanings, but of effect on the patient).

6. *The Analyst's Response to the Supervision Hour*

The analyst's responses were to accept the supervisor's viewpoint on the unanalytic impact of actions that served defensive rather than therapeutic needs. He berated himself for "acting like a traffic cop," "trying to rub her nose into it," "slapping her wrist," and he brought out his concern that this was his way of handling the sexual attraction that the patient, a good-looking woman, who stated in many ways that she was available, had for him. His remarks served to close the door on those thoughts and keep them both "down to business." In all of this the supervisor suspected that the analyst was going further than need be in showing the depth of this propensity, carrying it, furthermore, into the kind of *mea culpa* position that could serve to protect him from the supervisor.

SUPERVISION HOUR 9 (ANALYTIC HOURS 37–41)

1. *The Analysis*

In connection with a dream representing her father's erotic interest in her and mother's anger over that, the patient had many associations to her difficulties in having a wholesome, enjoyable relationship with her father, memories of her father drunk, and the mother's reaction to her own menopause with admonitions to the patient and her sister to go around the house more covered up than had been their wont. This developed into transference themes, the patient's reluctance to confess critical thoughts of the analyst lest she appear ungrateful, concerns about excessive dependency versus autonomy and independence, the issue of being involved with the analyst (wooing him) versus trying to put some distance between herself and him, and reservations about coming to the analysis—reluctance to find out more about herself, with an awareness of sexual feelings that were coming up that would be hard to take. She was at the same time reunited with her ex-fiancé, but with a desultory, troubled sexual life and discomfort especially over love play. She felt burdened by a sense of obligation to the ex-fiancé, which he found ridiculous.

After an interpretation of how the patient always felt that she let men down, she "got off the hook of the transference," bringing up many nostalgic associations to pleasant childhood memories, all suffused by the feelings of how irretrievably gone those idyllic states were.

2. *The Analyst's Understanding of the Analytic Material*

The analyst (in a somewhat stilted way) tried to distinguish feminine and masculine stances in the patient on the basis of the posture she assumed on the couch and then to relate these to the themes of dependency (more feminine) versus independence (more masculine), wish for help versus wish for autonomy, etc. He saw also the struggle to woo him versus the need to distance herself, her inability to convey her affectionate transference feelings and her defensive wondering whether she should come at all. He also noted her efforts to identify with him as the helper, and her guilt feelings about letting people down.

3. *The Analyst's Activity*

The analyst felt he had handled the patient's dream somewhat ineptly, that he had been too "intrusive" in bringing the patient back to try to associate to the dream text, which deflected her from the pursuit of many day-residue-linked fantasies. He was pulling for an explicit acknowledgment by the patient of the erotic tugs in the transference. He also very aggressively pursued "resistance interpretations," took up the ambivalences expressed in his conceptualization of the patient's analytic material (see 2, above), and pursued the interpretation of the patient's life behavior—that she worked to let men down, especially those with whom she was involved sexually.

4a. *The Supervisor's Understanding of the Technical Analytic Issues*

Nothing recorded relevant to this category beyond what is also covered in the next category, of understandings communicated to the analyst.

4b. *The Supervisor's Pedagogic Interventions*

The supervisor felt that the analyst's mode of "intrusiveness" in pursuing his interpretation could indeed artificially aggravate a beginning eroticized transference. He also indicated that the analyst's readiness to bring the patient back to the topic could be experienced by the patient as "too much guidance" (just like her family). He felt the analyst was too aggressive in the pursuit of "defense interpretations"; they were not needed so often. In fact, the analysis in general seemed to be moving along pretty well, and the analyst did not have to intervene as much as he did. The supervisor also indicated how concerned the patient was about the unrealistic nature of some of her feelings and how the analyst's comments might put her on edge rather than facilitate verbalization.

5a. *The Supervisor's Understanding of the Analyst's Personal Involvement*

The supervisor was concerned about a perfectionistic streak he felt he detected in the analyst, reflected, for example, in the way the analyst kept insistently returning to berate himself for his "error" of undue "intrusiveness." (Or perhaps this was a way of warding off expected or feared criticism from the supervisor?)

5b. *The Supervisor's Therapeutic Interventions*

The supervisor showed the analyst how his aggressiveness with defense interpretation could help control his countertransference feelings of attraction to the patient—a countertransference response to the patient's burgeoning erotic transference (the "wooing" of the analyst).

6. *The Analyst's Response to the Supervision Hour*

There was agreement between analyst and supervisor that things were going pretty well in the analysis, and the analyst, who was not inclined to be optimistic, felt pleased he had a "good patient."

SUPERVISION HOUR 10 (ANALYTIC HOURS 42–46)

1. *The Analysis*

The patient was more intensely occupied with her ex-fiancé, practically living with him. Their sexual relationship was still overtly troubled, neither seeming clearly to enjoy it. The patient was aware of a more complicated and mixed array of feelings in relation to him. In addition to her admiration, she was also irritated and jealous in regard to his "philistine tastes"—his materialistic orientation (and his greater life successes?). Her combined envy and disdain were expressed in her complaint about herself as an "unsuccessful philistine." When she was with her ex-fiancé she struggled with the impulse to cut loose and have affairs with others, though she was also resolved to curb such impulses and stick with him and work in her analysis.

With regard to her analysis, the patient was wondering critically whether she was reaching some kind of plateau, and just covering old ground in rehashing her feelings of not really being able to be close to her ex-fiancé. She talked about a very eligible friend who will not give the girls a tumble no matter how hard they try, dreamed reproachfully about her ex-fiancé doing wrong or bad things, and expressed a real loneliness for home and mother, though tempered by the feeling that her drunken father spoiled everything and that she would not want to share her mother's affections with him.

A good deal of analytic work was done with a very transparent oedipal dream (transparent to the analyst, that is). The patient associated to the note of aloneness and loneliness on which the dream ended; from that to the idea that it would be like death or suicide to get married; from that to an episode five years later where the patient experienced a dissociated state in which she came close to killing herself after a sexual relationship with a young Army officer (who actually saved her from the almost-suicide); and a final sequence of associations to an oedipal triangle on the job, with its dominant note of oedipal competition.

2. *The Analyst's Understanding of the Analytic Material*

With regard to the patient's description of her current life and her feelings about the analysis, the analyst felt that the patient was telling him she was giving up current gratifications in the hope of getting more than she had ever had before out of the analysis, while at the same time she was not at all convinced that it could or would work. He saw reproaches to himself in the statements about the eligible friend who would not give the girls a tumble.

3. *The Analyst's Activity*

The analyst worked particularly intensively with the long and very transparent oedipal dream the patient brought. She was not immediately aware of these significances; he worked interpretively with the associations along these lines.

4a. *The Supervisor's Understanding of the Technical Analytic Issues*

The analyst brought process notes of the week's analytic material amounting to nine single-spaced pages. He did not read them, but used them to refer to on occasion during the course of an extemporaneous presentation to the supervisor. He left the notes with the supervisor at the end of the session. The supervisor saw that the sequences in the notes often differed from those presented in the verbal account in the supervision. The verbal presentation had been more of an associative theme-linked synthetic account to the supervisor, but it had undoubtedly also skewed the picture somewhat for him. (These observations are more germane to the supervisor's effort to understand the mode of presentation of the analytic material within the supervision than to his understanding of the meanings of the analytic material itself.)

4b. *The Supervisor's Pedagogic Interventions*

The supervisor took up with the analyst his failure to inquire into the nature of the patient's specific difficulties; he had neither inquired into her specific sexual behaviors, nor the anomalous feeling tone with which she announced these experiences. The analyst tried to justify his reasons for this at some length. The supervisor sketched out for the analyst the pattern of transference and resistance that he detected, which he called the "homework theme"—the patient assigning herself the task of being a good girl, living an organized life, returning to her ex-fiancé as her "duty," all with the expectation that she would be rewarded by the analyst. The underlying question would be, "How long do I have to be good?" The supervisor saw all this as the beginning crystallization of the transference neurosis pattern. The supervisor and analyst discussed together the circumstances under which this would begin to be interpreted and to what extent. The supervisor noted things that could be picked up and conveyed to the patient which would have a facilitating rather than dampening effect on the development of the transference. The supervisor was concerned about a tacit contract that might be developing between patient and analyst, for the patient to express her sexual feelings elsewhere (with the ex-fiancé) and be a dutiful girl working in the analytic hour with the analyst.

5a. *The Supervisor's Understanding of the Analyst's Personal Involvement*

Nothing recorded relevant to this category beyond what is also covered in the next category, of understandings communicated to the analyst.

5b. *The Supervisor's Therapeutic Interventions*

The analyst at first interpreted the supervisor's suggestion that he concern himself with the manner in which the patient described her sexual experiences and their content as a pressure to intrude on the patient's "privacy," and he linked this concern to his reaction against possible voyeuristic tendencies in himself. The supervisor focused on aspects of the perfectionistic needs he saw in the analyst—the analysis seemed to be developing quite well with only miminal interventions necessary on the analyst's part, but there seemed to be an overriding need not just to adhere to sound technique, but to strive for an especial elegance. The supervisor then coupled this observation with the analyst's acknowledged attitude of intensified restraint (as a self-perceived reaction formation against any possible voyeuristic tendency in himself). The supervisor warned too of any temptation in the analyst to collude with the patient in her implicit contract (to keep her sexual impulses out of the analysis), which collusion he might be seduced into, as a protection for himself against unwanted erotic counterresponses.

6. *The Analyst's Response to the Supervision Hour*

The analyst seemed very receptive to the supervisor's concerns. He felt indeed that he might be struggling with voyeuristic tendencies of his own. He also compared his work here with that in his other case. There he was much too active, seduced by the patient into repetitive wrangles, feeling constantly challenged. Here he was, by contrast, succeeding in being more restrained. His difficulties with the other patient might be an additional factor contributing to his efforts at restraint with this patient. The analyst was also very interested in and responsive to the supervisor's overall formulation of the nature of the developing transference and resistance pattern.

SUPERVISION HOUR 11 (ANALYTIC HOURS 47–51)

1. *The Analysis*

The patient reported dreams she could not remember, linked somehow to one of her father kissing her in an unfatherly way. Maybe she did not want to remember her dreams; she was finding it hard indeed to be cooperative. In response to the analyst's interpretation of her feelings of disappointment and being on a plateau, the patient made excuses for the analyst: *he* was following the proper procedure for psychoanalysis; it was not his fault she could not free-associate. Then there were dreams indicating that her relationships with men were awry, and associations to unconsummated flirtations.

A main event of the week's material had to do with the weekend absence of the ex-fiancé to visit his parents. The patient was relieved that he was gone, and engineered a sexual adventure with someone she picked up at a party. She was tense until she could accomplish this and then felt "so good it almost hurt." But afterwards she couldn't sleep. She wondered why she relapsed into an old pattern. When her ex-fiancé returned with a thoughtful gift, she felt guilty. She associated to her one-time shame and embarrassment over her body. Now it felt nice to be complimented. She brought up a primal-scene memory and how revolted she was by the noise her parents made.

The patient dreamed of an old-fashioned key three quarters the height of the analyst's door, filled with crawling things (spiders) and also gold. She dreamed of a spider with a wedding ring around one of its legs. She wondered why she was not married to her ex-fiancé—they were married in all but name. When the analyst dealt with some aspects of this theme of sexuality and involvement, the patient at one point sat bolt upright, asking if the hour was close to over as she had to urinate urgently. It *was* just about over, and the patient fled to the bathroom.

2. *The Analyst's Understanding of the Analytic Material*

The analyst felt uneasy. He no longer had the sense of steady movement in the analysis. He could see a growing isolation between the patient's analytic hours and her life outside; she was forgetting her dreams and she said she even forgot the hours after she left. The analyst wondered whether he had become too interested in the dreams for their own sake and had let the thread of analysis slip. He discerned a transference pattern of teasing and not giving, with him as with the boy friend. He saw the dreams of the key and the door, the spider and the ring, as caricatures of aggressive, masculine sexual proclivities. He had failed during the hours with the patient to consider the patient's possible sense of loss over her ex-fiancé being away for the weekend.

3. *The Analyst's Activity*

The analyst worked interpretively with the patient's sense of disappointment, of being on a plateau, and also with her difficulties in getting involved with anybody with whom she had sexual gratifications.

4a. *The Supervisor's Understanding of the Technical Analytic Issues*

Nothing recorded relevant to this category beyond what is also covered in the next category, of understanding communicated to the analyst.

4b. *The Supervisor's Pedagogic Interventions*

The supervisor pointed out that the patient was letting both the analyst and herself off the hook. She was telling the analyst he was doing the right thing; she did not want him to change or do any more to help; she had no such expectation. Also, the way the patient was making the analysis into "work" was really antithetical to analyzing. He pointed to the transference situation that could be approached interpretively. There was a clearly uncomfortable train of thought of the patient's, her difficulty in cooperating with the analyst, her inability to remember most dreams, the dream of her father kissing her in an unfatherly way—all of these with discordant affects that could be made the center of intervention. In this connection the throwing of the rings in one of the dreams was likened to the "key game" people play—all transference elements in the patient's efforts to avoid becoming aware of the burgeoning involvement with the analyst. According to the supervisor, the focus of the patient's transference dilemma was her attempt to keep her analysis and her life outside apart, which only worked fitfully as they kept inevitably drifting closer together again. The analyst was not completely aware of all this; he had not fully appreciated the patient's sense of sexual arousal and concern to control it, which spilled through in the sudden urge to urinate.

5a. *The Supervisor's Understanding of the Analyst's Personal Involvement*

The supervisor felt that the analyst was clearly (consciously) disapproving of the patient's continued sexual acting out.

5b. *The Supervisor's Therapeutic Interventions*

The analyst reproached himself for having missed some of the themes (covered in 4b). "Why didn't I see that?" The supervisor asked: Why the self-reproaches? Was the analyst marking himself down for having erred (the supervisor having the perfectionistic striving in mind); or did the analyst want to look into why he might have missed these themes (the supervisor having in mind his feelings that the analyst's disapproving judgment concerning the patient's behavior perhaps was getting in his way)? The analyst replied he wanted to know why he had missed these themes, but he did not pursue this thought.

6. *The Analyst's Response to the Supervision Hour*

The analyst had taken up "fairly directly" with the patient what he and the supervisor had talked over in the preceding hour—the theme that the patient was doing her part, but what was the analyst doing. This turned out not to have been very effective.

SUPERVISION HOUR 12 (ANALYTIC HOURS 52–56)

1. *The Analysis*

The patient began the week by stating that her mother was having a D & C and would have to have a hysterectomy if a cancer was found, as suspected. She mentioned no feelings in connection with this, and never returned to the subject all week. Rather, she was preoccupied with her recent casual weekend romance (with an Air Force officer), which she could not shake. She talked of earlier life experiences when good appearances hid inner corruption. She talked about the Japanese, who were polite on the surface, but whose bitterness showed after you got to know them. She had learned a few phrases in Japan, just enough to get into trouble because people thought she knew the language. She came to an hour in little-girl clothes and associated to her childhood—the bad marriage of her parents and her own role as mother's confidante because, unlike the other children, she gave no advice (she had found out that people generally do what they want to do anyway).

The patient dwelt on her new affair, the partying with the officers, their drinking and acting like Casanovas. She just could not resist her growing involvement with this new boy friend, which was made the more possible to her, it turned out, because he was leaving soon for Viet Nam. She tried to tell her ex-fiancé about this new fellow, but found it difficult; he reassured her and urged her to go to sleep (just as she had tried to tell things to the analyst, with the same implication that she had not succeeded there either). The patient became growingly aware that she was willy-nilly getting more involved with the analyst, and redoubled her efforts to keep her distance. She turned down an Easter vacation visit with her parents because she was loath to miss the analytic hours. She asked the analyst to change an hour for her and reproached him for not having taken care of her request more expeditiously. When she came to the changed hour, she blocked in it, with several long silences.

2. *The Analyst's Understanding of the Analytic Material*

The analyst was growingly aware during this week of the patient's increasing involvement with the analysis and with him.

3. *The Analyst's Activity*

The analyst tried to work with the patient on her pattern of "being good," rather than analyzing, as a defense against analyzing. The patient protested this formulation. She could not very well be handling things just by "being good" because tensions kept building up in her and had to be discharged. The analyst began to touch on the patient's growing involvement in the analysis, how she had come to "get herself straightened out" and was instead finding, to her dismay, how much more involved things were becoming. He tried to point also to the patient's defensive struggles against the involvement; but he did all this in a way that he (correctly) felt to be somewhat too intellectualized and didactic, too "talky."

4a. *The Supervisor's Understanding of the Technical Analytic Issues*

Nothing recorded relevant to this category beyond what is also covered in the next category, of understanding communicated to the analyst.

4b. *The Supervisor's Pedagogic Interventions*

The supervisor indicated how the analyst was using one aspect of supervisory suggestions but leaving out the defense and transference aspects of the patient's acting out. For example, the analyst had stayed on the "being good" line but had not yet brought in the patient's efforts to control her involvements with the analyst by "discharging elsewhere." The supervisor explained how what was here called "being good" was not just compliance, but also displacement in the service of resistance. The supervisor emphasized how the patient's complaint that her ex-fiancé would not listen to her was also meant to apply to the analyst. The supervisor pointed, too, to a resistance pattern of tacit understanding (which the patient induced with her mother, various boy friends, the analyst with regard to the requested change of hour, etc.): the patient would state things very briefly or even just by allusion—if the other person wanted to help, he would pick it up and say something about it. The supervisor also felt that in some ways the patient was obeying the letter more than the spirit of the basic rule. She would tell the analyst many things, but without listening to what she was telling and trying to reflect on what she was saying.

5a. *The Supervisor's Understanding of the Analyst's Personal Involvement*

Nothing recorded relevant to this category beyond what is also covered in the next category, of understanding communicated to the analyst.

5b. *The Supervisor's Therapeutic Interventions*

The supervisor raised with the analyst the question of how much he was acting like the ex-fiancé, who did not want to hear the patient's confessions. Was this a reflection of his countertransference, his unwillingness to "intrude"? (Was his "forgetting" to change the hour expeditiously related to this?) The patient in turn made use of the analyst's inactivity and silences as a tacit agreement that they did not need to talk about such matters—and the supervisor here linked the patient's silences, her intra-analytic behavior, and her new affair.

6. *The Analyst's Response to the Supervision Hour*

The analyst misunderstood the supervisor's interest in the discussion of the countertransference issue, as if the supervisor were only encouraging him to overcome his own reluctance and confront the patient with her withholding.

SUPERVISION HOUR 13 (ANALYTIC HOURS 57–61)

1. *The Analysis*

The patient told the analyst, as if in passing, that the D & C confirmed that her mother had cancer of the uterus and would require a hysterectomy. When the surprised analyst confronted the patient with her absence of feeling over this distressing news, it turned out that the lack of feeling was only an apparent lack. The patient had a difficult time coping with such feelings. She said, "The fear of death disturbs me." Her associations led her to the thought that as long as her older sister was around, a bit of her mother would always be with her and she would be able to keep from feeling the loss of her mother. To her, cancer was equivalent to dying.

With her ex-fiancé, the patient was trying to talk about breaking up the relationship. There really seemed no future to it. She was at a point with him where either they would break up (which she felt they should) or marry (which she felt she could not). She was still failing in her efforts to tell him about the other affair which was still going on in an on-and-off manner. She did not really like the shallow people and the empty drinking parties the other man took her to. Her ex-fiancé was positively impressed by the patient's increasing directness and openness in expressing her feelings with him (all the distress she felt in the relationship).

There was a dream that involved the analyst, called the "tassel dream" because there was a long tassel in it with the name Mary on it, which the patient pronounced to sound like "marry." The tassel led associatively to a tassel the patient's sister wore in a picture taken of both of them with their father when the patient was about eleven. There were associations again to mother, who had a long history of gynecological difficulties which had led to recommendations of a hysterectomy some twenty years earlier, but this had always been avoided because she "wouldn't be a woman anymore." The patient felt the same way. There were references to the patient's periodic depressions and her chronic phobic propensities.

2. *The Analyst's Understanding of the Analytic Material*

The analyst felt he was getting a sense of the pathology of the patient in the area of affect expression. In relation to the news of her mother's cancer, she seemed unwilling to face the sad side of life. The analyst was shocked at first. He felt his own countertransference welling up, and he wanted to shake the patient up, saying, "What's the matter with you?" When he did take up the seemingly absent affect and found it really much more present (just deflected and covered), the analyst was struck by the patient's "childish ability" to seem to accept a substitute gratification in order not to feel a real loss (as long as sister was alive, she would not miss mother).

3. *The Analyst's Activity*

The analyst did take up with the patient her "absent feelings" concerning the serious news about her mother. He found it hard to deal with the complex defenses against affect that the patient offered. At one point he became involved in trying to link the patient's dilemma with her ex-fiancé with her dilemma with the analysis, and her feeling that she wanted to buckle down in analysis with her feeling of being unwilling to look, as shown in the work with the tassel dream. He became very involved in the top-heavy complexity of what he was trying to say.

4a. *The Supervisor's Understanding of the Technical Analytic Issues*

Nothing recorded relevant to this category beyond what is also covered in the next category, of understanding communicated to the analyst.

4b. *The Supervisor's Pedagogic Interventions*

The supervisor worked the whole session with the analyst on the handling of the patient's defenses against affect. He showed how the analyst's somewhat convoluted interpretive efforts came from being too ambitious and attempting to crowd too many disparate things into his interpretations. He should take up affective shifts more directly. And he should try to separate out what the patient talks about with him from how she talks about it; such an interpretive tack could lead the patient to an awareness that an unwitting motive was the wish to avoid feeling deeply. The supervisor also indicated that the analyst might well find an avoidance of good feelings as well as sad feelings by the patient. He warned the analyst that the patient might respond to such interpretive work with the feeling that the analyst just wanted to make her feel bad.

5a. *The Supervisor's Understanding of the Analyst's Personal Involvement*

Nothing recorded relevant to this category.

5b. *The Supervisor's Therapeutic Interventions*

Nothing recorded relevant to this category.

6. *The Analyst's Response to the Supervision Hour*

The analyst readily agreed with the supervisor's feelings that his interpretive statements were overambitious and overcrowded. He agreed too with the thrust of the supervisor's suggestions on ways that shifts in affect could be taken up much more directly. Throughout this whole supervision hour, the supervisor felt less in contact with the patient and not really concerned with how well *she* was doing, but rather much more in contact with the analyst and the problem he wanted to work on.

SUPERVISION HOUR 14 (ANALYTIC HOURS 62–66)

1. *The Analysis*

The patient began the week by mentioning her mother's surgery, but indicated no reaction to it. She described her own menses and her clotting with an intellectualized objective disinterest. She thought her clot "perhaps contained an ovum." She talked about her abortion, what a horrible experience it had been (the rusty tools that were washed in the sink in front of her, the infection that resulted, etc.). The patient laughed as she told about it and also laughed as she told about the sordid affair that abruptly ended after the abortion.

The patient felt her life was disorganized. She was suffering from insomnia, depression, and a sense of instability. She was compulsively knitting a sweater for her mother, and associated on and off to her mother. She tried to combat her feelings with various acts of denial, wearing new springlike dresses to each analytic hour (just sent to her by her mother as a "care package"). The patient's Air Force boy friend had just left for Viet Nam and she was more affected than she thought she would be. She still could not separate from her ex-fiancé, though she was more and more convinced that she should. He would be upset and cry and lose weight just as he had the earlier time when she had tried to break off with him, and she would be too guilty. Besides, there was a great security she felt in the relationship. But she just could not think of him as the father of her child.

The patient also talked of her depressed period at age seventeen, which came on in connection with an uncle dying of cancer. Again she talked of mother's cancer, describing it quite objectively, but as the analyst worked with this tone, the patient did become more aware of the depth of her denial and avoidance. Her sister was also a denier, and the sister's most recent letter had not even mentioned mother. And even when the mother called to tell the patient about the operation, they were "just chit-chatting."

2. *The Analyst's Understanding of the Analytic Material*

The analyst formulated the patient's material as indicating a crystallizing mother transference. It seemed to be the patient's implicit hope that he would understand without her having to say explicitly what goes on, and that he would "send her packages." He felt that much of the phallic talk the patient indulged in seemed to defend against oral conflicts. He felt that the patient was exhibiting a whole array of intellectualized defenses against her feelings, but by the end of the week seemed more aware of the depths of her denial and avoidance, especially around the issue of mother. He was struck by the pressured, strained quality of her laughter.

3. *The Analyst's Activity*

The analyst worked persistently with the patient's defensive denial of affects. He pointed out the discrepancy between the patient's laughter and the horror of the abortion story. He picked up the "objectivity" with which she talked about her mother's cancer. In each instance he focused on the disturbance in the affects while avoiding the content. When in response to the analyst's repeated comments, the patient finally admitted that "if she did not laugh, she would cry," he could point to the evidence of her tension in her kneading her fingers together—at which point the patient withdrew, embarrassed.

4a. *The Supervisor's Understanding of the Technical Analytic Issues*

The supervisor was struck by what had become the analyst's characteristic way of reporting, presenting the week's material as a single event, as if frozen in time, rather than as an unfolding process. For the rest, all his observations and understandings were communicated to the analyst.

4b. *The Supervisor's Pedagogic Interventions*

The supervisor focused on the analyst's handling of the patient's defenses against affect. He showed how when the analyst commented on inappropriate or absent affect, the patient tended to feel reproved and scolded. This could be picked up and put into the series of the patient's denials, the analyst's comments, the patient's feeling reproached. Similarly, the patient tended to misunderstand the analyst's interpretive efforts as implying that she "ought to feel bad." This reaction too would need interpretation.

5a. *The Supervisor's Understanding of the Analyst's Personal Involvement*

Toward the end of the supervision hour, after the analyst offered a detailed account of his altered feelings toward the patient, the supervisor felt that the analyst's attitude had become more "motherly" (as opposed to the previously discerned more erotic countertransference). This new feeling was not communicated to the analyst at this time.

5b. *The Supervisor's Therapeutic Interventions*

The supervisor was struck by the tone in which the analyst commented on the patient's incongruent affective states. He observed that there was a note of "primness" in the analyst's voice, a disapproving tone.

6. *The Analyst's Response to the Supervision Hour*

The analyst seemed sad and thoughtful in response to the supervisor's comments on his seemingly disapproving, "prim" tone. He felt "it might be so." Later in the supervision hour he came back to talking about the "prissiness" (his term) the supervisor had picked up in his tone of voice. He recalled now how "outraged" he had been at the patient the previous week over her apparent attitude toward her mother. This week he felt sad and touched by the patient. He traced in detail the shift in his range of feelings toward the patient from his earlier concern about a possible sexual attraction to his current view of how sad and limited she was.

CHAPTER VIII

Application: The San Francisco Project—The Supervisor at Work

EMANUEL WINDHOLZ, M.D.

The San Francisco Project was conceived as a study based on each weekly report as it was received from the supervisor. We explored only data that were available to the supervisor, keeping pace with him and thereby avoiding being influenced in our judgments by hindsight. The four members of the local group in San Francisco (DeBell, Jacob, Wallerstein, and myself) devised the schema, developed at length in the preceding chapter, for the condensation of this material. It was impressive that after making two slight revisions, we could easily accommodate the great variety of supervisory observations into our schema. As we each read the supervisor's weekly report, we simply marked his notes with numbers ranging from one to six, and the major events of both the analytic and the supervisory process were codified. Each member of the team brought to our biweekly meeting his sample of the codified process notes. The regular comparison of the four versions convinced us that our classification and condensation of the data produced a reliable document that could be used for systematic research study.

It is impossible to convey in a few words the usefulness of this schema.

Comparisons of the categories can be made along both vertical and longitudinal lines. Sequentially, as we followed the data in one category of each session over the course of several weeks, patterns of change in that dimension became clearly apparent. As we proceeded with this classification of the supervision reports, we discussed some preliminary conclusions about the supervisory process. It appeared that very adequate information was available about both the course of the analysis and that of the supervision. However, we realized that the notes could be best studied only through a comparison of their data in the several categories over a longer stretch of time.

A simple quantitative approach to the data was suggested by DeBell when it became obvious that there were striking differences in the amount of information accumulated in the different categories at various times. For example, marking the frequency of items under category 4a, he discovered that the supervisor made a special effort in the reports of the first six supervision hours to convey in a very detailed manner his thinking about the course of the analysis. Later on he made no such effort in that direction. The number of his didactic teaching interventions, on the other hand, soared in the ninth hour and remained high through the fourteenth. It was easy to correlate this to the appearance of the analyst's marked countertransference reaction noted in the eighth supervision hour! This could be displayed graphically in a diagram.

Throughout these years, as Chairman of the Study Group, I had to perform the task of warning the participants against reducing our discussions to an invidious second-guessing of the supervisor. It was difficult to resist the temptations to find better retrospective explanations based on our accumulated individual experiences. We would speculate about the possibility of filling in some missing links which would become available through receiving subsequent additional data. Such efforts, however, were not very rewarding, and I have avoided second-guessing of the supervisor in my systematic study.

At the conclusion of his report on the tenth supervision hour, the supervisor expressed concern that many things may not have been reported by the analyst, and he made a special effort to report more fully himself, after the eighth hour, by taking some notes during the supervision hours. He was not altogether pleased with this procedure saying, "I am content to go along for the time being, but I wonder how satisfied I would be with the analyst's reports if I were not taking notes and concerned about making a summary from them for the Study Group." The reports are centered primarily on the shifting transference-countertransference constellations. This is obviously not accidental. This initial phase of the analysis was under steady pressure from both the patient and the analyst. While the supervisor reported progress in the analysis, he was faced at the same time with continuous difficult issues. These took up the substance of his reports and are most instructive for our understanding of these problematic aspects of the supervisory process.

The San Francisco Project reflects comprehensively the events occurring among patient, analyst, and supervisor. It is an indispensable guide for an intensive study of these correlations in the original process notes. The supervisor described with great accuracy the interactions in the triadic system. Guided by the project, I could draw conclusions about the contribution of each participant to the emerging constellations. Shifts in the supervisor's attitudes could be identified and became meaningful as a continuing adaptation of his teaching to the needs of the student-analyst. In order to provide the reader with the evidence on which I have based my conclusions, I have liberally quoted the pertinent data verbatim from the original notes.[1] The following accounting, based on the supervisor's process notes of the first fourteen supervision hours (Chapter V) and our schematization of these according to the categories of the San Francisco Project (Chapter VII), is an illustrative exposition of some of these correlations:

The patient's erotization of her relationship with the analyst was evident from the very beginning of her analysis. Her habitual tendency to sexual acting out became quickly associated with the transference. The patient's dependency needs evoked panicky feelings, which she attempted to master through casual affairs. This problem took up the supervisor's attention from the start, since it interfered with the establishment of the analytic situation. While his teaching was directed to this "analytic problem," the supervisor was also aware of the analyst's own emotionally determined responses.

The analyst contributed his share to the patient's initial difficulty in developing a therapeutic alliance. He drew attention to his feelings about his own problems, and aroused the supervisor's curiosity about them, as early as the first supervision hour. When the supervisor asked him what he had been doing about his observations, he answered, "Nothing"! Since he stressed his inactivity, that he did nothing, it sounded to the supervisor a little like a protestation, and it evoked another question from him. He asked the analyst if the stress on doing nothing meant that he had been told by someone to keep quiet during the initial phase of the analysis. "Well, not exactly, but perhaps," answered the analyst. He added that "he knew his own tendency in psychotherapy was to be rather too active, to jump onto things as soon as he saw them, and he was trying to hold this tendency in check."

Once, during the second week of the analysis, this tendency appeared more

[1]These have, of necessity, been subjected to minor editorial changes, but every effort has been made to retain the original meaning.

serious. He seemed to become impulsive. When the patient countered the announcement of his forthcoming vacation by saying that she planned to be away for Christmas, the analyst counterreacted, telling her that she would be charged for the missed sessions. The continuity of the analysis was further affected by the analyst's several absences just at the start of the treatment. The supervisor felt uneasy about these absences and reported that, since the analyst himself seemed aware of this problem, he had refrained from commenting on the possible undesirable consequences of such interruptions. This may have been the first evidence of the supervisor's tendency to deal gently with the analyst's problems in "analytic terms."

As the patient's resistances increased, the supervisor himself became more active. He still tried to deal with this as an "analytic problem," but it soon became obvious that it was also a "teaching and learning problem." Knowingly, or intuitively, the supervisor felt he had to help the analyst control his tendency to active behavior. For example, in the third supervision hour, the supervisor tried to teach the analyst how to deal with the patient's silences. The analyst was inclined to break them up rather than wonder about the silence itself. The supervisor's intervention at this point did not effect immediate change.

In fact, in the next supervision hour, the analyst forgot in his verbal presentation to report about the silences altogether, and the supervisor became aware of them only as he was reading the analyst's written notes. The analyst had to look into his notes before he agreed that the patient's silences were indeed lengthening. This was one among other evidences of the analyst's initial difficulties in dealing with the patient's resistances. In this same supervision hour the analyst commented on his own perception of his unhelpful reactions. When the patient surprised him by revealing that she thought the agency that had referred her for treatment was paying part of her bill, he reported that he intervened "brusquely." The supervisor, listening to the analyst taking himself to task, wrote: "I noted to myself that he *has been very meticulous* about the handling of the case in its beginning phase, and while his handling of the case has been quite adequate, I thought I would note to myself the possibility of *overconcern about making mistakes*" (italics added). These features of the analyst's behavior influenced the supervisor's teaching activity. Looking over the analyst's notes, the supervisor made still another important observation. The patient expressed concern about how she would obtain help if she could not bring herself to talk about what was on her mind. She felt more helpless, but also more demanding.

The supervisor adapted his teaching to the analyst's needs. He sketched for the analyst the following transference paradigm. The patient's silences and remonstrances against herself for not saying everything that came to her mind represented an invitation to the analyst to force her to talk. He warned the analyst of the danger of his counteracting in the transference.

He obviously feared that the analyst might find this a pitfall. This was the first verbalized hint of the analyst's potential countertransferences. The supervisor went to great lengths to show the analyst how to deal with the patient's silences. The analyst reacted to the supervisor's teaching with a question which indicated that he may not have fully grasped the supervisor's point. "He asked specifically if he should be *interrupting* these silences *now*" (italics added).

We can identify the following movements through tracing the interactions in the triadic system. The patient was afraid to reveal her eroticized transference. The analyst perceived her fear, and responded with attempts to help her. He encouraged her to talk. This was a countertransference reaction, gratifying her wish to be forced to talk. Such countertransferences are common in every analysis. They are usually transient, tending to disappear as soon as the analyst understands the nature of the patient's resistances.

In this case, however, the analyst's countertransference was multiply determined. He found it hard to tolerate her silence, and responded with his habitual "activity." He may have needed to relieve his own incipient feeling of helplessness. This, in turn, tended to interfere with the learning alliance and to diminish the effectiveness of the supervisor's teaching. The supervisor intuitively went beyond the "teaching objective" by responding to the analyst's need for help to control his countertransference propensity. He warned him not to counteract. This, however, may paradoxically have intensified the analyst's concern. The following week the analyst pulled back on the intensity of his investment in the analysis.

The supervisor's description of the new problem in the fifth supervision hour can be paraphrased as follows: During the week, the patient had talked at length about many distressing events, particularly her inability to stay with or to leave her ex-fiancé. She would be stiff in intercourse, and he would be furious at her unresponsiveness. He would then cry as a way of winning her back. When he persisted in having intercourse, she became hysterical. In that same week, she canceled one appointment with the analyst because of sickness, and then was late to another, calling in to say that she could not get her car started. As she left that hour she remarked that she still needed to get her car started.

The supervisor was impressed by the patient's lack of demandingness, her apparent willingness to just "put up" with her distress. This, however, included the analysis. The supervisor described his concern as follows: "I said in a figurative sense there is no patient here, in that neither the analyst nor the patient seems to convey much empathy for the patient's actual distress." He compared the patient's attitude toward and lack of expectation from the analysis to her interactions with qualities in her father, who was often not there when she very much needed him.

After having described the patient's resistance problem, the supervisor turned his attention to the analyst. He said, "The patient's projecting a father imago onto the analyst could also include identifying with what she would construe as his objectivity toward her problem." He followed this up by raising the potential transference-countertransference issue, asking "if there was anything in his behavior, in his effort to be analytically correct, that leads him to overstress objectivity in his attitude, possibly to the point of conveying indifference." We are impressed by the supervisor's properly guarded wording, pointing out that the analyst's behavior could well be "correct," and that its possible reinforcing effect on the patient's transferences remains only a tentative hypothesis. The supervisor's unusually tentative formulation was a further adaptation of his teaching to what he felt were the needs of the analyst. The analyst may have felt intimidated by the supervisor's warning not to counteract in the transference. The supervisor had been very gentle. Now he became overprotective.

Was the analyst's "objective coolness" only a countertransference, responsive to the patient's need, gratifying her defense transference? Or was he also motivated by his action tendencies, his difficulty in controlling his urge to break up her silences, a reaction to the supervisor's warning? When he concluded his presentation, the supervisor observed, "The analyst looked thoughtful as he listened to my comments, but made no direct response to them. Nor did I act as if I expected any from him." He implied that he was just using this opportunity to teach the analyst about the dynamics of the patient's character defense. Why did he question the analyst about his possible countertransferences?

At the end of his report on the fifth supervision hour, the supervisor noted: "In the meantime, the patient is talking steadily, filling in a good deal of her background, indicating her willingness to work, for instance, on dreams, and showing a bit more psychological-mindedness than we had anticipated at the beginning." Her "willingness to work" and her talking steadily were an important change, compared with the silences of the previous two weeks. The analyst said that he "keeps feeling that the patient is coming more under stress." Was he asking whether he would have to become active again? The supervisor answered that he would "have to keep aware of the necessity to intervene at some point." This was already implied in his assessment, namely, the desirability of changing his "coolness" toward the patient.

In the sixth supervision hour an important change occurred in the analyst's performance. He appeared to have excellent empathic rapport with both the patient and the supervisor. At the same time, there was a change in the form of the analyst's reporting, which may be relevant to our understanding of his good performance. The supervisor had commented, in every supervision hour, on the analyst's lengthy notes. He had suggested in the second hour that the analyst shorten them to a maximum of one page. The supervisor looked at the notes later in the hour to identify some data, or sequences, and possible associative connections. He seemed, however, not taken with the need to read them in such detail.

In the sixth supervision hour the supervisor made two comments about the form of the analyst's reporting. He introduced his own report with the observation that the analyst's presentation was "completely oral although he had detailed notes on each hour typed and placed them on my desk. We started right in talking about what had been going on and *I did not look at the typed hours at all"* (italics added). A later comment was about the sequences: "I did not comment to the analyst, in part because I did not see it clearly until I started to dictate this note, that he had crossed the same point in his interaction with the patient three times in his telling it to me, each time adding more data."

The central theme of the analyst's presentation in the sixth supervision hour was that the patient had verbalized her sexual feelings toward him for the first time, a painful experience for her. This was reported by the analyst only after he presented many other problems, like the patient's returning to her ex-fiancé, her missing an analytic hour, etc. It only became clear later that she missed the hour *after* she had revealed her sexual feelings toward the analyst. Now the meaning of her missing this hour became obvious to the supervisor, as well as her subsequent sense of hopelessness. The supervisor concluded his report of this supervision hour by saying that "while the analyst's account was completely nonsequential (as is mine!), I had the feeling that I had a grasp of the overall situation." This was a shift from his previous attitude concerning the need he felt to check up on the sequence in the analyst's written notes.

Further evidence of the helpful effect of their oral communication was indicated when the analyst, at one point, remembered certain events from the patient's childhood which confirmed in an impressive way the accuracy of the supervisor's observations. The patient had a tendency to be "general" in her account of her sexual life with her ex-fiancé. The supervisor told the analyst that the patient and the analyst were both acting as if she had told him about her sexual experiences when, in fact, she had not. The analyst suddenly associated the following childhood memories:

She had told him how she used to keep things general and avoid communicating with her teacher in an (orally) explicit way. The teacher, however, had caught on to her particular way of communicating in writing, making general allusions as if the teacher would know what was specifically referred to. It is interesting to note that the analyst, like the patient, preferred communicating in writing. This could have been on his mind since the shift to verbal reporting occurred in this supervision hour. It may have been another determinant of his impressive association.

In the sixth supervision hour the supervisor offered another parenthetic remark about the analyst. In connection with his feeling that the patient was "going too fast," the analyst revealed the following fantasy: He felt like the Wizard of Oz, and he was concerned that it was too soon for the patient to see the mechanics of how the Wizard's illusions were created. The supervisor explained to the analyst that these were projections of his ideas. "Perhaps the patient was going too fast for him, not for her." He laughed with the analyst, who was embarrassed about his fantasy, and reassured him, saying that "he must feel that the analytic process was a fragile affair and that if the patient would see how it works, she would become immune to the 'magic.'" He added, parenthetically, "It occurred to me that this might be one reason for the analyst's obvious efforts to be delicate in his handling of the case." Apparently the analyst's concern over losing his full control over his impulses made him distrustful of himself, suspicious that his own unconscious wishes might surface. The patient, of course, contributed to the analyst's discomfort. Her incestuous ideas were close to consciousness, emerging easily in association to the analyst.

In the seventh supervision hour the supervisor was conspicuously passive, as if he wanted to permit the analyst to conduct his work without too much guidance. Since they had spent half of their time discussing the analyst's research endeavors, there was also less time available for supervision. The reported progress achieved during the previous week was, however, impressive.

The form of their communication in the seventh supervision hour was kept oral. It was the supervisor who suggested that the analyst should simply tell him what had been going on. The analyst's report indicated he was unusually empathic with the patient. She was in distress. She had broken off her current affair! She was back with her ex-fiancé. The analyst helped her to tolerate her fears, to verbalize her transference, and she linked this all to her father. She broke into tears for the first time. The supervisor, mostly just listening, praised the analyst in his report: "his interventions seemed to the point, tactful, and adequately sensitive. . . he was able to help her over some anxious moments when she was stuck."

At the conclusion of the seventh supervision hour the analyst's apprehension reappeared. This was significant in the light of subsequent developments. It indicated that he was uncertain in maintaining the appropriate use of his empathic capacity. He told the supervisor that he thought the patient was afraid he would become seductive, or overinterested in her, and not able to control himself if she should "let herself go." As we shall see, this was a reflection of the analyst's fear that he could let *himself* go, his concern that he might respond to the patient with sexual feelings of his own. He concluded this from the following material:

The patient had stated that she was afraid to "let herself go," when referring to a friend who had given her a "very sweet kiss." She did not want to stop him from doing this because she might hurt his feelings. But if he indicated he wanted to go to bed with her, she would not know how to handle that. The supervisor corrected the analyst's understanding of the implications of the patient's conflict. He said that the patient feared the analyst "might mistake her interest or sense of attachment to him and would sexualize this (projection)." In such a predicament, she would be stuck, i.e., not wanting to hurt him or lose his help.

This explanation of the patient's projection may have reassured the analyst concerning this issue of self-control. The following day, however, his behavior disclosed that he still had concerns in this realm. The patient told him about her birthday, and the analyst reported to the supervisor in the eighth supervision hour that "*he doesn't know why* he did it, but he asked her how old she was. He then congratulated her on her birthday, for which she thanked him" (italics added). He did it spontaneously, but this relaxed attitude could have been counterphobic, since the report indicates that he was also upset by his slip. As we shall see, the analyst's relationship to the supervisor now changed somewhat.

Let us now explore the sequence of events in the eighth supervision hour and their impact on the supervisory process. The analyst opened his report saying that he "would sort of summarize the developments for me, and I asked him if he did not prefer to report in that way rather than having me read what he had written. He said he would. . . ." This time it was the analyst who took the initiative to continue the oral communication, thereby eliminating a return to the supervisor's procedure of checking up on him from the written notes. The supervisor did glance at the notes after the analyst left, "filling in some details," but also checking up on one of the analyst's self-confessed "mistakes" which sounded exaggerated. This tendency to berate himself was the most obvious sign of the analyst's transference to the supervisor. It alternated with the tendency to berate the patient for impulses that were really his own.

After the analyst described how he congratulated the patient on her birthday, the supervisor wanted to comment on it, but the analyst indicated that there were other problems that concerned him, and the supervisor "let it pass." We can infer that the analyst diverted the supervisor's attention from this slip. However, the circuitous way in which he explored the effects of his slip indicated that he indeed was distressed by it. Instead of asking the patient *directly* how she reacted to his slip, he wondered if she was concerned about his reaction, or had some hesitancy about how he *would* react to the news of her birthday. This seemed a projection of his hesitancy.

The patient went on to say how difficult it was to talk to the analyst—a familiar theme. The analyst helped her relate this to her sexual feelings. She associated this again to her father, became anxious, wringing her hands. The patient's resistances returned the following day, and the analyst "thought he had better *bring her back,* but he was afraid he did so *rather sharply"* (italics added). The patient reacted with increased anxiety and the supervisor agreed with the analyst that, by his intervention "at a point where he might be reaping some of the effects of his interpretation, he in effect stopped the patient from going on." This specific observation of the supervisor was incorporated almost verbatim in the formulation that the analyst constructed at the end of this supervision hour in order to explain the dynamics of his own countertransferences.

The analyst agreed with the supervisor and, mocking himself, he dramatized his behavior by holding up his hand, saying that he had "acted like a traffic cop." It was the first of a series of actions in which he first blamed the patient and then turned the blame on himself. The supervisor commented on the sequence of interventions: The analyst's interpretation first deepened the analysis, but his later rebuke aborted this process. He felt the analyst "seemed to get the idea but did not go further into what might have led him to do that until closer to the end of our hour." By that time the analyst was getting involved in his *mea culpa* attitude, and was more influenced by his transference to the supervisor.

The paitent spent the following weekend alone, in the absence of her exfiancé. She "had a horrible Saturday," obviously missing the analyst, felt lonely, very anxious, and called a distant friend with whom she had once planned to have an affair. The analyst again agreed with the supervisor's observation that the patient had wanted to call him. The supervisor linked this to the patient's conflict between sexuality and dependency and her reaction to the transference interpretation. The analyst, however, seemed more interested in exploring his own reaction, and introduced his report on the next analytic hour by calling his behavior a countertransference.

He continued his report by saying that the patient felt better after the weekend. She did not know why, except that "she had become interested in things other than herself." The analyst reproached her for getting over these feelings, referring to the transference. He then said he felt as though he had given her "a slap on the wrist." He was very dissatisfied with himself, and this was the reason the supervisor checked on his intervention in the written notes after the supervision hour. He discovered that the hour did not look as bad as the analyst had made it out to be. Why did the analyst exaggerate the difficulties? The conclusion seems obvious. After the supervisor had agreed with him about his first mistake, the analyst started to blame himself. He exaggerated his second mistake, thereby protecting himself against further criticism. His self-accusations could be in the service of disarming the effectiveness of the supervisor.

Referring to this mistake, and the analyst's previous remark about it, the supervisor asked him what made him think of countertransference. The analyst returned to his fear of his sexual impulses, which he had revealed earlier when he misinterpreted the patient's apprehension at the conclusion of the seventh supervision hour. He sketched for the supervisor a transference-countertransference model which matched, in a way, the one constructed by the supervisor in the fifth supervision hour, except that the supervisor's model centered mainly on the patient, the analyst's more on himself. He may have wished to demonstrate that he could teach himself, at least about his countertransference. The analyst said he had taken a position with the patient "like a stern taskmaster, and indeed linked it to the traffic-cop-like remark that I had called attention to. . . and he wondered if it was not his way of handling the sexual attraction the patient had for him. . . . His remarks. . . had the effect of closing the doors he had opened with his own interpretation." Describing this effect, he paraphrased the supervisor's previous explanation. He added, "she is a good-looking woman who says in many ways that she is available." He believed also that his remarks were aimed at "keeping her little and thus less sexually threatening." To the supervisor, it perhaps appeared to be an intellectualization, and he expressed his doubt by telling the analyst that what he said sounded plausible, "but I wondered if he was convinced that it was. He said he thought it was. I just nodded and let it go at that."

The supervisor's doubts about the accuracy of the analyst's interpretation of his countertransference did not prevent him from using it as valid when he later incorporated it in his teaching of the analyst. He was very careful, however, always applying the identical terms used by the analyst, and thereby avoiding introducing any interpretation of his own. The analyst added new terms and new meanings in each successive supervision hour, as he continued his self-analysis. The supervisor followed suit, adding to his teaching the new meanings introduced by the analyst. However, in this eighth supervision hour, the supervisor made very few comments, and none about the countertransference.

In the ninth supervision hour there was a continuous exchange of observations between the analyst and the supervisor. Various topics were touched upon. Some were explored further and related to previously discussed material. At the end of the ninth supervision hour, the supervisor wrote, "We both agreed that things were going pretty well and the analyst, who is not inclined to be optimistic, thought he had a good patient. I recalled he turned down the previous case which had been offered to him."

The optimistic outlook was significant, indicating that the possible stalemate between the analyst and the supervisor which had threatened in the eighth supervision hour had given way to better communication. In fact, progress continued side by side with the analyst's emotional involvement with the supervisor and its unfavorable effects on the analysis which gradually became apparent. The patient spent a lot of time with her ex-fiancé, struggled against and finally had intercourse with him, not knowing if either "he or she enjoyed it." She had the feeling that they were drifting apart. She had a problem with foreplay, which the supervisor thought the analyst could have asked about. The supervisor also inquired about the patient's other affairs, and whether they had terminated. "The analyst said he thought so; she had not mentioned them."

The central theme which interested the analyst was the patient's need to remain independent or autonomous, which paralleled the analyst's struggle to remain autonomous and independent of the supervisor. This tendency became apparent as the analyst opened his report in the ninth supervision hour by continuing his self-criticism. He said "*he hadn't handled* a dream in the first hour *very adroitly*" (italics added).

The report on the eighth supervision hour indicated a diminution of the analyst's empathic rapport with the patient. The analyst's attention was centered on his countertransference which interfered with the learning alliance. The supervisor's previous observations about the analyst's meticulous handling of the case and his overconcern about making mistakes were not only confirmed, but these patterns were intensified. This appeared to be an indication of the analyst's transference to the supervisor being acted out in relation to the patient. First, as reported in the sixth supervision hour, the analyst seemed to have reacted favorably to the supervisor's protective attitude. He became more independent of his written notes, but possibly also more ambitious. He maintained and even improved his analytic skill, but gradually his apprehension returned toward the end of the seventh supervision hour. Since the supervisor became more passive, the analyst may have missed his support. His reaction to congratulating the patient was excessive. Did he have extreme expectations of himself? His perfectionistic streak later became very obvious.

We can conclude that the analyst's involvement with the supervisor became more *manifest.* His transference to the supervisor became more ambivalent, which put his performance into a delicate balance. He was dissatisfied with the intervention which brought the patient back to her dream. The analyst, as before, presented his own interpretation of his countertransference. He said he was "intruding," which interfered with the patient's associations about her father. He added that "he got more sexual feelings expressed in the transference." This last conclusion was not supported at this point by any material reported by the analyst so far. However, if he was "intruding," that would indeed be interfering with the patient's "autonomy"!

The supervisor now made his first comment about the countertransference, refocusing it in terms of its effect on the patient. He was very careful, saying that "he made a *little bit more* of the point that such an intrusion itself could aggravate an eroticized transference" (italics added). The analyst's immediate reaction to the supervisor's comment was to assert his independence. As the supervisor put it, "The analyst listened, but *went right on* when I stopped as if to say *he did not really need* all that explanation" (italics added). The analyst was right to reject this explanation since, after the analyst went back and referred to his error of intruding again, the supervisor noted, "It struck me that the error was not all that bad to deserve this much attention." The supervisor now attributed the analyst's self-criticism to a characteristic trait, saying, "I think I have been detecting a *perfectionistic* streak in the analyst" (italics added). He did not communicate these observations to the analyst, who went on pursuing the theme of the patient's autonomy until, finally, the supervisor "wondered if his *constantly* bringing her back to a topic might be experienced by her as *too much guidance*" (italics added). The analyst agreed, and hypothesized about her retreating from incestuous feelings "toward this need for autonomy" which she stressed repeatedly, finally provoking from the patient the protest that "she did not want to find out any more about herself. . .which had to do with her sexual feelings." This could have been related to the analyst's silent protest against the supervisor's "guidance." By giving his patient "too much guidance," he may have provoked a verbalized protest from her and continued to enact with the patient his transference to the supervisor.

When the analyst indicated that he "had done a good deal of talking and pushing," the supervisor made his next interpretation of the analyst's countertransference. "I suggested there might be a link between his pushing the patient along defense lines and his feeling he told me the previous hour about wondering if he was *not a bit troubled* by his attraction to the patient. I asked if his pushing or prodding her to get down to business might not also be an expression of his wish to control these feelings in himself. The analyst agreed this might be so" (italics added). The supervisor made no references to the other meaning: the analyst's possibly enacting with the patient his transference to the supervisor.

In the last analytic hour the patient was reminiscing about childhood events, talking about poetry, etc. The supervisor asked the analyst what he had been doing with these observations. The analyst said he had just sat it out. "She was talking freely and nearly all the material was new." In discussing these events of the week it became clear to the supervisor that the patient had gotten off the hook of the transference.

The analyst introduced his report in the tenth supervision hour by announcing another change in the form of communication. In the ninth hour he had offered a verbal summary; now he had prepared a written summary, having gone over his notes prior to meeting the supervisor. This must have prompted the supervisor to write his extensive note to the Study Group at the conclusion of this hour. The analyst's report revealed that he was now more eager to cooperate, but was still hampered by the continuing focus on his transference to the supervisor. He repeatedly tried to anticipate what the supervisor might say, frequently in terms of his countertransference, linking it to some of his "unconscious" wishes.

Still another addition to the list of the analyst's interpretations of his countertransference was *voyeurism.* As he became involved with describing several dreams, he reminded the supervisor that the patient had had other dreams involving looking through a window, which was a reference to *her* voyeuristic tendencies. At one point the patient reported having had intercourse with her ex-fiancé over the weekend, and that it "did not bother her or make any difference." When the supervisor asked the analyst if he had inquired about this, he said he had not, and began to justify his reasons for not doing so at some length. He had misunderstood the supervisor, whose question was intended merely to indicate his interest in the patient's "anomalous feeling tone." The analyst, feeling guilty, thought he should have inquired into the details of her sexual life. The supervisor said the analyst "seemed to be afraid of *intruding* on her private experiences" (italics added). This was a term which had been introduced by the analyst in the previous hour.

The analyst looked oddly at the supervisor as he proposed a new interpretation of his countertransference: "Maybe what he was trying to avoid were some voyeuristic tendencies of his own," and he associated this with the (old) window theme of the patient. To reinforce his theory, he described his reaction to the patient's story about some old letters, written to her ex-fiancé. She was struck by how free and affectionate they were. "As she read them they seemed almost vulgar to her." The analyst then said he had asked her in what way they were vulgar. He was upset by his own question, because he asked it "rather unreflectively." He felt he should have been more careful in inquiring about such a subject. The supervisor, reporting about the question, remarked that the analyst commented about these events from his notes. It was not clear whether the analyst had actually made written observations about his countertransference when he said his question "might have been an *intrusion* of some *voyeuristic* impulse" (italics added).

The analyst combined here the previous explanation of his intrusion with the new idea of his voyeurism. This new evidence of his attempt to be so meticulous in his formulations of his countertransference—maybe even in writing—finally prompted the supervisor to comment. First he told him it would be hard to ascribe any specific meaning to these formulations because "the analysis at this stage seemed to go very well with minimal intervention" on the analyst's part. The supervisor continued, ". . . there seemed to be an overriding attitude not just to adhere to a sound technique, but to strive for a *kind of elegance—a kind of perfectionistic tendency."* He followed up by again accepting the analyst's term about "his own possible *voyeuristic* tendencies which amounted. . . to a *reaction formation* resulting in an intensified restraint on his part" (italics added).

The analyst's response was a combination of agreeing with the supervisor and dropping the sexual implications. His formulation resembled what he had already reported in the first supervision hour, namely his tendency in psychotherapy "to be much too active." Now he elaborated, referring to his first supervised case, in which he "had been seduced by the patient into wrangles with him—feeling constantly challenged. He said in this analysis he was trying to slow down and not intrude unless he was certain." While confirming the supervisor's comments about his "intensified restraint," he now stressed the characterological roots of his fear of "intruding." As if again in agreement with the supervisor, he continued, "and besides, the analysis seemed to be going well this way," which allowed him to put aside further delving into the countertransference.

At this point the supervisor brought the analyst back to a theme he had introduced in the beginning of this tenth supervision hour. He called it the patient's "homework." Her temptation to have affairs with other men, after returning to her ex-fiancé, permitted the conclusion that she was embroiled in a resistance to the transference. But she was going to stick it out with her ex-fiancé, and work in her analysis. The analyst seemed pleased with these observations, and added material that further confirmed the supervisor's theme. As he continued to bring up new material, this also proved how deeply the patient was getting involved with the analyst. The supervisor thought he could see the "beginning of a crystallization of transference" into "a transference neurosis, at least in its early phases."

There appeared to be agreement between them about this favorable development, when the analyst again raised the typical question: whether he should do something about this. The supervisor told the analyst, "it sounded to me as if he were asking if I thought he should interpret and *destroy* this development, implying that he would rather *keep hands off*" (italics added). The analyst confirmed this, "saying that it was his fear I would recommend that he *plunge into it*" (italics added). This misunderstanding—projection—exposed again the degree of the analyst's need to keep controlling his activity, to remain most careful with his interventions.

At the end of the tenth supervision hour, the supervisor returned to the "homework" theme, linking it to the analyst's countertransference. Since the analyst had "mentioned his restraint as possibly referring to a reaction against voyeurism," the supervisor noted that "the patient was living out a kind of *contract* she made with him to take her sexual feelings to her ex-fiancé and do her work in the hour with him" (italics added). Here, as in the fifth hour, the supervisor outlined a transference-countertransference paradigm. Equipped with the analyst's interpretation of the countertransference, he proceeded to describe the analyst's contributions to the contract. He could be very explicit. He reminded the analyst of his (the analyst's) suspicion "that one of his unconscious motives might be that he would wish her to do just that to keep him from being tempted." The supervisor concluded his statement again with a reference to a "father image." The patient told of an incident, reported in the ninth supervision hour, when her sister was crying and telling the mother, "All right. He was drunk," referring to the father. Associations to the mother, insisting that the girls go around the house "more covered up," appeared. In this tenth hour, the analyst reported that the patient thought of going home, called her parents; the father answered and sounded drunk. The patient knew instantly that "she could not go home." The supervisor linked the analyst's restraint to the "theme about fearing her *father's 'uninhibitedness'*. . . . I emphasized that I was just bringing these possibilities together for him to look at, . . . but he seemed quite grave as he reflected silently about the matter for a moment. He then jumped to another topic altogether" (italics added).

Indeed, the analyst was reacting with obvious discomfort. It must have called his attention to the supervisor's previous elaboration of his countertransference in the fifth supervision hour and of his contribution to the patient's "contract" with him. The supervisor did not imply that the analyst was *intentionally* reminding the patient that his restraint was to protect her against his becoming seductive, like her drunken father. Yet the analyst behaved as if he were afraid that such a wish was revealed in his defensiveness. The analyst was fully aware of the relation between his behavior and such possible countertransferences. He was afraid his "unconscious" was playing a trick on him: Was an impulse coming through just when he felt completely in control of himself?

We realize the new knowledge about the analyst's struggle with his transference to the supervisor, and the supervisor's conflict with his reactions to the analyst, made the events reported in the fourth and fifth supervision hours retrospectively more meaningful. Their hidden influence on the supervisory process now became manifest!

At the end of his report on the tenth supervision hour, the supervisor wrote a note to the Study Group, raising questions about the analyst's reports. He wrote that he was taking notes during the supervision hour, which he did not like to do, but felt he needed to in order to prepare summaries for the Study Group. He characterized the analyst's reports as being an "associative, theme-linked, synthetic account" which made "a kind of sense, and I can see what I think are significant trends and pick up opportunities for teaching." He noticed that the sequences reported by the analyst in the supervision hour were sometimes different from those reported in the analyst's typewritten notes. The supervisor was aware of the possibility that many things may not have been reported in the verbal accounts. This could also explain the change in the length of the supervisor's reports. Starting with the eighth supervision hour, these reports became twice as long. The first seven reports never exceeded five typewritten pages. Each of the following seven was at least ten pages long.

The major event reported in the eleventh supervision hour was that, as the patient and the analyst temporarily drifted apart, she seduced a "good-looking stranger." Resuming her acting out, she was "wondering why the relapse into the old pattern." This remark further demonstrates her concealment of the transference implications of her acting out. The supervisor made several attempts to show this to the analyst, discussing dreams related to these themes. The analyst listened and understood, but his need to work out his relationship to the supervisor continued.

The analyst was aware of the possibility that he contributed his share to her finally "relapsing" into the old pattern. He opened his report in the eleventh supervision hour saying he had "an uneasy feeling that he could not fully justify. He felt *the ball* had been *dropped* somewhere" (italics added). He seemed justified in suspecting himself of an error, since he had misapplied the supervisor's teaching in a particular manner. "He began by saying he had touched fairly directly on what he and I talked about during the last hour—the theme that she was doing her part, but what was the analyst doing?" The patient reacted as if she were aware of the analyst's concern about his work, possibly his "cooperation" with the supervisor. "She tried to excuse the analyst, who she knew was following the proper procedure for psychoanalysis. It was not his fault if she could not free-associate." Referring to the analyst's interpretation of her feeling of disappointment at being on a plateau, the patient said she "was not really complaining, just informing him about her inner state of mind." The analyst correctly explained to the supervisor that the patient reacted to his interpretation by trying to get him off the hook. He was not aware of having invited her to do that. We can recognize the following reasons: The patient was acting out the transference, and the analyst felt uncomfortable about bringing this to the patient's attention. She would react with anxiety, and he could not maintain his present "restraint." This, in turn, would expose him to the supervisor's criticism, which he would rather avoid.

The supervisor continued to confront the analyst with the patient's resistances. He explained the patient's motivations, hidden behind her verbalized excuses for the analyst's failure to achieve better results. The supervisor concluded, "She was getting not only him off the hook, but herself as well." He paraphrased this to the surprised analyst: ". . . not only did she tell him he was doing the right thing, but she specifically did not want him to change and do more to help her." The analyst resisted change, and had difficulty in helping her more. This, however, fitted into her needs. The old theme of her having no expectations from the analysis now acquired a new and different meaning. The supervisor, continuing with his exposition of the implications of the patient's behavior, said, "There were no expectations that he should meddle in her inner state and there were the references to her father's unfatherly behavior." The supervisor reminded the analyst again of the "formal contract," showing him the one important link he had missed. "She was cooperating by making a tacit bargain." The analyst confirmed this. The patient "tried to bring notes in order to remember her dreams[2] and felt she *should* cooperate more" (italics added).

It was at this point that the analyst again revealed his involvement with the supervisor. He was "dissatisfied with himself and frowned, wondering why he did not see that and pick it up. Having in mind the perfectionistic pattern I had noted previously, I wondered aloud, 'Why the self-reproaches?' " This was the first verbalized allusion to the analyst's emotional involvement with the supervisor. The analyst bypassed the issue, returning to the factual mistake. "He said he saw it clearly now; he did not know why he did not see it before during the hours." The supervisor said, "I could not tell from the way he put that whether he was *merely* marking himself down for having erred, or whether he wanted to look into *why* he might have missed these themes" (italics added). Of course, the supervisor was in a position to surmise, since he did know of the "perfectionistic pattern." He just wanted to verbalize what was evident to both of them, leaving it up to the analyst to draw his own conclusions. This is the clearest example of the supervisor's management of the analyst's transference to him.

The supervisor reacted to the analyst's intense interest in his self-analysis in a manner that reflects his continuous awareness of the danger of his own involvement. Here again, by offering the analyst a choice, he left up to him how far he would wish to look into his own problems. The analyst avoided the topic of his transference to the supervisor. He said he was interested in his having missed these themes, and he suggested another difficulty which may have interfered with his analytic work. "He thought perhaps he had been too much interested in the dreams she brought for their own sake, and had let the thread of the analysis itself slip."[3] As the analyst acquired greater control over his fear of the supervisor's criticism, he could listen more and learn more from his teaching. He was still reluctant to apply all that he had learned, and the patient took advantage of this difficulty and more easily maintained the "tacit agreement" between them.

We recognize from the report on the twelfth supervision hour that the analyst was able to follow the supervisor's explanations about the patient's ability to "obey the letter but not the spirit of the basic rule." This was not unlike the analyst's continued tendency to obediently transmit the supervi-

[2]See, below, the reference to the analyst's research on dreams. If she sensed this, her writing to remember dreams was also to help the analyst. This would confirm further that cooperation was "work."

[3]The supervisor reported in the seventh supervision hour that he and the analyst discussed for half an hour "a matter having to do with the analyst's research ambitions until he seemed satisfied." We do not know the extent of the supervisor's interest in this activity, and its possible influence on their relationship.

sor's words to the patient. He had done this quite literally in the previous week. Now, he said, "he worked with her on her pattern of 'being good' as an alternative to analyzing." This was only half of the patient's problem. The analyst still avoided the other half, which was clearly defined as "homework," "contract," and "tacit agreement." The supervisor noted to himself, "it seemed the analyst had stayed on the 'being good' interpretive line but had *not yet* brought in the patient's efforts to control *her involvement with the analyst* by 'discharging elsewhere.'" This last phrase was a quotation from the patient's reaction to the idea presented to her by the analyst that being "good," for her, was easier than analyzing. She protested that it was "because tension kept building up and had to be discharged." This, of course, referred to her affair. She had tried to tell her ex-fiancé about it, but he merely "reassured her and urged her to go to sleep." The supervisor pointed out the implication. She succeeded neither in telling her full story to the analyst nor to the ex-fiancé. This became an important feature, permitting the supervisor to show the analyst more about the patient's unconscious expectations. Her silence about the details of the affair, and the analyst's silence, reflected his agreement that she should not talk about it. Parenthetically, the supervisor noted to himself that the patient's unconscious expectations were "perhaps a *correct understanding* of the analyst's countertransference, his unwillingness to intrude" (italics added). There were, however, no verbalized comments about the countertransference.

The analyst still hinted at his having "pushed things too far and fast." One of the patient's associations "ran to expectations on her part that, if she would let herself be more open, the analyst would prove untrustworthy." Since this was not borne out by the patient's material, the supervisor asked him to support this understanding of the data. The analyst said he had "gotten the idea from me during the last hour." The supervisor simply turned the analyst's attention to other meanings of the patient's associations, ignoring the attribution.

The countertransference issue receded gradually into the background, and could be looked upon more and more in terms of its meaning to the patient. The analyst recognized she was increasingly involved with the analysis and with him. The new meaning of the "tacit agreement" now became apparent: an invitation to the analyst to help her. This was a new "expectation" on her part. "If he wanted to help her go into this he would say something." Accordingly, the supervisor reminded the analyst that now her "being 'good' amounted to being quite bountiful indeed with her sexual favors."

The thirteenth supervision hour was conducted in a climate of relaxation. The supervisor was surprised, noticing in the beginning that the analyst brought up a matter for discussion which had nothing to do with the case. We can presume this may have been administrative. The supervisor reported his experience in the past had been that "when the analyst raises such issues it is because he expects to differ with me." It surprised him even more when the analyst agreed with him.

He did not offer the supervisor his written notes. "Indeed, at the end of the hour I had to ask him to leave them." Perhaps we should not agree with the supervisor's interpretation that "this seemed merely a matter of oversight"; it may have been unconsciously motivated. The supervisor was still very much aware of the selectivity involved in a purely oral and summarized form of reporting. This was noted by him again in the next supervision hour.

At this point an external event intruded into the patient's analysis, contributing to a change in the analyst's relationship to the patient. He had reported in the previous hour that the patient's mother was going to have a D & C. In the thirteenth hour the analyst reported that the mother did have cancer of the uterus, and would require a hysterectomy. Most of the analytic data were related to this event. The patient's defenses against affects were directed not only against her feelings about her mother's operation and possible death, but also her own preoccupation with the shallowness of her life in general. "There was a lot of depression not far from the surface," but she was jumping around from one idea to another. She herself used the expression that she was "trying to keep moving," and would bring up "humorous" recollections in a sudden change of mood.

The analyst tried various ways to confront the patient with these defenses, but met with little success. He was eager to show the supervisor he had tried out his suggestions. He even went on to read a portion of an hour, in answer to the supervisor's probing on "how he thought about approaching" the defenses. When the supervisor told him he thought he was trying to be too ambitious and crowded too many things into his interpretations, the analyst "nodded instantly." The supervisor demonstrated a more direct approach. After agreeing with him, the analyst wanted to show him "how he had done something like that in regard to the mother's call about having cancer."

These interactions, however, did not interfere with their communication, and a good learning alliance was in evidence. The supervisor closed his report, saying, "It was clear that we were in agreement about what had to be done next." The most impressive change, however, was in the analyst's own attitude toward his countertransference. He laughed when he told the supervisor "he felt his countertransferences welling up," seeing that the patient was unwilling to face the sad side of life. He felt like saying, "My God, what's wrong with you, girl?" It was unusual for the analyst to have a sense of humor about such feelings. His freedom was undoubtedly determined by the different nature of his countertransference. It was a sign of his compassion; he was not overconcerned about the patient and seemed very comfortable. This fitted into the total picture, since the change was not limited to this aspect of his relationship to the patient.

The fourteenth supervision hour represents a culmination of the new trend. The analyst was in good empathic contact with the patient, and was able to follow most of the supervisor's suggestions. The patient's associations seemed much more appropriate, and ranged freely from present conflicts to important memories. The central theme remained her reaction to her mother's operation and her denial of affects. The analyst thought now that he was more like a mother to her, and the supervisor noted to himself that the analyst's attitude had become "motherly." The patient's recent boy friend had left town, so her affair was terminated, and she was again in conflict about her relationship with her ex-fiancé.

The supervisor noted the same tendency to "represent the week as a single event. . .frozen in time." He was repeatedly under the impression that the analyst had concluded his report of the hours, only to discover "this happened in the first hour." Once, when he went over an hour and read the material, the supervisor asked him about "*the tone* in which he commented" (italics added) on the patient's inappropriate affect. The supervisor reported, "It seemed to me to have a note of *primness* about it. I mentioned this to him. He looked sad and wrinkled his forehead and said, 'It might be so.'" When the analyst commented also on the disapproving tone he used, he called it prissiness instead of primness. He said he was aware of his difficulties in dealing with material of this kind. In discussing the analyst's preoccupation with phrasing his comments in a particular way, the supervisor demonstrated this was another manifestation of the analyst's striving for perfection, and he applied words the analyst had used about himself, saying that this preoccupation was, "in itself. . .kind of *prissy* or *precious*" (italics added).

The analyst returned spontaneously to the supervisor's observations about him before the conclusion of the hour. He mentioned musingly that this week his feelings were more sad and touched by her as he felt her limitations. "He reminded me that his first feelings toward the patient were of concern about sexual attraction. He said these feelings had *disappeared entirely* as it became clear these were *just his fantasies* and that the patient seemed like a much more sad and limited person" (italics added). The image of her being "sad and limited" was apparent all the time as she struggled with her dependency needs. The preoccupation with the possibility of his sexual responses appeared only after the analyst became more involved with the supervisor. The fact that the analyst could now recognize that his concern about "sexual attraction" was based on his fantasies indicated a significant change toward greater freedom in his relationship to the supervisor.

The sequential study of the data clarified the vicissitudes of two specific features of this supervision: the patient's deficiencies of motivation and the analyst's so-called countertransference. Some of the determinants of each were uncovered and resolved. The dovetailing of the patient's and the analyst's defensive needs created difficulties in understanding their effect on the analysis and the supervision.

The patient's difficulty of motivation was partly an avoidance of the conflict arising from two trends: her eroticized transference and her dependency needs. At a point when she started a new affair she was able also to tell the analyst she did not want to change and he should not do more to help her. Her acting out the transference and her ability to *verbalize* her lack of expectations coincided, which was not accidental. The characterological roots of this attitude as an identification with her father were clearly delineated in the fifth supervision hour. The analyst's conflicts were rooted in two contradictory character trends: his overactivity, which he could control only with difficulty, and his striving for perfection. He needed guidance to avoid overactivity, which, however, would be perceived as criticism. The supervisor had to steer an even course between these two dangers.

Another pitfall the supervisor had to avoid was the choice between protecting the patient and thereby at times criticizing the analyst, or protecting the analyst and thereby at times neglecting the patient. Dealing with the analyst's countertransferences was an especially difficult task. The analyst's self-revelations were a unique feature of this supervision. Their management was very effective; the supervisor carefully avoided interfering with a process that had the function of a self-analysis. This contributed to the resolution of the analyst's transference to the supervisor. It appeared as if the analyst used the supervisor as an "analytic superego," which plays an important role in the resolution of the transference in the training analysis.

Some of the supervisor's interventions inadvertently perpetuated the process he was intending to stop. The Study Group considered this a characteristic feature of supervision and designated it as a "regressive process." We came to this conclusion after studying the example from another case of a "crisis in supervision," reported by Paul Myerson. He presented us with excerpts from a case of supervision of a student-analyst who was making good progress in analyzing his first patient, a young woman, until a "crisis" developed. The patient, unaware of her fantasy wish to have a baby from the analyst, reached a so-called "realistic decision" with her husband to become pregnant. The analyst was not concerned to explore the determinants of this decision since he did not recognize the major acting-out component in it. Lack of experience could be the most important factor in the analyst's lack of concern when his patient acts out the transference. This was the analyst's first case, and he looked upon the patient's wish to become pregnant as "natural." There were, however, several evidences that made us suspect that his opinion may have been a reflection of his countertransference. Moreover, the pregnancy was linked to a consequent change of residence which could well have resulted in premature interruption of the analysis.

We are, however, less concerned with the actual situation and would like mainly to consider the conditions under which such a regressive process becomes manifest. The assumption that the analysis would probably be interrupted permits us to consider this a potential "crisis" in supervision. It necessitated interventions which would forestall the possibility of the pregnancy, which indeed appeared imminent. The supervisor was, however, very reluctant to interfere "actively." This was contrary to his "philosophy of supervision" which was to teach the analyst how to arrive at his most appropriate intervention by himself. In this instance, the supervisor felt compelled to depart from this usual approach, and he expressed his concern and indicated to the analyst what steps had to be taken to counteract the patient's planned acting out. After the first attempt, the analyst reported that his patient "failed to listen." Subsequently, forced by the supervisor, he pushed his interpretations more forcefully with the patient. At the same time, the analyst complained to the supervisor: "We have a problem." The patient in turn complained to the analyst; she felt he was too forceful in his pressures and was "brain-washing her." This stepwise progression was completed when the patient conveyed to her husband that their plan for an immediate pregnancy was not realistic.

As we follow this "regressive process" we see it moving from one person to another, coming ultimately to the supervisor, momentarily even overcoming him and then being reversed along the line, first by the supervisor, then by the analyst, and ultimately by the patient. We did not look upon this event as an actual "crisis." We concluded that unless specifically perceived and focused on by the supervisor, such processes often run their course unnoticed and remain hidden within so-called "normal" supervision.

We concluded that good supervision is characterized by the capacity to recover readily from such transient "regressive processes." The reports of this supervisor should protect us from an oversimplified view. We should be particularly aware of the possibility that tensions do not originate only from the patient's resistances. Even these may have only triggered tensions created within the teaching-learning constellation. While in this supervision the analyst's transference to the supervisor may have been more intense, it exists in every supervision. We learn from studying such reports how these tensions are acted out with the patient.

The diagnostic considerations that must be applied in the exploration of this process have to take into account the sources of tension within all three of the individuals involved. Acting out, for example, may be an inevitable feature of a particular patient's neurosis. This certainly applies to our patient: acting out was her habitual problem. However, she resumed her acting out at a specific point in her analysis, which was not a mere coincidence.

Moreover, the analyst contributed to her acting out, which was by that time linked to the transference. Since the analyst himself was enacting with the patient his own transference to the supervisor, there were multiple sources of layered tension. The supervisor's accurate reporting of the adaptation of his teaching, and of his way of dealing with the resistances, was a reliable guide to identifying these sources of tension.

CHAPTER IX

Application: The San Francisco Project—
The Analyst at Work

PEYTON JACOB, JR., M.D.

HOW THE ANALYST WORKS: THOUGHTS OF A SUPERVISOR

A supervisor is called upon to know many things—to be an "expert" in many areas of psychoanalysis. Not only is he expected to be well grounded in psychoanalytic theory and technique, but he should be a clinician of proven ability and, in addition, he is supposed to be able to impart his knowledge and skills to his students. He certainly should know how *analysis* works. Though a serious beginning was made at the Marienbad Congress in 1936 (Glover, 1937), the study of the therapeutic process only recently has been receiving an emphasis—both clinical and investigative— worthy of its central position in psychoanalysis. How the *analyst* works is even less well studied. Ferenczi (1928), Fliess (1942), and, more recently, Abrams (1972) have been among the few who have contributed directly to this topic. Earlier literature was devoted mainly to the problems of the countertransference, to the neglect of the area of the analyst's work in the "conflict-free sphere." Papers on empathy (see Greenson, 1960; Kohut, 1959; Schafer, 1959) are filling in this gap, as are papers on the working and the therapeutic alliance (Greenson, 1965; Zetzel, 1956). Yet there is little written on the more normal aspects of the integration by the student of so many levels of theoretical conceptions into a final system of work habits—his own "working style." Perhaps it is our occupational bias to look for the psychopathology to the neglect of the more normative processes. Do we need the help of the experimental and educational psychologists to give us a fresh look?

This occupational bias is of special relevance to psychoanalytic supervision, as we are constantly presented with the problem of differentiating a lack of knowledge of theory and technique from problems due to the emotional involvements of the analyst. The transient identifications with a variety of instinct-defense constellations that are so necessary for empathy may mislead us into assuming a pathology greater than is actually present. For example, an enthusiastic reporting style, in which there is what I call a "momentum of identification" (cf. Arlow, 1963) may be misleading to the supervisor in just this way.

A candidate was analyzing a woman who had a particularly strong character trait we called "militant independence." The patient "took over" the analysis, plowing through dozens of dreams with her own associations and interpretations without allowing the analyst to say a word thereto. The analyst and I had many discussions as to how to draw the line between a more normal, facilitative autonomy and this pervasive defensive stance. We also discussed the feelings of impotence it gave the analyst. One day, as fate would have it, the furnace filter was being changed at the moment the analyst was in my small waiting room, causing a sudden, noisy flow of air. The analyst's first remark to me was: "Gee, I felt like I was in one of the space capsules just being launched." The ensuing material confirmed my initial notion that this was the analyst's announcement of a particularly frustrating week, having been "forced" by the patient to be more passive than usual. I will not attempt to go into how much I felt the analyst's residual conflicts about passivity contributed to the technical problem of the moment; I felt this patient would have tested any analyst to the limit by her dogged independence. My point is that a supervisor could overemphasize the analyst's feeling of helplessness as an *identification* with the patient's fear of passivity—the motive for the defense. In this instance the supervisor was silent about the reference to the space capsule, as he did not want to make the analyst self-conscious about such "meaningful chit-chat." On the other hand, the supervisor used this communication in making the decision to go on with the work on the analyst's conscious, professed feeling of helplessness as a countertransference signal affect. When this was done, the *patient's* fear of passivity could come under scrutiny.

Some analysts prefer to be less aware of how they actually do their own work. They fear that their intuitive approach will be interfered with by too self-conscious an introspection. The very fact that these countertransference signal affects are indeed countertransferences, even though transient and useful in the service of empathy, may make some hesitant to reveal to themselves or to others this one crucial link in the understanding of our patients. But I ought not pursue any further the details of our resistance to the study of our own work habits, as this could carry us far afield.

In spite of these resistances, the supervisor, probably more than the average practicing analyst, still needs to know how he works, including his idiosyncracies, and how an average expectable analyst *should* or *may* work. He is repeatedly making a comparative judgment of how he would have done it after he hears how it was done. But most of us are conscious of *only some of the final steps* in the mental processes that guide our therapeutic actions. There is far more. The analyst has to perceive, screen, and organize all that goes on in an evolving fashion. There have to be initial tentative hypotheses, actions based on them, and with results emerging from these actions, a new revision of the hypotheses. All that is known about this particular patient as a unique individual (manifest verbal content, observed behavior, and available *subliminal cues*) and all that the analyst knows about general theory and technique may be utilizable in the *never-ending revisions of some sort of current synthesis.* What are the intermediate steps that go on silently and almost instantaneously from the perception of new data to an assessment of relevancy to an integration?

Though the contributions of Hartmann and others regarding the conflict-free sphere of the ego are acknowledged as central to psychoanalytic ego psychology, relatively little work has been done detailing the more normative aspects of the many ego functions, or what could be called the organization of various ego substructures. It has remained for psychoanalytically trained experimentalists to follow through on some of these theoretical implications. George Klein and his co-workers have tried to bridge the gap between the psychological laboratory and psychoanalytic theory. In my opinion, their work has significance beyond that of the study of perception and cognition, as I feel there are far-ranging implications for learning theory in general, and for the learning theory of highly specialized interpersonal skills, such as analyzing, in particular. In his book *Perceptions, Motives, and Personality* (1970), Klein covers a large segment of his professional work. He writes: "The unifying theme is motivated cognition. The book deals with the interplay between a person's simultaneously active motives and the conditions that support or undermine effective perceiving" (p. ix). He develops the concept of "cognitive styles," and states:

> . . . that people differ in self-consistent modes of effective environmental encounter. Individual differences are treated as arising in part from different, developmentally molded cognitive styles. Each in its own way has

> proven itself effective in the person's history, yet none is more or less effective than the others by any absolute criterion of "perceptual truth." Several dimensions of cognitive style proposed in these papers imply a view of the nature of personality structure itself: that it is misleading to separate cognitive events from those that reflect "personality" and to speak of their "interaction." Rather, personality embodies stabilized dispositions of perception and cognition—or what we refer to as "cognitive style." Stable modes of cognitive control are thus presumed to reflect basic personality invariants [p. 10].

I have been interested in how the analyst "works" for over a decade; when I became acquainted with Klein's concept of the "cognitive style," I felt it fit elegantly as an explanatory substrate for what I call the particularity of the analyst's "working style." Timewise, of course, a person's analytic working style has developed much later, as the technical and conceptual contents obviously have been learned as an adult. However, in a given individual, his dominant cognitive style has had its formative influence on all stages of his education throughout his life, and casts its shadow on how he learns any new task. To refer to some of Klein's specific experiments (see Chapter 5), if the subject (now our analyst) is more of a "leveler" than a "sharpener" in his perceptions, this "filtration" (my term) will undoubtedly diminish the range and sensitivity to novel stimuli in the analytic situation. These and many other experiments have demonstrated a consistency within a given person of patterns of perception, and were correlated with other ego control mechanisms and certain personality traits. Klein points out that there is a parallel, an analogy, to the defense systems of the ego, but by no means an identity with them.

I shall not give a point-by-point comparison of how each of Klein's experimental results might be useful in understanding how the analyst works, but I would like to mention one area worthy of further study. Subliminal perception, or what he prefers to call registration out of awareness, is getting the attention of other psychoanalytically oriented experimentalists (Fisher and Paul, 1959). Freud, of course, was aware of the use of "neutral" or "peripheral," or "incidental" perceptions (not necessarily out of awareness) as day residues which become a convenient focus for channeling the pathway to the more highly cathected content in dream representations. Recent experimenters with registrations out of awareness have found clues to basic conflicts and references to transferences to the experimenter in tracing the fate of these stimuli. A next step I am suggesting would be devising some way of assessing how the analyst deals with the flood of stimuli directed at him which come from various levels of awareness. We are all familiar with the initial screening of the manifest and latent verbal content and the gross nonverbal communications. These perceptions per se are "conscious," but their screening and assessment of relevance are determined by many nonconscious factors. The analyst's cognitive style is an ever-present general influence on this screening process; his mental "set" that has been developing as he followed this or that transference or resistance is a more specific screening factor. In addition, there are the myriad subliminal cues, the precise fate of which we do not know. No doubt many nuances of empathy, intuition, "hunches," etc., are ultimately explainable by the way the unconscious ego assimilates and integrates all of these perceptions and registrations. To return to Klein again, he states: "Because perception is a cognitive event, an elaboration by schemata, it follows. . . that under certain conditions of release from reality contact registrations may be recruited to conceptual realms quite different from those that ordinarily dominate waking attention. . ." (p. 260).

Granted that he has drawn his conclusions from data relative to mescalinization and dream consciousness, as compared to ordinary waking states, I would add at this point that analysis is also a kind of "experimental situation." Both the analyst and the patient have developed a special form of consciousness, the well-known free-floating attention of the former, and the free-associative state of the latter. Of course they are not gross changes as in mescalinization, but they are controlled, regressive ego states, more open, it is to be hoped, to a broadening of cognitive style propensities and to sensitization to and utilization of the subliminal registrations on the one hand, and the interaction of these with the more highly organized ego functions of both parties, on the other. When both patient and analyst can coordinate their respective "split egos" in a productive interaction, we are describing an effectively functioning working alliance.

My attempts to extrapolate from the results of such experiments to how the analyst works in his clinical situation are only a tentative excursion. Perhaps I am asking the impossible in wanting to know in detail how such an intricate ego substructure is organized, as if it were the complex circuitry of a computer. I hope to stimulate further thought on the tedious process of the gradual shifting of our knowledge of analyzing from that of an art to that of a science. If we go back to the more familiar territory of the consulting room, we can become more aware of what basic psychoanalytic concepts we characteristically use, how they are integrated into the actual work situation, and what hierarchy of priorities of the many technical principles exists. For example, explaining the tact and timing of a simple interpretation may be very complex; Bornstein's classic discussion of alternative interpretations to the phobic child (1949) is an excellent example. How good a system of storage and retrieval of data do we really have? The data of historical facts, transference behaviors, etc., it is to be hoped, have many "valences" of potential "fit," a fitting into the many shifting contexts so characteristic of the analytic process. Or do our data have only a few "valences" that fit into a few simplistic and prematurely closed formulations? I shall describe in the next section a crude teaching experiment of my own which explored some of these considerations. I conclude this section with a deceptively simple statement by Ferenczi (1928):

> One gradually becomes aware how immensely complicated the mental work demanded from the analyst is. He has to let the patient's free associations play upon him; simultaneously he lets his own fantasy get to work with the association material; from time to time he compares the new connexions that arise with earlier results of the analysis; and not for one moment must he relax the vigilance and criticism made necessary by his subjective trends.
>
> One might say that his mind swings continuously between empathy, self-observation, and making judgments. The latter emerge spontaneously from time to time as mental signals, which at first, of course, have to be assessed only as such; only after the accumulation of further evidence is one entitled to make an interpretation [p. 95].

SOME FORMATIVE FACTORS OF THE ANALYST'S "WORK-EGO"

I wish I could give a more complete description of what goes into the formation of this suborganization in the ego, called by Fliess (1942) the analyst's "work-ego." As for some of the general formative factors, talent and training are as obvious as the nature-nurture duality. But which talents are the more crucial, and how do we measure them? Every selection committee struggles with these questions. Empathy, intuition, psychological-mindedness, tact, integrity (not just in the moral sense), ability to view one's self and also one's own ego functioning, the ability to suspend one's judgment while at the same time collecting and integrating data, are on all of our "checklists." Most of these qualities are "givens" by the time we see our applicants; how much they can be altered by the personal analysis and educational experience is an unknown. On the training side, each candidate again comes with his own idiosyncratic set of theories and principles that may or may not be well integrated into the way he actually practices psychotherapy. Various Freudian (Abrams, 1972) or other models of personality development and organization may be there with all varieties of misunderstandings and inexactness.

Compare, for example, a candidate who comes from clinical psychiatry, steeped in diagnostic syndromes, replete with all sorts of justified or unjustified ideas of etiology and prognosis connected with certain symptoms, to a research candidate who is less clinically but more research-oriented, perhaps less driven to "cure" than his colleague with a medical heritage. Their "third ears" will be tuned to different frequencies!

The school of thought of our applicant's favored or feared teacher may be firmly set as a positive or a negative model. There are factors related to more general influences of his prior education, such as the impact of the varying methodologies of the natural sciences he has studied. Bernfeld (1944) traced the influence of the school of Helmholtz on Freud's model-building; our modern applicant is exposed to many such modeling influences. The medical student may, for whatever reason, choose the model of an infectious disease, a tumor or hyperplasia, an endocrine dysfunction, an embryological maldevelopment, unconsciously and inevitably then transferring the old medical model to the new analytic situation. I will not go further into more archaic "models" such as religious and demonological ones!

On another level of conceptualization are factors such as the relative balance of verbal and nonverbal contributions to thought processes. I happen to have mechanical hobbies, and I often "think" in spatial-physical-dynamic images, and I use mechanical metaphors. Sometimes this is an asset; sometimes it is, rather, a liability. I have had relatively inarticulate candidates do excellent work by being in good empathic contact with their patients; their interpretations are often of a simple, direct, and accurate kind that surpasses the style of a more articulate fellow student whose explanations are on a high level of abstraction, but more usable in communication with me than in interpretations to their patients, in whom they may rather foster intellectualizations. Not so incidentally, the former, less articulate candidate, often has trouble with supervisors who are highly verbal, and mistakenly believe the candidate to have a poor conceptual grasp of theory and process. I rely on "an operational test," that is, I await the patient's responses to the seemingly "too simple" method.

There are a whole host of factors we can identify in how an analyst works that are related to his psychoanalytic training in general and to courses in psychoanalytic technique in particular. I would like, but find it difficult, to outline a "hierarchy" of these factors that can be considered to constitute an ideal conceptual framework. But whether we like to recognize it or not, I believe all of us have our own (mainly unconscious) hierarchal organization perceiving, screening, measuring the relevancy of observational data, and finally leading to action for that moment in analysis.

Each year from 1960 through 1967, when teaching the beginning course in psychoanalytic technique, I began by conducting a small teaching experiment. The "experiment" was more for pedagogic than research purposes, but contained the potential nucleus of a scientifically sophisticated study. I asked the new students to listen to a ten-minute portion of a patient's analytic hour, and I instructed them to write what they thought about the material. I told them I was intentionally not giving them more specific instruction. After I collected their responses, I began my lecture on "The Analyst's Work." I discussed what could be various conceptual organizers in this "suborganization of the analyst's ego functioning." These were of course my abstractions, arrived at by the armchair method, and would not necessarily reflect just how such screening and organizing functions existed and operated in any given analyst's ego. I told them I felt a study of how the analyst works was pertinent to psychoanalytic education in general, and to psychoanalytic technique in particular.

My admittedly arbitrary and incomplete list of scanning criteria consisted of about 25 items in five overall groups. The first was the most theoretical and abstract (and least usable?) of the groups, and, as might be guessed, consisted of the five metapsychological points of view. Next came the influences of training in psychoanalytically oriented psychiatry, as most of the students were just out of such residencies. It contained items such as diagnostic syndromes, developmental phases, points of fixation, the "complexes," and the like. (Listening to residents "talking shop" supplied most of the items in this group.) A third frame of reference was a catchbasket of what I called "the larger patterns." This referred mainly to how various psychoanalytic pioneers have viewed the overall organization of the ego, or some central, prominent, organizing tendency. It included "character types" (Reich and others), "ego identity" (Erikson), "personal myth" (Kris's "larger screen"), the self and object imagery spectra (Jacobson), and various pervasive, unconscious fantasies that served as individual organizers (such as the "Wizard of Oz," "Pinocchio," "Feminine Moses," etc.). A fourth frame of reference was another catchbasket of "smaller patterns," such as various instinct-defense constellations, points along lines of derivative development, pivotal dreams, slips, screens, and even anniversary reactions. This group contained dynamic content often "worked on" with a patient in day-to-day interaction. The fifth frame of reference was a set of basic operating principles in psychoanalytic technique; a sampling follows: linkage and integration of the past/present/transference; interpretation of defense before instinct and of surface before depth; the analytic stance of being "midway between the three institutions"; and especially the awareness of transference-behavioral processes as contrasted with manifest verbal content material.

In the second seminar, I returned his response to each student after I had had a chance to "score" it myself. The students were then invited to review their own productions in the light of these various frames of reference and their subcategories discussed in the course, and even to add to my list of "conceptual organizers" and "scanning criteria." The scorer had to keep in mind that the frames of reference would be multiple, to some extent hierarchically organized, and sometimes more implicit than explicit. For example, an attempted reconstruction would obviously include genetic considerations, but might make use of screens, or "reconstructions upwards."

Besides being used as an introductory lecture in which I attempted to give an overview of the course to come, I was trying to stimulate the students to keep in mind how they *work* and to become aware of their growth and integration of newly learned principles.

It was not surprising that, in spite of the limitations of the unstructured test and my arbitrary set of scoring criteria, I was able for the most part to pick out the better future technicians. There was, of course, a wide range of responses. I did not pay too much attention to the adjudged "correctness" of a given formulation, as indeed the sample of material presented to them was small, but I placed greatest emphasis on the breadth and integration of the frames of reference used in this scanning process. There were marked contrasts in the broad sweep of some, and the constricted view of others. In a number of instances I was able to validate these kinds of observations several years later when they came to me for supervision. I marveled at the consistency of their work patterns, and felt that their academic training (which I in no way underestimate) solidified and expanded the talents of the "born therapists," but unfortunately did little to free those who were severely restricted.

I trust that the reader will not take these 25 conceptual organizers and screening criteria as representing a fixed system of mine which reflects either how I work or how I review my supervisee's work. As I have indicated, they are tentative and incomplete, and outside of the didactic experiment. I do not use them to "score" a supervisory hour as to whether this concept or that principle has been central to the task at hand. Such a method of supervising would indeed be clumsy and would no doubt distract from smoothly following the trends of the "live" case. On the other hand, I hope these kinds of conceptual organizers and technical principles are integrated in my work-ego and the supervisee's work-ego, and can become conscious when some difference in our respective approaches becomes apparent. Not making use of an opportunity to make a genetic interpretation, for example, would cause me first to silently review the situation and reflect on how the student may in fact be correct according to his working system, if it is indeed working. To give a linguistic analogy: In learning a new language, various rules of grammar are consciously struggled with until they become automatic; neither teacher nor pupil may be aware of the rule again until it is broken. The analogy breaks down, of course, in that each analysis is unique, and only basic principles can be taught. Here I must resort to Freud's chess analogy. Can we as supervisors discern a *reasonable* "strategy" of our student, after we have assured ourselves that he has adequately mastered the opening moves? Or do we rather try to impose our own favorite strategies (embedded in our own conceptual organizers and central technical principles) on him?

Assuming an adequate background of courses in psychoanalytic psychology, psychopathology, and developmental processes, the theory of technique offers the student the best "how to do it" training in the classroom. Of course, we try to avoid a "cookbook" approach and emphasize general principles. But could we, or should we, try to arrange a kind of priority of these principles and assess their relative importance? Differentiating behavioral processes in the transference from the manifest verbal content of the analytic material is a distinctively psychoanalytic operation, and stands high in my hierarchy of governing principles. This should apply to the *analyst's* actions as well as to the patient's. It is an unfortunate paradox that experienced clinicians take such basic truths so much for granted that they fail to deal with them forcefully with their students. Integrating the ebb and flow and circular feedback of the material from the past/present/transference (Lewin, 1959) also has a high place in my "system." Rules about interpretations that involve surface and depth, defense before instinct, reconstruction upwards, and the like, are all teachable concepts, but in their application they are affected more by some of the "givens" in the student's aptitude, such as tact and psychological-mindedness, than by classroom experience. Often such classroom experience merely makes theoretically understandable what our talented students and earlier gifted clinicians have been doing all along. Loewenstein (1951) quotes Hartmann telling of an interpretation by Freud which he (Loewenstein) now calls "reconstruction upwards." Likewise, the technical papers of Ella Sharpe (1930), for example, demonstrate implicitly principles more recent technicians advocate explicitly as they apply what they have learned from "modern" ego psychology.

But I must emphasize that my groping excursion into this incompletely explored but complex set of organized ego functions is only to give the reader a sample of my thinking, to point out the need for more systematic and sophisticated studies. I am repeatedly in awe (and sometimes frustrated!) at the relative autonomy of such ego subsystems. There is, of course, evidence that the newly learned patterns overlay, do not replace, the older, and, as with instinct-defense constellations, are subject to "regressions." A prosaic example is the use of inexact name-calling such as, "This patient is too narcissistic to be analyzed," in lieu of a more forward movement on the part of the analyst into a study of narcissistic resistances (Kohut, 1971). When a candidate does not understand and regressively uses a less sophisticated model or principle, a supervisor may jump to the conclusion of the presence of a countertransference; the student may prefer to have this "diagnosis" of neurosis rather than the more painful acknowledgment of ignorance. Both may exist, as I consider "dumb spots" to be *locus minoris resistentiae.* In our shorthand, blind spots find dumb spots in which to reside.

One implication of these thoughts is that the earlier education of our future analysts on a higher level of conceptual and technical sophistication would avoid "fixations" on inaccurate models and misconceptions of basic principles that so many applicants have when they arrive at our institutes, and to which they then regress in times of stress. And it must be evident by now that by stress I do not mean only the emotional stresses of the transferences and countertransferences, but the intellectual stresses of trying to screen and assimilate the flood of perceptions from varying levels of the analytic material, of struggling to integrate them with the freshly learned concepts from the classroom, as well as the handling of the shifting roles from that of analyst to that of student and supervisee (see Ekstein, 1967).

THE WORKING AND DEFENSIVE STYLES OF THE ANALYST

With this lengthy introduction, I would like to suggest the use of two catchbasket terms for the evolving or final patterns of work habits of a given analyst. Those patterns that apply to the way the analyst works (for "good" or "bad") when in a relatively conflict-free state, I would call the "working style." The first two sections of this chapter have been devoted to developing the meaning of this rubric. For the sake of simplicity, I have arbitrarily placed all other work habits that are discernibly influenced by the personal conflicts of the analyst into the category "defensive style." The latter term is admittedly also broad, covering persistent character traits, transferences of the analyst, as well as reactions to the transferences of the patient: countertransferences, counterresistances, counteridentifications. I have chosen the word "defensive" in the label because, as Fenichel (1941) has pointed out, defenses of the analyst are usually more frequent and significant than forthright instinctual responses per se.

Another way of defining these catchbasket terms is by the method needed to correct the "errors" in each category. This corresponds to our ubiquitous "teach or treat" dilemma, being applied to the working and defensive styles, respectively. Categories 4 and 5 in the "San Francisco Project" follow this same dichotomy, as didactic teaching (category 4) is directed at the working style, whereas "all other forms of teaching" (category 5) are directed at alleviating personal problems, including those of the defensive style.

At this point one might reflect back on my extensive reference to Klein's research to see where his conceptualization of the "cognitive style" fits into my terminology. He has stated that ". . . stable modes of cognitive control reflect basic personality variants" (1970, p. 10). If I may paraphrase Klein, he considers perceptual attitudes or styles concepts derived from experimental data, and defense mechanisms concepts derived from clinical observation. These are two separate but often parallel functions of ". . . the ego control system as a whole" (p. 159). Thus the relatively stable characteristic modes of perceiving would be automatically "built in" to what I call the working style, whereas characterological defenses, though also often stable and relatively fixed in pattern, would more likely become involved in the transferences and countertransferences of the analyst, and hence would be classified as part of the defensive style.

Before we can judge a given technical maneuver or interpretation as determined by an emotional problem of the analyst, we must understand as many of the machinations of his working style as possible. And before that, we should also know how we work, as well as how any average-expectable good analyst may work. As outside observers, we may initially misjudge an "intuitive" therapist, but after prolonged observation we may learn, for example, that his delay in making an "obvious" interpretation was based on a valid hunch that was explainable only later on in the analysis. Please do not confuse this delay in judgment with a completely passive attitude on the part of the supervisor. Indeed, trying to understand the analyst's conduct of the analysis invites an active, though usually silent, speculation on the myriad determinants, not only on what we think of as dumb spots and blind spots, but also the *successful* methods used by the young analyst. In addition, we need an awareness of how our teaching style matches, or mismatches, the working, defensive, and learning styles of our future colleague.

I have been asked to justify this too neat and artificial dichotomy; it is true that the styles overlap. The word "style" itself may have the connotation of some superficial and idiosyncratic quirks that could identify an analyst. I hope my discussions in the first two sections of this chapter convey how complex our work in fact is, and how much remains to be done not only to understand and conceptualize it, but to ascertain the optimal formative factors that would help us in the selection of candidates and in the development of our curriculum. As I have implied before, is our medical heritage, with its various models, often inappropriate when automatically and unconsciously transferred to analysis, a greater handicap than we want to admit? Should more up-to-date Freudian models (see Abrams, 1972) be taught earlier in the curriculum, during or even before a psychiatric residency? Is it heresy to question the traditional requirement of a psychiatric residency as a prerequisite for all medically trained psychoanalytic applicants? Once a candidate comes to supervision, are we unaware of just how pervasive and constricting inadequate models can be for his development? A "going for the negative," as Ella Sharpe (1930) puts it, can be due to the particular defensive needs of the analyst, but as Abrams implies, it could also be an inadvertent reflection of his earlier training.

The following section on the application of the San Francisco Project to a study of how the analyst works may seem at this point disappointingly simple in view of my reference to such a *highly complex suborganization within the ego that ideally has a stability in its adherence to principles of high operational priorities on the one hand, and a flexible adaptability to the ever-shifting currents at varying depths of the analytic process, on the other.* The problems studied in the sample presented here are fairly typical of an early phase of analysis by a candidate, not quite a beginner. The same phenomena are discussed in much greater detail by other authors in this monograph, but my perspective is one of emphasis: *explore the working style.* First, what features of this working style can be identified? Second, what work habits are facilitating the analysis? Third, can we discern some of the formative processes that have led to the development of this particular working style? (Because of considerations of personal privacy, our data in this monograph are necessarily limited regarding the personal training and experiences of the candidates being supervised.) Only after such a review should we try to delineate in parallel fashion what I have called the "defensive style" of the candidate and reach for the countertransference labels. In this, I am in no way trying to minimize the inevitable presence of countertransference phenomena, but I am trying to avoid a premature closure on the educational problems of our students, and, as an important by-product, alert us all as to how little we know about how we work in the relatively conflict-free sphere of our egos.

APPLICATION OF THE SAN FRANCISCO PROJECT

The usefulness of a new scientific tool is determined by an operational test in a variety of situations. The San Francisco Project is essentially a screening and organizing instrument which renders clinical data more easily retrievable; and through being retrieved into various groupings of related phenomena, the ongoing patterns can be more easily discerned and be made to stand out in heightened relief. A study of how the analyst works could thus be facilitated by the "schema," and certain patterned work habits brought into focus. The San Francisco group, first individually, and then as a team, scored and compared results on the supervision process notes according to the described "schema." I then rescanned the supervisory hours 1–7 for data relevant to the emerging working and defensive styles, with some clues as to the eventual differentiation of these two styles. The majority of the data were retrieved from the two categories, 4 and 5, as 4 contains the "didactic" teaching, while all the other kinds of teaching are grouped under category 5. However, what the analyst did (category 3) and his understandings of the analytic process (category 2) reflect also on his working and defensive styles.

I shall illustrate this application by a brief summary of data gleaned from these supervision hours which are relevant to the two styles; however, the descriptions are gathered first as work patterns only, without undue emphasis on their correctness or possible distortion. Unfortunately, as the supervisor's reports become more problem-oriented as the analysis progresses, some of the facilitative work may be obscured. But even if we focus on the therapeutic problems, for example, a genetic interpretation that we may disagree with as to content or timing, we can see that at least the analyst makes genetic interpretations! Now I realize this might seem absurdly simplistic to a sophisticated audience habitually immersed in the complex problems of psychoanalytic education, but I am trying to get the reader to become more explicitly aware of the breadth (or lack thereof) of appropriate frames of reference a given student may actually use in clinical practice. And the use of a narrow set of operational principles may be in contrast to the candidate's ability to rattle off comprehensive definitions of the five metapsychological points of view in a seminar discussion. We all have had the experience of surprises in both directions—on the one hand, the bright classroom students who prove to be clinically inept, and on the other hand, sometimes a plodding student who suddenly blossoms in the clinical situation.

In the supervision process notes under study, our analyst begins with a self-observation on his work habits. He believes, or he was warned, that his previous experiences as a psychotherapist might tend to make him overactive, and he is consciously trying to correct for this. He reports not only his patient's verbal communications, but her nonverbal ones as well (dress, demeanor, manner of speech, etc.). Later, there will be a question raised of how well he integrates what he sees with what he hears. Much has been made in this monograph of the quick rejoinder by the student-analyst to the "captive audience" statement of the patient, to which he announces his planned future absences. Shortly after, there is a second quick reply to her answer that she might be absent, too; the analyst's response is that she would of course be charged for such missed hours. It seems to go unnoticed by the analyst that this is a highly charged bit of "banter." This raises a host of possible alternative explanations, and these are explored in considerable detail in the other chapters in this monograph. "Banter style" is my label for this interaction, not the supervisor's or that of the other observers. It is descriptive; it is obviously overdetermined, and it may or may not be grossly pathological or detrimental to the analysis; but it is stylistic, and we should first try to understand it in a more neutral fashion, even though we can quickly see it as a "loaded" interchange.

The supervisor senses then a lack of "demand" on the part of the patient in her interactions with the analyst, but the analyst does not report it or seem to notice it. The analyst focuses on aspects of missing content rather than noting or interpreting the resistance implications of the omission. Is he making a "natural beginner's error" of concern with data gathering in lieu of focused awareness of transferences and resistances? Or, is not a minimum of data gathering a necessary beginning step? Note that this questionable work habit could be facilitative, a dumb spot, or a blind spot; one needs more evidence to make a judgment. In the third supervision hour the analyst has repeated his skipping over the resistance of silence, in spite of prior advice on this issue from the supervisor. We could at this point wonder why he has not "learned." Is this related to his problem about learning, his countertransference, or a *continued belief* in his search for content? A shift from content-oriented to process-oriented listening is a difficult turn to make. Furthermore, when to shift the patient's attention from his own (narcissistically valued) content to a process of resistance (another narcissistic wound) is a highly individual matter of tact and timing. But back to our analyst: he arranges for further interruptions, though telling the supervisor (defensively) that he knows they are bad for the progress of the work. One could say he seems to be not too aware of the effects of *his* behavioral processes (i.e., absences) as contrasted to his "content" (i.e., interpretations per se). Thus the supervisor is more aware of the operative transferences and resistances than is the analyst, and he begins to make more comprehensive formulations about the case than does the analyst.

At this point we are confronted with one of the problems of the method of study, that of the inevitable "double condensation" in the selection, first by the analyst as he reports to the supervisor, and then as the supervisor selects what observations to report to the research group. Taking the latter's reports as representative and not narrowly selective, it seems that the analyst is becoming more concerned about making technical mistakes, and he prefaces a description of what he has done in the analysis with defensive remarks designed to anticipate and perhaps forestall criticism. The relationship between the analyst and supervisor becomes a focus of attention, and the analyst is "distracted" from his work with the patient. The supervisor has sometimes been described as being in a "Janus" position, looking both at the patient and the analyst. But I feel that the analyst's position is the one that is more emotionally charged than the supervisor's because he has to deal with the impact of the patient's transferences while being aware his work is being judged by the supervisor. In these first hours of supervision, it is difficult to assess just how much the distractions of the "normal" supervisory process itself interfere with the analyst's more usual working style, and also how much he might wish or need to distort his reporting of his work out of his fears about being judged. Such assessments are of course better made after a more extensive longitudinal review of the analyst-supervisor relationship.

The "nodal" supervision hour 5 arrives. In the reported material, the analyst does not deal with the patient's not dealing with a missed hour. In reference to the past/present/transference paradigm, he focuses more on the present and past, as does the patient, and theorizes to the supervisor on an emerging pattern of identification. (As noted earlier in this chapter, keeping tab on how a student appropriately integrates these three spheres gives an index to his style and quality of work; of course, it must be carefully tailored to the technical needs of the particular case.) The disagreement of the supervisor with the analyst on the type of identification is one issue; a separate issue is again the seemingly simplistic one that patterns of identification are valid ways to organize material. We may be able to see that the difference in the way analyst and supervisor formulate the identification patterns is due to what type of data is considered more relevant: content or behavioral processes. The supervisor naturally places more weight on the latter, and that is a measure of his greater experience. Now we are faced with another problem: If the analyst persists in his probably erroneous formulation, how serious could the cumulative errors become, and what is the optimum teaching tactic? For example, if he persists in his "mother-identification" image of the patient, his interpretations of her subsequent "transferences" to him would be slanted in that direction; this would change her "free" associations, whether she is receptive or resistant. In this instance the supervisor tells him that he senses the patient both projects a father imago onto him, and identifies with the father's masochistic attitude toward the abusive mother. Should the "cumulative error" be allowed to go on, assuming the supervisor is correct, until the analyst learns better from his experience? Will the analyst be distracted by an open disagreement with his supervisor? Or will the analyst simply be put back on the "right track"?

That a supervisor is faced with these types of decisions from moment to moment in every supervisory hour is old-hat to us. But since my primary focus is not on supervisory tactics, I have added this seeming digression to bolster my general plea for less activity on the part of the supervisor, since I believe that what goes into an analyst's formulations and actions is far more complex than is indicated by an answer to a question as to why he did what he did. As I have tried to explain at the beginning of this chapter, the unreported and unreportable (i.e., subliminal) stimuli to which the analyst is exposed significantly influence his final actions. When the analyst and supervisor have a peer relationship, the effects on the analyst's work of differences in day-by-day views of a case may be minimal, as contrasted to when their relationship is on a more hierarchically authoritative basis. These considerations, among others, have prompted me to attempt to make explicit what should exist implicitly—a "supervisory pact." This implicit pact could be imagined as an explicit conversation between the analyst and supervisor, as follows:

Analyst: I'll tell all of the manifest content, that I feel to be dynamically pertinent, of what happens between me and my patient. Since selection of data is inevitable, trust my judgment as to what is dynamically important. I do not know all of the determinants of how I select my data, but at least initially, hear me out!

Trust my judgment also to tell an optimum amount of my personal reactions to these verbal and nonverbal interchanges. I shall try to do so in the service of learning how to use signal affects, rather than in the service of a split transference (if in analysis), or in the service of resuming my "analysis" in disguise.

All of this, including the fear of being graded, is secondary to the work of analyzing and of learning about analyzing.

Supervisor: I promise to try to preserve your autonomy as far as possible, both in conducting your analysis of your patient, and in conducting your own self-analysis.

My observations on your personal equation will be minimal, only in the service of the work, and limited to observing phenomena directly pertinent to your work, not a "wild analysis" of the genetics of your problems.

Let us first just work and suspend judgment. If we work as outlined above, the judgment of your ability will become mutually self-evident.

Let us both consider that we are on the frontier of psychoanalytic knowledge; we both are students. It is granted that I have had more experience, but an overemphasis on the student-teacher relationship will detract from a mutual exploratory attitude toward this unique "experiment in nature": your case.

But back to the nodal supervision hour 5, where the analyst and supervisor are discussing their different views of the patient's identifications. The supervisor continues with the implications of the patient's identification with the long-suffering father, and how it emerged in the transference as the patient's lack of expectation of help, even though in reality she was indeed suffering. The supervisor has also noted an "overobjectivity" on the part of the analyst; is this a fulfillment of the patient's expectation of no help? This "coolness" is also taken up in much detail elsewhere in this monograph. Though at first glance it may denote a seeming lack of empathy, it seems a much more complex and less clear-cut issue at this point, and explanations range from a technically necessary soft-pedaling of the transference, to an insensitivity to it or a strong defense against it. It is also consistent with "bantering" as a character trait. Once again I am saying, let us observe this "coolness" as a manner of working, and delay judgment, granted that it is highly overdetermined on the part of the analyst, and has an as yet undetermined effect on the patient. The supervisor does deal with it as a didactic problem, pointing out it meets a "no-expectation" expectation of the patient. (In more technical language, this is a transference gratification of a special sort, a permission to have a transference defense, which is also a defense transferred from her past.)

In the following supervision hour the supervisor again notes how the patient escapes from the immediate transference material to her outside life, and how the analyst follows suit. That there is a *concurrence* of these patterns is undeniable; that it is *dynamically a collusion* of defenses is less certain, though of course this possibility could be of great significance. The picture clarifies somewhat when the analyst tells the supervisor he feels he has been going too fast for the patient, "like the Wizard of Oz, with the illusions exposed too soon." Has the analyst been all along more aware of transference phenomena than we have given him credit for? His caution may be technically justified since his patient indeed gets overly quickly involved with men in highly ambivalent ways.

As the patient's sexual thoughts about the analyst become conscious, or rather expressed, she misses an hour, and then is depressed. The question remains unanswered: Was the "collusion" of the analyst and patient to soft-pedal the sexualized transference an unconscious defense on the part of the analyst, a correctly planned (or intuitively carried out) titration of "dosage" by him, or a blind obedience to a mistaken ideal image of a "neutral" analyst? It should be noticed that the supervisor recognized that the patient was indeed in a bind: if she sexualized the relationship to her helper, the analyst, she might feel compelled to avoid it by flight, and then she would lose his help.

So I come back again to a suspended judgment about the complex determinants of the analyst's "coolness," though descriptively it is a part of his style for this patient. I must acknowledge at this point that we are still limited in the depth of our knowledge about how this analyst works. Perhaps the beginnings of this supervision can reveal only the most general features; a more advanced candidate with a less defensive stance vis-à-vis both his patient and his supervisor might well be more revealing about how he works. A promising new method of research, "consensual analysis," devised by Windholz (as quoted by Weiss, 1972) may offer additional avenues of study into how the analyst works. And then again the indispensable source of data may be the oldest one: the experienced analyst with a high talent for self-observation, especially for observing his ego functioning, who would at the same time have the courage to reveal his "trade secrets." Were I to instruct him how to go about his task, I would find it difficult to improve on Ferenczi's (1928) outline. A courageous and sensitive example of how a supervisor works is given in Chapter V, and should be an inspiration to us all.

In conclusion, I believe that the application of the "schema" used in the

San Francisco Project demonstrates that significant data relevant to the purposes of this study of "The Analyst at Work" can be readily retrieved. I used the instrument to screen the supervision material in order to selectively highlight data on how the analyst worked. In evaluating the "yield" of the data thus collected, I have tried to discern the frames of reference and the guiding principles that determined the way this particular analyst went about his work. Some of these frames of reference are admittedly simplistic and elementary. I consciously have tried to see them as positive or at least as neutral work habits, relatively unaffected by the personal conflicts of the analyst. I am sure that this has come across as a defense of the analyst's chosen technique, though in many places I have also tried to indicate where "dumb spots" and "blind spots" could be (co-)operating. But I justify my methodological procedure of a temporary favorable or nonjudgmental stance on the grounds that it may open our eyes to conceptual frameworks, guiding principles, and new techniques we may be blind to because of rigidities and dogmatic adherence to our own operational "set" or principles. Is the analogy of the scientific study of acupuncture too far-fetched? If we are open-minded, we *may* uncover entirely new vistas in neurophysiology, even if accompanied by massive suggestion admixed with hocus-pocus. The hackneyed and inexact view of technique, that "the analyst's unconscious has to get in touch with the patient's unconscious" *does* have *some* merit as a *beginning* of an exploration of how an analyst works. But this must be followed by our newest experimental techniques, the help of our theorists who are abreast of newer integrations, and the field tests of experienced technicians and clinicians. I do not agree with those who feel that something mysteriously vital is *lost* when we convert our art into a science. Some "art" of course may still remain, and must be given due respect. But how the analyst works is no exception, and we should strive for clearer and clearer explanations.

REFERENCES

Abrams, S. (1972), Freudian models and clinical stance. *Psychoanal. Quart.*, 41:50–57.

Arlow, J. A. (1963), The supervisory situation. *J. Amer. Psychoanal. Assn.*, 11:576–594.

Bernfeld, S. (1944), Freud's earliest theories and the school of Helmholtz. *Psychoanal. Quart.*, 13:341–362.

Bornstein, B. (1949), The analysis of a phobic child. *The Psychoanalytic Study of the Child*, 3/4: 181–226. New York: International Universities Press.

Ekstein, R. (1967), Omnipotence and omni-impotence phases of the training process. *Internat. J. Psychiat.*, 4:443–448.

Fenichel, O. (1941), *Problems of Psychoanalytic Technique.* Albany, N.Y.: The Psychoanalytic Quarterly.

Ferenczi (1928), The elasticity of the psychoanalytic technique. In: *Final Contributions to the Problems and Methods of Psychoanalysis.* New York: Basic Books, pp. 87–101.

Fisher, C. & Paul, I. H. (1959), The effect of subliminal visual stimulation on images and dreams: a validation study. *J. Amer. Psychoanal. Assn.*, 7:35–83.

Fliess, R. (1942), The metapsychology of the analyst. *Psychoanal. Quart.*, 11:211–227.

Glover, E., Ed. (1937), Report of the fourteenth International Psycho-Analytical Congress. *Internat. J. Psycho-Anal.*, 18:72–123.

Greenson, R. R. (1960), Empathy and its vicissitudes. *Internat. J. Psycho-Anal.*, 41:418–424.

——— (1965), The working alliance and the transference neurosis. *Psychoanal. Quart.*, 34: 155–181.

Klein, G. (1970), *Perceptions, Motives, and Personality.* New York: Knopf.

Kohut, H. (1959), Introspection, empathy, and psychoanalysis: an examination of the relationships between mode of observation and theory. *J. Amer. Psychoanal. Assn.*, 7:459–483.

——— (1971), *The Analysis of the Self.* New York: International Universities Press.

Lewin, B. D. (1959), The analytic situation: topographic considerations. *Psychoanal. Quart.*, 28:455–469.

Loewenstein, R. M. (1951), The problem of interpretation. *Psychoanal. Quart.*, 20:1–14.

Schafer, R. (1959), Generative empathy in the treatment situation. *Psychoanal. Quart.*, 28: 342–373.

Sharpe, E. F. (1930), The technique of psycho-analysis. Seven lectures. In: *Collected Papers on Psycho-Analysis.* London: Hogarth Press, 1950, pp. 9–106.

Weiss, J., Reporter (1972), Continuing research: the modification of defenses in psychoanalysis. *J. Amer. Psychoanal. Assn.*, 20:177–198.

Zetzel, E. (1956), Current concepts of transference. *Internat. J. Psycho-Anal.*, 37:369–376.

CHAPTER X

Supervision Hour 5: On the Supervision of the Supervisor

RUDOLF EKSTEIN, Ph.D.

The study of the supervision process, the range of differing possibilities for the ordering and comprehending of the supervision data and of asking questions about their value, is in itself an *enabling process.* We mean to improve teaching and learning techniques in the field of psychoanalytic training, and thus it might be worthwhile to imagine a situation which is not as yet general practice in psychoanalytic institutes. I am referring to the training of supervisors via seminars or direct supervision of their supervision. The first approach to such an undertaking is usually one that brings us together for the purpose of "studying supervision." Soon such an approach will invite considerations that make us move beyond objective study and into attempting earnestly the supervision of beginning supervisors of students who are to become psychoanalysts. The supervisor of these beginning supervisors would have to deal with material which is two and three times removed from the original events. He will hardly observe the patient and the analyst-to-be directly. He will, at best, see condensed summaries of analytic hours. He will not directly observe the supervisor and his candidate, and frequently will have to react to data supplied to him by the new supervisor, who will report to him verbally or in writing what has happened between him and the supervisee, and what he thinks happened between the supervisee and the patient. It would hardly be sound clinical practice, nor actually scientifically relevant, if he were to try to utilize video tapes or tapes of all these actions in order to be an effective supervisor of the new, young teacher.

I am attempting, therefore, to imagine what kind of issues he would have to consider during one particular session with his supervisor-trainee, and what uses he could make of the material available to him. The supervision specimen I imagine him to have before him, possibly preceding his conference with the student-supervisor, or, having it reported to him during the session, consists of the fifth supervisory session of the supervision process that is the focus of this monograph, imagined here to be the work of our student-supervisor with his supervisee, the student-analyst. This fifth supervision hour is one in which they deal with four patient hours (hours 19–22), the particular week's clinical work. The data he has in front of him are, of course, not "complete." The patient's free associations about a certain event are also not "complete." Inasmuch, however, as these are the *productions* brought up during a specific session, they are the *material* of that hour, and must be utilized regardless of whatever else is known or unknown.

I consider myself now for a moment as an outside observer, and I realize that I work with third-hand data: the supervisor's condensed and selective account of the analyst's condensed and selective account of the patient's material and the candidate's interventions; and the supervisor, too, brings us but a selective account of the supervisory conference itself, the student-analyst's way of using the student-supervisor, and the supervisor's way of responding and trying to be helpful. It is left somehow to my imagination and skill as to whether I want to consider the selective material as a rationale and/or a rationalization for the different learning and teaching options employed.

As I listen to the content of this supervisory conference, I start to play with my own impressions in such a way that I do not commit myself instantly to a specific answer, but rather, I want to develop the available range of possible answers, *possible options,* for each of which I have, in the beginning, but imperfect evidence. I might consider such play with thoughts as trial actions. Trial action would lead to trial prediction, and finally to technical action itself, that is, a special teaching intervention or nonintervention which is to lead in the final analysis to an improvement in the analytic techniques of the new analyst and in the teaching techniques of the new supervisor.

The student-supervisor's notes read as follows:

The analyst told me there were only four hours this week because the patient had called in sick. He handed me the notes, but I did not look at them, as he described briefly what had gone on during

> the week. He mentioned that the patient continues to talk, and I recalled (several hours after our meeting) his stressing that although she was absent for an hour, she made no reference to it the next time. She had called in to say she would not be coming.

I wondered why the supervisor had chosen not to look at the analyst's notes, although I had the impression they were required as preparation for the supervisory conference. But I chose to think I should make no reference to them, noticing that the analyst's patient made no reference to the missed hour, and the analyst himself did not take up the fact that she had missed an hour, or even seem to wonder about the nature of missing a session. I realized that I thought of my curiosity as a kind of critical observation, which, if expressed, might find the student-analyst touchy, and I chuckled at the thought that he too preferred not to intervene at that moment in his session with the patient. I also noticed that the supervisor thought of this only several hours after the meeting with the student. The question then is when one ought to intervene or not, and I noticed the struggle between the wish to keep the session objective and the awareness that the conference ought to go beyond the objective written data to a more personal and direct exchange. His not reading the notes might be the supervisor's attempt to get nearer to the student, while his reluctance to take the initiative might express the wish to keep matters objective and somewhat distant. I continue now to study the supervisor's process notes:

> He said she came in the following hour wearing a bright summery dress although it was one of the coldest days of the year. There was no mention of this either. The following day the patient could not get her car started and called in to say she would be late. Since the analyst's secretary was ill, he took the call himself. She identified herself by the diminutive of her name, the analyst noted, like a little girl. The conversation was straightforward, but again when she finally came only five minutes late she did not mention this unusual event. When she left that hour she said, "Well, I still have to get my car started," leaving the implication that she must have come by some other means.

The focus of this segment of the supervisor's process notes is on the patient. We find a very observing analyst, who gives us an excellent account of the salient events, and indicates a certain capacity to notice data pertinent to the developing transference paradigm. In spite of the wintry day, he tells us she wears a bright summery dress, a dress which perhaps says something about the analytic situation rather than about the climate. Over the telephone, she identifies herself with the diminutive of her name, and gives evidence then of the importance of the hour for her as she is but a few minutes late; though she could not get her car started, she tried so hard otherwise. All this is observed, recorded, and reported, but it is not used by the analyst vis-à-vis the patient. The supervisor himself chooses to record in his own notes what he observes about the student-analyst, but he stresses that he also chooses not to use his own observations as he states:

> While summarizing most of the details of the hour, the analyst quoted this remark, but gave no sign of why he thought it significant. In context, the remark struck me as implying that she had fulfilled her duty to the analyst by getting to her hour and now had to go back to deal single-handedly with her *own* problem. I wondered to myself if the analyst had heard this too.

Actually the supervisor too permitted the analyst to fulfill his duty by bringing all the material to his conference with the supervisor, but if the supervisor would not help him with the observations and implied inferences, he too would have to go back to his patient with his own technical problems still to be solved.

Do we deal here with three levels of the very same problem? The patient experiences her transference feelings and struggles with, and against, them. She wants to be dressed as if it were spring, but it is freezing outside. She wants to be called by her first name, but hears no reaction. She wants to be on time, at least to do her duty to live up to the demands of the analysis, but she cannot get her car started. The analyst does not help her to get the car started, to get the analytic process going, to face and to understand the eroticized transference and her struggle against it. The supervisor, up to this point, remains an observer; he waits objectively. The analyst dutifully reports, is an excellent observer, but he too cannot get his car started, to use the patient's simile. Could the supervisor help him to get the car started, and when will he choose to do so?

What are the options of the supervisor's supervisor? So far, putting myself in his position, I suggest the material is governed by a kind of objectivity, a kind of coolness on the part of the analyst, and a cautious, rational way of discussing the material in the supervisory situation—mainly on an intellectual-cognitive and a detached, observing level. What might be the supervisor's hesitation? Why does he not take up the analyst's seeming passivity? Does he wait for the analyst's questions? Does he believe he should not take the initiative lest he contribute to an increase in learning resistance? Just as the patient arrives in her lovely summery dress and tries to make herself likable, the analyst tries to show the supervisor his own attractiveness, so to speak, as an objective observer, as a good analyst who understands the material. But then he does not help to get the analytic situation going; he leaves the patient feeling that she must leave the hour, since she *still* must start her car by herself.

It occurs to me that this analyst is in a phase of supervision where, rather than being able to focus on his own (learning) problem, he must focus solely on the patient's problem, discerned through the material at hand, and he does not yet make himself a vital part of this material, nor does he see yet his part in the supervision conference. The supervisor is most likely thinking of the fact that he is just dealing with the fifth conference, and I—as I imagine having met the supervisor for this first conference between us—feel in a similar position. I have the choice of waiting for a situation where a supervisor starts to have questions about his work—his own work—or of taking matters up now when I can do this on a didactic level only, without real emotional impact and without my contribution stemming from a consciously felt need of the supervisor, who rather keeps matters on such an objective level.

As I continue to study these supervisory process notes, I read:

> The analyst also mentioned that the relationship with the ex-fiancé was coming much more into the picture. Also her distress about being unable to stay with him or leave him alone was becoming more important. The ex-fiancé was out of town, and she was longing for him, but she felt that when he came back she would be unable to get together with him. The analyst linked this up with other events in the patient's life she had told him about, particularly a memory relating to her teens when her father, who was usually long-suffering with her mother's excessive drinking and extravagant spending, one day, as the patient recalled it, was choking the mother on a couch in the living room when she came across them. She was used to her parents' quarrels and sympathized with her father because the mother really treated him badly (it was only the mother who talked about divorce). She was shocked to see the violence.
>
> We discussed this memory briefly. The analyst had been trying to see in it some explanation for the patient's difficulty with her ex-fiancé. The memory, along with other incidents we had been discussing, led me to suggest in passing that it might have some characteristics of a screen memory relating possibly to primal-scene material.

This material, again an objective account of patient material, an attempt at understanding the dynamics, shows us a young analyst who as much as possible keeps out of the situation, and sees the material either in genetic terms or in terms of the patient's present life situation. The patient is shown as wavering back and forth in her longing for the ex-fiancé and in her ability (or inability) to stay with him, and we hear of her reflections in earlier hours concerning father and mother. The analyst is quoted here for the first time as interpreting in linking up this material with earlier observations, and we now find that the supervisor too becomes active. He also focuses on the material, and he stresses the possibility that the memory concerning father's and mother's quarrel on the couch and the choking incident functions as a screen memory. The student-analyst sees it more as a kind of genetic displacement indirectly describing her current difficulties with the ex-fiancé.

Here we find supervisor and student engaged in a collusive *folie à deux* inasmuch as they both look at this material as if neither had anything to do with it, had any place in it, or was *meant* by it. The student leaves himself out as the central character, and thus also indicates his wish to leave the supervisor out of the material. It is as if he were to say to us that the patient talks about her life in an objective manner as if she were not in an analytical situation, and that he, the student, brings this material to the supervisor as if he were not in a supervisory relationship. The supervisor, in turn, seems to accept this challenge and is willing to discuss the material objectively. It is as if both of them were looking through a window, a kind of one-way-vision room, observing the patient and studying the material without the patient knowing that there is an analyst, and without the analyst acknowledging that there is a supervisory situation. Am I to start now and ask the supervisor whether he had any questions about his work with the young analyst, or am I hesitating to do so because I expect his questions might be merely academic, that is, about clinical data rather than about his teaching technique? But I notice that the supervisor now becomes more concerned with his own activity, and he actually goes back to the process notes the analyst has prepared, as he records:

> Later in this hour, after I had looked over the typed material he had given me, I tried to help him clarify his thinking that the patient was revealing a considerable identification with her mother. He based this inference partly on her shock at seeing the violence toward her mother and on parts of several dreams in which she put on clothes (incidentally, summer dresses) that belonged to her mother. He reminded me that the mother was generous to a fault and would give her, as the patient said, "the shirt off her back," if she knew she liked it.

As the material veers away from analyst, from ex-fiancé, and from father to mother, and to the patient's identification with her mother as a person who is described both as generous to the daughter and as unresponsive and nongiving to the father, it seems clear to the supervisor that the analyst's stress on the mother identification works to put the material out of focus. The supervisor writes:

> While I saw what led the analyst to his opinion, I was not impressed that it was the most important feature in the material. As we talked about his thinking regarding the material, especially after I read it, I kept noticing the even way in which the patient told her story. In connection with her ex-fiancé, whenever they tried to have intercourse, she would become so stiff that he would get furious about her unresponsiveness. Once he walked out on her, then came back. The ex-fiancé would also cry as a way to win her back. They finally decided to give up trying intercourse. (The analyst also mentioned to me in passing that the first fellow she had intercourse with, she had deliberately tried to get pregnant by in order to win him back from another girl he was interested in. This information is in the history, not mentioned by her in the recent hours.) The last time she and her ex-fiancé had intercourse she was unwilling, and when he persisted she became "hysterical."

The young analyst is correct in stressing the identification with the mother, who cannot "respond" to the father, infuriates him, but at the same time works to keep him. The story is actually a beautiful description of the transference situation, and the supervisor becomes more and more aware of it. The patient describes her desperate attempts to keep her lover, once even having tried to get herself pregnant in order to compete with another girl, but all her desperate attempts notwithstanding, she indicates she could not "get the car started," or "the intercourse going," and that the lover would end up infuriated with her unresponsiveness. Actually, as she gives this account, she describes in reverse how, in spite of all her efforts, she cannot get sympathy from the father imago—the analyst in the transference—sympathy for her distress, a distress toward which he remains objective and which he does not interpret in terms of the transference—as if she were offering no more than an objective account of her past and of her current life situation rather than a clear-cut appeal to him. The endless attempts possibly to sacrifice herself sexually, with the implied fear of being hurt thereby, as indicated in the example of father's violent outburst toward mother, give a clear picture of her interpretation of the analytic situation, her beginning involvement in this situation, and the specific development of her transference neurosis.

The supervisor understands all this, and as the analyst gives him an "objective picture" of this analysis, he must feel increasingly that he has made himself into the "captive audience" by this presentation. The patient, too, as she discusses her problem without being consciously much aware of her distress, her anxiety, and her attempts to appeal to him, has made the analyst into a *captive,* but *objective audience;* and both the supervisor and the analyst seem to react to all the material with *objectivity.*

Am I now, the outside observer, as I imagine myself to be the supervisor of the supervisor, also but a captive and objective audience? Of course, the outside observer, as long as he does not enter the arena of interaction, as long as he does not intervene, does not challenge, and does not try to get to the bottom of all this, also must become a captive, objective audience who can but play with possibilities, though he would prefer to arrive at workable trial formulations from which teaching interventions could be suggested. This style of working—coolness and objectivity—suggests a kind of *folie en masse* involving all of us: the young analyst, his supervisor, and the outside observer, who has to choose now between the role of the researcher of supervisory methods and the one of supervising the supervisor. I am using as alternative between these two polar roles that fantasied choice which I actually am unable to make, in order to stress the point that "objective research" in supervisory methods must be transformed into *action research.* Only action research allows for the development of methods of verification concerning the options advanced and the theoretical models underlying them without which the process of clarification remains always incomplete.

What are we to think of the analyst's coolness, his objectivity? Indeed, it may strike us as an inappropriate reaction, and perhaps as an inappropriate nonreaction. Are we to think of it as countertransference? It might be true that he does not see this material as transference material, but may merely view it in genetic terms; or he may see it in terms of the patient's attempt to deal with her reality situation; or, he may see no more in it than the patient's historical, literal and concrete, account of the doings of her father and mother, respectively her own current conflict with her boy friend. If the analyst were to do no more than that, we might perhaps be justified in suggesting that he suffers from a *blind spot,* from an inability to really see the true nature of the patient's productions. We could then speak of the analyst's countertransference proper.

But we could also think that his objectivity is a defense of a completely different kind, not a defense against unconscious conflicts he himself has with parental imagos of the past, but that he is trying to ward off a present attraction to this particular patient, and that he experiences her material as seductive—for example, the bright summery dress on a wintry day, and all the coy allusions as she identifies herself on the telephone by the diminutive of her name. In this case we would be understanding his objectivity much better if we were to relate this reaction formation to his having an unrecognized erotic transference response to the patient.

To the degree that the described coolness and objectivity do not really give a true picture of the interaction between him and the patient—and we must always remember that his report is *selective* and does not bring us all that happened during that hour—we may suggest that his style of reporting could also be understood as a reaction to the teacher, who perhaps also is experienced as cool and objective, and with whom he identifies—a reaction that permits him to make the teacher into a captive audience and at the same time to keep the learning problem away from himself while showing himself as a knowing and intellectual student. His particular selection of the material could be looked upon as a transference reaction to the teacher, a *learning resistance* by means of which he tries to keep the teacher away from his own true problems in learning. He exhibits his knowledge "objectively" rather than searching for genuinely troubling questions. He plays the good and obedient student who lives up to the presumed tenets of scientific objectivity which he wrongly considers to be proper analytic neutrality.

But these are not all the possibilities we must consider as we search for teaching options which are to help the supervisor free himself from his captivity. To the degree that this "coolness" might also be an expression of the student's own symptomatology—possibly even his current transference reaction to his own analyst—we might speak of it as a character resistance, a problem that indeed will yield only in his own analysis, a reaction that cannot as yet be tapped in the supervisory process, and may at the same time be so deep as to make learning very difficult, at least temporarily. If that were the case, both supervisor and the supervisor of that supervisor would have to remain the captive audience of a distant drama which must first find some kind of a solution in the student's personal analysis, at which time there will then finally be enough psychic energy freed and available to a meaningful learning relationship via the process of supervision. If the latter is true—a notion that has tempted many a supervisor to suggest to the learner that he take the issue at hand up in his own analysis—how is one to assess it? How can one establish an eventuality which on occasion would have to lead to grave decisions concerning the stability of the total training situation—and would lead us out of the supervisory process into administrative decision-making? Many a captive teacher has freed himself from such a dilemma by transferring it to the Institute's progression committee, or the like.

As I imagine myself to be this supervisor's supervisor, I have done at first what one usually does as one listens to a patient or to a person whom one supervises. I have identified myself tentatively with the presentation that is made, and I have searched for an answer to the questions that have been brought to me, albeit in a disguised and indirect way, by trying to understand what it was that the person reported to me about: the material about his supervisee, and through it, about the latter's patient. But as I listen with the *third ear of the supervisor,* I must ask myself questions concerning the supervisor himself, his way of assessing the patient's material, the meaning the analyst's work has for him, and his own pedagogic interventions; respectively, I must check his work, the nature of his interventions, through watching the student analyst's capacity to respond to these pedagogic interventions.

The supervisor, of course, will usually not merely react to the data on the page, the description of the analytic interviews. Rather, as he develops a picture of the meaning of the material, he will combine the overview of the analytic process with the insight he gains from the supervisee's specific appeal to him. Is this material brought to him solely to make him into a captive audience, an admirer, a confirmer, an endorser of the technique? Is the material combined with explicit or implicit questions the supervisee has about the data, about himself, his technique? It is this combination, I suggest, that will help the supervisor determine what to consider as the dominant problem, what he ought to select for the focus of their work, what his response ought to be, and what overall pedagogic appoach he is to take.

It is possible that an inexperienced supervisee may not even see the trend of the material; even though he has described it well, he may not see the common denominator that should lead him to a specific assessment of the transference and resistance situation. If that is the case, the supervisor may well try to think of this as a *dumb spot,* and for a while may choose to behave *didactically* and use explanation, description, and discussion of the case material. The supervisor may learn to travel between the Scylla of considering everything as countertransference, a blind spot, and the Charybdis of considering everything as lack of knowledge, a dumb spot.

In this particular case, the supervisee's emphasis seems to be on successful reporting, on the exhibiting of his intellectual understanding of the case, on his perhaps unconscious wish to use the supervisor as a captive audience. This may lead the supervisor to decide that he wishes to stress the interpersonal relationship between supervisor and supervisee, and he may now move into the foreground of their mutual consideration of the student's *problems about learning,* rather than his *learning problems.*[1] He may underline for himself, as I think this particular supervisor did in his own mind, that there is an issue of objectivity and coolness, and may see this as an expression of a specific transference reaction to the teacher. I am inclined to imagine that he ponders whether this is caused by a specific and delimited transference reaction to the teacher, or whether he is dealing with a deep-seated characterological issue that probably cannot be resolved in supervision. Should he wait? Should he remain the captive audience for a while, and should he be satisfied with a merely didactic level of interaction? It seems to me that this supervisor frequently chooses the option of waiting and of playing it along didactic lines. Should he on the other hand become more direct, and decide on a teaching technique that stresses the fact that the learner

[1]For the distinction between problems student-therapists have with their supervisors (problems about learning) and problems they have with their patients (learning problems), see Ekstein and Wallerstein (1972, Chapters 9 and 10).

seems to have no specific questions to ask, seems not really concerned about any of his activities except trying to impress the teacher with his comprehension of the material? Is the student's resistance style his current learning style?

Suppose I suggest to the supervisor that he take up with the student the issue of "coolness," of his objectivity, which really is not psychoanalytic neutrality; a situation may develop in which the student will now *explain* his coolness as a defense against his erotic feelings toward the patient. We would then ponder whether through this he inadvertently reveals a kind of compliant apology, a defensive maneuver, whether this quasi-confession about countertransference should really be seen as a kind of promise of submission, an expression of his wish more to please the supervisor than to learn from him. How is one to differentiate between such a confession in the service of the learning resistance and a genuine admission of intense feelings that interfere with the analytic work? We realize, indeed, that much of the differentiation will have to do with the question of whether the coolness, the objectivity itself, will yield during supervision to a freeing of emotions, and will lead from a pseudo-scientific detached attitude to a full learning involvement.

It may even be true that the student, even though all these possible connections are explained to him, is unable to see the transference, to accept the very concept of transference, and that all that is his way of defending himself against the very countertransference and/or transference reactions vis-à-vis his patient. Such a situation, of course, becomes more complicated if the student is in the throes of his own transference neurosis vis-à-vis his training analyst, which flows in turn into the supervisory situation. To what degree an oblique reference—such as a question as to whether this material more properly belongs in the student's analysis or in his supervision—will be helpful depends on the supervisor's capacity to proffer such a reference as an expression of actual helpfulness rather than as an expression of his own feelings of helplessness as a teacher—against which he musters the defensive alibi that the student is unsupervisable, an analogue of the difficult, and often only pseudo, question as to whether someone is analyzable or not.

It could even be that this student is already beyond his own personal analysis, but has residual character problems that require further analysis. When and how is the supervisor to convey this to his student? I certainly—as I imagine myself to be the supervisor of this particular supervisor—would not believe that this should be an active issue so early in learning. I would want to wait until the student has achieved sufficient insight to permit us to move such a question into the foreground of our pedagogic activities.

I suppose that my preferences as supervisor of this particular supervisor would be to have him go along with me, thinking of these several models as trial thoughts along the pedagogic axis and pleading for deferred action. Have I now, by choice, also become a captive audience? Or am I contemplating ways of participating and of initiating action, so that I can move from paralyzed objectivity to the neutrality of the analytic supervisor, which is not inactivity at all, but rather the technical stance conducive to maximal potential helpfulness to the student?

As the supervisor continues to report to me, I see how he slowly does get involved in the material, in the work of the young analyst, and becomes concerned about the technical inaction that seems to be based on an exaggerated objectivity rather than on the kind of interpretive helpfulness which is derived from true psychoanalytic neutrality. The supervisor writes:

> My point in recording these details here is that the patient talked about these and other matters about which she must have felt distress in a way that did not invite the analyst to be sympathetic or to help. There appeared to be very little of what I would call "demand quality" in her speech during the hours. One might say she allowed herself to expect very little of the analyst, but put up with the relationship, including the problems of getting there when the car would not start, without complaint.

The patient's plea for help is disguised as the willingness to do whatever she has to in order to secure the analyst's acceptance. It is as if she suggests she knows it is expected of her to grow up, love, deliver the expected associations in the analytic situation, cope with life undemandingly. The student-analyst, too, seems to think he must become an analyst without ever making demands on the supervisor, and his objective account of what happened in the analysis could almost be considered a kind of parallel event, inasmuch as he too has to get there to become an analyst (i.e., to help the patient), even though his own analytic car does not get started. It seems to me that the supervisor clearly starts to focus on the student's dominant problem, albeit disguised and hidden. He states his impression of the analyst as follows:

> In this connection, she described in the last hour of this week her first meeting with her ex-fiancé. She could get no sympathy from him. He seemed so objective at a time when she needed somebody to be on her side against the world. It was after this statement that the patient left the couch with a smile, saying she still had to get her car started.

At this point, I was just about to tell the supervisor he ought to make use of his accumulating insights and take the teaching initiative. He ought to challenge the student as he makes these issues clear. But as I read on in my study of the supervisor's notes, I saw he was catching up with my own internal preoccupations, and that my impatience was premature or, at best, an identification with the supervisor's dilemma. He continues:

> I called the analyst's attention to my observations, noting that the qualities she was acting out seemed to be closest to those she had described in her father (whom she also described during these hours as being absent much of the time during her early adolescence when she felt she very much needed him). After the analyst saw this pattern, I moved a bit further with him in two directions: I wondered if there was anything in his effort to be analytically correct that led him to overstress objectivity in his attitude, possibly to the point of conveying indifference. On the other side, I noted that I thought it very likely that the patient's projection of a father imago onto the analyst could also include identification with what she would construe as his objectivity toward her problem.

It is here, for the first time, that the supervisor chooses between two possible actions—to describe this material simply as transference material, or to stress that the patient's activities reflect a realistic evaluation of what she deduced about the analyst. The supervisor chose to link the material both with the past and with the current behavior of the analyst, and wondered whether the analyst was aware of the difference between coolness and objectivity on the one hand, and analytic neutrality on the other.

I wished he had stopped here and waited for the student's reactions. But I have the impression that the supervisor felt he did not make his point strongly enough and needed to be more active in order to pull the student out of his "objective stance":

> I said that the patient may not really feel herself to be a patient because neither she nor, as she perceives it, the analyst conveys much empathy for her actual distress. I linked to this figurative observation the lack of demand quality in the hours and the patient's apparent willingness to put up with the difficulties in coming for analysis without complaint.

It is clear that the supervisor tries, as I think he should, to put the emphasis now on the analyst's activities rather than on the meaning of the material the patient brings. What will the analyst do now? Will he be able to focus on himself and his own activities? Or will he turn to the patient's material? Will he react personally to the supervisor or, more impersonally, to the implication of the supervisor's remark? I would think that at this stage of the game the analyst would try to maintain his present learning stance by returning to the meanings of the material itself. We cannot expect immediate reactions after all. The supervisor's comment must be considered a seed which may bear fruit some day. It is not unlike many an interpretation that has to be made repeatedly before there is change in the material and genuine insight.

Let us return to the supervisor's notes in order to see the immediate result of his intervention.

> The analyst looked thoughtful as he listened to my comments, but made no direct response to them. Nor did I act as if I expected any from him. He did comment on the patient's character and resistance problem reflected in this behavior, and we discussed possible ways in which he could interpret this attitude when it seemed relevant to do so. The analyst continued to feel that the patient was coming more under stress, with which I would agree, and he would have to keep aware of the necessity to intervene at some point. In the meantime, the patient was talking steadily, filling in a good deal of her background, indicating her willingness to work, for instance, on dreams, and showing a bit more psychological-mindedness than we had anticipated at the beginning.

I suggest that the student is willing to take up the supervisor's attempt to put the focus on him by means of discussing his own problem, once removed, as a problem of the patient's. The possibility of his having character problems as a young analyst, or also resistances to learning, is now clearly in the open, not directly, but protected, by describing these unconsciously as the patient's problems. But much of learning and teaching through long stretches of supervisory activities must be carried out on such a level, a distance device by way of which more genuine insight can develop ultimately.

I feel in tune with the supervisor, except that I toyed for a moment with the question as to whether he was wise to make no comment whatsoever on the student's giving no direct response to his remarks. As I see myself with this supervisor, I would be inclined to tell him that I considered that new choice, but then decided in favor of his. However, I would want him in turn to consider the alternative choice, since the ongoing analytic process will anyway later allow the option for the second choice as a practical and useful alternative in the teaching process.

How does the supervisor end his conference report? He tells us:

> Another theme the patient talked about is worth mentioning. At one point she described her older sister as being more of a mother to her than her actual mother. The sister was quite compulsive and ritualistic. The patient recalled a childhood memory of being so angry with her sister that she ran down the stairs and kicked her in the stomach. There were in her dreams several references to stairs, and suggestive hints of pregnancy

fantasies and fears of being damaged in intercourse, none of which was interpreted by the analyst, who continued to handle the hours technically in a very adequate manner.

As I read these lines I wondered who was the compulsive and ritualistic substitute mother? At whom was the patient so terribly angry because she felt she was not treated right? From whom did she expect expressions of retaliation if she expressed her anger, leading to its suppression and the avoidance of demands? The supervisor only confirms the problem the patient has in dealing with the analyst, and he sees the analyst's unwillingness to respond at this point via interpretation, that is, by proper technical action. I am just about to take up with the supervisor the question of why he thinks the analyst continues to handle the hour technically in a very adequate manner. Does he simply mean a compulsively competent way of handling it? Does he wish to say that he sees no place of entry for himself, having been warded off earlier, as already described? What is his problem as a supervisor? As he submits the material to us, he must free himself from the wish merely to demonstrate his capacity, and he must give up the coolness and objectivity of a kind of supervisory reporting which makes for captive and admiring audiences. Objectivity and coolness of the type described in this material would ultimately lead to alienation from the material. Psychoanalytic neutrality as we see it would, on the contrary, lead to reflection and to appropriate technical action. The supervisor knows that there is no shortcut to the enabling process of supervision or the research on supervision. The study of his material cannot yet yield precise and reliable techniques. Perhaps if it is linked up—beyond data research—with action research, we shall be able to help him develop more teaching options than he had before. This, in turn, will give the student more learning options. But is this not exactly the nature of the psychoanalytic enabling process? The interlocking of treatment, of training, and of research permits the enabling process to move toward the widening of options.

REFERENCE

Ekstein, R. & Wallerstein, R. S. (1972), *The Teaching and Learning of Psychotherapy*. New York: International Universities Press.

CHAPTER XI

The Supervision and Treatment As Seen from the Analyst's Perspective

HOWARD SHEVRIN, Ph.D.

Although only made aware of the Supervision Study Group's labors following its completion, and more than a few years after the events examined in this monograph, as the analyst I consider it my task in this chapter to provide, as best as I can, a special perspective—one that moves between past and present, between my experiences as a candidate and my subsequent experiences as a graduate analyst, between my earlier days as a researcher and my later experiences as a seasoned (perhaps chastened is the better word) researcher, between my experiences as a supervisee and my subsequent experiences as a supervisor, and, last, between my experiences as a staff member without administrative responsibilities and my later experiences as an administrator.

Time may not always mellow, but it inevitably adds burdens which finally lower one's eyes to the level at which one's elders have been peering at reality for some time. What I smiled at, berated, and attacked in my analytic youth, I discover is too often now my portion. It is thus with a bittersweet taste that I undertake this reconsideration of an early piece of work, part of my apprenticeship, as it has been investigated in this monograph. I will devote my attention in this chapter to the scientific, educational, and factual aspects of the research with only an occasional lapse into personal allusion. In Chapter XIV I devote myself to a more personal reaction to the study. This chapter will deal with the overall setting of the study and with a detailed presentation of the analytic material related to the supervision of the first 25 analytic hours which were covered in the first six supervision hours.

THE STUDY AS RESEARCH

It sometimes happens in research that what starts out as a pilot study intended to help us across a small patch of unexplored water is launched instead across an ocean of difficulties. Thus, a tugboat is made to do the work of an oceanliner. It is my impression that this fate overtook the current study, for this is the only way one can account for the fact that methodological decisions made initially and maintained throughout the research were out of keeping with the two research programs on supervision which constituted the two main approaches to supervision compared in the research. The decision was to base the study on the supervisor's process notes in which the supervisor summarized: (1) the analytic sessions as presented by the analyst (often orally), (2) his own evaluation of the analytic material, and (3) the supervisory session itself.

The San Francisco approach, based on a broad and comprehensive method, requires—as Wallerstein points out (Chapter I)—independent data for the analysis and for the supervision: The method requires a comprehensive, separate, and independent study of two sets of data—the analysis and the supervision "in ways that make possible the study of. . . the major substantive issues of psychoanalytic supervision." Only in this way can one begin to answer a crucial question: How well has the supervisor grasped the analytic process? In the San Francisco schema, this is mainly embodied in category 4a, *The Supervisor's Understanding of the Technical Analytic Issues.* Ideally, one would want tape recordings of both the analytic and supervision hours and the thoughts obtained independently about the two parallel processes from both supervisor and analyst.

Similarly, the Fleming-Benedek approach (see Chapter VI) had to be modified because their method depends on video and audio tapes of supervision sessions in order to study closely the interaction between supervisor and analyst.

> The records of *A*'s (analyst) report to *S* (supervisor) about the events in the analysis varied, depending on whether *S* read *A*'s summarized notes or *A* presented his material orally. *The account of the interaction between* S *and*

> A. . . *varied in the amount of evidence given on which* S *based his inferences and evaluations of* A*'s work. The specific form of* S*'s activity with* A *also varied in the detail with which it was reported. Sometimes it was summarized so that the sequences of stimulus and response were not available and, therefore, the effect of supervisory teaching could not be so easily identified in relation to a given episode* [italics added]. I came to the conclusion that these "process notes" did not provide as adequate data for responding to the question, "What happens within a supervision session?" as a transcript of one electrically recorded [Chapter VI, p. 123].

We are confronted right at the start with basic limitations in the primary data as seen from the point of view of the two methods to be applied to the data. By deciding to rely entirely on the supervisor's process notes both as a source of information about the supervision *and* the analysis, the Study Group made it impossible to arrive at an independent assessment of the supervisor's understanding of the analytic process or to have an accurate account of what happened within the supervisory sessions. The strength of this study must, therefore, lie in the richness of its many-sided examination of a limited and inherently flawed body of data by a group of experienced and knowledgeable supervisors. To borrow a metaphor from music, it is more in the *reading* of the score than in the score itself that the value of the study resides, more in the *possibilities* than in the certainties. Nevertheless, the consequences of these limitations in the data will be discussed below.

Aside from the data base for the research, a question must also be raised about the balance in the research design itself, which focuses narrowly on the supervisor-analyst relationship, and on a blurrier view of the analyst-patient relationship out at the periphery, both as seen by the supervisor. If, however, we draw on the insights developed by Ekstein and Wallerstein (1972), we learn that the supervision process is set in the broader context of the institution in which it is conducted, with its administrative policies and traditions and with its research as well as teaching needs clearly in mind.

The model Ekstein and Wallerstein propose is that of the clinical rhombus. We find the patient, therapist, supervisor, and administrator at the four corners of the rhombus with the manifold relationships possible among them represented by the lines constituting the periphery of the rhombus and its diagonals. There are several potential segmented triangles: supervisor-therapist-patient; supervisor-administrator-therapist; supervisor-administrator-patient, etc. As Ekstein and Wallerstein note:

> The personal aspects of this clinical rhombus will. . . be experienced by each of the participants in a different way, since each of them—student, supervisor, patient, and administrator—has a different place in the hier-

> archy of interrelationships. We are talking not simply about the variety of human relationships which exist among four people, but about those stratifications of the relationships which reflect the different functions that the participants carry [pp. 12–13].

Strangely, there is no discussion in any of the chapters in this monograph of the *clinical rhombus,* a model of obvious relevance to understanding supervision. Moreover, in addition to the excellent rationale offered by Ekstein and Wallerstein, we can adduce a further reason for taking carefully into account the administrative, training, and research contexts of the study: distortions in communication can only be appreciated when we know something about the reality prevailing at the time of communication. In analysis we go to great lengths to preserve a constant, clear, and neutral environment because we know that only in this way can we be sure to identify the patient's unique way of experiencing the analyst and the analysis. Even then we must be alert to countertransferences, suggestions, real events of moment, and, in fact, the role of reality factors in general in the patient's life. No analysis exists in a personal and social vacuum. As Lewin and Ross (1960) have warned:

> The "ecology" of the [psychoanalytic] school is a necessary part of the "analytic material" of a present-day training analysis. It is not always easy to sense. . . the last thing a deep-sea fish could discover is salt water [p. 233].

Insofar as one of the main goals of the current study is to distinguish between the analyst's emotional and intellectual shortcomings—or those shortcomings for which he might need further analysis and those for which he could benefit from supervision—it is essential that the social, personal, and administrative dimensions of the environment in which the supervision was taking place be known.

In summary, as a piece of research the present study must operate within severe limitations both with respect to the limited nature of its data and the weakness in its design. At the same time, it is a unique and valuable undertaking, mainly because it brings to bear on the problem a wealth of supervisory experience. I found myself admiring time and time again the quality of clinical thinking, while wishing that a broader and firmer foundation were present to sustain these exercises in inference. It appeared to me that my contribution should try to strengthen the study precisely where it was weakest. My original process notes, with some reconstruction of my feelings and thoughts at the time, might make up for the limitation in the data. With respect to the research design, I could add my recall and understanding of the broader institutional context of the study and how this affected the supervision and the analysis.

THE INSTITUTIONAL CONTEXT

Psychoanalytic education is a complex, demanding, and gradually evolving process. In the past twenty years, two full-scale assessments of psychoanalytic education have been conducted, each ending with sobering conclusions about the problems involved (Lewin and Ross, 1960; Goodman, 1977). It matters greatly in what institutional setting this education is undertaken. In the first psychoanalytic study, Lewin and Ross (1960) expressed concern over what they referred to as the "syncretisms" of psychoanalytic education. By "syncretisms" they were referring to problematic combinations of roles and functions in psychoanalytic education. They followed *Webster's Unabridged Dictionary* in defining "syncretism": "Egregious compromise. . . that is illogical or leads to inconsistency; uncritical acceptance of conflicting or divergent beliefs and principles" (p. 46). They applied the definition to psychoanalysis in the following instructive manner:

> . . . the psychoanalytic educator has advanced gradually to the fact that education and the psychoanalytic procedure exist in two worlds and that psychoanalytic education, as a concept, is a syncretism. . . the two models "psychoanalytic patient" and "student" complement, alternate with, and oppose each other. A psychoanalytic treatment is *sui generis*. The education introduces a parameter for the therapeutic procedure, and the analytic procedure an even larger one for the education. The institutes are unavoidably trying to exert two effects on the student: to "educate" him and to "cure" or "change" him. Hence, the student as a phenomenon fits into two conceptual frameworks: he is the pedagogic unit or object of teaching and the therapeutic unit or object of psychoanalytic procedure [p. 47].

The issues identified by Lewin and Ross continue to reverberate in the Goodman (1977) report's more recent assessment of psychoanalytic education and research. The "tripartite system of psychoanalytic education" (training analysis, supervision, and seminars), however, is considered to be optimal and, in fact, the recent commission conducting the assessment recommended a "closer educational integration of the training analysis" (p. 45). There were dissenting voices, one participant in the discussion recommending that the candidate's required personal analysis be acceptable if conducted by any recognized analyst rather than by a training analyst (see

Shevrin, 1978). The reasons for avoiding syncretisms in analytic education are convincing, although they may be impractical. As our appreciation of the depth and delicacy of the transference in analysis has increased, and as the length of treatment has grown from months to years, the necessity to protect the treatment from extratherapeutic influences has grown accordingly. The work of analysis is difficult enough without complicating it by having the analyst play vital decision-making roles in the analysand's professional life. A direct conflict is involved between the neutral, though not indifferent, role of the analyst and the role of an evaluator of one's progress as a candidate.

If the syncretism of analysis and education creates special problems, then the existence of still another source of syncretism must further complicate matters. Yet this was precisely the situation existing in our institute, which was part of a larger psychiatric institution. Training analysts were not only members of the institute education committee, but were directors of the hospital, psychotherapy and diagnostic service, psychology discipline, and research department. Moreover, the unique institutional arrangement guaranteed that, with few exceptions, all analysands worked in settings administered and controlled by training analysts. Most candidates divided their time between two or three settings, so that it became highly unlikely not to encounter one's training analyst or supervisor elsewhere in the institution. At any given time at least half the complement of training analysts served in important administrative posts. Their influence was widespread and felt throughout the institution. Candidates were well aware that their relationships with their administrator-training analysts at work had significant bearing on their relationships with their training analyst-administrators on the couch, in the institute classroom, and around the education committee table. All these considerations applying to training analysts applied with only slightly lesser force to analytic supervisors, who were all training analysts themselves wearing another hat. The clinical rhombus in this setting behaved more like a clinical accordion that tended to collapse on itself—supervisor, training analyst, and administrator met in the same person; patient, candidate, and subordinate could be the same person playing different roles. Your supervisor might be your administrator in another context, while the administrators of the institute might also be your administrative supervisors over in the hospital, outpatient service, or research. Candidates were identified by their training analysts and associated with their analytic "siblings." They looked forward to their analytic terminations and eventual graduations as the time when they could join their training analyst-administrator's "convoy" or clique. These "convoys" were made up usually of one powerful training analyst-administrator, several satellite staff, and a number of ex-analysands. These "convoys" grew and were nurtured by the exercise of administrative—and what must be called —analytic power. I distinguish the two sources of power because analytic power is exercised through the analysis itself rather than through a formal administrative channel; and this is especially true when the analyst has real power to exercise through extra-analytic channels, which he did in many instances in our institutional setting.

These considerations concerning training analysts and analysands are equally applicable to institute supervisors, all training analysts, and their supervisees. The awe in which training analysts and analytic supervisors were held was not altogether an unrealistic idealization in our institution; indeed, in their administrative influence on professional career development, money earned, attractive work opportunities, and progress in analytic training (usually taking the form of good control cases), training analysts and analytic supervisors wielded enormous and largely unqualified power. The only limitation on this power was that enforced by the counter-ambitions of other colleagues, and thus the vital significance of having supporters or "convoys." The presence of this treatment-administrative syncretism greatly exacerbated the effect of the education-treatment syncretism, for both training analyst and supervisor were, in effect, the candidate's employers, who had a decisive voice in the candidate's promotion, salary, and work responsibilities in the institution-at-large.

The power priorities in this complex institutional setting rated clinical work first, education second, and research a poor third. This was especially the case for nonclinically based research. The psychoanalytic institute had an excellent record in supporting research candidates and obtaining waivers for them. At the same time, it was also evident that the institute did not altogether escape the ethos described in the Goodman report (1977, pp. 103–136). The research candidate for whom research was as important as clinical work was somehow suspect. In particular, it was not easy to see how he might move into a significant "convoy" position in an institution in which research appointments were not only few, but relatively powerless and without substantial influence. The researcher's power relationships extended beyond the institution to like-minded colleagues elsewhere; within the institution—with the exception of the director of research—he was a drone, good for occasional fertilization, but without any lasting impact and devoid of importance as a presence. Ironically, in this particular study, research exercised a powerful but largely subterranean effect on the supervisor. The supervisor knew of the research from the start and was both a research subject and participant investigator. The candidate and the patient were unwitting subjects. The Study Group truly constituted still another power locus directly affecting the supervisor and indirectly affecting the candidate and his patient, which cannot easily be represented in the form of a rhombus. If it is also borne in mind that the members of the Study Group included a number of quite senior and nationally noted figures, then one can readily conclude that the Study Group was of some weight and influence on the supervisor and, through him, on candidate and patient (Figure 1).

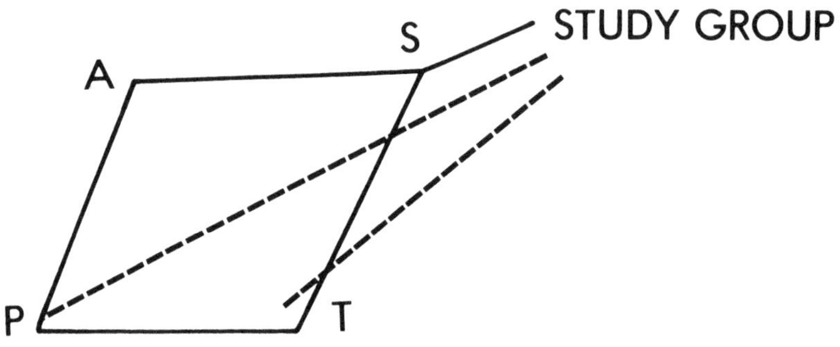

FIGURE I

The four corners of the clinical rhombus may be defined as follows in terms of identifiable roles:

P = patient — control case — research subject
T = analyst — candidate — research subject — supervisee — employee — researcher
S = supervisor — training analyst — education committee member — researcher — research subject — employer
A = chairman, education committee — director of institute (Let us assume that the responsible administrator in the clinical rhombus is the chairman of the education committee.)
Study Group = supervisor of supervisor-researcher

The patient as a control case had a special role vis-à-vis the analyst-candidate and the institution subsidizing her treatment. She was aware of this subsidization (although as will be seen below, she distorted this information). She was unaware of her role as a research subject.

The therapist was conducting an analysis in which the contract involved the psychoanalytic institute and the institution-at-large, to both of which he was responsible. To the psychoanalytic institute he was responsible as a student, and to the institution-at-large he was responsible as an employee. To his supervisor he was responsible as a student; but since his supervisor was also, in this instance, his chief administrator, he was in actual fact employed by him. The therapist also wished to continue his research and to apply it to analytic patients (more of this later, and in Chapter XIV). He was aware of all these roles and of their potential contradictory interaction. He was, however, unaware that he was a research subject.

The supervisor was not only concerned with the supervision of the case, but with evaluating the candidate's progress for the education committee. He also evaluated the progress and capabilities of the candidate as his employee.

Last, he was aware of treating him as a research subject while he himself was also one, a unique and difficult-to-assess complication of the supervision process.

The official administrator in this instance could wear his mere two hats with a sigh of relief. The Study Group, insofar as it monitored the supervisor as the supervision progressed, was in effect acting as a supervisor as well as a research group. Indirectly, they were influencing the candidate and his patient (the broken lines in Figure 1).

Clearly, the clinical rhombus must be extended into at least three planes: (1) the clinical plane, (2) the institutional-administrative plane, and (3) the research plane. This three-dimensional model must be superimposed on the two-dimensional clinical rhombus in order to represent this complex, multifaceted situation.

Finally, a word needs to be said about significant administrative changes occurring at the time the supervision studied in the monograph was taking place. There were major changes in the leadership of the institution-at-large as a result of which some training analysts and supervisors left and others were appointed in their place. These changes reverberated throughout the institution, not least within the institute, causing difficulties for candidates, especially those in analysis and secondarily those in supervision. Will my analysis be interrupted? Will I need a different supervisor in the midst of my case (an eventuality that occurred in this particular case)? Will the good teachers (much prized by candidates) leave? When the parents are busy separating and divorcing, the children are distressed, guilty, angry, and —most of all—cautious and circumspect. Political cleavages are never clearer and the need to be on the right side never more essential, especially since the cleavages in the institute and the society are also present in the parent institution, so that not only one's candidacy but also one's job might very well be at stake. Clearly this made for difficult circumstances in which to be analyzed or supervised. Lewin and Ross (1960) cite Ekstein's reference to the older, patriarchal training groups and how occasionally their problems are present in contemporary institutes, "complicating the 'reality' in which the training analysis takes place" (p. 232). Lewin and Ross quote an analyst who experienced the older, patriarchal, and highly syncretistic training in which "students, teachers and analysts met each other constantly. . . . It was difficult for them and us to keep reality and fantasy apart. The negative transference remained in many instances unanalyzed and 'reality' gave excellent rationalizations" (p. 232). One can only add that this situation would be made all the more difficult by the syncretism of administrative control over the candidate in his role as a staff member. Parenthetically, in my own experience it is not only that negative transferences may remain unanalyzed, but that negative and positive countertransferences are acted out in the institution-at-large along with the analysand's positive and negative transferences. Tacit agreements develop as to what is reportable and, if reported, how it is to be understood, i.e., in terms of certain agreed-on judgments of colleagues and factions. It might, in fact, be argued that in any institution serving any purpose the same kinds of forces would be at work. I do not at all doubt this and have seen it for myself. However, the critical question from the point of view of this study is: How did these forces impinge on, distort, and perhaps disrupt the normal, expectable course of analytic training, and, in particular, the supervision and treatment under scrutiny?

THE STRUCTURE OF THE SUPERVISION

The supervisor was one of the candidate's main administrators, with whom he had dealings over issues of work arrangements, salary, and career advancement. The candidate devoted a considerable portion of his time to research in which he was responsible to another administrator; it was for his clinical work that he was responsible to the supervisor as an administrator. Thus, the candidate's performance as an analyst had implications not only for his training in the institute, but also for his advancement in the larger institution. His job as well as his training partly depended on this supervision. The institute had assigned his supervisor without apparently taking into account the multiple roles played by one supervisor in the candidate's professional life.[1] In a certain sense, the circumstances were comparable to those in which an employer expects an employee to take a series of tests, presumably for the employee's enlightenment, but the results of the tests will be available only to the employer. I must underscore this point because it introduced a contaminant into the purely *educational* relationship not ordinarily found in supervision, even though it could be argued that in the long run one's analytic supervision will have bearing on one's career and income-producing capacity. The point is that it does not do so at the time, and the supervision is not immediately and directly involved in these matters.

The patient, as already described, was not only a control case acceptable to the institute, but was registered as a patient in the institution-at-large. In this latter role, the patient was under the jurisdiction of the director of psychotherapy, another training analyst and member of the education committee, who was, therefore, concerned with the patient's progress in these two respects. In complementary fashion, the candidate was responsible for the patient's treatment to the education committee, and as a staff member in

[1]As we shall learn in Chapter XIII, the supervisor also had a personal reason for assuming the supervision. The personal dimensions of this complex relationship will be dealt with in Chapter XIV.

the institution-at-large, he was responsible for the patient's treatment to the director of the psychotherapy service. The candidate, as a recipient of a research waiver, felt a responsibility to think of his patients as potential research subjects. Actually, although unaware of that fact, both he and his patient were research subjects. When it is recalled that the supervision was taking place in the complicated political atmosphere described above, it becomes apparent that the structure of the supervision was Byzantine in its ramifications for patient, candidate, and supervisor. No significant issue could present itself with only one clear facet—the candidate's education; each issue was inherently multifaceted, presenting a difficult challenge to understanding and resolution. Only rarely (in Chapters V and XIII) are these aspects alluded to, and nowhere are they given full consideration. Yet, they must have played significant roles. One is reminded of the comedian Jimmy Durante, who would pull an elephant behind him by the trunk across stage, and when he would be asked where he was taking the elephant, would reply, "What elephant?" Unlike Jimmy Durante, who knew what he was about, the Study Group appeared to be in ignorance of the elephant it was dragging behind it.

We shall now turn to an examination of the supervisory and analytic material. In this examination, an effort will be made to identify the influence of the different syncretisms just described and how they might have changed the understanding of the supervision itself. In addition, the material will be examined from the usual analytic and educational standpoints.

SUPERVISION HOUR 1 (ANALYTIC HOURS 1–3)

On the whole the supervisor thought the opening hours of the analysis went well, as did the first supervisory session. In particular, the supervisor stressed that the analyst was not overinterpreting, but resorting to "mildly facilitating comments." There was evidence for the patient's developing investment in the hours. Of some concern was the analyst's maladroit introduction of a forthcoming absence on his part at a point in the hour when the patient was referring to him as a "captive audience."

From the analytic process notes, two additional issues of some importance emerge: (1) the patient's references to affairs with younger men and her fear that a debauched life lay ahead for her, (2) the abrupt change in the content of her associations following the analyst's mention of his forthcoming absence. Her first thought on the couch was of a nineteen-year-old youngster whom she liked, but had to inhibit her interest in, because he was an "inappropriate" partner. In the second hour there was a long reference to the film *La Dolce Vita,* and her identification with a writer in the film who ended up debauched, an end she feared for herself. She recalled that as soon as she learned about her appointment with the analyst, she called her ex-fiancé, perhaps, she felt, with the hope that the treatment might work to bring them together. Then, after commenting how hard it was to talk in this intimate way to a stranger, she suddenly began talking about her "awful" apartment—"how cold and ugly it was with no curtains on the windows." At the end of the first hour, she took the analyst by surprise when she removed the napkin from the pillow, crumpled it, and searched out his wastebasket, where she deposited it. Although I suspect it was unclear to me at the time, it would seem that she thought herself to be an awful person, given to evil impulses, who must clean up after herself. She had hinted broadly at what made her think this about herself: her strong sexual urges that somehow led her into debauchery, especially with younger men.

The impact of the analyst's announcement of his absence was dramatic. After telling him of her plans made prior to the analysis to visit her sister for the upcoming holidays, entirely new material entered her associations dealing for the first time with the family's constant moving around during her childhood and how her sister took these moves much better than she. No sooner would she be settled in, than the family would move again. The patient reported at this point that the room had begun to spin. In fact, she had introduced talking about the family moves by referring to earth tremors she had experienced abroad. Lamps would begin to sway, and they would need to sit under the furniture. As she left the hour, she repeated the days I would be gone and asked me where I would be going.

Clearly, the patient was much affected by the news of the analyst's absence. Although it was actually too early to be sure, the patient had announced two major themes: (1) she felt bad about her inability to control her sexual impulses toward younger men, and (2) she was deeply affected by disruptions in her attachments.

Were I to look at these hours from the perspective of someone who has since that time analyzed a number of women, I would find myself concerned about the patient's reactions to lying down on the couch and assuming a passive posture—physically and emotionally—which might account for the emphasis she placed on her interest in younger men, with whom she could play a much more controlling and active role than with her peers. I would entertain the hypothesis that countering the news of my absence with one of her own was an effort to maintain her dignity in the face of what seemed to her to be my arbitrariness, much like her father's, whose career needs resulted in many dislocating family moves. I would not have placed the patient so quickly on the couch, nor would I have announced my absence in the midst of an hour. I have found it valuable to explore in advance the meaning of the couch, especially with women patients, and have never found it to be without intense, ambivalent significance. My practice now is always to announce any change in analytic routines at the beginning of the hour so that the patient's reaction can be judged freshly rather than assessed in mid-hour after much has already been said by patient and analyst. I would have benefited by a discussion of these issues in the supervision.

SUPERVISION HOUR 2 (ANALYTIC HOURS 4–12)

Because the supervisor had been unavailable for two weeks, eight hours were discussed in this one session. Mainly, the supervisor stressed the patient's struggle over dependency and the apparent absence of any indication of her expecting anything from the analyst. The supervisor hypothesized that as the patient was becoming more aware of her helplessness in her life through the analysis, she experienced this as "jumping from the helplessness of the fire in her life into the frying pan of the analysis and were very much afraid of her impending dependency on the analyst." The supervisor concluded that the analyst was handling the case well and was experienced by the patient as perhaps giving her too much, thus making her feel helpless. The supervisor made mention of the length of the process notes and recommended that the analyst devote a maximum of one single-spaced page per hour.

Before commenting on what the process notes of these sessions brought to light, it is necessary first to discuss the supervisor's reference to the length of the process notes, for this was the first allusion to what would become a running battle between supervisor and analyst. Here, for the first time, the candidate's role as a researcher clashed with the supervisor's style of supervision, which depended on relatively brief notes. This clash would also have reverberations on the candidate's role in the supervision as the supervisor's administrative subordinate. The supervisor's response to the analyst's resolve, with some fluctuation, to keep relatively lengthy notes (averaging over the course of the time dealt with in this monograph approximately one and a half single-spaced pages per hour) was not to read them at all, or at most to glance through them at the end of the supervision as a check on the analyst's oral report in the session. The analyst would undertake to summarize the sessions orally at the beginning of each supervisory session. One important consequence of this standoff was that the supervisor did not have a detailed knowledge of the analytic sessions prior to the supervision. Another important consequence was that the analyst's oral report could much more readily be influenced by the ongoing dynamics of the supervisory interaction. Both consequences resulted in a much less clear contribution of the analytic material to the supervision process. The candidate made careful notes which he would use as the basis for dictating a detailed note each hour right after the hour. He prided himself on his discipline in doing this and felt that the notes were potentially useful research data. It is of interest to note that Ekstein, as quoted by Lewin and Ross (1960), recommended that ". . . the student submit . . . prepared material which I read, if possible, ahead of time. This material, our common knowledge about the main events of the analytic week, is then the basis for a free, spontaneous discussion in which the student is encouraged to bring up his own questions and problems" (p. 262).

There was much material in the analytic hours on the patient's current love relationships in which she was sleeping with one fellow while fending off the entreaties of other fellows who lived in the same building. She found herself tempted by a younger boy with whom she necked, but refrained from having an affair because their age difference kept him from being an "appropriate" partner. She enjoyed "wildness" in her relationships with men, by which she meant running risks of pregnancy, maintaining several relationships concurrently, and doing daring things like bathing naked near a waterfall where she could have drowned—this right after having had intercourse. She continued to experience much ambivalence about coming to the sessions and was, at one point, painfully aware of this. She forgot to come to an appointment, believing it was in the afternoon rather than in the morning. She was especially unhappy about her lapse because that morning she recalled her first dream and so much wanted to tell the analyst about it. The analyst commented, ". . . in the first hour you had mentioned how much you wanted and needed treatment and yet how hard it was for you to describe your troubles. It was like yesterday and today; you so much wanted to tell me the dream and yet somehow you became confused about the time and did not come" (hour 5). Her response to this was to agree, but then to talk about how she had been trying to do things right lately, but she had, for example, not been studying enough. Her thoughts then took her back to her teasing flirtations with the four fellows in her apartment building. We may surmise from this that she heard the analyst's comment as a criticism to which she responded by saying indirectly that she would try to do better, but this was followed by a return to thoughts about teasing men, which strongly suggested that this pattern would continue with the analyst.

The patient related much tragedy and near-tragedy in her love life. One of the first involvements was with a young man who left her for a girl friend. She undertook to win him back, even going to the extreme of getting pregnant by him and having to undergo an abortion when he continued to reject her. Her attachments to men, like to her ex-fiancé, were painful and highly conflictual. There was some reason to believe that this pattern emerged after she left her parents to live away from them. There was one highly significant dream in which she saw her mother behind a glass panel pointing to a wedding band on the wrong hand. The patient related that her mother was an overly generous person, ready to give her anything, including this ring. She also related the glass panel to a window in the family summer home where she would spend summers with her parents and where she could have stayed rather than living by herself; but she did not wish to live with them. She spoke of her father as someone she greatly admired, recalling warmly the games she and her sister played with him when he would roll on top of her and her sister would then roll on top of him. But her mother was always criticizing him and warning her against men. Like mother, she had suffered at the hands of men, and there were more than strong hints of wanting to turn the tables but feeling great guilt over her castrating wishes. Yet, there was her frustrated and perennial ex-fiancé, as well as the desirous and thwarted young men in her building. Would the analyst begin to emerge as a potentially dangerous male who had both to be propitiated and frustrated? A dream of a black cat, her first dream, was associated by her to an old phobia for spiders, and was the first indication of a possible projection of her powerful oral-aggressive wishes, which one could hypothesize were directed mainly at men.

The process notes document this theme of hostile behavior toward men in some detail, and must be placed alongside the theme of dependency stressed by the supervisor. There was certainly evidence for this dependency, as cited by the supervisor, but there was much else in the material the analyst was hearing, experiencing, and writing up in his notes, which was not getting into the supervision process. The patient's early experience of the analysis was likely compounded of her competitive, hostile, and sexual conflict with men and her conflict over dependency. She did not want to become attached to a man (e.g., her ex-fiancé, the analyst, her father) because of her hostile and incestuous wishes, as well as by reason of her fears over dependency. At this stage one had to surmise that it would have been hard to separate these two sources of conflict and to weigh their relative importance. It was clear, however, that the supervisor had made his choice—dependency. The rationale for this was unclear. In this sequence we have the first clear indication of a bias and selectivity that continued to affect the supervision itself. This selectivity may have been influenced by the supervisor's neglect of the process notes which documented the patient's struggle with men and the oedipal sources of her difficulties. More speculatively, one could wonder if the administrator-supervisor and employee-candidate syncretism might not have made any issue involving competitiveness more difficult to deal with, thus contributing to making dependency more of an issue than it really was, or at least making it hard to weigh that issue along with the oedipal issue.

SUPERVISION HOUR 3 (ANALYTIC HOURS 13–15)

The supervisor made note of the cogent and concise oral summary given by the analyst of the week's events. He read the notes part-way through and commented that the patient "did not seem to need even as little intervention as he was applying." (For these three hours the notes were a page and a half in length. The analyst had made four comments in the first hour, three in the second, and two in the third.) The supervisor took up for the first time the patient's attitude toward men and marriage, for the patient had commented at length about her cynicism toward men in general and psychiatrists and psychoanalysts in particular. She reported a recent affair with a married psychiatrist who argued that he would not be unfaithful to his wife if he had been analyzed. Whereupon she mentioned that a girl friend of hers was sleeping with an *analyzed* psychiatrist, married and the father of four children. Her lover replied that the analyzed psychiatrist probably did not feel as guilty as he did, presumably because of his analysis. The supervisor pointed out that there was nothing in her account of her affairs of any sexual pleasure or interest in her partner's pleasure. The analyst raised some question about the patient's psychological-mindedness. Last, the analyst mentioned another upcoming absence to the patient, who showed little overt reaction. The supervisor discussed with the analyst the "likely way in which the patient's increasing transference feelings might show themselves."

The questions raised by the analyst concerning the patient's psychological-mindedness were the tip of an iceberg. The analyst was becoming increasingly concerned by the extent of the patient's acting out and how close to home it was getting. She seemed, in effect, to be saying, "Why should I invest myself in you and this treatment? You will turn out to be as corrupt as the rest of them." Marriage was a trap, psychiatry and psychoanalysis a cynical façade behind which lurked considerable hypocrisy. When the analyst pointed out to the patient how she was emphasizing the difficulties and possible dangers in getting involved with people, she denied this by saying, "People were really the fun things in life." Yet, her life belied this. In retrospect, I should have made my comments much more specific and related them to men in particular and not to people in general; furthermore, I should have related my comments to her current difficulties in talking to me (e.g., forgetting an hour when by her own account she had an especially important dream to tell me, in fact, the very first of the analysis). I do not think I would now agree with my supervisor that I should have said even less. At the time, as best I can recall, I was cautious because I was surprised and a little alarmed by the extent of the patient's acting out. She seemed to be saying, "Don't expect too much of me; I'm doing the best I can considering how totally unreliable you are likely to prove." It remained to be seen if this acting out was primarily a defense against dependency needs, as the supervisor had previously suggested, or was an expression of great hostility toward men. What the analyst felt most directly was the latter. In the long run, both might prove to be true at different levels, and each would be available in time. The supervisor's approach was to advise the analyst, "Take it easy. Facilitate but do not interpret. The less you say the better. She is talking easily and productively."

What made it hard for the analyst to convey his concern about the patient's hostility toward men (and him) and the way it was expressing itself in the analysis? What made it hard for him to convey his worry about her acting out and its impact on the treatment? These are not easy questions to answer, especially after the passage of so many years. Tentatively, it could be argued that the analyst's absences so early in the treatment were a disrupting influence for the supervision as much as for the analysis. The supervisor was taken by surprise by these announcements. It should be noted that the supervisor himself was unavailable during the start of the analysis and had notified the analyst about this before they began. This had been a surprise to the analyst. Although the analyst certainly knew about his impending absences, he had to surprise the patient with them, as in fact he did the supervisor. The analyst may have been acting out against the supervisor through the patient. This sequence of action (by supervisor) and counteraction (by analyst) must have focused considerable affect on this aspect of the analytic process, while leaving other, perhaps especially pertinent, material off to the side. For the patient the lesson in all this may have been an old one: men mistreat you, leave you, they put their own needs first (like father), they are hypocrites. Although one would anticipate that the relationship with father was affected by earlier separation difficulties with mother, one would doubt that these difficulties were at all available at this stage of the treatment. One would surmise that analyst and supervisor were involved in a struggle that had its origin outside the supervision itself. There were certainly other contacts in which they interacted, disagreed, discovered significant differences to exist between them, and these must surely have affected the supervisor-analyst relationship. In fact, this was the case, and will be described in Chapter XIV.

SUPERVISION HOUR 4 (ANALYTIC HOURS 16–18)

In general, the supervisor believed the hours to be going well. He noted that the analyst had been ". . . very meticulous about the handling of the case in its beginning phase, and while his handling of the case had been quite adequate, I thought I would note to myself the possibility about overconcern about making mistakes." At another point he noted, ". . . the analysis was moving in a proper way, considering the interruptions." (As in the previous supervision hour, the supervisor glanced at the notes quickly, although each hour was reported in less than one and a half pages for the second week in a row.) Recorded in the notes were the first clear indications of the patient's growing concern about her difficulties in talking to the analyst and how she would benefit from the treatment if she could not bring herself to talk. She likened the problem in talking to the analyst to a problem in talking to "authorities," like her boss and her father. Yet, once she reached this point, she backed off from further exploration. The supervisor noted, ". . . she was refraining from talking about something. . . and the analyst tried in a properly nonspecific way to help. She went on to talk about how difficult it was for her to stop smoking and eating too much with no implication at this point or later that she was asking for help from the analyst. There are some hints of a fear of dependency on the analyst." The supervisor suggested that the analyst could deal with her difficulty in following the basic rule by resorting to ways of "facilitating her communicating without getting into an authoritarian position with her." The developing transference seemed to involve "the patient's fear of dependency, but also making of the analyst an authority with whom she found it difficult to talk."

In reviewing these three hours from the process notes, the main focus that emerged was the patient's surprised reaction to the news that it was not the community clinic where she first went which was subsidizing her treatment, but the analyst's institution. Although her status as a control patient had been explained to her in the first hour and the nature of the fee made plain, she had apparently needed to distort this information so that she would not be beholden to the analyst or his institution. Just before telling the analyst her mistaken understanding about the fee, she had described how guilty she felt in not contributing more to the community, especially since now her treatment was being subsidized by it. Her first association following the correct information concerning her fee was that she worried about people who did not know how to take care of themselves and she likened herself to them. She then mentioned her boss who went around looking like he needed someone to look after him, and she did worry about him. But he must like it that way. When asked how she saw herself that way, she talked about her own "sloppiness" and desire for comforts. She switched, after a pause, to talking about a little contretemps with a man at work, an artist, who was furious at her for doing his job for him. In the early part of this hour, prior to the exchange about the fee, she had been talking at some length about people who did not benefit from treatment and how you really have to rely on yourself. It was fairly apparent that she did not like receiving a supplement from me. Again, the issue was complex: Was it because of the fear of dependency, or because she was being put in a position of being beholden to a man? Evidence for both was present, and there did not appear to be, as yet, a way to assess the different weights to assign to these two sources of conflict. For example, in a subsequent hour (17), she recalled spending a "fun month" with father while both were attending college and mother was away. He helped her with her term papers, and she recalled one in particular which was "torn to pieces" by a woman professor. There was a reference to a boy she liked years ago who was beneath her in status and who had since been diminished in her eyes. But she then complained about being "really bad" because she was not talking about things she should in the analysis. She did not seem to be able to change the "repetitive patterns" in her life. It was hard to talk to the analyst, although she had talked very readily to the psychiatrist who evaluated her at the community agency. She returned to her theme: she must do it herself. It seemed like she vacillated between reflecting on the problem she was now becoming increasingly aware of about talking to the analyst while cautioning herself that she must really depend on herself.

In the third hour in this series (hour 18), which followed the analyst's absence for two sessions, and during which she came for her first hour at the regular time, she started out by talking about her problem with "authority." She just could not talk readily to people in authority, including her father. She felt she did not want to bother them or appear ignorant in their eyes. When she was asked how these thoughts might apply to her difficulty in talking to the analyst, she said she did not know why she would see me in that way at all, considering that the analyst was "just a voice behind her." She had first thought that analysis would only take a few weeks, but she could now see why it sometimes took years, implicitly referring to the difficulty she was encountering in talking to the analyst. But then, after a pause, she went on to talk about an incident at a previous job when she was made "bottom man on the totem pole." Toward the end of the hour she referred to a spoof on analysis in which the analyst was referred to as "Doc." She added in a very earnest tone of voice that she knew she was here to get help, and it was not going to help her if she simply did not talk about the things she had on her mind.

In retrospect, I would have been inclined to have been much more active and readier to relate issues more directly to the transference were I doing this analysis today. There were several opportunities. Certainly the patient's misunderstanding of the way the fee was paid lent itself to further exploration which might have led to some beginning recognition on her part of the degree to which she did not wish to be beholden to the analyst. It was certainly true that in the expressive psychotherapy I was doing at the same time and for which I was no longer supervised, I was far readier to interpret similar issues, and did so and with success. The patient was suddenly talking less about her affairs and more about the analysis; the transition from one to the other was provided by her previous reference to her affair with a psychiatrist and how he believed that, were he analyzed, he would do the same thing but feel less guilty. She was finding it hard to talk to the analyst because, I suspect, he could not be trusted to abide by his avowed standards. He was an "authority" who would prove arbitrary and hypocritical. Yet she was also eager to be in analysis and found it hard to abide the analyst's absence. It was "fun" to spend that month with father when mother was away, but it was generally hard to talk to him and he was the source during her growing-up years of constant dislocation. Separations were engineered by father. We could see in this some hint of the intrusive role of father in the early mother-child relationship. But the understanding of this issue was some time off. More immediately at hand was the patient's enormous hostility toward the analyst as a man, so much so that she could not believe he was responsible for her lowered fee any more than she could accept her ex-fiancé's kindness to her. She would treat him shabbily, refuse him sex while sleeping with other men. (Later in the analysis, beyond the period covered by this study, the patient confessed how during intercourse with him she would struggle desperately against yielding to the urge to scratch and maul him; what she resented most of all was his "sticking" her with his penis.)

As mentioned in the comments for supervision hour 3, the analyst was feeling more and more embattled. He felt the patient was already proving difficult, but he was being reassured that he was handling the beginning "properly." It was important to the analyst that he continue to proceed "properly" in view of the complex roles he and his supervisor were playing with each other and in view of the gunfire that could be heard daily coming from the hilltop positions of the institute and the institution-at-large. One moved carefully toward graduation as through a mine field, at least those who did not have a guide to lead them through the safe routes. There was thus constant interaction between the supervision process and the larger institutional events.

SUPERVISION HOUR 5 (ANALYTIC HOURS 19–22)

These hours became of special interest to the Study Group, and their exposition will be presented in greater detail than the previous ones.

The main point stressed by the supervisor was the "even way in which the patient told her story"—for example, when describing her problem in having intercourse with her ex-fiancé and her near-hysterical reaction leading to her decision to stop having intercourse with him, the supervisor stressed, ". . . the patient talked about these and other matters about which she must have felt distress in a way that did not invite the analyst to be sympathetic or to help. There appeared to be very little of what I would call 'demand quality' in her speech during the hours. One might say she allowed herself to expect very little of the analyst, but put up with the relationship." On the basis of this interpretation, the supervisor felt that the main current problem was not derived from an identification with her mother as the analyst was supposing, but that "the qualities she was acting out seemed to be closest to those she had described in her father (whom she also described during these hours as being absent much of the time during her early adolescence when she felt she very much needed him)." The supervisor then wondered if the analyst was encouraging this acting out by trying to be too "analytically correct" so that he was overstressing objectivity "to the point of conveying indifference."

As I reread the supervisor's interpretation, it was unclear to me if he meant that the patient was identifying herself with her father, was displacing (or projecting) these characteristics onto the analyst, or both. He continued: "On the other side, I noted that I thought it very likely that the patient's projection of a father image onto the analyst could also include identification with what she would construe as his objectivity toward her problem." This statement seemed to imply the presence of what some would call "projective identification"—she was projecting her objectivity derived from an identification with father onto the analyst and then identifying herself with that objectivity. The main evidence for this understanding derived from the patient's lack of "demand quality," her willingness to put up with difficulties in coming to the hours (e.g., in hour 22 the patient's car broke down and she took a cab to the hour, but only mentioned this at the very end, just before leaving).

The analyst's response to this supervision was to look thoughtful, according to the supervisor, but to give no immediate response. However, the analyst emphasized that the patient appeared to be coming under more stress. The supervisor agreed and advised the analyst "he would have to keep aware of the necessity to intervene at some point. In the meantime, the patient was talking steadily, filling in a good deal of her background, indicating her willingness to work, for instance, on dreams, and showing a bit more psychological-mindedness than we had anticipated at the beginning."

With respect to several dreams the patient reported, containing references to staircases and hints of pregnancy fantasies and fears of being damaged in intercourse, the supervisor noted with approval that these were not interpreted by the analyst, "who continued to handle the hours technically in a very adequate manner."

For the first time the supervisor was raising some serious questions about the analyst's conduct of the analysis concerning: (1) his understanding of the material, and (2) his handling of the transference. Yet, despite these shortcomings, the supervisor believed the analyst continued to handle the hours, from a technical standpoint, in an adequate manner. I shall give a detailed presentation of each of these hours.

In the first hour (19), the patient came in with a dream written down because she wanted to be sure to remember it. She recalled she could not tell me the very first dream she had in analysis at the time that she had it because she forgot to come that day (hour 5). The ambivalence in this statement was obvious; she feared forgetting once again and guarded against this by writing the dream down. As the transference was intensifying (at whatever level) she was at the same time fighting it. The dream itself was as follows:

> She was going through a closet with pretty summer dresses in it. Some belonged to her mother. One of these she put on. Then the dream seemed to shift to a large building which was sort of a combined office and apartment building. She was going down this staircase. As she described this she used the pronoun "we," apparently indicating in this way that there were several people there, at least several girls. They needed to get around some water. She seemed to be in this tub, something like a plastic basin which was round and tippy, although she did not find herself afraid or uncomfortable. As they approached the bottom of the staircase, there was a lake and the boat caused a "tidal wave" which they had to get across. Everyone somehow seemed to be in boats. Someone seemed to be telling a story about catching fish, and if the fishline got around you, it might cut you. All the time this was going on, they were descending the stairs. This girl was gossiping about a boy friend who recommended two kinds of birth control devices. It was not exactly clear to her what this was about. She seemed to be criticizing this fellow. Her boy friend was at the bottom of the stairs. He was a nice-looking man who had a broken arm.

She added, in one of her associations to the dream, that she had asked her mother in the dream if she could put on one of the dresses which she knew would turn out to be too big for her. Her mother agreed, as she had anticipated. Yesterday, she wore a suit her mother gave her for Christmas (the dream was reported in mid-January). She also recalled a photo she had seen of the governor's wife at the governor's inaugural ball. She had just written a paper on a subject which reminded her of her mother. A number of other associations related the staircase to pleasure (e.g., she always liked to run upstairs and downstairs), injury (e.g., wrestling with her older brother when six and cracking her head on the bottom step of a staircase; her sister-in-law who, when pregnant, liked to jump off a staircase, and her mother would become "frantic"; running down the staircase at home when she was younger, and in a fury kicking her sister in the stomach).

There was much material in a recent hour on taking her mother's place: spending a month with father while her mother was away, competition with women at work for a top spot. These efforts were usually followed by some negative outcome: a woman professor tore apart the paper father had helped her with; she lost out on the job. Here, in this dream too, putting on mother's dress led directly to symbolic sexual activity (the staircase) and impending disaster—a "tidal wave"—a good oceanic image of maternal retaliation. But there was also indication in the dream of getting cut by the fishing line, which suggested a fear of actual harm in intercourse. Later in the hour she associated the birth control reference in the dream to a time when she and her psychiatrist lover improvised a birth control foam applicator which indeed had cut her. It is also of interest in this connection that the boy friend in the dream had a broken arm. Thus, sexual involvement with men brought with it two dangers: (1) retaliation from mother, and (2) attack from men and against men. But there was also a powerful element of excitement and frustration in all this, as if she reacted counterphobically to these anticipated dangers. In one association she remarked how much she liked to swim and that a doctor once commented that her toes had almost become webbed from so much swimming. Insofar as the dream equated water with sex, she was indirectly conveying how ready she was to court the danger of the "tidal wave." It is also useful to recall a memory in which she ventured too near the edge of a waterfall right after having had intercourse with a man whose profession was the same as her father's.

Nevertheless, even though she herself believed that the dream had to do with sex (in her associations she said she had heard that water is supposed to be related to sex) and she confessed to having real problems with sex, there was little she could say about her problem with sex. In fact, she said things were "fine" with her ex-fiancé, except she did not want to sleep with him and was looking for other sexual liaisons, which weren't satisfactory either. But, she "has not been bothered lately" with her sexual problems! A clear link to the analyst was present in the form of an association by way of another dream about a building similar to the one in the current dream in which the doors had gold handles like the door to the analyst's office. In this same context she recalled a film in which a boy goes off with a prostitute and his girl friend is understanding, which the patient noted was the reverse of her relationship with her ex-fiancé. She could not be sure whether his loyalty was due to his belief that she would get over her problem or it made no difference to him. (It may be recalled that she had also made reference to the fact that her father never was the one to ask for a divorce, even though her mother was often unfaithful to him.) This was another bit of evidence that an oedipal conflict was being re-enacted. The analyst was supposed to be "indifferent" to her promiscuity and to accept her not "sleeping" with him (i.e., not sharing her sexual secrets with him) if she were to identify herself with the oedipal mother and have father for herself. However, even this partially fantasied re-enactment had to be paid for in the real coin of pain and suffering—her feeling she was "really bad" and deserved to die (the near-suicide at the waterfall, the "tidal wave" awaiting her at the foot of the pleasure-giving staircase).

The following hour (20), the patient called in ill but made no reference to it when she came for her subsequent hour—this interruption might have signified the distress produced by the previous hour. No doubt this should have been commented on by the analyst. Interestingly enough, the material picked up where she left it in the previous hour. Her thoughts turned to adolescence. She developed early, at twelve or thirteen. Just as she was getting acquainted with boys, the family made one of its many moves, and the father had to go off for an undetermined time. She felt that was a time when she most needed her father; her mother provided her with little guidance. There were various delinquent acts, vandalism, and even rape in the crowd she ran around with. She herself "lived in terror" around boys, which one suspects goes along with two symbolic references to danger and intercourse that occur in this hour—a very nearsighted actress girl friend of hers who she feared might fall off a staircase on stage, and one of her sisters who was a sleepwalker and once fell off a staircase and hurt her head.

When she grew silent at one point, the analyst wondered if she was then thinking of things she could not share with him. She revealed that she was thinking about her mother's infidelity while her father was away. It was confusing to her, but she supposed that was how people acted when they were lonely.

Despite the fact that we were still in the opening phase of the analysis, it might have been helpful to have pointed out to the patient how she was in some ways acting in the very way toward her ex-fiancé as she saw her mother acting toward her father. The risk in so doing, in view of her intense ambivalence about the treatment itself, would have been to endanger the treatment. It could also be argued that the analyst, through taking up such things as her illness, might have found ready derivatives of this material in the treatment relationship. The supervisor was concerned about the patient's lack of expectation from the analyst which the analyst may have been playing into by not taking up the matter of her canceled hour. The question to be raised concerns the bearing of actions on the working alliance as well as on the transference. A patient who does not come or withholds her thoughts is challenging the working alliance, although it may be in the service of certain transference needs. There was a shakiness to this beginning which argued for caution. True, the analyst may have contributed to this instability by his absences, which paralleled father's absences when she was growing up. But the patient's pattern of unstable, unsatisfactory relationships with men was established long before the analysis, and indeed it was for that main reason she entered analysis. In the previous three supervision hours, the supervisor's emphasis was on a subtle facilitation of the patient's communication and for the analyst to stay away from any interpretive approach as yet. The analyst, for reasons already cited, felt under a strong compunction to abide by this proper conduct of the analysis.

In the next hour (21), she arrived looking inappropriately summery in a sleeveless, bright blue dress. There was another dream:

> There was a whole bunch of people in an institution, probably a mental institution. One woman figured in the dream, a Muriel C., with whom she used to work. She is a divorcee. This other woman had on a suit belonging to Muriel. Muriel said, "That's my suit. I don't care if you wear it as long as you know it's mine. I know it's mine because it has a big flower on it that fits the square of my jaw." A young couple in another building across the way started to fight. They ran out of the building. They could see her through the window. The woman was very afraid of the man. Once outside, however, they calmed down. She came over to them and the man went back into the house.

Muriel emerged as a tough-minded individualist who actually out-competed the patient for a job some time back. The patient in that instance backed off from the competition and literally invited Muriel back after Muriel had quit the job. She admired Muriel for her ability to raise two boys after her divorce, supporting herself on the proceeds from land she had inherited from her father. Associations to the mental institution in the dream (a transparent screen for the analyst's office and building) led to memories of fighting and divorcing couples, which finally touched on her parents. Her mother was always wasting her father's money, keeping them constantly in debt. She recalled them quarreling over money and her father pushed her mother against the couch and hit her. At the time the patient became quite frightened. She herself then commented that the same pattern was repeating itself between her ex-fiancé and herself. Whenever they would go to bed together she would become "real stiff." He would get mad and walk out. He would return shortly and scream at her for being unresponsive. She would become terrified because she would think that he would beat her. But he never did. It was she who then actually made the decision about their not having intercourse. She acknowledged that these were very hard things for her to talk about especially to someone like the analyst, a person in a position of some authority; she liked to think of her parents as peaceful people and her life as good rather than "rotten." But it was getting easier to talk about these things now.

When the analyst attempted to pursue the meaning of her father's violence further, the patient stiffened on the couch and seemed to clutch at her face. She said she always felt that what her mother did was horrible. In some ways she deserved what she got. What scared her was that there seemed to be no answer to the problem, they (her parents) were tied to each other. They somehow needed each other. At one time she told her father that if he didn't like her, he should divorce her mother. For some reason they could not get away from each other. Perhaps it was the kids, perhaps it was their love, or perhaps their hate. It was like her ex-fiancé and herself. She could not live without him or with him. She just did not know why it was hard for her to admit these things. Her mother had done some very horrible things and had been no credit to her father. Nevertheless, it was never her father who talked of divorce; it was always her mother. The patient was crying. All her life she could remember her mother bitching at her father. She would always get under his skin, and he would not seem to let it bother him.

Father emerged as the wronged party and mother as an exploitative, irresponsible, and unfaithful wife. In addition, she acted irresponsibly toward the family, providing little guidance for the patient during her difficult early adolescent years. Yet father was also away and the perpetrator of the traumatic family moves. It appeared that in the transference the patient was reviving competition with mother for father's attention, almost literally wishing to be in her clothes, yet backing off from the competition and anticipating a terrible outcome if she were to succeed. The analyst thus appeared to be in the position of the tolerant father, distant and preoccupied but capable of sexual violence if pushed too hard. There was the haunting recognition on the patient's part that she might be repeating this parental pattern with her ex-fiancé. There was still no recognition on her part of the same pattern in the analysis. One could hypothesize that transference gratification derived from coming to the hours, talking about her sexual escapades in mother's clothes, as it were, and in reliving life with father in the person of the tolerant analyst. As always appeared to be the case with this patient, there were undertones of a much more somber theme having to do with mother's sense of abandonment by father, as well as the patient's participation in that experience. Mother's infidelity might then be seen as her retaliation, and so also the patient's. Yet this was a distinct and different theme from the oedipal one. For example, in her relationship to her ex-fiancé, the oedipal re-enactment seemed far more central than the earlier oral conflict. Which of these conflicts was uppermost in the transference was hard to tell, although here too the oedipal configuration seemed closer to the surface, although ultimately which represented the more significant fixation and source of conflict remained uncertain.

It was in the subsequent hour (22), the last in this series, that the incident over difficulty with her car occurred, as a result of which the patient called early to forewarn the analyst she might be twenty minutes late. Actually, she arrived only five minutes late. She spoke to the analyst on the phone and introduced herself by the diminutive of her first name. A good portion of the hour was devoted to talking about the fellow who had jilted her for another woman, a friend of hers. She had recently visited his mother and discovered he was about to publish a book. She found that she felt nothing toward him anymore. The last time they had intercourse she was unwilling, and when he insisted she became hysterical; she started screaming. Shortly thereafter, she started to talk about this "young boy" with whom she slept last summer and who was one of the main instigations for her seeking treatment. This young man called her last night; she was sure he wanted to become reinvolved with her, but she was fearful of this. Ostensibly, he called to ask her for pills to keep him awake while he studied for his exams. Actually, this fellow's older brother had gotten a girl pregnant recently. When this brother called the patient, not so far back, he mentioned quite a few things, but failed to mention his having gotten this girl pregnant. When the analyst pointed out that she too had difficulty in talking about important things, she began to talk with hesitation about her continuing struggle with her ex-fiancé. She started to cry. She did not know what there was to talk about in connection with that. When she was not with him, she felt she needed him all the time and she called him up. However, when she was with him, she wanted to get away from him. She was reminded of the TAT card showing an old couple. She got choked up on that one too, and did not know why. Mainly, the patient appeared to be conveying her helplessness in the face of her conflictual attachment to her ex-fiancé, which she was beginning to liken to the relationship between her parents.

SUPERVISION HOUR 6 (ANALYTIC HOURS 23–25)

The next supervision hour and analytic sessions might help us to see how the analysis fared after what appeared to be a failure in empathy on the analyst's part, an unfortunate falling in with the patient's own lack of expectations. For this last set of hours the order of material will be reversed and the analytic notes will be presented first. Furthermore, for the first hour (23), the actual process note made at the time will be quoted at length followed by comments. After the presentation of the analytic notes, the supervisor's notes on the supervision will be summarized as they bear on the analytic material.

Analytic Hour 23

1. After a considerable pause during which her stomach grumbled loudly, the patient said haltingly that she has been thinking about her relationship to her ex-fiancé but was having a hard time knowing what to talk about.
2. I commented that, in view of what she has already described about

her problems in her relationship with her ex-fiancé, it may have more to do with her difficulty in knowing what to tell *me* than in talking about it.

3. Rather quickly she replied she had been giving some thought to that problem today—the problem of how to talk to me. On the job, for example, today she was going around talking to people about their work and socializing easily with them. However, there is one man, the production manager, whom she has always found it tough to talk to. He is a dynamic man who is "in motion all the time," whom she admires very much. With other people she finds it easy to converse, yet she would rather talk to him than to others. She finds it hard to be relaxed with him.

4. I encouraged her to talk more about this.

5. She said after a brief hesitation that she really does not know what to say to him. She does not want to say anything stupid or silly. Second, she is sexually attracted to him even though he is not good-looking. It is rather the kind of man he is that sexually attracts her. She admires his goals, his ideals, his principles, and his striving to attain them. He is not sitting around complacently. Then she grew silent. In a genuinely questioning tone of voice she said she did not really understand her difficulty in talking with me. Perhaps this difficult time she has talking with me is really more important than what she is talking about. Perhaps the two are tied up together: if she knew why she had a hard time talking with me, maybe she would not have such a big problem with what she could talk about.

6. I was quite frankly taken aback by this apparent insight. My reaction, I guess, was "chicken." I said that certainly our interest was in the problems she felt brought her here as well as in what would make it hard for her to deal with these problems here.

7. The patient became silent for a considerable period of time. She confessed she really did not know what was making it hard to talk with me. She could go off and talk about other things, but she does not know if she would be going in the right direction. Yet, it has not been as hard talking here lately as it was in the beginning. She feels that we have been working together successfully and getting somewhere. I seem to be able to pick out the things that are important in what she is saying and make it easier thereby for her to talk about other things that are important. She became silent again, and I commented that she offered the production manager as an example of someone she found it hard to talk with although she very much wanted to talk with him.

8. She admitted she was puzzled by this because he is not in a particular position of authority with respect to her. There are several who are higher up in the company with whom she finds it easy to converse. Somehow she relates it to his vitality. Yet even this characteristic is not true of everyone she has trouble talking to. For example, her father is not a par-

ticularly vital-appearing man. Actually, today she did better in her conversation with the production manager than she had before. She usually cannot talk to him at all; today she was able to talk some business matter over with him and not simply converse. She talked to him about how she would like her own work to be more meaningfully related to the work of the company. These are issues she could not easily talk with him about before. Then, without any apparent transition, she said that the analysis had been making her nervous. Is she afraid of finding out some things? For about ten years she has had regular periods, but this last month her period was a week early. When she comes in here she finds herself getting "real nervous." Analysis is a very different kind of thing to do. If she has what she considers to be a good session here, she feels very good the rest of the day. Her problems do not seem so unbeatable. There is this girl friend of hers who is about to go into treatment, and she told her ex-fiancé the analysis seemed to be helping the patient. This encouraged her to seek treatment for herself. At this point, quite suddenly, the patient half sat up on the couch and seemed to straighten out her back. She then lay back down.

9. I asked her about this.

10. She commented that sometimes she gets the shakes in here. She does not know if it is because it is cold or because she is nervous (actually, the office was a little on the chilly side today). She thought it would go away if she sat up.

11. When I asked her if this had happened at other times, she said that it had. Mainly the shakes seemed to be situated in her chest. It's like an uncontrollable spasm or shaking which somehow she associates with stage fright. (I recalled at this point that she referred recently to a girl friend of hers from her teenage years who was an actress and, because she was nearsighted, there was fear she would fall over the stage scenery and particularly, the staircase.) She went on to say that occasionally when she voices her opinion in front of people who might take offense, she gets the shakes like that. Following this remark the patient fell silent. Then she started to talk about her ex-fiancé and how he would be home tonight and she is looking forward to having a good time with him tonight. She certainly hopes things will work out, although she is afraid they might not. It is as if she is waiting for "disaster" rather than really expecting a good time. When she thinks of her situation with her ex-fiancé, she finds somehow that she is thinking "cold-bloodedly" about how she got into it. Yet, she knows that she is not really this cold-blooded about it but has become quite involved.

12. I took this occasion to say that perhaps she *tries* to look at it in that way.

13. She agrees that she does but does not believe this is too good an idea.

14. When I wondered why she would want to look at it in a cold-blooded way, she said perhaps she thinks it might be easier to understand then.

15. I said that I wondered if it was not also a way she thinks one does things in analysis or perhaps what she believes to be my attitude about the right way to do it.

16. She denied this and, to my knowledge, this was the first thing I had said with which she had taken open issue. She said that the psychiatrists whom she has heard talking about their patients talk as if they were really involved with them. Even though it may be more of a study for them, it certainly does not sound cold-blooded. Then, after a very considerable pause and in a markedly different tone of voice, having the character of a confession about it, she said, "Dr. Shevrin, I have a hard time talking to the production manager because I want to sleep with. . . that's the reason in talking to you and my father. . . I can't imagine. . . " and she trailed off. Shortly after this, the hour ended.

The analyst's reaction to her insight (paragraphs 5 and 6) is of special interest. Why was he "taken aback" and feel he responded too conservatively? As already mentioned, there was a considerable investment in conducting a "proper" analysis and getting it under way in a "proper" manner. The supervisor had been at pains to point this out on several occasions. Yet, there were also strong hints of other feelings on the part of both supervisor and analyst. The supervisor was becoming alarmed at the analyst's overmeticulousness, while the analyst, despite all of his efforts to conduct a "proper" analysis, introduced such technical impurities as absences announced in the midst of an hour. It was as if both supervisor and analyst were working under self-imposed restraints that neither fully accepted. These restrictions may in large measure owe their power to the general context in which the supervision was taking place—the need for both to be careful with each other in the light of the real complexity of their personal, administrative, and political relationship to one another—all of this quite apart from any transference and countertransference issues that might also have been present.

Nevertheless, as the subsequent material shows, the patient was not deterred by the analyst's caution. She was complimentary to the analyst (paragraph 7) and intent on undertaking the hard, reflective work so difficult for her. She stressed how important the analysis had become for her and reported a psychosomatic symptom—her period arriving early, which she attributed to her increased nervousness (paragraph 8). At a later point in the session, she suddenly sat up and described this as the "shakes" and attributed it to her nervousness in the hours (paragraphs 8 and 10). The analyst's association to her allusion to stage fright as like the situation she ascribed to her adolescent actress girl friend who was nearsighted and might fall off the staircase on stage was, it turned out, not so far off. The patient was clearly struggling over lying down on the couch in the analyst's presence and with her sexual excitement. This was a forbidden wish. The next derivative to appear in her associations was to her relationship with her ex-fiancé with whom she hoped things would work out, but she feared "disaster." Her thoughts here follow along her dreams in hour 19, as if there were a hidden sequence: taking over mother's role (wearing her dress), having intercourse with father (going down the staircase), all this leading to disaster (the tidal wave). The impending disaster is signaled by a sudden rush of anxiety which results in her sitting up, thus obviating her yielding to the incestuous wish.[2] Another defense was indicated in her reference to how she felt herself thinking cold-bloodedly about how she got into her relationship with her ex-fiancé in the first place. At the same time, she realized that she had become quite involved with him (paragraph 11). Here we have a disguised allusion to the analytic relationship itself. She tried to be "objective" but knew she really was not. When the analyst asked her why she tried to look at it objectively, she said it might be because it would then be easier to understand, implying that her strong feelings made it hard for her to think clearly. When the analyst, as if having in mind the supervisor's comment in the previous supervision session, asked if it were not her view of the way analysis was supposed to be done, the patient denied this; in fact, she said that in her experience psychiatrists talk about their patients as if they were really involved with them. In light of these reflections on the patient's part, it would seem that the supervisor's interpretation about the apparent objectivity of both patient and analyst, with the patient expecting little from the analyst and the analyst perhaps supporting this attitude, was not confirmed. Instead, the patient conveyed her belief that the analyst was involved, but she was fearful of this involvement and of her own involvement, which had a clear sexual focus. It is also important to note how readily, under the impact of anxiety, she resorted to action—in this instance, sitting up. This was consistent with a pattern of acting out already well established as a characterological recourse before treatment.

Finally, the patient arrived at her insight—relating her difficulties in talking with her boss, the analyst, and her father. Again, the analyst may have turned "chicken" because he permitted the hour to end without making any comment on the patient's good work.

The patient did not come to the next appointment. When she came (hour 24), she explained she had mentioned several hours before that she might be late because of examinations. However, she did not come at all. Life had

[2]In hour 21 the patient stiffened on the couch not long after describing how she would become "real stiff" in bed with her ex-fiancé. She was talking about her mother's mistreatment of her father.

become uninteresting and she was "bored with the idea" of spending the rest of her life with her ex-fiancé. Marriage would be the end of having fun, although she acknowledged she was not much better off now. When the analyst called attention to her skipping the last hour, she replied that she thought it had been understood she would not be able to come because of her examinations. In any case, she could not have made it that day. Although she pursued it further, she could not relate her absence to the previous hour. The analyst, still perhaps being "proper," did not do so either. She spoke in a general way even while she was mentioning that her evaluating psychiatrist had pointed out to her that she avoided things by not getting into details. She acknowledged there were things she must not be wanting to talk about.

The patient appeared to be in full retreat from the insight of the previous hour, from the greater openness with the analyst, and from the intensification of the transference which was obviously occurring. Again, we can see how readily the patient resorts to action—skipping an hour—and how it served the purpose of disrupting the flow of the analytic work. In retrospect, I would very likely have interpreted the reasons for her skipping the hour after first wondering if she herself had any ideas about it. Yet, there would still be a danger inherent in this approach because any such interpretation would have served to intensify the transference at a time when the patient was clearly indicating that it was proving too much for her. This, of course, is always the problem with acting out. Perhaps it *was* still too early in the treatment to chance such an interpretation.

The patient ended the hour by emphasizing that her life seemed boring to her and lacking in purpose. We can surmise that this "boredom" was a defense against the powerful feelings and conflicts she had been more bravely confronting the previous hour.

In the next hour (25), the richness of the patient's material resumed. She came in with a "bunch of dreams" and wondered why it was easier for her to talk about dreams than about "things":

> In the first dream she was running up and down the street in some city. Then she was in a building where there was a meeting of "office people." Her boss was there. She ran out of cigarettes and she went to his apartment to get some. The apartment was next to some beach or river or lake. It was a crummy apartment. She found one moldy old cigarette. She went into the bathroom and there she found a figure under a sheet. It was some girl she knew. Suddenly they were in the hospital. People were getting tonsillectomies and they were all under sheets. She too was under a sheet. They were all awake and she was surprised they were not put to sleep for the operation. She complained about this, saying, "How do you do it awake—that's horrible!" They gave her some Pamperin, which is a

> drug for cramps and didn't do much. She was told not to worry. Then all of a sudden she realized she had no tonsils, and she woke up.
>
> In the second dream she was in some attic apartment. There were many rooms and hers was the middle one. There was a bed in the middle of the room. Surrounding her were huge, monstrous spiders. [And here the patient indicated with her hands how big they were, approximately eight to ten inches in diameter.] They had long legs, but she was not afraid. She did not want any around. Somehow she made sure not to see any before she went to bed. There was more to this dream, but she could not remember the rest.
>
> The third dream she recalled was "all mixed up." She was at a resort at a swimming pool. She was standing on top of a lifeguard tower or a ladder. Someone made a remark to her that had a double meaning, and she replied with a risqué retort. There was this fellow there with a handsome masculine physique who grabbed her and threw her in the swimming pool. Then suddenly they were in this high-school locker room. She found drugs and needles in her locker with the thought in mind that someone had put them there. They were going to this motel room. They had to go down an elevator which turned into a trolley car going downtown on a schedule. They found themselves in the Orient at a souvenir shop. They had just three minutes before the trolley returned to the hotel, which they did. Following this the patient woke up.
>
> Before this dream, however, she had another one in which she had sexual intercourse with her ex-fiancé. Then, quietly, she added that she was sleeping next to him that night and refused to let him have intercourse with her although she dreamt about it.

It was clear from the patient's comment that telling the analyst her dreams was preferable to free-associating in the hour itself and running the risk of getting into dangerous waters. Yet her thoughts about the dreams inevitably led into some of the same material, for example, the dream about having intercourse with her ex-fiancé after having actually refused to do so with him. In a certain sense, this paralleled her unwillingness to talk freely in the hour with the analyst, while describing rich dreams to him in which she already knew what she was going to say. She could not abandon herself in the analyst's presence any more than in her ex-fiancé's presence.

The tonsillectomy dream led back to childhood memories involving her older sister, who had a tonsillectomy at the same time as the patient to keep her company. The patient ate her sister's applesauce after the operation, and her sister never forgave her for it. In a later association to the dream about the handsome swimmer, a sister again figured as the wife of a brother-in-law toward whom the patient had sexual inclinations. Toward the end of the hour the patient became noticeably nervous, kneading her hands and complaining about never having had such "sexual dreams" before. She tried to figure out what "binds her up" with her ex-fiancé. She somehow associated him with her mother. She always needed some person around she could turn to. As long as there was someone else around she did not seem to need him; but when she got bored or disinterested she always went back to him.

In this hour, one might begin to see some evidence for the direction of regression from the oedipal level of conflict. She could not take her ex-fiancé as her husband and have him be the father of her children because he was too much an incestuous object for her, as well as a male she envied. She withheld herself from him, both to avoid an incestuous tie and to frustrate him. She turned to other men for the same reasons and, in addition, to achieve sexual satisfaction. But these men were "uninteresting" to her because they were not incestuous objects. She must return to her ex-fiancé either to re-enact the same conflict or to regress to an earlier oral fixation in which he became like mother. (It is of interest that in her first dream, a girl friend figures who was once thought to be homosexual but recently got married. Also her tonsils were "great big ones, like marbles.") We can also begin to see the same situation developing in the analysis with the analyst emerging more as a father figure; as soon as this threatens to become too real, the patient distances herself, does not come, and then returns, but no longer ready to deal with the earlier, more direct sexual implications.

This sequence of hours may throw considerable light on the issues in the previous supervision hour. Derivatives of the oedipal conflict became more strikingly evident, as well as indications of an earlier conflict over dependency. As the issues emerged with somewhat greater directness in the analysis, reports of acting out diminished and the patient's ambivalent attachment to her ex-fiancé took center stage. She became aware of a significant parallel between her mother's relationship to her father and her relationship to her ex-fiancé. There were even intimations that she sensed some parallel in her relationship to the analyst. The patient made it clear that she did experience the analyst as being involved, but she was fearful and suspicious of this involvement. It was not his lack of empathy she feared, but his readiness to take advantage of his understanding for his own ends—presumably purely narcissistic ones.

In the supervisor's notes a sharper tone is heard. The supervisor continued to be impressed by the patient's efforts to avoid the analytic work, ". . . the patient was attempting to master problems as fast as she saw them as a way to minimize her involvement with the analyst." The supervisor warned the analyst about overlooking the fact that the patient was talking in over-general terms about her sexual experiences. He informed the analyst that the analytic process was a great deal sturdier than the analyst appeared to believe, judging from his cautious reaction to the patient's insight. He speculated that the analyst's view of the analytic process as too fragile might explain his "obvious efforts to be delicate in his handling of the case." He advised the analyst to pick up feelings as expressed in gestures as well as in words. For the most part the analyst listened, agreed, and provided the supervisor with material supporting his points. It is of interest to note that there was very little work devoted in the supervision to dreams, although they were reported in the hours. It is possible that the supervisor's reliance on the analyst's oral report, nonsequential in nature, resulted in a slighting of the actual content in the hours, in particular as it appeared in dreams, memories, etc. At times, the supervisor appeared to be implying that the analyst was responding more to the content of the associations than to the quality of the relationship. The supervisor appeared to emphasize the latter more, perhaps because the content was not as fully grasped by the supervisor. Obviously, it is the interaction of content with the quality of the relationship that results in an optimal understanding of the patient. But something in the structure of the supervision made it difficult for this interaction to emerge constructively.

CONCLUSIONS

At the start of this chapter I promised to view this study from three perspectives: (1) as a candidate and analyst, (2) as a researcher, and (3) as an administrator. In these concluding remarks I shall reverse the order and start with the administrative issues.

ADMINISTRATIVE PERSPECTIVE

Ekstein and Wallerstein (1972) underscored the importance of wise, judicious administration as providing a sustaining environment for psychotherapy training. It is implicit, if not explicit, in their argument that there be clear role distinctions between administrator and supervisor, supervisor and trainee. The very conception of a clinical rhombus is based on role and function differentiation. The power to give or withhold the rewards of an institution which is essential to administration cannot easily be combined with the offer of help and instruction related primarily to the needs of the student. The teacher (as also the analyst) should derive his power from accepted standards of performance in learning, shared by both teacher and student; for the administrator, on the other hand, factors quite apart from his relationship to the staff member may determine whether the staff member is promoted, given a raise, fired, etc. A grade, for example, represents the final outcome of a learning process and is not (or should not) be a reward or punishment in and of itself. Students consider as arbitrary the use of grades as rewards or punishments; however, when grades do represent the outcome of a learning process, students consider them fair and acceptable even though they may feel disappointed, but the disappointment is at their own failure rather than at the teacher's punitiveness. In order for this evaluation process to proceed neutrally and beneficially, the teacher should not have administrative power—the power to reward or punish performance often on grounds quite unrelated to the actual performance—because this serves to render ambiguous the learning task itself. The student has inevitably to be concerned about the career and bread-and-butter implications of his immediate performance; moreover, he cannot help but believe his behavior elsewhere in the institution involving his administrator-teacher must have some bearing on his learning relationship and vice versa. Essentially, the *conflict-free* character of the learning encounter is compromised. No learning situation is entirely conflict-free, but one should try to approach that ideal. Actually, the source of conflict should be in the student for his ultimate benefit and not in the environment, over which he may have little control.

Now, one significant consequence of administrator-teacher syncretism is that the student is placed in a regression-producing and infantilizing position. It is important to stress that this kind of regression-engendering circumstance is *not* the same thing as a therapeutic regression. For one, *neither* participant is aware of this consequence, least of all the administrator-teacher, who usually is relieved to be wearing his teaching hat and to be rid of his administrative hat for a while. He wants nothing better than for the student to treat him as a teacher so that he may more totally put aside for a time the nettlesome responsibilities with which administrators are always burdened. As an administrator myself, I have often felt this way, expecting of my students that they confirm my validity as a teacher, which to no small extent means joining with me in scotomizing my role as administrator. It is much harder for the student to do this than it is for the administrator-teacher. The student often sees the administrator's hat even when the administrator-teacher has tried to toss it behind his desk—and the student must perceive it this way. When a therapist not in formal training, for example, purchases a supervisor's time, just as a patient purchases an analyst's time, the quality of the supervisory relationship is quite different from when the supervision is part of a training program and certainly from when the supervisor is also the student's administrator.

When I referred earlier to regression and infantilization engendered by the reality of the administrator-teacher role syncretism, I meant that the student must constantly keep in mind issues of power. Let no one underestimate the prevalence of these forces in our society and in our psychoanalytic institutes in particular. They are as real as the list of analytic societies that have split apart and gone separate ways. In fact, I suspect that this kind of analytic fission is so potent because of the syncretistic fusion of therapeutic, educational, and administrative roles. The student can react in one of two ways to this syncretism: (1) shrewdly and manipulatively—weapons of all those who are powerless—and (2) submissively and passively. The latter is what I had in mind by infantilization; the former response is in some respects more adaptive, although it ends by producing cynicism and distrust that can only foment ultimate alienation. I would suppose that the failure of many graduates to join the American Psychoanalytic Association is one index of the degree to which they feel alienated. It is significant that many will continue their analytic work and think of themselves as analysts but will refuse to align themselves or participate in the formal organization representing analysis. In many instances this may be one consequence of their continued suspicion of analytic role syncretisms which play so prominent a part in analytic politics. This is more than "unresolved transference"—a self-serving explanation at best, an impediment to solving the problem at worst—rather, it is unresolved *institutionalized* role conflict, based on real social forces, which continues to alienate and infantilize.

To become specific, the candidate in this study was caught up in the consequences of an administrator-teacher role syncretism. On the whole, he was responding to this syncretism by efforts at submission and at the same time rebellion against the forces requiring this submission. The overmeticulousness noted by the supervisor was the candidate's effort to be careful and do as he felt the administrator-supervisor required (the more personal aspects of this will be formulated in Chapter XIV).

The candidate was quite aware, as he could assume the supervisor was, that the supervision was taking place in the midst of much institutional upheaval, involving both of them quite seriously, which would eventually lead to their departures. They both narrowed their focus to the work at hand in an effort to ignore the surrounding maelstrom. This could not and did not work; it was defensive in its very function and could only succeed at the expense of reality. In short, there were forces affecting the supervision which neither, for different reasons, could acknowledge. Instead, the very context and conduct of the supervision were affected. As a result, the Study Group—like supervisor and candidate—perforce had its vision narrowed to the *apparent* dynamics of the learning situation. But these dynamics were subject to significant influences quite beyond the teacher-student relationship. The administrative power of the supervisor was ignored and, as a result, the candidate's behavior was interpreted solely in terms of its possible emotional and educational resistances. Either an assumption was tacitly being made of an ideal supervisory relationship, or consideration of tact and politics made it convenient to do so. Neither basis serves the interests of research.

RESEARCH PERSPECTIVE

In my estimate there was more than a coincidence in the fact that the research was undertaken without informing the candidate or the patient of their roles in it, on the one hand, and the narrow focus of the study, on the other. As a researcher I am myself quite aware of the inclination to simplify and avoid complications. The charge is most often leveled by the clinician at the experimenter. But, in my experience, anyone doing research who becomes aware of the inherent difficulty and complexity of the phenomena he is studying is ready to simplify wherever possible. Sympathetically, we can understand this as an act of denial in the face of considerable challenge and complexity. The researchers were also concerned about not affecting the candidate's training and the patient's treatment, which they judged might be adversely influenced by knowledge of the research. It is ironic that analysts would take the position that knowledge withheld is knowledge without adverse effects; or that knowledge freely shared and mutually understood is likely to prove harmful. However, the very fact that the Study Group gave thought to this problem of informed consent at a time when subject and patient rights were not so firmly fixed in our professional consciousness as now reflects a significant sensitivity ahead of its time. Nevertheless, the decision to keep the candidate and patient uninformed requires understanding.

It could be argued that there was only one subject in this study—the supervisor, and his informed consent was presumably obtained; indeed, he took part in the planning of the research as well as its execution. But this argument would subtly underscore the role of institutional power in decision making. Both candidate and patient were charges or wards of the institution-at-large and of the psychoanalytic institute. The candidate was *in fact* a dependent both because of his position as a trainee in the institute and as a subordinate staff member in the institution-at-large. The patient was *in fact* dependent on the institution for subsidization of her fee, a fact which she needed to distort. It is quite human to feel that one's dependents are in one's care and that one must act for them in their behalf in order to discharge this responsibility. Moreover, often the realities of institutional practice require that decisions affecting many people be made in secret and without their participation. Most people in an institution are subordinates; they are hired to do a job. Matters may be explained after the fact or people may be prepared for certain eventualities, but the actual decision and decision making involve only a few highly placed, superordinate individuals. This latter model is in direct conflict with both the student-teacher model and the patient-analyst model, in both of which shared responsibility for a process is basic and in which it is further assumed that unconscious forces are the most likely to affect this process adversely.

I would conclude that the Study Group made its initial decision to keep both analyst and patient uninformed on the basis of the institutional model for decision making, not the educational or psychoanalytic models. It was mainly based on the exercise of administrative power rather than on the basis of shared responsibility. Perhaps this decision demonstrates in clearest form the nature of institutional role syncretisms in psychoanalysis. The administrator-supervisor was in a position to decide to use the case for research purposes without consultation with the candidate because there were also many other things he decided for the candidate. Would he have felt himself to be in that position if he were not the candidate's administrator? Or if the candidate had simply been purchasing his supervision? I would seriously doubt it. Nor should we overlook the analyst's status as a candidate, another role dependency in actual fact. Thus, the administrator-supervisor-training analyst-education committee member had still another basis on which to believe himself to be in a position to decide for the candidate and indirectly for the candidate's patient. The decision was, in institutional terms, a paternalistic act in both its best and pejorative senses. However, it is difficult for those who are decided for to see the tolerant face of well-intentioned paternalism rather than its somber shadow of arrogance. There is, indeed, a subtle infiltration of attitude into the manner of those who exercise power which must affect their relationships to their subordinates. Similarly, the subordinate's passive, rebellious, or manipulative attitudes form as a counterpart to those of his superiors. Thus, the withholding of information about the study does not mean that the study was not affected; rather, it was affected in ways that, unfortunately, cannot easily be identified. They are untagged contaminants. To some minor extent in this chapter I have been trying to place tags on these contaminants. It is perhaps a continued indication of the existence of the syncretism I am attempting to describe that I consider myself still unsure as to the basis on which the Study Group revised its position and decided to inform the candidate of the study and to request that he consult with his former patient.

Aside from the role of informed consent in the study and its implications, there are two other issues: (1) the data base and the research design, and (2) the candidate as a researcher. I have already touched on the problems encountered by the San Francisco approach and the Fleming-Benedek approach by limiting the data to the supervisor's recall of the supervisory sessions. This was still another—and I think fatal—narrowing of focus which again was influenced by the syncretistic process. The failure to pay attention to the broader institutional framework and to make it part of the research marks yet another consequence of syncretism. Last, a few words about the candidate himself as a researcher, about which more will be said in Chapter XIV. The candidate had an enormous interest in the case, not only from the standpoint of learning to be an analyst, but also from the standpoint of a researcher. Although our institute was quite liberal in its disposition to obtain research waivers for suitable candidates, like most institutes it made little provision for incorporating research into the training or encouraging it on any formal basis. Tacitly, it was assumed that the researcher-candidate would take the initiative, as in fact he had in obtaining his waiver. It was thus not out of keeping with this expectation that the candidate would have considered his control cases as possible research cases. His detailed process notes were, in effect, a promise he was making to himself that he would have data available for future use. These detailed notes, however, were a source of difficulty in this supervision. The supervisor felt they were too long and seldom read them through. He might at times read them through *after* the supervisory session, but this apparently was more for the sake of the research than for the supervision. Even when the notes were relatively brief, they were not read. One is tempted to suppose that the hidden research influences discussed earlier were focused on this issue of process note length. For the candidate his notes became the symbol of his research interests; for the supervisor-researcher (and research subject) they may have represented the intrusion of another and unwelcome research interest that reminded him of his own unshared research commitment.

TRAINING PERSPECTIVE

It would be correct to say that the burden of this chapter has been to describe a variety of ways in which the supervision as a form of training might have been influenced by forces beyond the supervision itself. In this last section it might be useful to identify at least one factor in the training itself that was of importance.

On more than one occasion during the supervision, the supervisor made note of the fact that the analyst was properly silent or refrained from interpretation and that the patient was appropriately productive, thus not requiring any intervention. The analyst was encouraged to make facilitating comments intended to foster more communication, but in this early state of the analysis he was to be wary of interpretations, although he certainly had to be sensitive to the patient's circumstances and have some idea of what was going on. On the basis of this empathy, he could guide his facilitating comments, but no interpretations were as yet called for. This approach was widely shared by other supervisors in the institute. In time I began to have some doubts about this approach. In fact, in my own psychotherapy and diagnostic work conducted at the same time as my analytic training, I behaved quite differently. Interprctations of the relationship between patient and therapist were often, I found, necessary and useful early in the treatment and indeed as necessary and useful in diagnostic interviews and psychological testing. I tried to present some of these ideas in a paper with a colleague (Shevrin and Schectman, 1973).

Gill and Muslin (1976) have also challenged this cautious approach to the role of interpretation. They point out, "...many analysts seem to believe...that the analyst's interpretations during the beginning stages of analysis must be limited and that, generally speaking, silence is desirable" (p. 780). This guideline, according to the authors, is based on an early opinion of Freud's that transference is not to be interpreted until it becomes a clear resistance. The authors propose that this approach was later superseded in Freud's own writing by one in which it is understood that although the patient may be talking freely, there may be "important evidence of transference resistance which would be desirable to interpret" (p. 787).

The supervisory approach was to encourage silence, judicious facilitation but little interpretive work in the opening phase. In this respect, the emphasis was on the old and—in Gill and Muslin's view—erroneous point of view concerning the role of interpretation in the beginning phase of analysis. Seldom in the supervision were different technical approaches discussed, or different options in understanding the material considered, nor was there recognition that the patient's communications might be simply confusing and difficult to understand at this point in the treatment. There was, in fact, one way to approach the data, one way to understand it; any mystery was a failure in such understanding. Certainly at no point were *researchable* issues considered—questions that needed further clarification in theory or technique. It was this approach more than any other aspect of the supervision that cemented the candidate's belief that he was to discover what the supervisor wanted and to try to do it. This was further exacerbated by the defensively narrowed focus of the supervision because of the administrative and research syncretisms.

As I look back at the time of the supervision, the image that comes to mind is of two people attempting to swim in a flood. The Study Group, ignorant of the flood, interpreted the swimmers' struggles in terms of their effects on each other based on one swimmer's account. The supervisor, inured to the flood and wanting so much to enjoy a swim, could only see his efforts as helping his companion to swim better, but could not acknowledge the impact of the powerful forces around him. The candidate, struggling to keep afloat, painfully aware of the flood and his supervisor's involvement in it, had to reach out for help while maintaining his own equilibrium.

REFERENCES

Ekstein, R. & Wallerstein, R. S. (1972), *The Teaching and Learning of Psychotherapy*. New York: International Universities Press.

Gill, M. M. & Muslin, H. L. (1976), Early interpretation of transference. *J. Amer. Psychoanal. Assn.*, 24:779–794.

Goodman, S., Ed. (1977), *Psychoanalytic Education and Research: The Current Situation and Future Possibilities*. New York: International Universities Press.

Lewin, B. D. & Ross, H. (1960), *Psychoanalytic Education in the United States*. New York: Norton.

Shevrin, H. (1978), The training analyst: a contradiction in terms. *Contemp. Psychol.*, 23: 929–930.

——— & Shectman, F. (1973), The diagnostic process in psychiatric evaluations. *Bull. Menninger Clin.*, 37:451–494.

CHAPTER XII

On Being a Member of a Supervision Study Group

PAUL G. MYERSON, M.D.

In this chapter I shall highlight the value for one's own supervisory work that can be gained from participating in a study group on supervision. The essential task of the COPE Study Group on Supervision was to develop what we came to call generic principles of supervision. This goal led the San Francisco group to develop an approach for systematically following the supervision process over periods of time. This is obviously a worthwhile endeavor, but the success of this or similar systematic undertakings depends on the sustained and dedicated activities of those relatively rare psychoanalytic educators who are well versed in research methodology. Most of us do not have these skills, but those of us who took part in this study profited greatly simply from the sharing and the discussion in systematic fashion of clinical experiences with our colleagues. Because I found these contacts so valuable, I have taken upon myself the role of propagandist to expound the considerable educational worth of establishing and participating in similar study groups.

Joan Fleming, in her discussion (Chapter VI), has indicated some of the difficulties that occur when a group of psychoanalytic clinicians and educators convene for the purpose of exchanging experiences. These difficulties reflect the competitive tendencies and narcissistic vulnerabilities that exist even in experienced psychoanalysts, but they can be mitigated if the leaders of the group keep reminding the participants of the purpose of the study, i.e., to enhance one's supervisory skills, to delineate what are the crucial diagnostic and procedural supervisory issues, and to ascertain the options for managing these issues.

The value of sharpening one's skills in diagnosis and methods of procedure in any clinical field is self-evident. It is almost equally evident—at least it should be to psychoanalysts—that there is a resistance to examining and modifying one's hard-wrought way of working, whether as an analyst or as a supervisor. This resistance is due in large part to the enormous complexity of the analytic and supervisory processes, which makes it hard to sustain an inquiring and open-ended approach to either analysis or supervision.

I emphasize this point because I don't want to oversell the value of participating in a supervision study group. Judging from my own experience, a participant in such a group may modify his approach to supervision, but it is unlikely that he will change it radically. I started out believing that the supervisee's growth as an analyst was enhanced if the supervisor was, by and large, enabling rather than confronting. In my present supervisory work, as a result of my involvement in the study, I am more likely than before to confront, but still prefer where possible to teach in a manner that minimizes the supervisee's anxiety. There are also limits to how far we can develop our supervisory skills. In our Study Group, considerable attention was devoted to discussing how best to listen to and to evaluate this particular supervisee's way of reporting. Our discussion of this has helped me to listen better and evaluate more appropriately what I am hearing, but I frequently find myself listening in my old, more haphazard fashion and evaluating what I hear in my old, more "intuitive," undisciplined manner.

With these reservations in mind, I shall indicate several ways that participating in study groups on supervision may improve one's clinical skills as a supervisor. If I were seriously to present myself as a case example of how contact with a study group influences one's ways of conceptualizing and coping with the supervisory process, I would need to present illustrations of my concepts and techniques of supervision prior to this study and compare them with my present modes of thinking and functioning. There are obvious problems in doing this; we have agreed in writing this monograph to focus our presentations on the one case of supervision we have thoroughly examined over the last several years. My discussion of the various supervisory issues I now find significant represents more the outcome of my experience with the Study Group than a systematic attempt to delineate the process through which I have changed.

The categories of supervisory activities in which I feel I have been most influenced through contacts with the Study Group are: (1) mode of listening and registering information preparatory to making a diagnosis of the analyst's learning needs, (2) methods for diagnosing the analyst's learning needs, (3) considerations in selecting the appropriate teaching procedures, (4) criteria for evaluating the effects of teaching procedures.

MODE OF LISTENING AND REGISTERING INFORMATION PREPARATORY TO MAKING A DIAGNOSIS OF THE ANALYST'S LEARNING NEEDS

I have here been most influenced by the Fleming-Benedek (1966) book and, of course, by Joan Fleming's contributions within the Study Group. In her discussions with the committee, elaborating on the principles set forth in her book, Fleming has presented a systematic way of listening preparatory to making an educational diagnosis. She suggests that when the supervisor hears the analyst's report of the analytic material, he should listen carefully for the responses from the analyst which he perceives as inappropriate and incongruous with the dynamic line and state of the patient's transference, then note the effects of the analyst's responses on the patient, and finally observe whether the analyst is aware of the inappropriateness of these responses and their effects on the patient.

This description of the method of organizing in one's mind the flow of the material in the supervision report is deceptively simple and might be viewed as just an elaboration on the obvious. It is in fact difficult to carry out in the actual supervision situation. I have found that it requires considerable discipline and training to listen in the manner Fleming suggests. It is difficult to avoid making a premature diagnosis of the analyst's learning needs and to refrain from intervening until the necessary information sufficient for the purpose has been gained, that is, until note has been taken as to whether the analyst is aware of the inappropriateness of his responses to his patient and of his patient's reactions to his responses. Because I have a tendency to try to minimize the tension in the supervision situation and because of my concern over what is happening in the analytic situation, I was—before my contact with the Study Group—and perhaps still am, likely to point out to the analyst in a didactic fashion what is going on between his patient and himself without observing sufficiently whether the analyst is mindful of the detrimental impact of his response or lack of one. I was apt to use the analyst's mistake as an impetus for a didactic intervention rather than as a signal to me to make further observations that might help me make a more accurate diagnosis of the underlying reasons for the mistake.

If the supervisor is able to refrain from his teaching intervention after he has recognized the analyst's mistake, he has the option of simply registering the information for further use, or of involving the analyst in a discussion about his understanding of his inappropriate response. In the latter case, the supervisor may be seeking additional information which will further his ability to diagnose the analyst's learning need, or he may be using a teaching procedure that calls the analyst's attention to the mistake he is making. In the latter case he is asking the analyst to reflect upon the reasons for his mistake rather than teaching him in a didactic fashion how to do psychoanalysis. I believe that involving the analyst in this kind of discussion may be a valuable method of teaching. It is one I have come to use more frequently since my participation in the Study Group. Nevertheless, this approach will often create a different type of supervisory climate than a more wait-and-see approach. It requires a well-developed supervisory alliance in order to be effective, and runs the risk with less secure analysts of increasing their defensiveness and interfering with their spontaneity.

I shall return to this issue later when I discuss the considerations involved in selecting the most appropriate teaching procedure. As I have suggested, a supervisor can observe whether the analyst is aware of his mistake and its effects on the patient without involving him in a discussion about why he made such a mistake. In recent years, I have frequently confined myself to registering the fact that the analyst is unaware of his mistake and its effects upon the patient.

When I do this I am in the position of any clinician who makes observations before he is ready to take action. Clinicians in any field can either overreact to or minimize the importance of diagnostic clues—*vide* the internist who insists on a complete and expensive medical workup for every simple complaint or the one whose optimism leads him to ignore the significance of persistent symptoms. I am here emphasizing the difficulty in confining oneself to just registering pertinent information without becoming either prematurely active or scotomatizing its significance.

In the first supervision session of the analysis under discussion here, the analyst described a response to his patient that it would be almost impossible for any supervisor entirely to scotomatize. The analyst clearly became anxious when the patient told him that she, upon entering analysis, finally had a "captive audience." He immediately announced he was shortly going to be away for awhile, and when the patient said she, too, was going to be taking a brief vacation, he told her in response that she would be charged for her time away. This is a significant "inappropriate response" on the part of the analyst, of which he seemed unaware, as he did of its effect on the patient. Before my participation in the Study Group, if I were supervising this student-analyst, I undoubtedly would have registered his response as inappropriate. However, it is likely that I would have attributed it to the analyst's initial anxiety and regressive reaction in starting the analysis and the supervision, and would not have kept this interchange as firmly in mind as a possible portent of events to follow, which I should observe with great care as I now would. At present I probably would not ask the analyst what he had in mind lest he take such questioning as criticism, but I would register his response as more than an initial regressive and anxious analytic reaction and as a rather serious "inappropriate analytic response to the flow of his patient's material" which he was not aware of and which might be indicative of major difficulties to come.

METHODS FOR DIAGNOSING THE ANALYST'S LEARNING NEEDS

Fleming and Benedek (1966) deal extensively with the question of learning problems in the analyst. In their chapter on "The Supervisory Process," they present a chart titled "Learning Problems Relevant to Transference Phenomena." This chart includes three general categories: failure of recognition and diagnosis (due primarily to inexperience and deficient theoretical knowledge); transference-countertransference reactions by the analyst (due to unresolved conflicts in the analyst); transference reactions to the supervisor. Under each of these categories, they enumerate pertinent subcategories.

The committee repeatedly used these categories to discuss the analyst's learning difficulties in supervision, frequently employing the picturesque rubrics of "dumb spots," "blind spots," and even "deaf spots" to designate the analyst's difficulties. The committee's interest in understanding the nature of the analyst's learning difficulties which derived from transference-countertransference phenomena was reflected in the content of the meetings organized with representatives from the various institutes, where we used countertransference difficulties as a taking-off point for several of the discussions.

I have found these categories of learning problems to be of increasing value to me in conducting my supervisory work, particularly where the analyst was having serious difficulties in maintaining a proper analytic situation. Where this continues to be the case over a long period of time, his blind or deaf spots become increasingly obvious. In the average fairly good supervisory situation, however, it is often difficult to make such clear-cut distinctions. There are reciprocal relationships between the various types of learning difficulties, and in practice one can observe mixtures of all three. For example, the more an analyst knows about the analytic process—the less inexperienced or "dumb" he is—the less likely he will be to manifest countertransference irritation to his patient's resistant and regressive behavior or be annoyed at his supervisor—i.e., he will be less blind and deaf.

One of the better analysts I have supervised recently manifested an overt annoyance to his patient's regressive narcissistic defenses against transference feelings. The analyst's annoyance did not interfere with the development of a quite good analytic situation, but it did lead him to give an unnecessarily critical tinge to his interpretations of this regressive behavior. His countertransference annoyance appeared to be a mixture of frustration over this patient's inability to look at transference feelings and a deeply felt, partially recognized irritation at the patient's narcissistic behavior. As the analyst became more experienced, as he came to understand that his patient needed to retreat from intense feelings, his interpretations became less critical and he was better able to listen to and consider alternate options for managing his patient's resistance. I found that an either-or diagnosis of "dumb spot" *or* "blind spot" was insufficient; rather, it was necessary for me to understand the relation between inexperience and countertransference reactions as they influenced his analytic techniques.

Mastery comes from living through difficult experiences. Experienced supervisors are experienced analysts who have become able, over many years, to be realistic about what is likely to happen in an analytic situation and adjust their expectations accordingly. There is a tendency for us to forget that the analysts we are supervising have not had this experience and that their expectations of analysis are inevitably unrealistic. If we do forget this, we are likely to make inappropriate diagnoses about their learning problems. Another quite gifted analyst I have supervised became disappointed and somewhat annoyed with me because his patient had not relived and worked through the "crucial infantile experiences responsible for her neurosis." His patient in fact had done very well, considering the complex nature of her character structure and a deeply embedded need to seek immediate external gratification rather than to look at the meaning of her behavior. I inwardly applauded the analyst's ambitious goals for his patient, which I believed would stand him in good stead with less difficult patients, and recognized that he would listen to my comments about the limitations of the analytic techniques only after he had analyzed many more patients and found out for himself what he could and could not accomplish through the psychoanalytic technique.

Supervisors will have different ideas about the correct analytic approach. These differences will lead them to make diagnoses about their supervisees' learning needs which are at variance with one another. Participation in workshops on supervision not only opens one's eyes to new supervisory options, but to new ways of understanding the analytic process. While these differences in analytic approach never explicitly led to major disagreement among the members of the Study Group, I can imagine, by adding to the group certain analysts I know, that disagreement about what is correct analytic procedure would indeed occur and that heated discussions would take place about the correct diagnoses of supervisees' learning needs. For example, an analyst who very actively confronts his own patient's regressive defensive reactions would presumably not evaluate the analyst's critical comments to the patient in the first example I cited in this section in the same light that I did. He might consider what I viewed to be the more reasonable aspects of his interpretations as a reflection of countertransference anxiety which resulted in an inability to be forceful enough. I bring this point up to indicate that as I have acquired more experience, not only from my own analytic and supervisory work, but from interchanges with colleagues both in the Study Group and elsewhere, I have found it necessary not only to review how I diagnose a learning need, but to re-evaluate what I consider to be appropriate analytic technique.

Trying to be as objective as I can in reviewing the influence of the Study Group on my diagnostic activities, I find I consider the analyst's transference and countertransference reactions more stringently than before my participation. In many instances, where the analyst is doing reasonably good analytic work, my diagnosis of a countertransference difficulty does not necessarily lead to a major supervisory intervention. Yet I not only hear and register the analysts' reactions in this light, but I am more clear about how their transferences and countertransferences influence their analytic technique and limit their options for furthering the analytic process. I am more aware both of the analyst's irritation and frustration with the patient's various resistances and of the analyst's fear of and difficulty in tolerating the patient's transference feelings of love and hate. While I have no way of knowing how I would react today if I had not participated in the Study Group, I am convinced that the impetus to conceptualize what I was doing in order to communicate with the other members of the committee and the need to comprehend their modes of conceptualizing have led to a considerable gain in my ability to tune in to this aspect of the analytic process.

CONSIDERATIONS IN SELECTING THE APPROPRIATE TEACHING PROCEDURES

This topic, of course, goes right to the hub of discussions on supervision. What is the best method of promoting the analyst's development, particularly when we are aware that he has significant transference-countertransference problems? Fleming and Benedek have direct and important things to say about this issue, which again have been influential in my thinking and have led me to re-evaluate my supervisory approach even where I do not always agree with what they are saying. As I have indicated, I have become much more aware of the analyst's transference-countertransference problems from my experiences with the Study Group. But becoming aware of a problem is one thing; deciding on the appropriate management of it is quite another.

Fleming and Benedek (1966) have concluded from their observations that the development of the student's self-analytic function is probably the most important objective in learning under supervision, and they advocate active teaching measures designed to enhance the student's associative and introspective faculties. They give an example of their active teaching techniques geared to this purpose (pp. 165–166). The patient under discussion was intensely involved in transference feelings toward the analyst which she defended against by asking questions of the analyst, e.g., about her health. On a number of occasions the analyst gave concrete answers to her questions and failed to encourage the patient to associate to why she was asking the questions. When the supervisor queried the analyst as to why he did not do this, it became evident that the analyst was ascribing his mistake to inexperience rather than to any reactions he might be having to the patient. On one occasion, when asked why he answered the patient's questions, he stated that because he had mistakenly considered that she had transferred feelings to him which she had for her brother, he should be responsive to her in order to help her view him as different from her brother. He indicated that he had a dumb spot. The supervisor told the analyst he ought to question why he repeatedly answered her direct questions.

> Analyst: I can't give you a dynamic reason at this moment. I can give you something that smacks of my being defensive, but. . . .
>
> Supervisor: Well, think about it, because I really think there must be something here that belongs to you, and it's contaminating with the patient. It's more important that you discover what this is than that you and I talk about it [Fleming and Benedek, 1966, p. 166].

The supervisor here very clearly indicated that there was a problem and that it stemmed from feelings the analyst had about himself as an analyst or from feelings he had about his patient. The analyst responded favorably to this confrontation of his countertransference difficulty and apparently, as judged from subsequent recorded material of the supervision, was able to discover what in his own reactions to the patient or to being an analyst was interfering with the analytic process. The supervisor here appeared to enhance what Fleming and Benedek have delineated as the most important objective in learning under supervision—the development of the student's self-analytic function.

Many supervisors—judging from my own reactions when I first read the Fleming-Benedek book and from conversations with colleagues about this technique—react initially by feeling that this approach is too intrusive, that it runs the danger of placing the supervisor in the position of a therapist confronting the analyst with his neurotic conflicts, and that it thereby increases the stress of the supervisor-analyst alliance and interferes with the analyst's ability to learn from the supervisor's other teaching procedures, and possibly inhibits his own potentiality for discovering his mistakes for himself. This group of supervisors would undoubtedly agree with the emphasis Fleming and Benedek place on enhancing the supervisor's self-analytic function, but would be concerned that the approach they delineate is not the most appropriate method for achieving this objective.

Fleming, I believe, would argue that one can only make an omelette by breaking some eggs and that an analyst who reacts unduly negatively to this type of confrontation has unresolved conflicts that, at the very least, require more self-analysis. These are cogent and, for me, almost convincing arguments. Yet I continue to have reservations about the universal applicability of this approach. I believe it requires for its effectiveness careful timing in the context of a good supervisor-analyst alliance, which not all supervisors nor all students are capable of establishing. Moreover, many students are still working through conflicts that affect their analytic work in their own analyses. This working through of transference and countertransference toward one's analytic patients may be delayed rather than enhanced by a too-active confrontation from the supervisor. To do full justice to this most crucial issue, we would have to examine both alternative techniques for enhancing the self-analytic function and the shortcomings—from the point of view of Fleming and Benedek—of interventions that fall short of letting the analyst know he has a transference-countertransference problem.

As I have stated earlier, a seasoned supervisor has the tendency to forget how little real experience with the analytic process the student has, even when he is working with a second or third analytic case. One has to live through enough situations where one's patient retreats to a sticky transference defense really to understand and appreciate that the patient needs to do this and is not regressing just because he wants to irritate the analyst. One has to analyze enough patients who rapidly develop a deeply eroticized transference to recognize this is a transference resistance that is serving to avoid the real analytic work. These reactions on the part of the patient will almost inevitably mobilize transference and countertransference responses on the part of the analyst, which, if he is inexperienced, will interfere with his work, either leading him to intervene inappropriately or causing him to overlook more appropriate methods for managing a transference defense or a transference resistance.

As Jacob, in particular, has stressed (Chapter IX), it may be valuable for the supervisor to demonstrate these inevitable movements in the analytic process pedagogically before focusing the analyst's attention on his own deficiencies. This approach does not overlook or de-emphasize the analyst's transference and countertransference reactions, but considers them—for operational purposes—secondary to his lack of experience. The case for this approach is that the analyst's working through of his conflicts is more likely to occur in a situation where the supervisor makes sure the analyst really understands the analytic process and the reactions of his patient which activate his countertransference responses, than in one where the supervisor confronts the analyst with these responses and encourages him to do some self-analysis or to go back into personal analysis. This pedagogic approach can include demonstrating the analyst's countertransference as part of the paradigm—that is, the supervisor can indicate not only the inevitability of the patient's reaction to the analytic situation, but the inevitability of the analyst's responses, thus implicitly suggesting to the analyst that his own reactions are expectable and comprehensible rather than reflections of neurosis. The relative effectiveness of the approach here advocated—when it is effective—stems from its pedagogic and encouraging nature, which is comparatively tension-free and which may promote integrated identifications with the supervisor.

There is no reason, of course, why a supervisor has to confine himself to any single teaching approach. Fleming and Benedek have demonstrated that it is possible in their hands to confront some students with their countertransference responses in a manner that does indeed enhance their self-analytic function.

In the supervision that is the subject of this monograph, the supervisor, after a period of listening to and registering the analyst's mistakes, came to the conclusion he had an important countertransference difficulty that was interfering with the analytic process. Not only had the supervisor noted the analyst's very early direct rejection of the patient's wish for a "captive audience," but he noted too that the patient subsequently appeared to have no expectations from the analyst or the analytic work. He concluded that the analyst, because he found the patient's wish for closeness too threatening, had behaved in "too cool" a fashion, which in turn had led the patient to hold back or withdraw from her desire for closeness. The supervisor attempted a variety of pedagogic techniques to teach the analyst what was going on, although one might argue that these were tried in an *ad hoc* fashion before the supervisor had the opportunity to appreciate the rhythm of the analytic process and consequently could not clearly demonstrate to the analyst how far he and his patient had progressed. The supervisor suggested to the analyst—tactfully to be sure—that perhaps he was behaving "too coolly," perhaps the analyst was more afraid than the patient of the development of the analytic process, particularly of the patient's transference reactions. Sensing that the analyst was anxious about opening up the issue of the patient's sexual reactions to him, the supervisor also urged him to probe actively into the patient's sexual fantasy life.

The supervisor here confronted the analyst with his countertransference reaction to the patient. One can question whether it was adequate to confront the analyst with the fact that he was having unrecognized feelings toward his patient and that this lack of recognition interfered with his understanding and handling of the case. Telling someone he is behaving "coolly" is more likely, I believe, to mobilize a sense of guilt or inadequacy which may lead him to attempt to counteract his behavior before understanding its meaning fully than it is to help him discover the feelings in himself that lie behind his coolness. Awareness of the significance of an affect is a better impetus to shifting to a self-analytic frame of mind than confrontation with behavior, especially when the inappropriate behavior has been pointed out in a context that indicates the behavior has probably been hurtful. The supervisor's subsequent interventions could be considered, in the context, more of a call to action than to self-observation. The supervisor's statement that the analyst seemed more afraid of the patient's transferences than the patient was implicitly a challenge to him to allow the patient to more fully express her feelings. The statement was a direct suggestion about how to proceed, which ran the risk of intensifying the analyst's anxiety because it occurred before the analyst fully understood the nature of the analytic process and before he was aware of what he was experiencing that caused him to be "cool" and was responsible for his difficulty in allowing the patient to develop her sexual transference toward him.

I have discussed this vignette not to criticize the supervisor, who I thought in general did excellent work, but to illustrate how this type of presentation to a study group exposes the participants to varying and often conflicting points of view about the most appropriate way to proceed. Both the Fleming-Benedek (Chapter VI) and the Jacob (Chapter IX) approach have considerable merit, but they also have limitations. I am still struggling to assimilate their ideas. If I were faced with a similar supervision problem, I would first try to make sure that I was demonstrating as adequately as possible the nature of the total analytic process, which would include the analyst's responses to his patient's reactions to him. Then, if I felt it valuable to confront the analyst with his countertransference problem, I would try to pay careful attention to our alliance and, in cautious stages, try to help him recognize what was responsible for his learning problem.

CRITERIA FOR EVALUATING THE EFFECTS OF TEACHING PROCEDURES

Evaluation of the effects of supervisory procedures is a task which is analogous to that of listening to and registering information preparatory to making an educational diagnosis. When we listen for the analyst's mistakes, we try to delineate the response from the analyst which we perceive as inappropriate and incongruous with the dynamic and state of the patient's transference, note the effect of this response on the patient, and observe whether the analyst is aware of the inappropriateness of his response and its effect on the patient. Difficult as this is, it is even harder to determine where our own supervisory teaching procedures are inappropriate, especially when we are even less sure of what is the correct way to conduct supervision than we are of how to conduct an analysis. But we can at least consider the possibility that our teaching procedures are inappropriate, ill-timed, or are made without an adequately effective supervisor-analyst alliance. And we can try to note the effect of our procedures on the analyst—to evaluate the success of our supervisory interventions, whether our intention is to increase his knowledge of the analytic process or to enhance his self-analytic functions.

The San Francisco Project, through the schema it has developed to categorize and record the supervision process over considerable sweeps of time, offers hope of ascertaining criteria that will be useful in evaluating the effect of the supervisor's teaching procedure. Windholz—using this schema—addresses himself directly to the effect the supervisor's techniques have on the analyst (Chapter VIII). From its review of the supervisor's process notes, the San Francisco subgroup suggests that the more confronting interventions I discussed in the last section mobilized reactions in the analyst that were indicative of considerable tension, probably reflecting transferences he had to the supervisor that would not be useful for the learning process. They indicate that the analyst revealed evidence suggesting he was momentarily shaken in the analytic situation, that he was reacting in an unnecessarily confronting manner to the patient, and was unnecessarily self-critical in the supervision situation. This was a reflection either of guilt activated by the supervisor's urging that he probe into the patient's sexual life or a reflection of his efforts to placate the supervisor, whom he saw as forcing him to move more quickly than he was prepared to. The analyst's attempts to confess his countertransference—which the supervisor felt were not altogether genuine—might be viewed in a similar light, intended either to mitigate his unnecessary guilt about having sexual feelings for his patient or to obscure the fact that he resented being forced to move faster than he felt ready to. Whatever these reactions on the part of the analyst might turn out to be—and in such a complex system as the one we are describing, it might be impossible ever to really know—they are indices of a "heated-up" supervision situation, and as such could serve to alert the supervisor to the importance of his re-evaluating his overall supervisory approach.

The problems of ascertaining and evaluating such indices in an ongoing supervision situation are obviously formidable. We are asking ourselves not only to observe the analyst's mistakes and his awareness of them, to make an appropriate and operational educational diagnosis, to select a teaching technique to help the analyst with his learning needs, but now to observe as well our mistakes. Moreover, we are far from knowing when the analyst's responses to our interventions—e.g., his self-criticism or his confessions—are indicative of a poor alliance, in which he is unable to learn, or when they represent the inevitable resistances that go along with new growth. The fact that someone's anxiety or guilt is mobilized by new understanding does not necessarily mean that he is unable to assimilate this understanding. In fact, it is our lack of understanding of how and at what rate our analytic students grow and develop as analysts that makes it so difficult to evaluate the effects of our teaching endeavors.

Fortunately, I have not set this last task for myself in this discussion, significant as I believe it to be. What I have tried to present are some of the questions—and the very partial answers—that have been raised for me through my contact with the COPE Supervision Study Group. I am convinced that the organization of similar groups can raise even more pertinent questions and find fuller answers to the complex problems involved in psychoanalytic supervision.

REFERENCE

Fleming, J. & Benedek, T. (1966), *Psychoanalytic Supervision.* New York: Grune & Stratton.

CHAPTER XIII

On Being the Supervisor Studied: Observations and Confessions

HERBERT J. SCHLESINGER, Ph.D.

BACKGROUND

The story of my relation to the COPE Study Group on Supervision may be of interest to those who will review the Study Group's work and who may wish to make their own assessment of the sample of supervision studied.

My own interest in studying supervision is part of a larger interest in psychoanalytic learning and teaching, an interest I have sometimes summarized to myself in the oversimplified question, "Are analysts made or born?" Are psychoanalytic skills teachable, or perhaps more usefully put, how and to what extent can one facilitate the learning of the essential psychoanalytic skills by a candidate?

In recent years this interest has focused on the supervision process. I have tried to study both by myself, and with the aid of small, *ad hoc* groups of colleagues, the handling of certain teaching and learning problems that occur regularly in supervision. These efforts to study supervision met with only indifferent success for a number of reasons: I found it very difficult to get colleagues, experienced supervisors, to focus on the specific issue I wanted to study—the use of the supervisory situation as a medium for teaching and the activity of the supervisor as a teacher. Rather than looking at the activity of the supervisor, as reflected in his process notes, the members of the groups seemed characteristically much more comfortable with looking at the activity of the student-analyst or his patient and in taking an evaluative stance toward his work. They were governed more by a clinical than by an educational attitude, and tended to resolve what I wanted to regard as teaching and learning issues in terms of the clinically discernible excessive difficulty of the case or ineptitude of the student-analyst. While these latter factors would, of course, have to be considered in any overall assessment, they tended to be used to preclude consideration of the nature, rationale, or quality of the teaching going on in the supervisory situation, which was my major interest in presenting the material.

The fact that the members of this group were all faculty of my own institute, and thus knew the candidate whose work I was presenting, made it easier to focus on him (perhaps also because he was not present at our discussions!) and also made it easier to consider factors outside the immediate supervisory situation in order to explain events in the supervision. However, I found it difficult to get the group to focus on conceptualizing the events in the supervisory teaching itself or even to be critical of the supervisor. Thus, after several unsuccessful ventures of this kind, I decided it was not possible to do it in this fashion or in that setting.

At about this time, Emanuel Windholz, Chairman of the COPE Study Group on Supervision, who had heard of my study efforts, asked to borrow my supervision notes to see if they would be suitable for the Study Group's purposes. Perhaps because these sets of notes covered relatively brief segments of supervision and reflected difficult problems, the Study Group felt they were not typical enough of supervision in general or expanded enough for their purposes. They asked me if I would be willing to make the same kind of process notes for my next supervision case to help them in their effort to devise ways of studying the supervisory process. I agreed, and the first fourteen of these weekly notes, together with an account of the "rules" I adopted in writing them, appear as Chapter V of this monograph.

While the Study Group was reviewing these notes, I did not take part in their discussions. But when they had enough material for their purpose, I decided to enlarge my role as subject and to study both the notes I had written and the several strategies of investigation being explored by the Study Group. Before giving up the exclusive role of subject and undertaking my own study of my notes and reflections about them, I thought it might be useful to try to reconstruct from memory the situation in which the supervision had taken place.

The following account, altered only to preserve privacy and slightly amplified for clarity, is what I wrote at that time. It is based on my reminiscences when I tried to recapture the way I had felt as I undertook this project and describes the various forces that impinged on the supervisory situation. I wanted to record my impressions in as uncontaminated a form as possible before reviewing some six months of supervision notes. I did not make this account available to the Study Group for approximately another year. It alludes to more material than is presented in Chapter V, since I prepared it after approximately eighteen supervision hours, while the Study Group decided to restrict its attention to the first fourteen.

OVERALL REVIEW AND CRITIQUE OF EIGHTEEN SUPERVISION HOURS (ANALYTIC HOURS 1-89)

PROCESS RECORDING

I have the initial feeling that I do not remember this supervision as clearly as I should, that is, not as well as I think I remember other supervisions I am currently engaged in. I am not sure whether to attribute this to my involvement in process recording in this case, which I believe has a tendency to take the place of memory. Perhaps I expect more of myself with regard to this case than others, or perhaps I do remember it well enough, and it will come back to me as I reflect about it.

I think I underestimated considerably the impact that making notes for the COPE Study Group on Supervision would have on me and on the supervision. First of all, I underestimated grossly the amount of effort and trouble it would be to prepare the notes I had committed myself to provide. It turned out to be quite a different thing to prepare such notes for an existing group of well-known colleagues than it was to prepare notes for my own curiosity, with only the hope that I could interest some group some day in looking at them with me.

Notes taken for my own purposes were prepared in a much more relaxed frame of mind and were allusive rather than a complete account, inasmuch as they were to serve merely as an aid to my memory rather than as an independent record of the supervision process. The task of trying to summarize what took place between the analyst and myself in a way that would permit others to follow this process (as well as the analyst-patient process, which I did not always see clearly), without becoming too involved in detail, has been considerable. I was as concerned about understanding and remembering for a third party as I was with the primary task of supervising. I cannot be sure just how much interference my divided attention caused. I think it influenced me somewhat in my behavior with the analyst. At the very least, my sense of spontaneity was affected, and my wish to demonstrate "teaching" may have been an intrusion. When I observe that the atmosphere between the analyst and me was "stiffer" than with other candidates, I wonder how much responsibility I bear for this.

My efforts to preserve my "objectivity" as the subject of study also led to some unanticipated difficulties. I found I was developing "transferences" to this Supervision Study Group that took the form of fantasies about how they would read and (mis)understand my notes. My thoughts would turn, during the supervision hour, to whether it would be possible to compress into a paragraph the essence of the problem I was having with the analyst and my thinking about it. I found myself wanting "to make very clear" to the Study Group what "really happened." These fantasies also made it difficult to be spontaneous in dictating the notes. As I imagined myself a member of the Study Group trying to make sense of what I had written, I felt I had to attempt to answer questions I could raise as a potential reader. One of the effects on the notes was to make them more organized, "rational," and smoother than they might otherwise have been. Perhaps my ordeal is only a replica of the anxiety of the candidate in presenting his material to the supervisor.

I could also not keep from considering at times whether my dual interest in the supervisory process was preventing me from functioning maximally effectively as a supervisor. This concern became more troublesome when problems appeared in the supervision that led me to wonder if the analyst would be able to work successfully with the case. I found myself becoming protective of the candidate, as if the Study Group were, in effect, an education committee. This was the case especially around the fifth supervisory hour in which I felt that there was some deficiency in the analyst's empathy with his patient. When I looked back on this period, I could see that I had not written it up the way that I was feeling it; I had to be protectively "objective." It aroused recollections of my experience with my local colleagues who had shifted so quickly and inexorably from the study of supervision to an evaluation of the less-than-skillful supervisee. Since the Study Group did not yet have the discipline of an organized research protocol to guide it, I thought they too might slip into just such an evaluative stance and fail to maintain the focus I desired on the teaching problem the analyst's difficulties presented.

These issues were all the more troublesome when I felt I had to take up with the candidate the possible deleterious effect on the conduct of the analysis of his own avowed research interest in his patient, feeling as I did that on this issue my own hands were not clean.

In looking back on these times, I can easily rationalize my reactions to the realistic and unrealistic problems I have been describing, but I think it more important to simply record them here without attempting to answer or dispose of them, since I believe that they represent some of the common, but not usually explicitly remarked hazards of studying supervision in this way.

PREVIOUS RELATIONSHIP WITH THE CANDIDATE

The candidate was no stranger to me. I had known him since he first began his psychotherapy training and I had been his teacher and supervisor in other contexts than at the institute. For some years, however, our relationship had been that of scientific and personal colleagues. At the inception of this case, my impression of his work with patients was quite a few years old, but I still recalled such characteristics as his persistence and seriousness of purpose. While not at all humorless, he takes himself and his work very seriously and becomes deeply involved in what he is doing. In his clinical work, before his analysis, he often tended to take a more somber view of the pathology of a patient than would his colleagues. He has a streak of stubborn self-righteousness, and when convinced that he is right, can become nearly unshakable. He is widely regarded as being very talented, even brilliant, very energetic and hard-working, and highly articulate. He has always had a strong interest in research and has done notable investigative work in several areas. I should add that the candidate has always rejected sharply any implication that because he also has an interest in research, he is therefore less interested in clinical matters. Indeed, he has always kept a considerable portion of his day for work with patients and has always done some teaching.

When I was asked to supervise the second case of this candidate it was against the background of a difficult experience with his first case (which was still in progress as of this writing). Further, I knew that this difficulty was not altogether of the analyst's making. The first supervisor had withheld for some time his approval for a second case, while the candidate himself was eager to get on with his training. Finally, after a prolonged discussion within the education committee, the first supervisor was prevailed upon to let the candidate try a second case. As one of those who had favored it, I was asked to undertake the supervision, and accepted. Thus, I felt under some pressure to justify my support of the candidate in terms of the demonstrated progress in the second case.

The candidate and I then reviewed the record of a case that was immediately available. While the case looked reasonably suitable to me, at least worth a try, the candidate demurred after reviewing the clinical chart in great detail, seeing dire implications in some areas of the intake evaluation that had not been gone into thoroughly. I thought he was probably overreacting on the basis of the difficulty experienced with his first case, and told him so, but saw no point in exerting pressure to have him take this case. I should add that such pickiness about accepting a case offered for supervised analysis is quite unusual in our institute, and there was some feeling on the part of those responsible for clinic case assignments that he ought to "cool his heels" for a while before a substitute case would be offered him. The present case became available before too long, however, and the candidate accepted it after discussing it with me. He raised no real objections to this case, although there were some open questions about the patient's early development that could have given rise to the same sort of doubts he had raised about the other. I entertained the possibility that it might be easy to get this particular patient into analysis, but difficult to achieve successful termination.

EFFECTS OF INTEREST IN STUDYING SUPERVISION

It was my hope in agreeing to present this case from the beginning that it would turn out to be a "normal" supervision with no serious problems so that the group could remain focused on the supervisory process, in particular on the activity of the supervisor. This wish to offer an "average expectable supervision" for study contributed to my reluctance to report my own feelings of uneasiness about the progress of the supervision as deeply and as soon as I felt them. It may also help account for some of my reluctance to move in faster than I did on what quite early began to look like serious evidence of difficulty in the analyst's work. I deliberately decided to see how far I could get in supervisory teaching by using essentially pedagogic methods. I also think I felt somewhat protective of the candidate before the Study Group. Leaning so far backward in regard to this issue, I think I probably did the candidate an overall disservice.

SUPERVISOR'S PREFERRED STYLE

I like to allow a candidate sufficient time and room to develop his own way of working with a patient and to help him to mature within it. I need to feel that I understand what is going on with his patient, but even if I don't, I will, if the candidate seems sufficiently knowledgeable and skillful, allow things to go on and hope to catch up after a while. I also like to develop an understanding of how the candidate conceives of analyzing and, if his understanding and technique are sufficient, to allow him to raise for himself the questions he would like to discuss. If a consultant-colleague relationship, rather than a teacher-student relationship is possible, so much the better.

I also like to step back from the day-to-day details of the case and look at the forest rather than the trees in order to help the candidate appreciate larger issues that may be implicated by the current events of the case. Thus the case may provide the opportunity for some more general teaching. Actually, if the progress of the case permits it, I find it difficult *not* to make use of it for such opportunistic general teaching, and occasionally will let such discussions get quite peripheral to the actual conduct of the case. Of course, if the candidate has something on his mind he wants to discuss, or if the case does not seem to be going well and I have doubts about his capacity to carry on, I try not to burden him with extraneous matters. Thus, while I "believe" in allowing the candidate to set the pace and take the lead in making use of me, I prefer it when I can be more active and raise and discuss issues that may not have occurred to the candidate at all. From another point of view, while I have no objections to a candidate making mistakes and learning from them, I do not feel it is right to simply let him go until he makes mistakes. I like to try to discuss with the candidate where the case is, where it is heading, to relate what we see to theory when we can, and to rely on nature for the "mistakes" that often enough provide invaluable teaching opportunities.

It is against this background of my preferences that I recall I have been less active as a supervisor in this instance than is my usual wont. I have alluded to some of the factors that may have interfered in this regard; I should add that perhaps the case is one that has begun developing slowly but naturally, and also that I may have been anticipating this candidate would be (i.e., it may have been *my* need that he be) a better analyst at this stage of his development than he, in fact, was.

TRANSFERENCE AND COUNTERTRANSFERENCE IN THE SUPERVISORY SITUATION

As I noted above, I have become increasingly uncomfortable about the supervision on several counts. Though the analyst prepares exhaustive notes we do not use (i.e., they are too long to be read and discussed during the supervision hour), he is also concerned to "give me the picture" orally and is very punctilious about his self-imposed task. I do not feel, however, that I am really in touch with what he is doing with the patient, and tend to feel that I am being held off at arm's length—defensively kept out of things. The "picture" he gives is often a synthetic account of the week, ignoring chronology. I am not acting entirely naturally with this candidate, a feeling I can relate in part to the nature of these presentations which make me feel I am being made into an "audience" for him. I have often felt it necessary to try to penetrate the obscurity of these "clear" reports and, detectivelike, try to find out what is actually going on. Yet I have felt constrained from directly taking up with the analyst the nature and the impact of his way of presentation.

I am not certain about all the motives that may underlie the candidate's behavior. He is characteristically a person who likes things well organized and can be quite argumentative in pursuit of an issue or when he believes a "principle is involved." But during this supervision he has been most courteous, though at times quietly stubborn, as by listening politely to me but not dealing squarely with the substance of what I have to say. I sense that he very much wants to be right and he is quite hard on himself when he detects a technical mistake or a facet of his countertransference. For my part, I find myself being more passive than is customary for me. As I think about it, while there have been a number of interchanges and discussions between us, there has been less give and take than with other supervisees, and the atmosphere has been "stiffer."[1]

I have described some of the factors that may have colored my participation in this supervision. After reviewing my supervision process notes and reflecting about them, I think I can discern some additional character traits and potentials for transference involvement that this supervisor brings to the teaching situation. I notice a wish to "give," which probably has part of its roots in insecurity about whether I really have enough to give to justify being an analytic teacher. "Giving" also has within it the sense of wanting to be a plentiful provider, to "stuff" the candidate who has come under my wing as well as to overwhelm the candidate with how much I as the supervisor have to offer, to awe him and show him how far he has to come in order to be enough like his teacher. Together with the defenses against them, these needs to feed, hold down, impress, encourage and discourage, could certainly influence the teaching process and shape the teaching situation and thereby the nature of the learning alliance. It may be worth studying how these traits may have colored the teaching situation, and how much their form or intensity may owe to interaction with specific detectable characteristics of the candidate.

I have known the candidate as a student and colleague before he applied to the institute, but in recent years he has become professionally independent. Now he returns to be my pupil once again. Part of my concern is necessarily with how well this reverse transition from comfortable colleagueship to teacher and student will be accomplished. I may have been influenced by the anticipation that the candidate's well-known "hard-headedness" and "show-me" attitude would manifest themselves early in supervision. Reacting to these anticipated challenges I could well have felt that I had better demonstrate (to the candidate as well as to the Study Group) right from the

[1]When I later actually reviewed the supervision notes, I noted that my level of activity varied and also that the target of it varied from relatively peripheral to relatively central issues in the supervision. Perhaps the impression of my own passivity has to do with the discomfort I feel in not taking up more directly my uneasiness about not having a better grasp of the case. I should add here that while I like to know where I am in working with a case and generally do, I do not need to be "on top of it" at every moment, but can tolerate periods when things are not clear and can await developments. In this instance, however, I often felt that things were happening that I ought to have known about and that the nature of the analytic situation was not clear to me.

outset that I still know more than he does. Contrasting with this anticipation, and my hopes (despite the first supervisor's negative report) that the candidate would be a better analyst at this stage in his development than he actually seems to have been, and hence possibly also a more vigorous opponent, was my surprise at the analyst's initial deference, especially surprising since I had been expecting more of a "fight."

But tendencies of the candidate that are reported in the supervision notes may be relevant here. The candidate's own efforts to impress the supervisor, to "give him the picture," rather than let him see the picture for himself from a sequential reporting of the hours, to demonstrate his own mastery of the analytic situation by developing and proving his own hypotheses, and to anticipate the analyst's criticisms by pre-emptive self-criticisms, can be seen as more subtle versions of the opposition I was expecting.

One could indeed study this entire supervision from the point of view of the transferences and countertransferences operative within the supervisory situation. The factors at work in the supervisory field would have to include as a minimum the character attitudes that enhance and that inhibit the supervisor's teaching, as these support and conflict with the supervisor's preferred style, his prior relationship to the candidate and his wish to show the candidate as better than other supervisors rate him, and his commitment to furnish process notes to the Supervision Study Group. The supervisor's growing distress as he finds himself kept out of meaningful teaching contact with the analyst by the latter's style of reporting, his "neutralizing" the supervisor's interventions, his investment in using the case for research, and his difficulty to be fully "open" in the service of learning would also have to be considered.

Questions for study might then be, if these inferences of underlying or superimposed transference-countertransference processes are substantially correct, just what was their actual impact on the supervision? In what ways did they interfere with the candidate's learning and development as an analyst? And in what ways did they possibly facilitate them? Are the supervisor's transferences and countertransferences within the range of the "average and expectable," i.e., not more than the candidate should be expected to adapt himself to? If they seem to intrude further or distort the situation beyond this point, what can be done about it? And when?

DETAILED REVIEW OF FOURTEEN SUPERVISION HOURS (ANALYTIC HOURS 1-66)

These questions were not answered at the time, and to a large extent they remain unanswered. As a first effort toward answering them, I reviewed the first fourteen supervision hour process notes I had written from the point of view of what I was trying to teach and the various factors that may have interfered with that teaching. The process notes could be approached in any number of ways, of course, and I knew at the time that within the Supervision Study Group different approaches and foci of attention would be tried. But I wanted to remain with my original interest in supervision as a teaching method, and within that framework concern myself mostly with the content of what I thought I needed to convey to the candidate. This review was also intended to be a first effort to reduce the amount of material I would have to deal with in studying the notes. Thus, these first brief summaries were to serve as a kind of thematic index to the teaching reflected in these notes and to the other steps in the analysis of the data that were to follow. In the context of the present monograph, the chief interest that these summaries may have is in what they reveal of the supervisor's "second thoughts" in looking over his notes.

SUPERVISION HOUR 1 (ANALYTIC HOURS 1–3)

I had some confidence in the analyst's capacity to carry the case without too much assistance, and so I suggested that he begin even though I did not yet have an hour cleared to see him on a regular basis. In informal meetings we could arrange I had the impression he was handling the beginning satisfactorily, the patient showing some usual beginning uncertainty, apparently dressing up for him, suggesting a probable tendency to eroticize the transference, a passivity-activity struggle imposed on this, and some readiness to develop hysterical symptoms ("whirling"). I asked him what he was doing about what he was seeing, and understood his statement that he was doing "nothing" to mean that he was trying to allow the analytic situation simply to develop. My comment about his having been told to "shut up" was a joking reference to what I had heard from his previous supervision. We discussed some of the issues about the beginning phase of analysis, and I discovered that we shared a common understanding about these. I tried to use the material to demonstrate some points I thought would be useful to him in detecting whether an analytic situation was indeed developing, and particularly about the flow of the patient's associations.

I did not anticipate that the analyst would be absent as much as he was or that he had an absence in mind so soon after beginning. I saw a hint of a countertransference problem in the way he seemed to vie with the patient regarding his and her absences and the problem of charging for missed hours. On the whole, however, I felt satisfied with the beginning.

SUPERVISION HOUR 2 (ANALYTIC HOURS 4–12)

I came to the hour without any conscious expectations of what I would have to deal with and was first struck by the lengthy notes the analyst had prepared. I suggested he try to shorten these since we could not possibly make use of such extensive material. I did not realize then that the notes represented for him potential research data. While I suggested on several other occasions that he shorten them, he obviously did not do so. I have not taken up with him the possible impact on his analytic work of simultaneously looking at the patient as a research subject. As I look back from this vantage point, perhaps it is because we each had an ulterior interest in what we were doing together. I heard in the patient's material her reactions to the candidate's absence, and in her dream of abandonment that might follow, her fear of becoming too dependent.

My interventions with the analyst were mostly in the form of technical suggestions having to do with his unnecessary questioning of the patient. My interest was to help him allow the analytic situation to develop, but for the most part I felt that things were developing satisfactorily.

SUPERVISION HOUR 3 (ANALYTIC HOURS 13–15)

I heard in the patient's material her distrust of the analyst, perhaps related to his absences ("unreliable"). There was material about her viewing herself as a liberated woman against which the accounts of her sexual difficulties with her ex-fiancé and her anxiety attack about staying with him had to be viewed. With the analyst, I found myself again suggesting less intervention on his part and that he try to understand the resistances manifested in her silences rather than simply prodding her to get going again, or picking up the topic himself in some way. I also noted in reviewing these hours that I did not recall how frequent his absences really were until I reviewed all of this material.

SUPERVISION HOUR 4 (ANALYTIC HOURS 16–18)

The pattern of the analyst being overconcerned with mistakes and bringing them up to me, as it were, for criticism, began to show itself. Perhaps the overconcern about mistakes has been a displacement of guilt about his absences, which certainly have been troublesome. Clearly the fluctuation in attendance has been difficult for the patient and himself; they have had more than the expected amount of trouble in getting together. In retrospect, I would weigh this problem more heavily than I did at the time. A pattern of silences also seems to have been developing, and it appeared the patient was not saying everything that came to her mind. The patient was ending an affair to resume life with her ex-fiancé. The material went from him to her father. I used the material to do some teaching in regard to the transference paradigm that seemed to be developing and how this might relate to what he might need to do in order to promote the development of the analytic situation. I also tried to show him that the patient's transference paradigm of creating an authority to resist would exert a pull on him to counteract. In retrospect, I think I may have stressed this out of a concern that the analyst would be likely to find this a special pitfall. I also note that, in contrast with her setting the analyst up as an authority, there was very little explicit "demand quality" in what the patient was saying. Though she talked about troubles, she did not voice any specific expectations of getting help from the analyst.

SUPERVISION HOUR 5 (ANALYTIC HOURS 19–22)

The material permitted me to sketch more fully an aspect of the patient's characteristic style of interacting out which I would expect a transference paradigm to develop; experiencing the analysis as something unpleasant that she had to put up with rather than something intended to be useful to her was part of this. I also tried to discuss with the analyst how he might be playing into this character attitude of hers. His attempt to be "cool" (possibly a countertransference inhibition of the attraction he later said he felt to her, or possibly reflecting insensitivity to, or a lack of empathy for, her situation) could support her in her attitude. I felt more disturbed by his failure to fully appreciate the nature of the situation and his contribution to it than I expressed to him. There was also a difference of opinion between us, as the analyst saw elements of her identification with her mother in the material, while I was more impressed by the qualities she shared with her father.

SUPERVISION HOUR 6 (ANALYTIC HOURS 23–25)

I picked up from the material the patient's pattern of "solving her own problems" in order to minimize involvement with the analyst about them, and also saw in the material the analyst's tendency to accept the patient's "generalities" and to make comfortable, presumably shared, assumptions about what they meant. I tried to stress with him that he had to keep in mind what he *did not explicitly know* and what the patient *did not tell* him. The analyst brought some confirming material about this tendency.

The analyst mentioned his surprise that the patient was going as fast as she was, and it became clear that she might be going too fast for him. His "Wizard of Oz" imagery suggested to me his feeling that he was not comfortable yet as an analyst (and perhaps felt like something of a fake). It also seemed to me that he felt analysis to be a very fragile affair that might be damaged irreparably by slight mishandling. I tried to reassure him about the latter and pointed out some of the implications and effects of these attitudes without labeling them countertransferences. I tried to link the developments during the week, including the patient's missing an hour, to the emergence of sexual thoughts in the transference, and also tried to make the more general point of how I thought this was dealt with within the patient's character structure. I noted to myself that he only slowly developed the events of the week, telling the same story several times, each time adding a few more details. I also noticed and called his attention to the fact that he did not use all the material available to him, tending to ignore what he saw in favor of the words that he heard. I felt more in contact with the patient's material than with the analyst, unlike the case in most of the other hours.

SUPERVISION HOUR 7 (ANALYTIC HOURS 26–31)

Following my feeling of being so closely in touch with the patient in the last supervisory hour and my increased teaching activity, I wanted to see what use the analyst might make of what had been discussed during that last hour. The analyst began with extraneous matters, but I let him go on until he decided to get down to the case at hand. I did not (and do not) know for sure whether my previous increased activity had had anything to do with this.

We did not have much time to talk about the case then, but the patient's material showed her fear of involvement with the analyst, whom she "did not know," and contained historical references to the difficulty in making attachments that would have to be broken. She had broken off with the boy with whom she had been having a casual affair; she was quite dejected. The activity-passivity issue was also contained in the alternating references to her having been confined with tuberculosis as a child and trying to break away from her mother at an early age. The analyst's interventions seemed to me adequate enough. The analyst himself noted a deficiency in his handling of the defenses and showed some capacity to correct himself.

In checking his notes later to refresh my own memory, I noted that his synthesis during the supervision hour presented the events of the analysis in a quite different sequence from the way in which they actually had occurred.

SUPERVISION HOUR 8 (ANALYTIC HOURS 32–36)

The analyst intimated he had a particular problem he wanted to talk about, and I therefore sat back to hear his summary while waiting for him to outline it. In the course of things, he mentioned that the patient had told him she was late one day because it was her birthday, and that he had congratulated her. The analyst was clearly uncomfortable about having done this, and as I recall now may have been anticipating a scolding. I let it pass, thinking I would come back to it, but forgot to. I was still waiting for what he particularly wanted to talk about, and this did not seem to be it.

The analyst tried to make a recovery, I thought, from the "birthday affair" and commented on the patient's difficulty in talking about pleasant as well as unpleasant things. This soon became linked to her difficulty in talking to people toward whom she felt a sexual attraction, including analyst and father and brother. Historical material from adolescence came out. In the next hour the analyst himself noted that he tried to "bring the patient back" too sharply when he thought she was wandering from the point of focus. I was not sure what his rationale was for doing so. In retrospect, I think it may have had something to do with his eagerness to control things better so as not to let his countertransference slip again. But the effect of his "bringing the patient back" was to step on his own toes and not let the patient respond to his transference interpretation, all of which amounted to a rebuke and a bit of intellectualizing. We discussed this issue at some length.

As I reread my notes it seemed that the analyst's rationale for his behaviors was quite unanalytic. The patient became anxious, cold, and phoned the first fellow to whom she had been once engaged and who was now residing in a distant state. The analyst seemed to persist in his rebuking stance and suggested himself that his own difficulty with his feeling of attraction to the patient might be at the root of his "traffic-coplike attitude." This had the sound of something that had been thought out, and while plausible, I did not feel there was anything for me to comment about in it. I did point out to him, again, however, the patient's failure to think of him as someone she could call when she was anxious, linking it to previous thoughts about the "lack of demand quality" in the hours. My own position was to encourage him to not push the patient, but to give her a chance to react to his interpretations. I also noted he was rather eager to call himself down and to be self-critical, which, in addition to whatever characterological roots, could be a way of forestalling and controlling the supervisor, through anticipating criticism.

SUPERVISION HOUR 9 (ANALYTIC HOURS 37–41)

The analyst began with self-critical remarks about his intrusiveness which, as on other occasions, struck me as somewhat exaggerated. But I used the occasion to try to show him he could be aggravating an already eroticized transference and there was no need to intervene here. Although the analyst had raised the question, I had the feeling when he stopped that he was brushing me off, as if he did not really need what I was telling him. On reflecting now, it may be, as I suspected about the last hour, that his own self-criticism was intended, in part at least, to ward off my potential external criticism.

On the same issue, the analyst noted at a later point that the patient reacted poorly to "guidance." The material permitted me to suggest that his repetitive intervening could be experienced by her as excessive guidance. I also tried to show him from the material some differences between masculine and feminine feelings, as distinguished from defenses against feminine feelings. The same material that gave rise to this effort on my part also suggested that the patient was wooing the analyst and defending against it, while the analyst seemed to be doing something reciprocal. When the analyst came back to the idea that he had been pushing the patient too much, I finally suggested his pushiness might have its source in an effort to control the kinds of feelings of attraction he mentioned during the last supervision hour. He agreed this might be so, but as with other discussions of countertransference, he did not seem too disturbed by the idea, nor did he take the opportunity to explore it further at this time.

In the next hour, the patient mentioned feeling obligated to have intercourse with her ex-fiancé, the analyst picking up intimations that she felt she let men down. This led the patient into nostalgic feelings about a happy childhood one cannot return to. The patient seemed to be free-associating fairly easily, and new material came up with which the analyst did not interfere. The analyst had some hypotheses about where the analysis stood. Our discussion got back to technical matters, and I tried to show him once again that his idea of a defense interpretation was to confront the patient with what she was *not* doing.

I showed him how the critical tone of such a focus could be softened by couching his remarks in terms of the obvious adaptive utility of her behavior. I also noted that there was no need to focus on the unrealistic quality of some of her feelings of which she was well enough aware. The analyst seemed fairly pleased with himself, the supervisor being less certain, not altogether clear about what was going on or why, though not enough to demur.

SUPERVISION HOUR 10 (ANALYTIC HOURS 42–46)

The patient was becoming increasingly involved with her ex-fiancé, reflecting displacement of feelings from the analysis. During a description I noted that the patient seemed to be engaged in "homework" from the analysis, and I tried to get the analyst to look at the pattern. He had some hypotheses about a different point, so I let him go on to develop them. But at the end of the hour he came back to what I had in mind, and I sketched what seemed to be an unconscious bargain the patient had struck with the analyst permitting her to express her sexual feelings elsewhere. He seemed intrigued with this idea, which was new to him. I also commented on some implications I had detected that, for the analyst, the suggestion "to interpret" meant "to destroy." He seemed to fear that I was telling him to plunge in and interpret this pattern away. I again tried to relate his declared preference for restraint to an effort to control his extratherapeutic interests in the patient, showing how the patient's behavior could be an effort to fulfill his unexpressed defensive intent. The analyst listened gravely to this suggestion. There was further support for what I was trying to get across in one interaction he reported, about which I suggested that he could inquire into the tone in which she described her sexual experience. The analyst misheard me as suggesting that he intrude directly into her protective privacy.

I also commented on the analyst's need for elegance, which also seemed to imply a reaction formation against "messing around." My own feelings after this hour were ones of uncertainty about what was going on with the patient, and I observed that the analyst's written notes were somewhat different from his oral presentation. In dictating this critique I wondered if my own increased activity during this and the last hour had something to do with my own feeling of growing uncertainty over where things stood.

SUPERVISION HOUR 11 (ANALYTIC HOURS 47–51)

The analyst seemed uneasy, feeling that someone had "dropped the ball." He added he had tried to use some of my ideas, but the patient had rejected them. I tried to show him from this material that not only was the patient getting him off the hook for her lack of progress, but also herself; she had an investment in continuing the status quo. I also tried to pick up and show him some missing elements in his use of our last week's discussion and amplified the "bargain" concept. I pointed to the patient's effort to make "work" of the analysis and the resistance elements in this. The analyst seemed dissatisfied with himself as he saw more clearly what I was pointing out to him, as if he should have been smart enough to have seen all this for himself. Further on in the hour there was an opportunity to discuss something in the way he gave transference interpretations, showing that her feelings could be the center of his interventions alongside her words. I pulled a good deal of material together to demonstrate this point.

It was only after this, however, that the analyst got down to what was concerning him: the patient had suddenly begun another affair outside of her relationship with the ex-fiancé. The analyst said he just listened to this material, but I had the impression that he disapproved considerably of her behavior. The patient told some dreams, and there was a good deal of material to work with—the analyst picking up the theme of sexuality versus involvement for her. When I went over the material with him, I tried to show him the transference elements in her efforts to avoid involvement with him. It was after this that the analyst mentioned, as if unconnected with our previous discussion, that the patient had had to flee from the office to urinate when he brought up the issue of sexuality versus involvement.

Again I noted increased activity on my part, and this time the analyst seemed uncomfortable too. Perhaps my increased activity led him to feel one-down and perhaps in this way reproduced the patient's feelings that she is always one-down with him.

SUPERVISION HOUR 12 (ANALYTIC HOURS 52–56)

The analyst said he was trying to use my formulation about the patient being good instead of analyzing. After listening to a good deal of material, I suggested he was using one aspect of what I had suggested but leaving out the defense and transference components of her acting out.

The analyst went on to say that the patient, in effect, could not get either her ex-fiancé or her analyst to listen to her story about what she was doing, and I had to bring the analyst back to the way he had reported this to make the point clear. Later the analyst did try to point out the patient's avoiding "involvement" with him, but he did so in a way that was very intellectualized and wordy, and he was quite critical of his own performance, with which criticism I felt in agreement. The patient reproached him for his slowness in taking care of her request to change an hour, and he seemed to get bogged down in a bit of an argument with her about this. Later I took the opportunity to associate to the material, linking her silences, the new affair, and the forgetting about the hour change. The analyst misunderstood the implication of what I was putting together, hearing me as urging him to confront her with her withholding. But my interest was to show him the pattern in which his unwillingness to intrude played into the patient's feeling that he was not interested and hence she could not tell him.

SUPERVISION HOUR 13 (ANALYTIC HOURS 57–61)

The analyst described the patient's reaction to news of her mother's cancer and his awareness of his disturbance at her "lack of feeling" about it. After listening to the material and discussing it a bit, we shifted to the affect problem. The analyst had noted the deficiency in the patient's affective response and her shifts in affect, but did not deal with them, addressing himself rather to the content of what she was talking about. My comments were about the overambitiousness of some of the analyst's crowded interpretations, leading to a discussion of how he might better deal with the patient's affects, especially the shift from one to another. I also tried to help him anticipate how the patient might respond if he would deal with her affects as I suggested he do. I noted that I felt more in contact with the analyst about his problems during this hour, though still not fully certain about what was going on with the patient.

SUPERVISION HOUR 14 (ANALYTIC HOURS 62–66)

I noted to myself that the analyst gave a static summary of the overall week as if it were but a single event. The material about the mother's cancer and the patient's abortion were told with inappropriate affect, which the analyst had picked up. The patient was feeling more disturbed. We discussed the possibility that there was in her wish to get rid of her ex-fiancé also a transference wish to get rid of the analyst. As he summarized the hours he seemed to be concentrating on the patient's denials and other defenses against affect. But when he read the material from his notes directly to illustrate what he had done, I picked up a tone of primness in his interventions, which I pointed out to him. He agreed sadly. He said he was aware of his difficulties in dealing with material of this kind, and I could show him that the patient acted as if she were aware that he disapproved. He also was not able to follow up her reaction to one of his interventions, which involved her behavior, and the analyst was chagrined to realize this. Later the analyst came back to his countertransference reaction, which he now called "prissiness," and linked it to his feeling of outrage at her lack of feelings about her mother. He noted the transition from his concern about sexual attraction to his present feeling about the patient as a sad, limited creature—a kind of concern that sounded a bit "motherly" to me. The hour ended with my coaching him once again concerning the way in which he had confronted her with denials of feeling, and particularly the necessity to evaluate her response to his interventions and to be prepared to follow them up.

SUMMARY OF PROBLEMS

To summarize the problems that seem to have shown themselves in the supervision by this time, I prepared this brief outline.

I. Reporting

A. Exhaustive notes, not so useful, taken for research rather than for teaching purposes.

B. Synthetic oral summaries guided by overall hypotheses and intended to give the supervisor the "picture." These summaries were nonsequential and did not give the supervisor the feeling that he adequately understood the material. They also led him to feel left out. Maybe they were unconsciously intended to produce this effect. The analyst made much of small details that fed into his various hypotheses.

II. Analyst's understanding of the case

A. The supervisor could not be wholly sure, inasmuch as he was limited by the nature of the reporting.

B. The analyst did not seem to have a full enough understanding of female psychology, nor did he seem to have enough empathy for the patient in her plight. He seemed unable to look fully at the world as she did, through her eyes.

III. Understanding of psychoanalysis as a treatment

A. Seemed to have a good intellectual understanding.

B. His character style interfered in that he tended to be too active, and instructive, formulating, rather than facilitating, and his reaction formations against intruding also hampered him.

IV. Countertransference

A. The supervisor was surprised at the constant interference of the analyst's insufficiently integrated counteractive sexual impulses and especially the reaction formations against these. The analyst's activity-passivity pattern encouraged the patient to think of him as the "right man" and at the same time direct her sexuality toward others. The analyst participated somewhat too easily in such unconscious "bargains" with the patient.

B. The analyst recognized some aspects of these problems but sometimes seemed to "confess" to them in order to ward off criticism from the supervisor about them. It was not clear to what extent the analyst could use the awareness of his countertransference to promote self-analysis rather than in the service of defensive efforts to suppress it.

V. Teaching

A. The supervisor expected the analyst to be more advanced than he actually seemed to be and was not particularly supportive or encouraging of the analyst.

B. The supervisor was too active, especially as he became more uncertain.

C. The supervisor wanted to demonstrate his "teaching" to the group and he did so too much. Instead of simplifying, he tended to complicate matters.

D. In retrospect, the teaching seemed scattered. Though some points came up repeatedly, the central themes were not sufficiently emphasized.

SPECIAL REVIEW OF SUPERVISION HOUR 5

When I became aware of the Supervision Study Group's particular interest in studying this hour, I examined it again and tried to see, from the point of view of countertransference, what I could add to my original account. I tried to reconstruct my own impressions of that time. I now inferred from my growing unwillingness to look at the analyst's lengthy notes that I felt there was something standing between us of which perhaps these lengthy notes were symptomatic.

I noted a developing pattern of conscious withholding in the patient's material, particularly in relation to the interaction with the analyst. Paralleling this was a growing pattern of nonresponsiveness in the analyst to the patient's behavior, and to her missing reactions to him and his activity—his absences, etc. I was also becoming increasingly aware of the analyst's "coolness," and noticed that he was thinking "centrifugally"—that is, making connections to the past, to larger issues, omitting, or at least underweighting, what was right under his nose and directed at him. My lengthy report of my concern about the analyst's "objectivity" that might be experienced by the patient as indifference, I think, stemmed from my growing concern about this problem and a need to help him to empathize with her in her relationship with him.

As I reread these notes I felt the impact again of his report that the patient left the couch with a smile, saying she "still had to get her car started." That comment epitomized to me her unexpressed feeling of the irrelevancy of the analysis to her concerns, and her making the analysis into another imposition to be stoically borne.

I may have misled the Supervision Study Group when, in my brief summary of hour 5, I noted that his coolness might be a reaction formation to the attraction he said he felt to her. I think I was entertaining the idea of a countertransference problem at this point, but the analyst did not "confess" to an attraction to the patient until supervision hour 8. In any event, I was not sure at that time whether the problem was a specific countertransference reaction or a more general characterological coolness. In supervision hour 8, the analyst's speculation about his "attraction" did not seem too convincing to me. What concerned me about the analyst was not the sense of attraction he felt for his patient, but the degree to which he had to defend himself against that sense of attraction. I wondered if I, as the supervisor, was doing anything that led him to try to be "purer" than he naturally would tend to be, to be less aware of the range of investments he had in this patient, and hence to be more in need of defenses and more susceptible to countertransference distortions with his patient. The extent of my efforts in hour 5 reflected the depth of this concern, but the form of my activity remained pedagogic.

SOME THOUGHTS ON PSYCHOANALYTIC SUPERVISION AND ON THE STUDY OF PSYCHOANALYTIC SUPERVISION (WITH EMPHASIS ON THE PROBLEM OF COUNTERTRANSFERENCE)

The entire experience of having my work studied and then trying to study it myself was in many ways unsettling. It led me to reflect often about supervisory teaching in general and my own work in particular. When the Supervision Study Group became concerned with the problems of countertransference in the analytic situation, I went back to my notes and reviewed them once again from this point of view. I had been aware of certain problems in my relationship with the candidate and wondered about the possible interactions between the analytic situation and the supervision situation. All this concern with aberrations in the analytic and teaching processes rather than with the teaching process itself made me feel it necessary, for my own sake, to formulate my position about supervising and then, against this position, to evaluate the possible distortions of the teaching situation that might have been introduced by transferences and countertransferences in the relationship between analyst and supervisor.

The following statement should be understood then, in part, as a reaction to the experience of being studied as a supervisor and, in part, to the additional experience of trying to distance myself sufficiently from the position of subject to be able to study my own work as a supervisor. Its significance in the context of this monograph may be less what it states as a credo than what it says indirectly about the experience of having one's supervision studied. This statement was not written for the Supervision Study Group and was not shown to them until about a year after the period of supervision studied.

It is my conviction that, in general, neither psychoanalysis nor teaching via supervision is a fragile affair. Neither the teaching alliance nor the therapeutic alliance is a hothouse plant that needs to be specially nurtured. If the patient is properly chosen and if the analyst does not interfere egregiously, the psychoanalytic situation will develop as a matter of course. It is a "natural" phenomenon. The teaching situation also develops "naturally" provided the candidate is sufficiently well analyzed and talented. It is the main task of the analyst and of the supervisor, respectively, to help establish the "average expectable conditions" for psychoanalysis and for learning about it. Part of this task is to see (or to "diagnose") whether it is possible to establish a viable, that is, a self-sustaining psychoanalytic situation or psychoanalytic teaching situation, and further to determine *what kind* of analytic or teaching situation is developing and what, if anything, the analyst or the supervisor may need to do to improve it.

I add this last hesitantly because I feel it would be better if at least the supervisor did not feel that he had to pay as much attention to the teaching situation as this statement might imply. The supervisor should be able to anticipate that he has an "average expectable candidate" before him, whose talent and skill ought to be commensurate with his official status in the institute, and that he is therefore free to teach in the style he finds most effective. I think the average expectable candidate should be able, under the circumstances, to adapt to the supervisor's teaching style, assuming that this style also is within the range of the "average expectable," i.e., not wildly idiosyncratic or such as to lead to great distortions of the teaching situation.

It is also worth remembering that by the time a candidate presents himself for supervisory teaching, he has already proved himself able to adapt to the styles of and learn from a multitude of teachers of widely varying adequacy. There is, of course, something new in the psychoanalytic supervision meeting. The candidate comes in order to learn how to work effectively with deeper layers of his own personality. He is at this time also a patient himself, somewhere in the middle of his personal psychoanalysis, and perhaps experiencing the transference neurosis. His usual adaptive and coping mechanisms have been challenged and are under systematic scrutiny. He may be more open to significant learning than he has been before, but he is also more open to regressive experiences and to displacements to the supervisory situation from his own analysis. But the period of training analysis prior to beginning supervised work, while it should have helped the candidate to "open up" so that he can experience and work at greater depth, should also have encourged sufficient reintegration to permit effective learning to take place in the classroom, in supervision, and with his own patients.

The teaching situation, like the analytic situation, is superimposed on several earlier selection processes, the purpose of which is to ultimately bring together patients and candidates (and supervisors) who are capable of therapeutic or professional growth within the range of the "average and expectable" of the psychoanalytic or supervisory situations. When a patient is poorly selected or a candidate is poorly selected, or poorly analyzed, special "parameters" may need to be introduced into the analytic situation or the supervisory situation, heroics of one variety or another that tend to distort the therapeutic or learning processes. It is always hoped that the need for these parameters will only be temporary. But the necessity for them and the effects of their resolution (or nonresolution) are special topics that are not our first-order concerns in conducting or teaching psychoanalysis. From a purist point of view, the apparent necessity for these parameters represents the intrusion of excessive interest in curing a patient or in salvaging a candidate.

The intrusion of a bias of this kind is understandable on humane grounds. But we must also consider that our basic commitment is to conduct an analysis or to teach a candidate how to conduct an analysis, and that there may be limits beyond which efforts to salvage the situation may not be worthwhile. As humane therapists or teachers we may feel we have no other choice than to help the patient or candidate through whatever means we can. But we should recognize that analytic and teaching values may have already been sacrificed, inasmuch as the prior selection processes, which should have obviated the need for such compromises, failed.

Psychoanalytic situations and teaching situations, or therapeutic alliances and teaching alliances, may be of different kinds. The relevant question about them is not "*Is there* a therapeutic or teaching alliance?" but, qualitatively, "What kind of alliance is there?" and, quantitatively, "How much of an alliance is there?" and, functionally, "How useful?" "Is it sufficient for the purposes at hand?" One formulation of a technical question that derives from this point of view is: "Is it necessary to improve the balance of resistive and facilitative factors in this particular therapeutic or teaching alliance (and how), or is it sufficient in its kind?"

I do not mean to imply that the therapeutic or the teaching alliance is a static affair. Far from it, I would expect that as the psychoanalytic or supervisory situation extends in time, the relationship between analyst and patient, or supervisor and analyst, will change, mature, and become more realistic, adaptive, and task-oriented, and less interfered with by transferences and resistances from either side.

If we could imagine an *ideal* (though perhaps nonexistent) psychoanalytic or supervisory situation, it would be one in which the analyst or supervisor could remain only peripherally attentive to the state of the analytic or teaching situation, in which the analyst or supervisor would not need to do anything *special* in order to bring about or facilitate the analytic or supervisory situation, since such distortions as might occur would be self-limiting or would be resolved in the course of ordinary analyzing or teaching activity. Within this view of the ideal analytic and supervisory situations, the countertransferences of the analyst could be considered quite benevolently. They might tend to interfere to a greater or lesser degree with the development of the psychoanalytic situation (and again I should emphasize, interfere with *how* it develops, not merely *whether* it develops). But the disturbance would be limited as the analyst became aware of his involuntary participation in the patient's life (and vice versa), understood it, and corrected for it. In the everyday, less than ideal, supervised analysis, the matter may not be so simple, though often enough the candidate can make use of his personal analysis as his primary resource in resolving his countertransference problems. Supervisors differ about whether to take up with the analyst his countertransference problems with his patient. I would prefer to put the question of *whether* a supervisor should deal with the analyst's countertransferences in terms of *when* and *how* he should deal with them, and with what expectation of success.

I believe that analyst's countertransferences of minor degree (preferably of no more than "signal" intensity) are inevitable. While persisting countertransferences may distort the development of the analytic situation (and if they are far-reaching they certainly will), a less pejorative way of putting it would be to say that they are one of the influences that shape the psychoanalytic situation. Put in this way, one could conceive that they might at times even have certain facilitating as well as inhibiting or distorting influences. It should be the analyst's and his supervisor's concern to see *how* the analyst's countertransferences manifest themselves and *what effect* they have on the analytic situation. The aim of their joint attention should not be to expunge the analyst's countertransferences or to inhibit them (if the latter is really necessary, perhaps the candidate should not become an analyst). Rather, the supervisor's main teaching focus in regard to countertransferences should be to help the analyst discover the nature of his "involuntary participation" in the shaping of the analytic situation, the kinds of stimuli he is responding to, the effect of his countertransference reactions on his patient, and the reciprocal effect of these reactions on himself.

It is my impression that more damage is done by extensive (unconscious and conscious) efforts to contain countertransferences (via repression, reaction formation, and outright suppression in particular), as well as efforts to rationalize them, than by countertransferences themselves (for the moment I am conceiving of countertransferences as having more to do with wish, impulse, or need than with the higher-order structures, channels, or ego mechanisms that are equally a part of them). It is thus the duty of the supervisor to help the candidate learn about his countertransferences, just as he helps him learn about the other influences that shape the psychoanalytic situation. Naturally, as with other topics in psychoanalytic teaching that touch on the student's narcissism or his self-esteem, issues of timing and tact must be considered centrally.

The supervisor must keep in mind the diagnostic question, "Is this a teaching problem or an analytic problem?" If the balance of countertransference effects is consistently more distorting than facilitating, implying that the candidate's capacity for self-analysis or assisted analysis is inadequate to resolve them, the supervisor may need to help the candidate become aware of the seriousness of this problem and to assess its implications. We must keep in mind that the problem of persistent and overriding countertransferences, like the problems in developing requisite skill and sensitivity, may for some candidates, prove to be beyond our capacity to influence favorably either through personal analysis, through supervision, or through didactic teaching. The administrative (i.e., selection and evaluation) aspects of supervisory teaching are implicated here.

We can take a similar stance toward the transferences[2] and countertransferences of the supervisor and ask at any point in the process: How strong are these involuntary participations in the supervisory process, and what is the balance of their facilitative and distorting effects? One could also ask, assuming that these manifestations of countertransferences and the defenses against them vary at different times, to what stimuli in the teaching situation are they responses? And if we could assume that ideally the supervisory situation would be better off without them, what can be done, and when, to minimize them?

In asking, "What is the effect of the supervisor's countertransferences?" we might ask, "How sublimated are they?" Do they have a general effect on the supervisory situation, coloring it without distorting it excessively? Or do they make for specific intrusions that interrupt the orderly development of the learning situation, i.e., do the supervisor's interventions have more to do with the supervisor's personal needs or biases than with the analyst's or the patient's needs? Do his biases lead him to ignore consistently features in the teaching situation or the analytic situation that are more important than those he stresses? Does the supervisor thus present a distorted view of the analytic situation to the candidate via such misplaced emphases?

On the other hand, and perhaps less noxiously, do the supervisor's countertransferences lead him to give more than is necessary, possibly to overload the candidate to the point of confusing him or giving him more than he can profit from at any one time? Or does he give less than would be optimal, or fail to give what would be optimal? From this last point of view, and considering the expected adaptability of the candidate, the supervisor's excesses, whether in negative or positive directions, might largely be irrelevant rather than noxious. We must also consider that the supervisor's excesses may not only place a cognitive strain on the candidate, but may stimulate him to be too passive in pursuing his own education, or to be aggressive or rebellious, to touch on but a few of the potential neurotic responses of the candidate. The candidate, of course, may in turn display transferences to the supervisor that stem primarily from his own unresolved neurotic problems, and these may also interfere to a greater or lesser extent with the supervisory mission.

This discussion has focused on some of the problems that may beset supervision—on pathology rather than on normal growth and learning. To summarize the kinds of problems that have been mentioned or alluded to

[2]I should make clear that for the moment I am using the terms "transference" and "countertransference" to include what many would prefer to call manifestations of character, as well as more specific transferences and countertransferences attributable to the development of a particular relationship with a given candidate.

and which could be focused upon in a study of the supervisory process:

1. What problems does the candidate seem to have with his case? We can conceive of problems of the following kinds: (a) He might lack knowledge, for instance, about psychoanalytic theory in general, or about the general principles of conducting an analysis, or about the early phases of an analysis, or about specific neurotic patterns unfolded within the analysis. (b) He might be insufficiently sensitive to the analytic material as it emerges and, though familiar with the theory from an intellectual point of view, be unable to correlate his observations with theory and conceptualize them. (c) He might be insufficiently empathic with the patient to be able to grasp the latent message of his statements or behavior. (d) He might be insufficiently aware of the degree to which he is intruding upon the analytic process, i.e., the degree to which his own activity, or lack of it, is influencing the patient. Behind this issue would lie the questions of whether the analyst is unaware because he has not been told, or has not been helped to know, or whether there is a countertransference blind spot. Also, there might be a problem about learning through supervision so that the supervisory relationship, rather than being facilitative, comes to interfere with the analyst's development. There could be a problem of transference, that is, in the teaching situation.

2. The supervisor could be having problems paralleling those described for the candidate. These also could be considered under the headings of lack of knowledge, lack of sensitivity to the psychoanalytic process as heard through another's report, or insensitivity to the learning needs of the student (i.e., lack of teaching talent), and could include dynamic interferences attributable to transference and countertransference reactions that affect his view not only of the patient-analyst relationship but also of the analyst-supervisor relationship. Not usually mentioned in such contexts, but also important, is the possibility that since the analytic situation and the supervisory situation are both human relationships, sympathies and antipathies which would not strictly speaking come under the heading of transference might also be interfering or facilitating. The concept of the "learning alliance" captures and perhaps blends a number of these issues. One not infrequently is able to learn from people whom one does not like, and occasionally from those one does not particularly respect. But probably the concept of the learning alliance is elastic enough to include such situations as special variants.

3. What kind of teaching activity should be addressed to the problem(s) seen? Since supervisory teaching is essentially opportunistic, it may seem to defy a systematic approach. At least, one cannot have a syllabus for supervision. But one can expect certain typical problems to arise with candidates of known degrees of experience and skill and be expectant, even as one is expectant in conducting an analysis, of developments that are more or less

certain to arise. The question of what one does about these developments, and when one does it, would seem to me to be among the issues that are discussable in working toward a general formulation of supervisory teaching.

All these issues are, however, confounded with the issue of supervisory style. Supervisors differ in their ways of working. Some prefer to wait, listen, offer general encouragement, and not interfere unless the analyst requests assistance or gets into a mess of some kind. Their teaching strategy would seem to be to let the candidate make his mistakes and learn from them, while the supervisor sets an example of patient acceptance modeled partly on the analytic stance and partly on a kindly, avuncular role. Other supervisors prefer a more active style; advice may be given freely, the supervisor may allow himself to react spontaneously and through his behavior exemplify not how an analyst should act while analyzing, but rather how an analyst listens and resonates with the patient's material. Some supervisors put themselves into the analyst's shoes and pay attention to the patient's productions more or less exclusively. For such a supervisor, the candidate may be experienced as a middleman—a third party who has to be tolerated between the supervisor and the patient. Other supervisors may prefer to attend to the candidate and his experiences as student and analyst to the relative exclusion of the patient. Their focus may be on the technical handling of the case or on the candidate's countertransference difficulties.

I could sketch other stylistic variants that I am sure would have live representatives without going beyond the bounds of what could be considered a useful supervisory style. I mean to exclude here, however, any reference to those supervisors who believe supervision is simply an extension of the personal analysis and who thus confound the therapeutic and teaching purposes.

Most effective supervisors probably have a range of styles in their repertoire and call on them as needed. Since we know that such stylistic differences exist, we must presume that each supervisor, within the style, or range of styles, with which he is comfortable, can very likely be effective (or ineffective) regardless of style. Thus we do not need to study clinical or supervisory material simply to discover that the supervisor has a style and that others might approach the teaching opportunities from a different stylistic stance.

4. The problem of evaluation: How can one tell if the supervisor's understanding of the candidate's problem was correct (or sufficient) and if the teaching activity (or inactivity) was correct, properly timed, and sufficient? The limiting factors—is the case sufficiently analyzable, and is the candidate sufficiently teachable (under the given conditions of this case and this supervisor), and is the supervisor sufficiently knowledgeable, flexible, etc.?—belong here.

CHAPTER XIV

On Being the Analyst Supervised: Return to a Troubled Beginning

HOWARD SHEVRIN, Ph.D.

As I considered what I might write about my experiences during the supervision and my evaluation of these experiences long after the supervision and the analysis had been completed, I found myself thinking of ballet. Sometimes, when watching ballet on television, I turn off the sound in order to watch the dance without the music. The dancing then appears like a spontaneous, unfettered creation emerging out of the dancer's impulse. Then I turn the sound up, and the dancing changes its aspect—it is closely married to the music. It holds to the beat and, though no longer spontaneous in any casual sense, it is for all that richer and more exciting because the music and movement together create a mutual significance neither could achieve alone. In analysis there is always the danger of losing oneself in the dancing and of ignoring the music—the sound of many voices seemingly out of earshot. In my previous chapter (Chapter XI), I pointed out how the research design of this study, in effect, ignored the music to concentrate on the dance. The supervisor's notes were made to do for the analysis as well as for the supervision; they ignored the social, administrative, and power structure within which the supervision and the analysis took place. In that chapter I tried to provide the music, and indeed the dance assumed a different significance and value. But I was not playing with a full orchestra, and it was simply my own variations based on recall and reconstituted from notes. Several times in my previous chapter I informed the reader I would be taking up some of the more personal aspects of my experiences in this chapter. I shall describe the dance, trying to give a picture of how it was experienced at the time, then I shall add the music as I now recall it. Often the dancer is so much at one with the music that he may cease to be aware of it even though his body reveals its presence. It is not easy to take note of all the forces affecting one's behavior. Only the changed perspective offered by the passage of time and subsequent experience make it easier to recall the dance and the music simultaneously. As Lewin and Ross (1960) characterized the atmosphere created by the education and treatment syncretism in institutes, the last element fish become aware of is the water in which they swim; the last element analysts find it easy to acknowledge is the social, administrative, and power structure in which we practice and educate. Of course, as training analysts, supervisors, administrators, and employers, we create the music others dance to, although we too often choose to interpret the dance as if it were a purely personal expression. Seemingly, the biggest fish have the greatest difficulty in realizing they are surrounded by water.

In brief outline, I shall first describe the events leading up to my contribution to this monograph, then I shall discuss issues of transference and countertransference in the supervision, and last I shall present some thoughts on the educational nature of the supervision.

HOW I FIRST HEARD OF THE STUDY AND MY INITIAL REACTIONS

I first learned of the research when I received a package in the mail whose contents surprised me. I learned from the enclosed manuscript that I had been the subject of a study on the nature of psychoanalytic supervision. These pages were written by one of the two supervisors of my second control case. He had supervised the case for two and a half years; the case was brought to successful conclusion a year later with the help of a second supervisor. At first I found myself utterly baffled by what I had just received, especially since not so long before I had prevailed on my first supervisor, when he was paying a visit to his old friends and colleagues, to let me show him my laboratory. In retrospect, I realized he seemed quite interested in finding out about the case he had supervised some time before, and I was pleased to tell him. He acted surprised by the generally favorable outcome I reported to him and asked me how I accounted for it, a question that surprised me in my turn. But during that visit he mentioned nothing about the supervision study, although the supervision and analysis were long over. Now I had before me a considerable number of pages of manuscript written by him on my case. The question, "Why was I not told?" leaped into my thoughts. How could *they* (whoever *they* were was not yet known to me) undertake this study without notifying me, without me notifying my patient? How could *he* (my erstwhile supervisor) do this to me? This first outburst of anger dissipated and was then replaced by a sense of hurt. I came to appreciate why the word *grievance* contains within it the word *grief*—for a grievance is based on loss, a loss of esteem for oneself and for others who have arbitrarily inflicted this loss. Naturally, I wanted redress for my grievance. Certainly something of that sort was in order—an explanation, perhaps even an apology. Instead I had this neat stack of pages in front of me.

After dressing my narcissistic wound, I calmed myself and considered the matter further. Clearly the main intent of what I had before me was to make a scientific and educational contribution; it was not to hurt or embarrass me. I too was a researcher (this is only one of the ironies)—were my hands so clean? One may, for example, refer to a clinical instance in a paper without consulting the patient—a vignette suitably disguised. In my experimental research it was another matter—the subject's consent was always explicitly obtained for the procedure itself and for the publications that might come out of it. But this study was of another order of magnitude —*the entire study dealt with this one supervision and this one analysis.* How could they possibly not have asked for my consent? I would certainly be well within my rights if I simply returned the manuscript with a brief note indicating my disinclination to give my consent to its publication, and that would be the end of it. Yet, I could also see that considerable work had been invested in the study. How could I deprive the field of this wisdom? Also, if indeed I had been made an unwitting and silent partner in the past, perhaps now I could be a conscious and active partner who might have something to offer. To my knowledge, nothing like this study had ever been attempted before.

Such were the waves of feeling and surmise that washed over me as I considered what steps to take. I decided to see in what way I could contribute. This set in motion a complex chain of events, lasting over several years, from which much could be learned about the sociology of science and education as practiced by psychoanalysts. This was my state of mind and resolve before I received, as in time I did, the balance of the monograph—a number of chapters, each by a different and noted contributor. As I read these new chapters, which included one by my supervisor in which he reevaluated his supervision, the analyst, and the study, I saw that I was dealing with a totally different kettle of fish. I now began to see clearly for the first time how utterly cowed I had been by the first package of manuscript. I had failed to see what now became evident in the light of these additional chapters—the study was flawed in design, data, and execution. As a result, what appeared to me to be a misleading view of the analysis and the supervision emerged. Only in one chapter by Jacob (Chapter IX) was there any extensive discussion of possible built-in biases and the narrow perspective that had been brought to the study.

The real dangers involved in the failure to consult with me and my patient were now brought home to me. Quite aside from the significant injury that conceivably could be visited upon my patient and myself, there was the study itself as a scientific and educational enterprise to consider. I insisted that I meet with the Study Group and present my serious concerns. In some detail, I spelled out my worries, many of which were subsequently elaborated (Chapter XI). The committee listened with the corporate ear of a group intent on following its own elected course no matter how favorably each individual might have heard my arguments. At one point I learned that some members of the Study Group wanted to consider publication with or without my consent. The time had come for decisive action. I wrote a detailed letter to the officers of the American Psychoanalytic Association enjoining them from publishing the monograph without my consent and my patient's consent or else suffer the legal consequences. I became painfully aware of the power of an institutional structure which had apparently swallowed up my colleagues and friends in the Study Group. But by this time I had resolved to stand firm. However, I recommended the appointment of a mediating committee which would assist the Study Group and me in working out the issues outstanding between us. This recommendation was eventually acted on and the ensuing mediation by Dr. Jay Katz was of vital importance; without it this monograph would not have seen the light of day.

I have gone into these matters in some detail on the basis of the same principle that has informed my previous chapter: the administrative, educational, and power context must be described if the supervision itself is to be understood. It can be seen from the foregoing that the same factors governing the uses of power were at work in the larger psychoanalytic institution of the American Psychoanalytic Association as in my local psychoanalytic institute and the psychiatric institution in which the supervision itself took place. The same implicit paternalism was at work in the Study Group, an official committee of the American Psychoanalytic Association, as in the supervisory context.

We are now ready to consider transference and countertransference issues in the supervision itself.

TRANSFERENCE AND COUNTERTRANSFERENCE IN THE SUPERVISION?

I have placed a question mark after the above heading to call attention to the fact that to apply the concepts of transference and countertransference to supervision is an extension of these terms from the therapeutic context in which they were discovered and put to use. We know a good deal about the therapeutic context which is constructed and developed in order to optimize transference manifestations and, as much as possible, to minimize countertransference or to make use of it as it emerges. The very goal of treatment is to encourage self-exploration through the medium of a unique personal relationship; this goal in itself encourages the emergence of transference and the concomitant development of a transference neurosis. Even so, the identification of transference and countertransference problems is not so easy for either patient or analyst. The same experiences must recur a number of times before we are confident about their nature. The transference emerges against the background of a real relationship between analyst and patient which is made up of the helping role of the analyst and his stable, personal characteristics as revealed in his treatment of the patient. We now no longer believe that the "slide" of transference is "projected" against the "blank screen" of the analyst; rather, the more apt image is of a figure seen against a ground which is a constant, although not unstructured in its own right. I have elaborated these perhaps obvious points because the implication I shall draw from them is not so obvious: in any situation other than analysis (including psychotherapy) the real relationship, the shared task external to the participants (rather than the self-exploration of one) and the social context assume much greater importance. In other words, what is in analysis the ground, assumes in nonanalytic relationships significant figural properties; as a result the regression necessary for transference to emerge is far more limited, and even if these transferences do emerge, they are much more difficult to discern because they are competing with other prominent figural elements. Interpretations of transference and countertransference are therefore hazardous and subject to much error. At the very least it becomes necessary to clarify what the nature of the real relationship is, what social context prevails, and what constitutes the nature of the shared task. As I have indicated in my previous chapter, in my judgment the Study Group omitted these factors, and with some considerable loss in understanding what had occurred in the supervision. These same thoughts apply more specifically to issues of transference and countertransference within the supervision. I shall try in what follows to describe this relevant administrative and power context, the personal relationship between supervisor and candidate, and the nature of the shared task. Within each section, I shall comment on possible transference and countertransference issues.

ADMINISTRATIVE AND POWER CONTEXT

There are two main aspects to the relevant administrative and power context: (1) the Study Group, and (2) the local institutional complex (the psychoanalytic institute and the larger psychiatric institution). Dr. Schlesinger has described the nature of his relationship to the Study Group and how he believed it influenced the supervision. He felt he tried to be too objective in his reporting of the supervision and protective of the candidate. His research collaboration with the Study Group also made him uneasy about the candidate's own research interest in the case and how this affected the treatment. I think the research had another significant influence which might really be another aspect of his efforts at objectivity—a hands-off approach, as if he were averse to tampering with the spontaneous evolution of the supervision so as not to introduce artifacts into its development. In addition, he had an accounting to make to the Study Group, whose members were his peers, and some his seniors in experience and stature. If he had to protect the candidate, it very likely was also true that he had to protect himself. Just as the candidate had to be concerned about his career, so did he need to be concerned about his. The supervisor would be less than human if, under these conditions, he did not try to put his best foot forward. His protective attitude toward the candidate seemed to drop away entirely as he felt the case was going badly. In effect, he appeared to be saying to the Study Group, "You see, it was not my fault." Last, the research task placed the supervisor in competition with the candidate with respect to the conduct of the case itself, the outcome of the supervision, and in the larger context of making a scientific contribution. All of these factors were mainly instigated by the Study Group's implicit contribution to the social context.

I have already gone into some detail about the institutional context in my previous chapter. Briefly, I stressed how the syncretism of educational and administrative roles freighted both training analysis and supervision with a burden of power relationships at cross-purposes with the intrinsic goals of analysis and supervision. This burden would further complicate transference and countertransference issues, making it more difficult for them to be resolved because they would be useful later (or at the same time) in the extra-analytic, extra-supervisory relationships between the two parties. The supervisor was the candidate's superior and not simply a colleague and peer. During the time of the supervision he had a decisive voice in the candidate's advancement within the institution-at-large. Within the institute, he played a role in deciding the candidate's fate. It is of considerable interest that the supervisor stood up for the candidate in the education committee when the candidate's first supervisor opposed advancing him to a second case. Something of the institute's ambience is conveyed by the way the candidate's evaluation was conducted: namely, at no point was this evaluation discussed with the candidate. Neither his first nor his second supervisor nor the education committee informed the candidate where he stood. Further light is thrown on the attitude of at least some members of the education committee when Dr. Schlesinger reports how, after the candidate had turned down a first referral for his second case, the advice was to have the candidate "cool his heels" for a while before being sent a second case to consider. This is simply punitive. But punishment appropriately administered can be educational. However, even this likelihood was obviated by the fact that the punishment itself was kept from the candidate. Had he "cooled his heels" for a year or so (a not unusual time to wait; it was the time I had waited for my first control) the candidate would have to have *guessed* at what was going on. This ambiguity would have encouraged projections and other distortions, heightened anxiety, and, in general, would have been far from educationally beneficial. The advice to have the candidate "cool his heels" really represented the surreptitious use of institutional power in a faceless and unapproachable way. Without going into detail, this use of institutional power was fully implicated in the ongoing factionalism and convoy politics of the institution-at-large. The supervisor-to-be was put in the position of protecting and defending the candidate rather than being the person through whom the education committee could convey to the candidate its concern about him, which might then have cleared the air for a healthier beginning to the supervision. Instead, the supervisor entered the supervision in the role of an education committee member who had been put on the spot. It would seem to me the supervisor would also feel that the candidate really owed him a debt. It was a debt the candidate, however, had no knowledge he had incurred. There is a hint of this attitude on the supervisor's part when he reveals how disappointed he was in discovering that the candidate was not as advanced as he had anticipated. In other words, he had thought he had put himself in the position of protecting and defending a candidate who would show him to have been right in his judgment; instead, he might end up proving him wrong. This has clear personal and political implications and parallels the same kind of problem the supervisor must have had in his relationship to the Study Group. Certainly these matters would have had an impact on the purely educational purpose of the supervision, and in my view, they did. The supervisor's office was thus filled with many lurking shadows and a babble of voices in the background as far away as San Francisco. Dr. Schlesinger was looking over his shoulder at figures he knew well were there; the candidate at best may have felt their presence in the case of the education committee.

Now I must come to a difficult and delicate matter—the first supervision. It is important to deal with the first supervision because what happened there apparently set the stage for the second supervision. Dr. Schlesinger describes the first supervisor as dissatisfied with the candidate's long notes and his argumentation with his patient. Dr. Schlesinger adds that he himself was surprised that the patient was assigned as a control. As I mentioned earlier, I had already waited for a case well over a year—perhaps "cooling my heels" even then for some unknown misdemeanor. Although I had misgivings about my first case as an analytic control, I accepted the case. As Dr. Schlesinger notes in Chapter XIII, he himself had some doubts concerning the patient's suitability as a first control case. Now I must come to an especially difficult and painful point. Here the music I must play will seem discordant and harsh, but it was there at the time for all to hear. My first supervisor had never informed me of his impression of my work. Very quickly, my first control gave indication in the treatment of his difficulties with analysis. Despite my reporting of this material in the supervision, my supervisor was insistent on a classical analytic approach in which I would deal with oedipal issues.

How could this be, one might ask? A seasoned training analyst and supervisor was not responding to material of this kind reported by the candidate? My supervisor was a very elderly person, who would often drift off during the supervision sessions. Two other candidates had requested and were granted transfers from him to another supervisor. In the Goodman report (1977) a section is devoted to the problems of the aging analyst. The problem is real, and my experience of it was disturbing. I considered requesting a transfer myself, but did not feel secure in my standing with the education committee. My request might be interpreted as a sign of querulousness and disrespect. Here it must be recalled from my previous chapter that I was not safely ensconced in a convoy. My first supervisor was a powerful voice on the education committee and himself very much a part of one of the contending factions that drew on his support. As presented by Dr. Schlesinger, the dancer is the candidate who was having trouble with his first control, possibly a difficult patient, and with his first supervisor; his notes were too long, he argued with the patient. The music tells us the patient was difficult; the supervisor was drifting off during the supervision and was a key figure in institute and education committee politics. When we put the dancer and the music together we can see that the odds were heavily weighted against the candidate. But it is important to note that the candidate was not at all explicitly aware of these odds.

I approached my next supervision and the selection of my second case with something less than perfect confidence and trust. It was indeed hard to distinguish in myself what was distinctly personal from what was a realistic appraisal. I might add that other candidates were in the same fix, although we did not know it at the time because candidates were, on the whole, locked into private worlds and felt that communication about their circumstances would be a violation of their analytic confidences or would be seen as "anti-analytic" or "acting out"—that dubious, all-purpose concept which is too often used as a weapon in the political struggle to enforce compliance. Usually, the accusation hurled at one or another staff member and an occasional obstreperous candidate was that he or she was "anti-analytic," which did not really refer to differences in theory or practice, but to political malfeasance—an action or a public statement at variance with the wishes of the prevailing analytic power faction.

On the whole, the administrative, educational, and power context within which the supervision was undertaken was hardly optimal.

PERSONAL CONTEXT OF THE SUPERVISION

The supervision started well over ten years ago, and meanwhile much has happened. My current view of my supervisor is different from what it was then; in fact, my opinion has changed with the reading of his account of the supervision. The Rashomon experience always has a chastening effect on one's narcissism. The truth as one sees it can only be identified with the whole truth by an act of arrogance.

I had already known Dr. Schlesinger for a number of years prior to the supervision. As already mentioned, he was my immediate superior, had supervised my psychological testing, and had been my teacher. When people have had to deal with each other over such matters as salary increases, work assignments, and career development, differences crop up. I always had the highest regard for him as a clinician and as a thinker; we did not always see eye to eye on the bread-and-butter issues. His style of administration was distant to the point of aloofness; his philosophy was to say as little as possible, play his cards close to the vest; but he always managed to accomplish a good deal for his staff. One was given to understand that the fewer questions asked, the better. I have always been an inveterate question-raiser. Our temperaments did indeed clash on occasion. I wished he were different, and I'm sure he wished I was. I greeted the news that he would be supervising my second control with mixed feelings: he had a reputation as an excellent clinician and a skillful supervisor, and yet I also knew that we did not always get along. There was a subtlety and finesse about him that made me feel awkward, gross, and clumsy in his presence. He possessed a rapier wit that penetrated and deflated affectation and pretension. There was no doubt something formidable about him. For this and for the other reasons I have detailed above, I counseled myself in advance to be on my best behavior in the supervision. As a candidate I was dependent on him for advancement up the ladder toward graduation; as a staff member I was dependent on him for career advancement as my administrative superior. I started the supervision with many misgivings, great anxiety, and a self-imposed commandment to make every effort at pleasing my supervisor. I was going to be politically "wise." It is rather an irony that Dr. Schlesinger regrets I was not "a more vigorous opponent." That was exactly what I had expressly forbidden myself to be.

One misunderstanding concerned my interest in research. I was, of course, totally unaware of my supervisor's decision to use the supervision for research purposes. However, I also felt that I had my own research responsibilities. I took seriously the fact that, after much travail over it in my analysis and several unexplained postponements, I was granted a research waiver by the American Psychoanalytic Association. Although I disagreed then (and continue to disagree) with the policy that nonphysicians, in order to have full training, must plead a special case, beyond their clinical interests and talents, I was prepared to fulfill my research commitment and was troubled by others who viewed the waiver cynically as the only means to the end of full training available. This was especially so because I was painfully aware of the great need for psychoanalytic research and how few people were doing it. I must confess that at the time I was fanatical on this point. Perhaps my fanaticism was fed by my sense of isolation in a clinical setting in which many of my colleagues were suspicious of anyone spending a good deal of time doing research. Actually I have always done a fair amount of clinical work—psychotherapy and diagnostic testing—and had established a decent reputation as a clinician. I had, for example, been asked to be a psychotherapy supervisor. When I finally was cleared for controls, I looked forward to starting them not only for the clinical experience, but also for their research potential. Ideally, I would have liked to tape-record the cases, but in the atmosphere at the time, this was not possible. So I took the second best course of keeping fairly extensive process notes. I jotted down occasional notes during the hour and from these notes dictated in the five or so minutes after each hour how the hour had gone. My aim was to be as thorough as possible. The notes were about one and a half single-spaced pages per hour in length; occasionally they would exceed two pages. I was proud of these notes because I thought of them as making it possible for me to come as close as I could to a record of the analysis, and as such they constituted invaluable data. I was also aware of the possible problems that might be created by having a "research attitude" toward the patient. Would this affect my capacity for "free-floating attention" or dull my sensitivity to the patient's feelings? I felt convinced I had a special responsibility as a research fellow. I knew I would have only a few analytic patients in my career, fewer than most practicing analysts because of my research and teaching interests. Each case was important and irreplaceable. On this point I was ready to defy my supervisor, although I also knew from my fellow candidates that supervisors' practices varied—some encouraged long notes; others wanted no notes at all. Ironically, I have sat through many a long, continuous case seminar while the candidate presenting read endlessly from his notes (perhaps my aim was to inflict this on my supervisor!). A page to a page and a half of single-spaced notes per hour was not uncommon. In my own subsequent experience as a supervisor, I have welcomed detailed notes and have discovered that it takes at most ten to twelve minutes to scan through five to seven pages for a week's work. In a continuous case seminar I am currently conducting, the presenter has been able to read detailed process notes of six to eight hours in a little over twenty minutes and to allow for well over an hour of discussion in an hour-and-a-half session. It would seem to me to have been possible for my supervisor to have read my notes at the start of the session (or before the session, a not overly demanding expectation). Interestingly, there were apparently times when the supervisor read the notes *after* the session as a "check" on the candidate's oral report, so that there was occasionally at least time to read the notes—alas, not for purposes of preparation, but for purposes of research and apparently to "check" on the validity of the candidate's account. Clearly, the notes became a significant focus for transference and countertransference feelings and affected the nature of the shared work task, a problem to be treated in the following section.

I must add that I was prepared for indifference to my research interests from my supervisor. Over the years, I had never felt that he fully supported my research efforts, nor did he appear especially interested in my research accomplishments. In retrospect, I would judge that the reason for this attitude (assuming I perceived it correctly) was that my research was largely experimental rather than clinical in nature. His own interests at the time were largely clinical. He was also a very busy man, and what I identified as indifference may have been his preoccupation with much else. For whatever reason, the attitude I perceived helped create the anticipation that my own research interests would not be met with a sympathetic ear. Yet I had confidence in my ability as an investigator, which fortified my conviction that I must set my feet on that path. Little did I know that my supervisor was setting *his* feet on his own research path and was himself preoccupied with how his need to report to a group would affect his spontaneity as a supervisor! Moreover, it would be incorrect to overlook an issue mentioned previously, when discussing the impact of the Study Group—competition. Only my supervisor knew that both of us were interested in doing research with the clinical material. While he could look askance at my research interest, he was only mildly troubled by his own research interest as it might affect the supervision. He too was taking notes and dictating material on the supervision. Ironically, we were both inveterate note-takers and dictators, and for the same reason. My notes were rejected by him except for research purposes and checking. I think in particular the latter need must point to the supervisor's competitiveness, inasmuch as the same effort could have gone into reading the notes earlier, when it would have been helpful in the supervision.

When I look back at this particular aspect of my experience, I regret my stubbornness on this research issue. It is possible that at the time my insistence was more a way of preserving my pride in the one area in which I was reasonably confident. The proof of this may be in the fact that, aside from one small study on dreams, I have not done very much with the data. The struggle over this issue of research on analytic material, and my own expanding interests in another research area, shifted my research interests away from the case. Nevertheless, it is also true that the case went well, and I kept detailed notes until the end. I would not conclude from my experience that keeping detailed notes seriously affected my attentiveness or sensitivity. If they suffered, it was for other reasons.

Now I must come to the main misunderstanding, and it was indeed a sad one. In my eyes my supervisor was an especially sensitive, subtle, and fastidious person. He was a man of great economy of gesture, word, and deed. His wit was but one example of his parsimonious mode of thought: one word, one phrase, would do the job for several. It was a knack I marveled at and envied. He was also someone who rarely conveyed directly what he really thought about what you were saying; rather, he let you know what he felt by way of almost minute expressive signs around the lips, the eyes, and even the eyebrows. It was a vocabulary and syntax written in very small letters, but rather easily read once one adjusted one's sight. I sought mightily to find the right messages there by trying to emulate his spare style both with my patient and with him. As all this was going on inside me, my supervisor noted in his assessment of my attitude that he was perplexed by my fastidious, overly correct, meticulous manner. He saw me as "technically correct" but without much heart. I suspect now that this was my caricature of him, offered in a spirit of conciliation; it was also an effort to acquire what I admired through emulation. I will say in retrospect that the effort has worked to some extent and that I have internalized some of my supervisor's subtlety and economy; it was not all a defensive identification with a presumed aggressor. Nevertheless, for a time at the beginning of the analysis, my supervisor was looking at his distorted mirror image and wondering what was going on. It will be seen that this attitude on my part was consistent with the administrative and power context previously described. How much in my attitude was based on transference in the literal sense and how much on my appraisal of the reality remains hard to say either for me or, for that matter, for anyone.

There was another issue concerning the case itself. I was prepared for the patient's sexual difficulties. I did not think that a pattern present for a considerable number of years would modify in a matter of weeks. In fact, in the early hours the patient more fully informed me about the real extent of her casual liaisons. I remember distinctly on a number of occasions dreading going to my supervision hours because I would need to report on the details of these difficulties. I would note with a sinking feeling my supervisor's eyebrows semaphoring his displeasure. I was frankly puzzled by this. At the time I remember being convinced that his reaction was a moralistic one, although I was not sure if his displeasure was more directed at me than at the patient. I could not escape the conclusion that he felt that if I were a better analyst the patient would not need to act out at all. It was my fault that she needed to communicate in this self-destructive way. Were I better attuned to the patient's feelings, she would not resort to this way of showing how little she cared for herself and how little she thought the analyst cared for her. I remember my sense of futility, even despair at times, when I felt confronted by my supervisor's silent condemnation. It was of considerable interest to me when I read in his account how he had been careful to be objective in writing up his notes for the Study Group so that in retrospect he felt he did not convey the extent of his unhappiness with my work. He really was quite concerned about the analyst's conduct, and disappointed that I was not further along in my skills. These feelings did indeed come across, although I interpreted them rather differently: if I were as skilled as the supervisor, the patient would not have an unhappy moment, or at least these unhappy moments would be limited to the analysis itself.

With respect to this issue of moral judgment, it is clear that Dr. Schlesinger and I are at variance in view of his account of that matter in Chapter XIII. From his perspective, it was I who was "prissy" and given to moral condemnation. It would be correct to say that I was worried, at times alarmed, by the patient's acting-out propensities, at a loss somehow to empathize with how she felt when she had to behave that way, but to the best of my recall, I did not feel any moral condemnation. This may be still another instance of a painful misunderstanding between us which was not addressed during the supervision.

THE SHARED TASK

Jacob (Chapter IX) presents a thoughtful analysis of analytic working styles. He stresses that to know these styles is vital if we are to be accurate in identifying transference and countertransference issues. Jacob is thus identifying another factor in the "ground" against which the "figure" of transference and countertransference reactions has to be perceived. These same considerations apply to supervision with greater force because the work task is of a different order in supervision than in analysis. In addition to the institutional context previously described, the nature of the shared task as defined by the participants is of great significance.

Jacob provides a simple yet eloquent description of the agreement between supervisor and candidate:

> *Analyst:* I'll tell all of the manifest content, that I feel to be dynamically pertinent, of what happens between me and my patient. Since selection of data is inevitable, trust my judgment as to what is dynamically important. I do not know all of the determinants of how I select my data, but at least initially, hear me out!
>
> Trust my judgment also to tell an optimum amount of my personal reactions to these verbal and nonverbal interchanges. I shall try to do so in the service of learning how to use signal affects, rather than in the service of a split transference (if in analysis), or in the service of resuming my "analysis" in disguise.
>
> All of this, including the fear of being graded, is secondary to the work of analyzing and of learning about analyzing.
>
> *Supervisor:* I promise to try to preserve your autonomy as far as possible, both in conducting your analysis of your patient, and in conducting your own self-analysis.
>
> My observations on your personal equation will be minimal, only in the service of the work, and limited to observing phenomena directly pertinent to your work, not a "wild analysis" of the genetics of your problems.
>
> Let us first just work and suspend judgment. If we work as outlined above, the judgment of your ability will become mutually self-evident.
>
> Let us both consider that we are on the frontier of psychoanalytic knowledge; we both are students. It is granted that I have had more experience, but an overemphasis on the student-teacher relationship will detract from a mutual exploratory attitude toward this unique "experiment in nature": your case.

As Jacob further observes, "When the analyst and supervisor have a peer relationship, the effects on the analyst's work of differences in day-by-day views of the case may be minimal, as contrasted to when their relationship is on a more hierarchically authoritative basis." In fact, it is when the supervisory relationship is on a more hierarchically authoritative basis that the supervisory pact he describes is necessary. I have adequately documented the nature of the hierarchical basis of the supervisory relationship in this study. The freedom and openness on both sides called for by the pact is at best difficult under these circumstances. Rather, we must see how the spirit of the supervision developed and fared in fact.

The candidate's effort to convey the manifest content of the analysis to the supervisor was discouraged. His notes were left largely unread or read for research but not for purposes of supervision. To my knowledge, very few references were ever made to these notes in the supervision. Although it is plain that the supervisor was critical of the analyst's mode of oral reporting, he never made it an issue. Neither the notes nor the oral report came up for serious consideration as criticisms in the accomplishment of the work task. Rather, they were dealt with more in the nature of uninterpreted resistances.

The autonomy of the analyst in conducting his analysis was glaringly compromised by the secret research being conducted on the supervision. The candidate was not given the opportunity to experience that autonomy by being consulted in advance for his decision and for his patient's consent. Indeed, much of what I have described in my previous chapter as well as in this one documents the degree to which the candidate's autonomy as student and analyst was at the mercy of influences and actions beyond his ken: he exercised his choice of patients at some risk; his fate as an analytic candidate was affected by factors present in his extra-analytic work. In short, the supervision was working under severe handicaps with respect to Jacob's ideal supervisory pact.

I often had the impression that the patient presented us with no mysteries, nothing that our technique and theory were not up to handling. If something was not going right, then it was due to a failure in technique, understanding, or more likely the analyst's personality. I was frankly puzzled by the patient's silences, her delays in telling me about her escapades, her fears about getting involved in the analysis. Although my caution was partly dictated by my efforts to emulate the supervisor, it was also motivated by my desire to wait and see how the problems would be illuminated by further developments in the treatment. In time, this illumination occurred. It was not altogether that the patient experienced the analyst as indifferent to her plight as she felt her father to be, but rather that she very much feared her own greedy possessiveness: were she once to grab hold, she would not let go, and this would doom both herself and the analyst to becoming the victims of her oral-aggressive impulses. Better to play these impulses out piecemeal than run the risk of that fateful encounter. Indeed, the need to respond to the analytic stance as indifferent was a necessary defense against this further destructive involvement. Premature interpretation of this defense might well have precipitated even more abandoned acting out. But all of this can be said with the wisdom of hindsight. At the time I was simply puzzled by the patient and troubled by what appeared to be my supervisor's insistence that I must know what to do and understand fully what appeared to be a mystery at the time. I felt that there was no place for behavior that resisted understanding. In this respect, the supervision failed to consider that supervisor and candidate were at the "frontier of psychoanalytic knowledge." Jacob was, in fact, entirely right in raising the question about the analyst's concern over the patient's acting out, ". . . has the analyst been all along more aware of transference phenomena than we have given him credit for? His caution may be technically justified since his patient indeed gets overly quickly involved with men in highly ambivalent ways."

There were many difficulties in the way of establishing a mutual sense of a shared task—the Study Group, the institutional context, the personal context, and transference and countertransference reactions.

EDUCATIONAL VALUE OF THE SUPERVISION

What did I learn during the supervision in the specific, cognitive sense of the word? The supervisor stressed the technique of facilitating the patient's free associations rather than impeding their flow by questions or too verbose interpretations. This I found useful. Yet, the emphasis was more on what not to do than on what to do in its place. Attention was focused on a stance or attitude rather than on specific guidelines or principles. Mainly, the supervision felt like treatment and may have mobilized in me transferences, conflicts, and anxieties with sometimes regressive consequences. The supervision did indeed instigate a good deal of self-analysis, and in this respect may have been instrumental in stimulating much emotional learning. However, issues developing within the supervision were seldom directly and explicitly addressed. For example, if the supervisor felt I was being too condemnatory of the patient's acting out, this was never brought up as such, nor could I in turn feel free to bring up my concern about the supervisor's condemnation. Apparently my supervisor felt I was not being assertive enough in my own defense of my treatment, yet he never brought this issue up either; nor again could I bring up my need to satisfy him by emulating him. There was, in other words, a conspiracy of silence about significant issues, conscious and unconscious. The music was subliminal, but the dancers responded to it nevertheless. Although the supervision was unstructured and even unfocused, and was thus fostering an analytic-type relationship, the overriding social, political, and educational context was highly structured and fostered an explicit self-protective stance on the part of the candidate and the supervisor. We were like two fighters circling each other and not landing a blow while looking over our shoulders at our own seconds and across the ring at our adversary's seconds. Caution was the byword. I may be forgiven for using this pugilistic analogy; it is in keeping with my supervisor's several references to my lack of "fight" and his hopes for a stronger "adversary." I would suggest that the main transference and countertransference paradigm was of an aggressive, competitive nature in which pseudo-help and pseudo-acquiescence were ever-present dangers. These transference and countertransference manifestations were created both by the political context and the supervisory ambience that fostered a very special work atmosphere.

I wish the examination of this supervisory process had continued beyond the first sixty-six hours, especially beyond the first year, because things began to change about then. I quote from my note on treatment developments at the time of changing supervisors to convey some idea of where things were then so that the reader may compare it with how things were earlier in the analysis.

> The contrast in her way of dealing with the analyst's two vacations a year apart may give some idea about what has happened over the past year. Before the previous vacation, the patient was threatening to end the analysis by her sexual acting out with its danger of pregnancy. She was living with a roommate whose life style reinforced the patient's own and who often played the part of the "other woman" in the patient's acting out. She was not sure of herself as a professional and thought poorly of herself as a woman. The analysis itself was a necessary evil which was a major source of anxiety in her life. She continued to seduce her ex-fiancé into believing that something might still come of their relationship, just as she was inclined to seduce the analyst into believing that something might still come of the analysis if only he would be patient with her and tolerate her behavior. On the analyst's return she tried to hide and obscure her anger for having been left. In fact, not long before the analyst left on his vacation, she returned home for a brief visit, substituting her family for the analyst.
>
> Prior to the analyst's recent vacation, the patient was openly talking about her jealousy of the analyst's wife and her fantasy of being taken along with him on his vacation. This verbal access to her feelings went along with a total absence of promiscuous sexual behavior. In fact, now the patient insisted that only the analyst would do and that she had no interest in any other man, including her ex-fiancé. She no longer shared an apartment, having decided to live by herself, and discovered that she really did not need to depend on her roommate for company; her life ran much more smoothly without her roommate's disruptive presence. The analyst had now actually become of primary importance to her without altogether pre-empting her necessary involvement in her work, which she enjoyed very much. On the analyst's return, she complained at length about a variety of reverses which, on closer examination, were not of very great moment but were mainly intended to make the analyst guilty and concerned. Currently, this reaction to his return is being examined in the light of her persisting possessiveness. In a recent hour she insisted that the analyst must be a part of her "world only"; if he is in any way "outside" of it, he in effect is abandoning her and she, in turn, must reject him. She likened this to a childhood episode in which she joyfully threw herself at her father on his return home and was dismayed when he did

not catch her. She felt he should have known she would jump, and his not knowing this showed how indifferent and apart he was from her.

Mainly, the theme of possessiveness has been examined in the context of the father-daughter transference. The mother-daughter aspect of it has only occasionally been explored. The patient is very loathe to examine her clandestinely dependent relationship to her mother, and much remains to be done in this area. One would anticipate that the patient's readiness to resolve the transference neurosis and to make a suitable marriage (the main stated goal for which she came to treatment) will hinge on the thoroughness with which she can understand her wish to have a penis as reflecting not only her masculine protest, but her wish to hold on to an early infantile, omnipotent relationship with her mother.

This last development occupied the next phase of the analysis, and its resolution led to the termination.

The patient has provided the best conclusion to this chapter. In the last hour of the analysis she told me how the day before, a Sunday, she had been invited with her new fiancé to have breakfast with her best friend and her best friend's parents out at the parents' farm house, where the patient had spent many a wild weekend when the parents were away. As she was sitting on the couch on which she had slept quite often, she began to finger the top of a glass box on the adjoining night table. As she was conversing with her friends, her fingers worked into the box and she was then brought up short by the discovery that there was a ring inside the box. With the excitement of some premonitory feeling that something important was about to happen, she fished the ring from the box. As soon as she saw it, she knew she had found the ring her mother had given her, which she thought she had lost many months before. It was her mother's favorite ring, a family heirloom, and one her mother wanted her to have for her own wedding. She recalled an anxiety dream she had reported much earlier in the analysis, when she saw her mother behind a glass panel extending her fingers and pointing at this very ring. She would have none of it. Now she could accept it because she was no longer plagued by her fears of greed and possessiveness. She must have placed the ring there herself and finally, at this momentous time in her life, when she was about to finish her analysis and marry, she could retrieve it. I wonder if this episode does not provide the touchstone for her analysis and perhaps all analyses that end well: the patient knows where the truth is and will find it when the analysis has prepared the patient for the discovery.

A ring is a symbol of a return to the beginning, with the difference that, once truly completed, a new beginning is possible. This study of my supervision has taken me back to its beginning and has made it possible for me to complete something that had apparently remained unfinished. I am grateful for that opportunity.

REFERENCES

Goodman, S., Ed. (1977), *Psychoanalytic Education and Research: The Current Situation and Future Possibilities.* New York: International Universities Press.

Lewin, B. D. & Ross, H. (1960), *Psychoanalytic Education in the United States.* New York: Norton.

APPENDIX

Outline of Supervision Topics

Prepared by

ROBERT S. WALLERSTEIN, M.D.

I. COPE Study Group Goals

A. Not a research in supervision, but rather a survey of approaches to supervision, an experience survey (diverse local ecology of supervision, diversity of purposes and uses geared to varying local conditions).

B. Creation of supervisory syllabus, array of areas of knowledge to be acquired, techniques and capacities to be mastered (examples: meaning of basic rule and rule of abstinence, induction of psychoanalytic situation; nature of analytic process, formal and content aspects; strategies and tactics of analyzing, etc.).

C. (A later goal) Clearinghouse function of a national committee, systematic collection of data from institutes (in part via meetings with institute representatives); center for coordination and exchange of information about varying supervision practices and problems.

D. (A later goal) Survey of recent analytic graduates on their training experiences.

II. Supervision Issues

A. Goals for different phases of training, first case, advanced cases, first six months of first case, etc.

B. Issues of *pedagogical progression*. Where is the candidate in his training? What case is this? Where is he in the time sequence with this case? Early? Well along? Relation of the case—its difficulty, complexity, etc.—to the level of skill and experience of the candidate.

C. Issue of unsupervised cases. Should this be forbidden during training? Allowed? Encouraged? Required?

III. Prerequisites for Undertaking Supervised Work

A. Formal requirements—in relation to personal analysis, course work, examination or colloquium, etc. Clarification of quantitative and qualitative aspects. Should supervision be undertaken only after, or during the training analysis? Should it be required that one still be in personal analysis? Etc.

B. Emotional requirements (relative)—to the extent that one has not worked through and assimilated one's own experiences of anxiety, depression, envy, one's own paranoid propensities, etc., so that one has become able to tolerate such intense affective states, one's own understanding of patients will be largely intellectual and defensive.

1. These experiences come in part through one's own analysis, in part through experiencing responses to one's own patients: hence both a prerequisite to and an outcome of a successful supervisory experience.

2. Related supervision dilemma: pedagogic needs of student and his capacity to deal emotionally with the clinical problems being encountered do not necessarily run together; if one tries to push the student-analyst beyond his emotional capacities because of the needs of the clinical situation, one may create only disorganizing anxieties.

IV. Role of Institute

A. Organized, administrative body under whose auspices training program is conducted; sets rules, guidelines. Body to whom both the supervisor and the candidate are accountable, and from which each derives the legitimization and perquisites of their relationship. Supervision is not a "private contract."

B. Problems of the transferences to the supervisor in his administrative capacity.

V. Selection of Cases for Supervision

A. Varying institute requirements and practices; who finds and selects the case, institute, supervisor, or candidate? What kinds of cases are allowed and what kinds are disallowed? (E.g., one institute will not accept as supervised cases instances of conversion of psychotherapy into psychoanalysis.)

B. Issue of Analyzability.

1. Are candidates sufficiently experienced in their understanding of analytic material and analytic issues to adequately assess questions of analyzability?

2. Can analyzability be predetermined (during diagnostic evaluation process) in relation to carefully worked-out and specified, agreed-upon criteria?

3. Or, oppositely, is analyzability an intra-analytic issue? In this view, it would be the task of the beginning phases of the analytic work to assess this properly and, in marginal cases, to make the patient analyzable.

4. Need the patient be an analyzable (i.e., a terminable) case? What of taking cases that are good for learning even if not prognostically the best risks for treatment?

C. Relation to goals of analysis and to altering analytic goals and expectations.

Are sights set differently nowadays? Are different (i.e., sicker) patients now considered amenable to an analytic effort, in relation, incidentally, to the lengthening time span of the "average expectable psychoanalysis"? Relation of this to the issue of determination of analyzability.

D. Differential selection, first control cases, advanced control cases, etc.

E. Double problem of selection.

1. Selection of appropriate case for the candidate.

2. Selection of appropriate supervisor for the candidate.

VI. Problems of Reporting: What and How to Report

A. Methods of reporting.

1. Process notes of candidate's analytic work with the patient (to be sent for reading ahead? to be brought to the supervision hour?): (a) related materials: process notes by candidate of supervision session (to be checked by/discussed with supervisor?); correlated notes by supervisor of the same supervision sessions—for comparative study of understandings reached, etc.

2. Tape recording, use of tapes in therapy and/or in supervision: (a) to be listened to? (b) to be transcribed and read?

B. Selection, and therefore selective distortions, in reporting.

1. Effort to eliminate it (Kubie proposals, 1958)—use of tapes.

2. Effort to utilize it as a vehicle for understanding; we work with the selections we get, create a Gestalt, note the emphases, the gaps, etc.

C. Styles of reporting.

1. Differences in efforts by analyst to keep supervisor apprised of the whole flow of the process, and its context. Some candidates allow for the week's gap in the supervisor's contact with the material by reconstructing the whole context for him; others do not.

2. Differences in reporting (in this instance by two supervisors) as reflecting (a) differences in the two patients being treated by one candidate—the more diffuse reporting in the one instance reflecting the patient with the more diffuse and chaotic transference, the more focused reporting

in the other reflecting the more clear-cut transference unfolding that came through in the material despite the therapist's inexperienced handling of it; or reflecting (b) differences in the two supervisors and/or in the supervisory process they induced.

VII. Diagnosis and Evaluation

A. Problems of clinical diagnosis—the patient (relates back to problems of analyzability, V, B).

B. Problems of educational diagnosis—the candidate. For example, how does one differentiate between a circumscribed problem about learning (a deep resentment of status as a student, and therefore a defiant, careless, and disorganized way of presenting material to the supervisor) from a more pervasive character pathology (the therapist so compulsively bound and so obsessively guilty in his activities that he might have to present his material in this disorganized fashion to the supervisor as the projected demanding superego with whom he was ostensibly complying, and really defying, and from whom he was provoking punishment)? How do we test such alternative hypotheses within the supervision situation?

C. Consensus problem—in diagnostic evaluation and at all points in the process. By what criteria do we decide which of differing psychodynamic formulations or educational formulations of particular material, of a particular problem, is the more valid?

VIII. Theory of Supervision

A. Are there generally accepted generic principles of supervision? How idiosyncratic are the supervisory conceptual frameworks that we collectively are guided by? How diverse? Psychoanalysis offers a comprehensive, articulated general theory of personality formation and functioning, normal and abnormal; to a lesser extent it offers a theory of therapy and of therapeutic change. Is there even to that extent a comparable psychoanalytic theory of supervision or, differently, a theory of psychoanalytic supervision?

Proffered conceptual frameworks: (1) Arlow—Minutes of New York Education Committee.[1] (2) Rosen—Minutes of New York Education Committee (counterposed to those of Arlow). (3) Fleming and Benedek—their book (1966), also articles. (4) Ekstein and Wallerstein—their book (1972), also articles. (5) Jacob—materials circulated to the Study Group. (6) Myerson—viewpoint proposed in paper prepared for the Study Group. How congruent or diverse are these?

B. Relationship of this issue of a psychoanalytic theory of teaching (or a theory of psychoanalytic teaching) to a psychoanalytic theory of learning; or, less ambitiously, to at least learn more about the conditions under which the learning of particular content (method, technique) is facilitated and, *pari passu,* the kind of content (method, technique) that is thereby rendered harder to learn.

[1]Minutes available in Archives of COPE Study Group on Supervision, Central Office of American Psychoanalytic Association.

IX. The Teaching Process and the Learning Process

A. Distinction between supervision and therapy. Is supervision pedagogy or is it therapy? Patient-oriented supervision, student-oriented supervision, process-oriented supervision. To what extent should the analyst's emotional entanglements (countertransferences) be avoided or dealt with? To what extent should they be ruled out of the purview of supervision? Where is the line drawn? Is this different when the candidate is still in an ongoing personal analysis (to which problems can be taken back or referred back), as against when he no longer is?

1. Related question of recommendation for more analysis. As an aid to working out inhibiting work blocks, supervisory problems, or as a defensive move, an effort to move a supervision problem into the arena of personal analysis.

B. To what extent is there a (discernible) *parallel process* in the analysis and in the supervision? (See Tarachow vignette, August 1965, Minutes.) Is it "therapy" to thus point out similar behaviors and similar dynamics? Is such a confrontation itself therapy? Or, rather, to what extent does the answer to this depend on the purpose of the confrontation and the use made of it in either facilitating the flow of professional work or in exploring the ramifications of the candidate's character structure? Again, does one handle such issues differently if the candidate is still in personal analysis versus no longer being so? If so, why? Is it not still the same supervisory problem?

X. Ways of Learning, Learning Style, Learning Problems, Problems About Learning, etc.

A. Learning problems and problems about learning (Ekstein and Wallerstein). To what extent is this cognate with working style and defensive style (Jacob)?

B. "Blind spots" and "dumb spots" (Jacob)—problems of emotional block and of lack of knowledge.

1. Interpenetration: "dumb spots" as a *locus minoris resistentiae,* vulnerable to invasion by countertransference propensities, by "blind spots."

2. Disentangling for heuristic purposes. To what extent and in what order does one use each of these perspectives? Is it a general working assumption that it is a "dumb spot" rather than a "blind spot" until proven otherwise?

C. Problem of inexperience. A condition of each one of us to a varying degree at each point, with each kind of patient, but a special "problem of inexperience" when it is out of proportion to what might be expectable in the circumstance. Called "compulsive inexperience" (Tower). Issue of lack of aptitude or talent that can be confused with or covered over by "inexperience."

1. Related problem—defensive willingness to confess to countertransference difficulties (which are a more respectable badge among therapeutic

neophytes) rather than to inexperience or ignorance (felt to be shameful); the countertransference as a cover for learning problem or ignorance (opposite of the more usual concern).

D. Learning by *opposing* despite or to spite the supervisor. Link to problem about learning—acting out by the candidate against the supervisor; leading the supervisor toward particular conceptualizations and advice and then proving how wrong he is. (What is the degree of "healthy one-upmanship" in even so-called "normal" supervisions?)

E. Triangular competitive involvements in supervision.

1. Ready reactivation in supervision (supervisor, candidate, young hysterical female patient) of inherent oedipal dynamics; supervisor misperceived by candidate in terms of fear of competing, coercion to comply, etc.

2. Triangle with candidate, training analyst, and supervising analyst; bringing the personal analyst into the supervision: "That's not the way my analyst does it." Issue of split transferences.

F. Problem of conceptualizing the nature of psychopathology and of the therapeutic process designed to induce change; training the student to focus on the patient's neurosis rather than his reality.

G. Countertransferences and counteridentifications. Does excessive emphasis on the countertransference make supervision as teaching harder? Is this more so when the candidate is still in analysis?

H. Problem about learning. Deep resentment at continuing "student" status. Will such a problem mitigate on its own as the candidate moves toward graduation? May it therefore be bypassed in supervision? To what extent would this hamper effective learning?

I. Limits of supervision. Under what condition is more analysis an appropriate recommendation for the handling of work problems rather than a supervisory dodge, bucking supervision problems for solution by "more analysis"? What are the limits of what can be done within supervision, if we have no "easy out," no recourse to further personal analysis?

XI. Ways of Teaching, Teaching Style, Teaching Problems, Problems About Teaching, etc.

A. Personal variations in supervisory style. Different ways of teaching. Does a supervisor have a single, preferred teaching style, or is he able to, or does he feel it desirable to, adapt his way of teaching to the particular way of learning of the student?

1. Meshing of teaching style and learning style. The flexible student can adapt to the teacher's style, can learn from each, even those least congenial to him, can adapt to range from the most directively authoritarian to the most permissively democratic. But, can he learn equally effectively from each?

B. Degree of supervisory involvement.

1. Does supervisor tell the student only as much as *he has to* (with full

consideration of all the anxieties and the acting out that can be induced with whatever he tells the student), or, does he tell the student as much *as he can* (being guided, of course, by considerations of tact, timing, appropriateness)? (a) Supervisor can elucidate the patient's dynamics; (b) supervisor can indicate how he would have handled the situation himself; (c) supervisor can catalyze the candidate's associative process, eliciting *his* view of the patient's dynamics, of what he hoped to achieve in the way he handled the situation; (d) supervisor can try to understand (work out) the basis of the student's difficulties in understanding the dynamics, in handling the situation effectively; (e) even the simplest of these—explaining the dynamics—may be complicated, not accomplishable (if, for example, the candidate is caught up in a regressive sweep).

2. Degree of joint and interactive involvement. To what extent does the candidate try to formulate the psychodynamics and the tentative treatment strategy and tactic? To what extent does the supervisor? Do they discuss their individual formulations and try to achieve a consensus? Is it important (worthwhile) to elicit both the candidate's and the supervisor's initial understanding and compare them for concordance or divergence? Is this not indicated?

C. Degree of supervisory activity.

1. What is the appropriate degree and kind of supervisory activity? Ought this be different at a time of crisis or emergency? How aggressively, how insistently versus how tentatively, does the supervisor impart considerations? How much danger is there even in the most neutral of "helpful" formulations or explanations of the supervisor frightening or overpowering the student? How much compliance does the supervisor demand? How much room for disagreement does he allow?

2. Style in supervisory activity: (a) supervisor with clear-cut conception about meaning of material who tries to get the candidate to see it, conform to it, interpret in accord with it, with correspondingly less emphasis on drawing out the candidate's own ideas on the meaning and organization of the material (an analysis guided by the supervisor's conceptions) versus (b) supervisor who cultivates the art of analytic reflection about the material by the candidate through eliciting the candidate's conception, working from within the starting point of the candidate's understanding; (c) the two extremes of the intrusive supervisor who treats the patient through using the candidate as his puppet as against the other extreme of the supervisor who, in reaction formation against this, is unduly concerned, fearful, inhibited in his reluctance to "intervene" (read, "interfere"); (d) safety factor here against undue supervisory pressure in the fact that supervision is always a *retrospective* learning experience which dampens the directness and immediacy of the pressure.

D. Teaching problems and problems about teaching.

1. Supervisory rigidity, dogmatism, authoritarianism. The too strongly held conviction that there is a firmly established body of knowledge and analytic understanding to convey which can lead supervisors to pose as know-it-alls, to make sweeping ex cathedra pronouncements without really knowing the whole picture and forgetting that even though he, the supervisor, is the more experienced, the candidate has the more intimate knowledge of the clinical situation. (Supervision is an arena in which such characterological rigidity can be readily enacted; or the dynamic can spring from a reaction against the insecurity of the supervisor who feels burdened that he has to teach something to an individual who is closer to the situation, knows the material more intimately, etc.)

2. Related problem of supervisor who feels the "need" to give the candidate something, some increment of learning, preferably in each supervisory hour, so that the candidate stays contented with his learning; the same person does not usually feel the counterpart of this supervisory furor in his clinical psychoanalytic work. (The meshing of this problem with that of the student who has to have a feeling of closure and accomplishment about each supervision hour.)

3. Knowing how to learn the material of the case, how to elicit a clear picture of what is going on in the analysis, how to teach the student to present analytic material.

4. Capacity of supervisor to tolerate ambiguity, complexity, not knowing.

5. Capacity of supervisor to control frustrations, narcissistic injuries, etc., generated by the poor student who does not understand, who suffers from ignorance, lack of experience, countertransference involvements.

6. Ability and willingness of supervisor to take the time and energy to organize his material, reflect about the case, to give the candidate and the patient their due.

XII. Special Phenomena of Supervision

A. Contagion in the transmission of anxiety (up and down the chain from patient to analyst to supervisor, and back). The concomitant arousal of resistances to free communication up and down the line, and the resolution of those resistances among three people, each separately, complexly motivated to a particular predilective position (dependent on one's individual neurosis, reality position, "school" position as a candidate, etc.).

B. Regressive process in supervision. Similar in form though not in depth to that in psychotherapy and psychoanalysis. Importance of keeping it limited (see Myerson material, Minutes, August 1965).[2] Once set into mo-

[2]Minutes available in Archives of COPE Study Group on Supervision, Central Office of American Psychoanalytic Association.

tion, going from one individual to another (patient to analyst to supervisor) until reversed. A characteristic supervisory phenomenon, often manifest as a "crisis" in supervision. What distinguishes the good supervision is the capacity to delimit it and to recover from it. It can be a manifestation of the regressive pull of the situation when the supervisor is drawn into taking a therapeutic stance with the supervisee.

XIII. Role of Identification in Learning and in Teaching

A. Supervisor by his way of studying the analytic material and of conducting the supervision serves as a *model* for the candidate in his behavior with his patient; in his ways of introducing the student to modes of listening and weighing, without necessarily speaking and acting. Therefore, the personal tutorial encounter is central and cannot be replaced by even the most intense reading and individual or group study. Beyond his information-conveying and standard-maintaining functions, the analytic teacher helps the student (via identification) to bring his nascent analyzing capacities to bear (helpfully on the analytic problems of his patients).

B. Importance of good *supervisory alliance* in order to convey contents and to serve as a model for a way of approach to contents.

C. Neurotic aspects of identification; the issue of the appropriateness of the "*we* have a problem" approach.

1. The reality of the shared responsibility.

2. The neurotic aggression of the candidate toward the supervisor, reflecting either anxiety or psychopathy. The mix, then, of possible favorable and unfavorable connotations with respect to the strength and workability of the supervisory alliance.

XIV. Crises and Emergencies in Supervision

A. Definition of emergency. When is an emergency an emergency? When is active intervention on an emergency basis warranted and when does it represent a being drawn into a transference-countertransference bind or acting out-counteracting out? Whose is the emergency?

B. "Emergency" as an expression of a regressive process in the analysis; in the supervision.

C. Relation of emergency to supervisory responsibility for the welfare of the patient. To what extent can or must the supervisor assume this responsibility? When he does, to what extent does it overrun the teaching task? Need to distinguish between the real emergency, when the supervisor must intervene, and the pseudo-emergency, when active intervention ought to be avoided.

XV. Normal Learning and Normal Supervision

A. Lack of concepts or language to describe normal learning process. Tendency to conceptualize learning and the problems of learning in the language of psychopathology, which is familiar and which we feel we understand, rather than in terms of the processes of normal behavior, normal growth and change, of which we have so little understanding.

B. Characteristics of "normal supervision." To what extent does it consist just of the analyst's report of the flow of the analytic material, the supervisor's passive, analytically receptive listening, comparing it to the model he holds in mind of how the "average expectable analysis" should unfold, and indicating that matters are proceeding satisfactorily?

C. To what extent does the writing up even of "normal supervision" for purposes of exposition and discussion artifactually foster its consideration in terms of difficulties and crises faced?

D. Even with the most experienced, are there not (more or less frequent) crises of inexperience in our work? After all, the totality of anyone's experience is so sharply limited in the total range of patients seen analytically or candidates supervised.

XVI. Illustrative Case Material[3]

A. Windholz, April 1965, "Discussion of a Supervised Analysis—with Reference to Some Problems of Psychoanalytic Training": Patient who acted out a pregnancy and (somewhat prematurely) terminated her analysis. Impatient analyst who oversharply confronted the patient, based in part on the analyst's own unresolved residua in relation to her own neurotic conflicts around penis envy. Supervisor who found it difficult to help the analyst overcome her consequent difficulties in dealing with the sexual fantasies of the patient lest the analyst react in ways that would only evoke accentuated defiant acting out by the patient. Effort to distinguish in the conceptualization of the supervision problem between "acute countertransference crises" and "residual neurotic attitudes" in the candidate.

B. Myerson, August 1965: Analyst bending over backwards to be properly "analytic," inhibiting his activity, becoming thereby too passive in his dealings with the patient (as a reaction formation against his own natural active bent in psychotherapy—which he was trying to overcome). Patient who wanted to act out rather than analyze transference fantasies, through a so-called "realistic decision" with her husband to become pregnant. Analyst's attitude that this would be a good idea since they had discussed in seminars how much could be learned about the psychology of women by analyzing patients through a pregnancy. Candidate had thus regressively identified with the defenses of the patient, which he bolstered with intellectualization. Supervisor who felt momentarily regressively helpless to stop this collusive acting out between the analyst and the patient. Then an overcoming of the regression with the supervisor and a subsequent reversal all along the line.

[3]Material available in Archives of COPE Study Group on Supervision, Central Office of American Psychoanalytic Association.

C. Tarachow (vignette), August 1965: Candidate who gave up prized research time in order to take on an analytic patient who, however, treated the analysis most cavalierly, skipping hours, etc. In this the patient was re-enacting a life pattern; she had come to analysis having jilted a lover and she was now "jilting" the analyst. It was clear to the supervisor that the analyst was very irritated with the patient who was treating so flippantly the analysis for which he, the analyst, had given up so much. The analyst seemed unaware of his own irritation, which the supervisor then pointed out.

1. It is proper to point out the presumed irritation?
2. Is the candidate perhaps aware of it? Should this not be first ascertained?
3. If he is aware, ought one then to inquire into his understanding of its nature and source?
4. Or is he not aware, but with the question, able to come to the ready realization?
5. Or is he not aware, and needing to maintain this, responding to the question with a denial? Should the circumstantial evidences then be pointed out?
6. Or is he not aware, and displacing the conflict into a "symptom"—an inordinate fear of losing the patient (a projection of a vengeful desire to be rid of her)?

In the above sequence of steps, where does the supervisor stop in the progression? What are the proper limits of supervision here? Where does the supervisor become personally intrusive or professionally therapeutic?

D. Tarachow (vignette), August 1965: Candidate who consistently interprets the evident oedipal dynamics. Patient who does not respond to the interpretations. Supervisor who comes to feel that the whole analytic process is being experienced by the patient in stubbornly anal terms as a demand by an importunate mother for the surrender of the cherished stool—and that this is the more proper interpretive focus. Candidate who can be brought to "see" this but continues unable to use it effectively. It becomes clear that the candidate is doing the very same thing in supervision the patient is doing in the analysis; he is holding back his reports, coming late, etc.

E. Tarachow, November 1965: Analytically sophisticated, actress patient, who did not want surprises, wanted everything smooth, without eventful "bumps" in her life. The patient's fear of and wish for pregnancy and (transference) baby. Candidate who responds to the patient's discomfort by surprising her the very next hour with the announcement of his coming summer vacation plans. Issue of avoidance of surprises and of control that sprang to the forefront of the analytic material. Very energetic supervisor who vigorously pressed his formulations and his viewpoint on his student.

F. Debell and Weiss, November 1965 (both supervising the same candidate with a "problem of inexperience," a not knowing that was defensively covered with a knowing air): With DeBell, the candidate had all the necessary pieces in view, but seemed unable to integrate them into a meaningful Gestalt; he presented them piecemeal and unintegrated. The analytic situation was of a patient acting out with his girl friend his transference reproaches to the analyst for taking insufficient care of him. Themes of separation and enforced interruption through the analysis. The patient's response to the analyst's trips with a defensive denial of sickness, and therefore, of need for the analyst. The analyst's "unwillingness" to see the analytic consequences of his frequent interruptions of the analysis by his many professional trips. But the candidate was better than he looked at first blush. He would not have been able to give the supervisor all the material out of which the supervisor could meaningfully integrate the whole picture unless he, the candidate, "knew" more than he consciously allowed awareness of.

With Weiss, the candidate presented material that seemed hurried, pressured, compressed, chaotic. It seemed as if no one took a reflective look, considered the varieties of meanings, the alternative hypotheses that were possible in the situation. The supervisor seemed inundated by this process as well. The analyst seemed to be operating without any coherent image of an analysis and an analytic process (acquired somewhere along the line, especially in his own analysis).

Patients going differently, the supervisions going differently.

G. Schlesinger, August 1966: Patient whose whole life style, which characterized the analysis as well, was one of "It's better than nothing." By dint of the analytic work accomplished, the patient was enabled to behave significantly differently with her boy friend for the first time. Perseverative analyst, however, sees everything as a repetition of transferences out of the past, including the reality, which has elements of new behaviors. Pushes everything into repetitive transference interpretations that then blur for the patient any understanding of what is new and different for her. The supervisor making repetitive and, by now, impatient efforts to help the analyst distinguish the difference, transference from reality. Candidate who tries to learn, but again ends up doing the same old thing.

H. Myerson, August 1966: Patient who came with an eroticized transference and ready-made rape fantasies; every interpretation that touched on sexuality, no matter how tentatively, experienced by the patient as an assault. Intellectually gifted, somewhat rigid analyst, also somewhat insensitive and insufficiently empathic. Task of supervisor to keep the analyst from seeing the whole of analysis as just a process of making brilliant interpretations (phallic aggressions). Interpretive work needs to be set within the context of an empathic tuning in.

REFERENCES

Ekstein, R. & Wallerstein, R. S. (1972), *The Teaching and Learning of Psychotherapy.* New York: International Universities Press.
Fleming, J. & Benedek, T. (1966), *Psychoanalytic Supervision.* New York: Grune & Stratton.
Kubie, L. S. (1958), Research into the process of supervision in psychoanalysis. *Psychoanal. Quart.,* 27:226–236.

Name Index

Subject Index